THE DIGITAL
EVANGELICALS

THE DIGITAL EVANGELICALS

Contesting Authority
and Authenticity after the
New Media Turn

TRAVIS WARREN COOPER

INDIANA UNIVERSITY PRESS

This book is a publication of

Indiana University Press
Office of Scholarly Publishing
Herman B Wells Library 350
1320 East 10th Street
Bloomington, Indiana 47405 USA

iupress.org

© 2022 by Travis Warren Cooper

All rights reserved
No part of this book may be reproduced or utilized in any form or by any means, electronic or mechanical, including photocopying and recording, or by any information storage and retrieval system, without permission in writing from the publisher. The paper used in this publication meets the minimum requirements of the American National Standard for Information Sciences—Permanence of Paper for Printed Library Materials, ANSI Z39.48–1992.

Manufactured in the United States of America

First printing 2022

Cataloging information is available from the Library of Congress.

ISBN 978-0-253-06225-3 (hardback)
ISBN 978-0-253-06226-0 (paperback)
ISBN 978-0-253-06227-7 (ebook)

*To the memory of RHE,
the bravest of postevangelicals.
Requiescat in pace.
And to Miss D: sauveur ou destructeur?
Je ne sais pas.*

CONTENTS

Acknowledgments ix

Introduction *1*

PART I: *Media and Message*

1. Media Sincerity and Promiscuity: Origins 33
2. Evangelical Media Ecologies from Print to the Internet 46
3. Evangelical Theories of the Digital 71

PART II: *Authenticity Construction across New Media: Case Studies*

4. #FareWellRobBell: Heresy Discourse and the Horizontalization of Authority 101
5. Feminist Publics and the Progressive Evangelical Blogosphere 122
6. Instagram, Authenticity, Affect 147

PART III: *Local Technologies in a Global World*

7. Emerging Midwestern Evangelicals and Digital Media 173
8. Media Ambivalence in Emerging Evangelicalism 203

   Conclusion: Zoom Church, Cancel Culture, and the Exportation of Evangelical Media 238

Appendix 261

Glossary 275

Bibliography 307

Index 355

ACKNOWLEDGMENTS

WHAT IS A BOOK BUT a vast, interpersonal network—a media artifact so thick with intertextual links and hooks and interpersonal gestures that even a massive bibliography fails to do justice to its debts? Thanks first and foremost to Candy Gunther Brown, Steven Selka, Daniel Suslak, Anya Peterson Royce, Kathryn Graber, Aaron Stalnaker, Bharat Ranganathan, Kate Netzler Burch, Alexandra Cotofana, and Adam Prusinsky for reading and commenting on chapters at various stages of the book's fruition. I've had the brilliant luck of working with Allison Blair Chaplin, my editor at Indiana University Press, and am thankful for her constant insight and unyielding patience with this first-time author. Thanks also to the three reviewers who helped shape the book for the better.

Many people and institutions offered resources, publication venues, funding, and research assistance along the way. Thanks to Russell McCutcheon, Mike Altman, and the University of Alabama's religious studies department for publishing "New Media (and) Ritual" on their departmental blog. Anderson Blanton edited and published "ePrayer and Online Prayer Rituals" in "The Materiality of Prayer" project hosted by the Social Science Research Council's *Reverberations: New Directions in the Study of Prayer*. "Media Ideologies, Contested Authenticities, and Socality Barbie" appeared both in *The Bulletin for the Study of Religion* blog and the University of Chicago Divinity School and Martin Marty Center's *Religion and Culture Web Forum*. Thanks to Matt Sheedy and Emily Crews, respectively, for their editorial oversight on these pieces. *The Religious Studies Project* hosted "The Invention of the Emerging Church Movement" and "The Inauthenticity of New Media" essays. *anthro{dendum}* (formerly *Savage Minds*) published "Theses on Method: New Media, Social Technologies, and the Anthropology of Digital Worlds." Thanks to Adam Fish for bringing this piece into existence. Although rehashed and recombined in interesting ways, the theories I experimented with in these public scholarship pieces have structured this book. Multiple travel grants and stipends provided by the University of Antwerp UCSIA, the Indiana University College of Arts and Sciences, and the University of Notre Dame's Institute for Advanced Study sponsored travels for me to speak about my work and network with other researchers. I'm indebted to Darrin Rodgers at the Flower Pentecostal Heritage Center in Springfield, Missouri, for the assistance in tracking down archival data on revivalist media and televangelism.

I presented research featured herein at several institutions. Recognition goes to Deborah Whitehead, panel chair of the *Media, Gender & Religion* conference at the University of Colorado, Boulder, in 2016, who provided feedback on chapter 5, and to Lisa Sideris, who wrote a thoughtful response to chapter 3 at Indiana University's *Presence and Absence* conference, hosted by the Religious Studies Graduate Student Association in 2017. Thanks to Amanda Koch and Rachel Coleman for inviting me to speak about progressive evangelicals on their panel at the Indiana Association of Historians conference in 2014 and for commenting on an early draft of research on evangelical television media. Thanks (again) to Kate Graber, who responded to a theory of digital evangelicalism, in its earliest iterations, at the Anthropology Graduate Student Association conference in 2015. I benefitted from feedback on a talk on evangelical neoliberalism in the digital era at the University of Antwerp's UCSIA graduate colloquium in 2017. Gratitude goes to Jennifer Olmstead and Paul Oslington for the extended interaction with this piece. Conversations with Pamela Klassen at the University of Toronto's *Media Fever!* conference, way back in 2013, also shaped my ideas about religion, television, and digital media. Most recently, I gave a Zoom talk on evangelical responses to the COVID-19 pandemic at Pennsylvania State University. I can't express how much interactions with fellow panelists and audiences at these events shaped the trajectories of my research.

Digital media have reconfigured how scholars collaborate. I'm appreciative of Ilana Gershon, a trailblazer in the field of social media studies, for the email correspondence and inspiration. Her writing's extensive influence on this project will quickly become evident below. I'm thankful to all those I've consulted with online. Every few months someone in my vast academic social network posts something about the pitfalls involved in defining evangelicalism. Too many friends and colleagues are involved in these fascinating discussions, typically hosted via Facebook comment or Twitter thread, to cite them all. But I'm especially thankful for the insightful exchanges and comments among Mike Altman, Elesha Coffman, Kristin du Mez, Janine Giordano Drake, and Daniel Vaca—to name only a few. Beyond scholarly Facebook debates, I'm grateful to Shannon Schorey for the recommendations for sources on the history of technology, religion, and the Internet; to Ryan Bachman, for the long conversations about how digital media might be altering the pastoral profession; to Krista Dalton, for consulting about religious feminists in the blogosphere; to the Facebook, Instagram, and Twitter communities through which I was exposed to more work relevant to my studies than I imagine was ever possible in previous eras of communication; and to Daniel Jones, for always alerting me to new books and bringing scholars of religion together by way of compelling Facebook thread discussions.

Social networks run deep. As a master's student at Missouri State University, John Schmalzbauer and Martha Finch proselytized me into the study of religion, everyday life, and American culture. Later at Indiana University, I joined a stimulating intellectual community that included American religion scholars like Candy Brown, Winni Sullivan, Lisa Sideris, Steven Suslak, Cooper Harris, and Sarah Imhoff. The contours of my academic work are shaped by scholars whose books I read in graduate seminars, and later for comprehensive exams, people I had the privilege of interacting with on a personal level. At regional, national, and international conferences, receptions, dinners, and other events, conversations with Christian Smith, Gerardo Marti, James Bielo, Amy DeRogatis, Heather Curtis, Grant Wacker, Andrea Jain, Arlene Sánchez-Walsh, Anthea Butler, Kate Bowler, Grant Wacker, Thom Tweed, Russell McCutcheon, John Modern, Katie Lofton, Sean McCloud, and Brad Stoddard—among many, many others—nurtured and stoked my interests. I'm grateful for camaraderie with fellow early career #AmRel scholars, including but not limited to Dana Logan, Sarah Dees, Andrew Monteith, Sonia Hazard, Charlie McCrary, Jeffrey Wheatley, Michael Altman, and Benji Rolsky.

I experimented with arguments that show up in the following chapters in most of the courses I've had the privilege to design and teach. Thanks to students in my courses at Indiana University ("New Media and Digital Religion," "Religion and Popular Culture," and "Religion, Ethics, and Public Life") and Butler University ("Understanding Global Issues" and "Introduction to International Studies"). These students thought hard with me about global digital technologies and the ramifications of habitual media. As digital natives, significantly more so than myself, these students alerted me to emerging media ideologies that were not even on my radar. Which is to say, from these students I learned a lot.

Networks tend to refuse the categories we place on them, existing, instead, as messily complicated social assemblages. I'd be remiss if I failed to acknowledge my ethnographic interlocutors and collaborators, many of whom are friends and confidants rather than generic ethnographic subjects. Thanks, most of all, to the Church on the Margins community for putting up with an anthropologist-in-residence in their midst for five long years—one who did either a lot of awkward standing around scribbling field notes or asking what must have come across as glaringly obvious questions about technology use. Thanks to this community for your radical inclusivity. Outside of Church on the Margins, I'm grateful to Rev. Mihee Kim-Kort for the coffee shop meetups and intelligent conversations. Thanks, Mihee, for being a model writer-activist-intellectual-parent-scholar. Appreciation goes to several bloggers who I encountered first through their online texts for allowing me to write about their writings, corresponding about the project over email, and on rare occasions meeting in person at events. Sarah Bessey, Emily Maynard, Daniele Vermeer, Dianna Anderson, Marian Williams, and Mihee Kim-Kort: I'm deeply appreciative to all of you for bravely submitting your work for strangers, like myself, to read and react to online.

Finally, I want to express the utmost of gratitude and love to my children, the most central and invaluable node of this complex social network. Thank you for your graciousness, endurance, and patience with me as I survived classes, conducted fieldwork and research, and spent long hours analyzing hundreds of pages of tweet lists and blog articles, pouring through fieldnotes, coding Instagram images, and revising chapters. I apologize for the fact that as a scholar of social media and ethnographer of the American Midwest, coming out of anthropologist mode has been, for me, somewhat difficult. Moreover, I must express that this whole thing wouldn't have been possible without you, that if it weren't for you all to begin with, I never would have had the drive to undertake such a project. Merci infiniment.

I dedicate this book to the memories of two of the most influential women in and on my life. To Rachel Held Evans, pioneering progressive blogger and theological pot stirrer par excellence. Although she left too soon, her work was a catalyst for the questions that drove me to research and write this book. And to my dearest Dawnetta. For whatever it's worth, I wrote this book for you. It was always only for you.

Bloomington, Indiana
March 2022

THE DIGITAL EVANGELICALS

INTRODUCTION

IF THERE IS AN IMAGE floating around on the **internet** that captures the complexities of religion in **the digital age**, it is Paweł Kuczyński's "Dinner" (2016). A Polish graphic illustrator and philosopher, Kuczyński trained at the Fine Arts Academy in Poznan. The award-winning artist is best known for his satirical political cartoons and illustrations. His visual works situate him as a cultural commentator and critic who addresses rampant social problems in complex modern and postindustrial societies. A quick survey of his artwork posted online reveals that **social media** frequently draws Kuczyński's attention as a subject matter. "Dinner" is typically Kuczyńskian in that it portrays a scene that is at first familiar but quickly grows more disconcerting the longer one observes its details (see fig.I.1).

In the background a white, seemingly middle-class family sits around a dining table. The family's body languages and facial expressions suggest sincere engagement in a religious ritual, likely a prayer of thanks before a meal. From there, the illustration's key symbols break with expectations. On the serving platter at the center of the table, in the place of a steaming pot roast or a baked chicken, sits an active internet router. A blue **WiFi** symbol rises out of the device. In front of each family member are not place settings, as one might anticipate, but tablet devices of varying sizes. The bluish hues of the screens are consistent with the WiFi symbol, signaling connectivity to (and communion with) the central router.

What to make of this disturbing scene? As with any image, the illustration is open to interpretation. When I show "Dinner" to undergraduate students in classes on digital religion and global issues, I ask them to pinpoint the main subject of Kuczyński's critique. Most responses gravitate toward one or two possibilities. Often, students identify that the artist's concern is heavy **media**

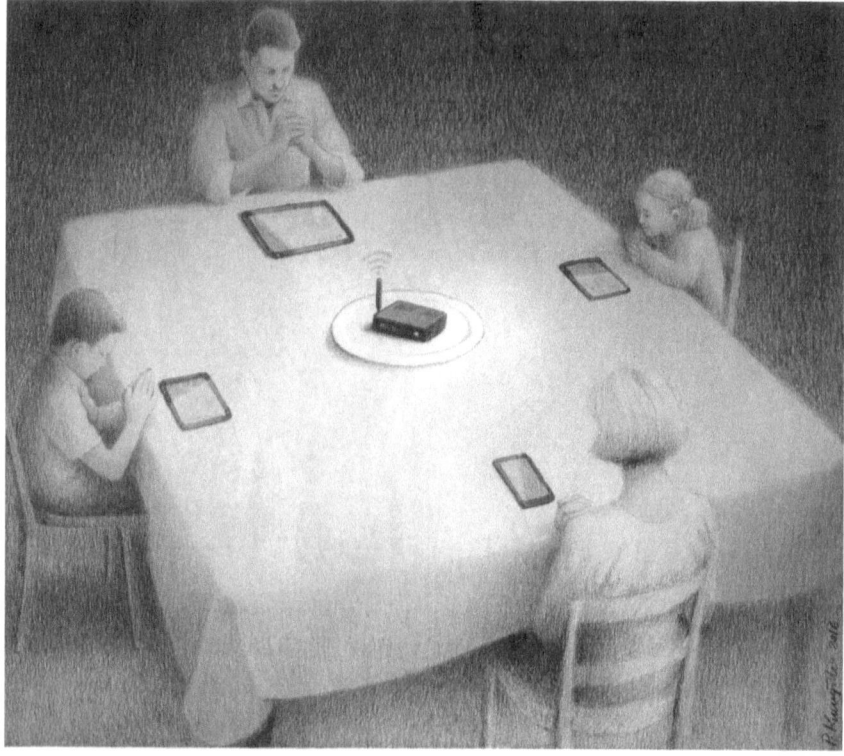

Figure I.1. The digital evangelicals. "Dinner," Paweł Kuczyński, 2016.

consumption. Students mention problems like "addiction," "obsession," and "overuse." This first interpretation makes good sense. Instead of lasagna or baked tofu, the platter serves up the router. In place of the meal, the family is about to consume information on their internet-enabled media devices.

A second, equally compelling reading of "Dinner" is that Kuczyński's nuclear family invests their devotional attention on the internet itself. Students wonder whether the mother, father, daughter, and son are praying to the internet rather than expressing thankfulness to God before consuming. Beyond simply spending too much time on social media or practicing media consumption rituals that verge on the addictive, this family has reified internet connectivity as divine. Kuczyński declares, "All hail the Internet! The Internet is God!" Were Kuczyński's family evangelical, and it might very well be, the internet would be its gospel. Either way one interprets the image—addiction vs. apotheosis, overuse vs. idolatry—the situation is dire. Regarding their communicative media and information technologies, these evangelicals find themselves in quite the conundrum. For the purposes of this book, "Dinner" identifies and foregrounds those digital evangelicals who are at the center of this study and names one of the evangelicals' greatest technological and moral predicaments. As Wendy Hui Kyong Chun (2016, 75) aptly argues, "New media are crisis machines."

Crisis, indeed. In the years of research that led up to writing this book, I started paying close attention to the many forms of public commentary on new technologies. Although not exclusively so, much of public commentary on **technology** is critical. Whatever "Dinner" means, for instance, it is difficult to argue against the claim that Kuczyński is criticizing new media use. Because all media, including the devices of mediation, are what scholars describe as "civilizational ordering devices" (Peters 2015, 5), I became particularly attuned to the critical public discourses that bemoaned the rise of social media and denounced its ubiquitous presence in public life. Scores of journalists and bloggers had written about contemporary technology's addictiveness.[1] Beyond Kuczyński, visual artists created stunning photographic montages depicting **cellphone** users as **disembodied**, distracted, and depressed.[2] Theorists of modern life credited the digital with the rise of public-facing **shitstorms**,[3] wherein online discursive noise, disturbance, chaos, and lack of respect loom large.[4] Even scholars of religion and technology took the time to mourn the internet's bringing about the end of civilized etiquette and the demise of interpersonal ritual and decorum.[5] At the other end of the spectrum, I observed how religious commentators, especially evangelicals, quickly adopted new media forms and pronounced them divinely ordained tools. Between the poles of the scathingly critical and the unabashedly optimistic, I assumed there was a more complex middle ground of interpretation and use. How were people adapting to the increased presence of new media in their everyday lives? Writing this book was my attempt to find out.

To study these changes, I conducted several years of ethnographic fieldwork in Midwestern religious communities to observe the place of new media in American lives. I learned that because of the peculiarly threaded histories of religion and technology in the United States, evangelical Christians, more than other segments of the American public, are arguably better attuned to the abilities of technological adoption to restructure religious authority and social and cultural order. My fieldwork as an anthropologist, online and offline,[6] confirms that evangelicals have much to say about the advantages and disadvantages of an increasingly digitally networked society. I discovered that across the range of commentaries produced on the subject, conversations returned time and time again to two interrelated concerns. First, in the **digital era**, will authority and order prevail? And second, in an age of hypermediation, complexity, and distraction, will authentic interpersonal communication become a thing of the past?

MEDIA: SINCERE AND PROMISCUOUS

This book's central argument is that within digital-era American evangelicalism, centuries of struggle between two opposing communication traditions have reached a culmination. On the one hand, the sixteenth-century Protestant Reformers instituted an influential, centuries-long paradigm of directness that despised mediation and championed the virtue of sincerity in communication. On the other hand, evangelicalism as a historically dominant Protestant subgroup subscribes to and actively develops a tradition of freely circulating texts and discourses. I refer to these overlapping yet frequently contradictory systems embedded within evangelicalism as **media sincerity** and **media promiscuity**, respectively.

To put the matter plainly, Protestant media sincerity is partial toward unmediated, embodied, and direct communication; privileges communal, in-person interactions and **face-to-face communication**; and advocates for people to mean what they say and say what they mean. This tradition prefers the media of its communication to be transparent, minimal, and trustworthy. It supports in-person congregational gatherings and distrusts communication over distance. It is this tradition of media sincerity, also described in anthropological scholarship as the **sincere-speech paradigm**, that has had a major hand in structuring Western communication patterns.

But evangelical Protestants find their high standard of authentic communication countered by an ingrained secondary impulse. Media promiscuity is equally powerful and distributes media artifacts widely in the service of the dual goals of replicating textual communities across distance and spreading the good news to the ends of the earth. In common use, "promiscuity" as a noun typically denotes a sense of unbridled or profligate sexuality. My adoption of the term builds on its association with indiscriminateness, hybridity, mixture, and propagation.[7] I prefer the term due to the idea of textual-reproductive transgression it carries with it but do not in my adoption intend to levy a moral criticism. Promiscuity herein refers to the propensity of new media to transgress the boundaries between elite authorities and new, emergent, nonaccredited voices (Cmiel and Peters 2020, 223). Promiscuity means that evangelical texts and utterances by design and implementation share as broadly and indiscriminately as possible in order to expand the kingdom of God, that is, to expand the evangelical community.

Evangelicalism necessitates promiscuous media. Indeed, evangelicalism's eagerness to share the gospel is entirely dependent on the promiscuousness of the various media it chooses to use. But the balancing contradiction posed to promiscuity by sincerity supports one scholar's claim that evangelicals "struggle with a whirlwind of competing imperatives" inherited from theological predecessors

(Elisha 2011, 2; cf. Lynerd 2014). Evangelicals "constantly wrestle with the forces that rule them" (Worthen 2016, 2). This book is about that struggle as it plays out in perhaps the most promiscuous technologies in the history of interpersonal human communication: new, twenty-first-century, internet-mediated, social **digital media**.[8]

How does that struggle play out? This book observes the tension between media sincerity and promiscuity as it has led to a crisis in authority and authenticity within evangelical circles.[9] This book explores how people in and around the loosely designated social network called evangelicalism negotiate that crisis.[10] Authority as a social phenomenon is always complex. Hailing from a Reformed Protestant tradition grounded in the rejection of institutional religious authorities especially complicates things for contemporary evangelicals. More on the imprecise definitional contours of evangelicalism later, but for now, dwelling momentarily on social theories of authority clarifies what is at stake in the struggle over power.

DIGITAL AUTHORITY AND AUTHENTICITY TROUBLE

Max Weber famously defined **authority** as legitimized dominance enacted through power. For Weber, **power** is "the probability that one actor within a social relationship will be in a position to carry out his own will despite resistance" (Weber 1964, 152; Horsfield 2016, 39). But legitimate authority in its purest form involves compliance to or acceptance of discursively skilled leaders beyond rote coercion or physical force (Lincoln 1994). Although too simple, Weber's theory of ideal-type leaders (of rational, traditional, and charismatic iterations) who exercise authority over compliant subjects is a necessary baseline. Are social media influencers contemporary versions of Weber's **charismatic authority**? Perhaps so if we can wrestle the idea of **charisma** away from being an innate, natural-born essence. But if, as Stewart Hoover (2016, 5–6, 27) writes, Weberian authority rests on a leader's plausibility in the eyes of his or her subjects, new media are radically altering the means through which everyday users of digital technologies both establish and perceive plausibility.

In his ambitious *History of Sexuality*, Michel Foucault redefines power fluidly as a "multiplicity of force relations," which emerge through social struggle and confrontation. In Foucault's model, the exercise of power occurs at various nodes in the social hierarchy rather than in a top-down, unilateral direction. The field of authority is much more contested in the Foucauldian paradigm than in the Weberian one. "Where there is power, there is resistance," Foucault writes, underscoring the dialectical distributions of power in modern social networks of domination and submission, control and opposition (Foucault 1978, 92–95;

Scott 1990). Foucault's work on the intricacies of power and authority lays the groundwork for **network theory** to follow.

Contemporary scholarship on digital religious networks builds on and critiques Weber's classic theory by approaching the issue of authority with more Foucauldian nuance. Peter Horsfield, a historian of media and religion, argues that authority is far more contextual, contractual, limited, and territorial than all-encompassing, as Weber previously depicted it. Authority is more tenuous, even fragile, since at any time digital audiences can simply refuse to participate or invest attention. Compliance in the digital age is different. According to Horsfield (2016, 46–47, 52), religious authority "lies not just in the power exercised, but also in the voluntary compliance with that power by those who are subject to it." And as Heidi Campbell, a pioneer of digital religion studies, confirms, authority online is now "marked by prestige, position, and perceived power by others" (Campbell and Garner 2016, 75). Religious authority, in short, must be constructed via the cultivation of followers. This construction is perpetually ongoing. Once achieved, authority is never final and may remain in a relative state of fragile contingency.

Three other concepts inform this book's approach to understanding shifting authority and the digital: **horizontalization, simultaneity**, and the **algorithmic**. First, a related challenge to traditional authority is that the internet can have a horizontalizing effect (Hoover 2016, 31). The internet relativizes and exposes users to (non)religious others outside of one's tradition of origin and places (non) religious collectives in a more or less level online marketplace of ideas. *The Digital Evangelicals* will challenge the claim that the internet is equal as a religious or ideological playing field, but the point that the internet has horizontalizing effects holds. The guiding questions are to what extent have these forces of horizontalization progressed? Are people becoming more open-minded to religious and cultural difference or have they simply transported their biases online? To what degree have determinations of the authentic become personalized and individualized (Wagner 2013, 202)? The effects of horizontalization, as we will see, are numerous. Horizontalization may afford greater freedom and awareness of diversity, on one hand, but it also enables **digital orientalism**, on the other, wherein people engage in essentialist and stereotypical rhetoric about various others encountered on the internet. Horizontalization's drive toward exposure also leads to the emergence of what I describe below as the rise of the **digitally buffered self**.

Second, the concept of **simultaneity** is another **affordance** of the internet that has recourse for religious authority. In her prescient *Twitter and Tear Gas: The Power and Fragility of Networked Protest*, technosociologist Zynep Tufecki (2017, 116–117) documents how microblogs, such as Twitter, allow messages to be shared to a group instantaneously or simultaneously in real time. It is increasingly easy to take for granted the ability to share a message with a sizable audience in the matter of mere seconds, but Tufecki urges readers not to overlook this radical affordance of social media. A tweet's simultaneity "may seem a trivial convenience," she writes, "but in historical terms, it is a powerful development." Social technologies do not simply create trendy new modes of communication. These platforms' affordances for instant communication are doing the very real work of "altering how we experience time and space." New media are reconfiguring the relationship between authorities and dissenters, providing novel venues of access to power and influence that were not previously available.

Third, one of the most subtle changes to authority in the digital era is that it becomes less anthropocentric and more posthuman. Intelligent digital networks and **meaning-making machines**, including algorithmic systems, increasingly influence access to information and activity on the internet. **Algorithmic-based authority** (Campbell 2020a, 24–37), in short, means that various informational structures are growing more influential as they curate which knowledge we take to be true or false, trustworthy or misleading. The very social perception of authenticity, then, is mediated by artificially intelligent algorithms that interface, invisibly, between human actors and personal computing systems. Algorithmic authority also refers to the ability of techno-informational systems to provide access to numbers. The most powerful digital entrepreneurs are those who have the means and knowledge necessary to exploit the algorithms for their own benefit in cultivating the largest online audiences possible.

One final point before applying the question of power directly to the digital evangelicals. Contestations about authority are inevitably, even if implicitly, about authenticity. To recall Weber, authorities may not be able to keep hold of power if they cannot retain legitimacy in the eyes of those subservient to them. To diminish something as "inauthentic" (or "unorthodox" or "heretical") is to attack the legitimacy and plausibility of a person, group, or idea. Within all newly introduced media ecologies, **the digital turn** included, structures of power and authority undergo negotiation and contestation. Implicitly, public discourse about media is frequently about the social order writ large. Within local evangelical congregations, one of several key ethnographic contexts for this book, such discourses concern not only social order in general but more specifically religious and ecclesial authority and control. Who gets to decide what is authentic or inauthentic? Debates center around which sorts of rituals, beliefs, and interactions are real and true, that is, authentic. This concern with the authenticity of religious media is no surprise. This book's findings support Hoover's (2016, 5) claim that "the power to assign things to the category of 'the authentic' is the primary power that religious authorities hold."

Digital era authority, to summarize, is far from straightforward. If power is the ability to get people to do things and behave how you want them to, the rise of social media and the integration of the internet into everyday life means that authority must be cultivated in novel ways. The power of traditional religious authorities has come under fire even as traditional authorities have migrated their institutions and influences online. Because of these horizontalizing, simultaneous, and algorithmic dimensions, evangelical authority in the digital era is under severe duress. In short, the widespread presence of digital and social media means that more and more evangelicals can now contend for what counts as authentic.

Emboldened by promiscuous affordances, digital media has strikingly paradoxical effects in that it both decenters structures of authority and reinforces existing nodes of power (Cheong 2013; Wagner 2013). As a dialectical network of contradictory forces, digital media can "emancipate and control, diversify and homogenize, empower and disempower, challenge and reproduce hierarchies, give voice and silence" (Mortensen, Neumayer, and Poell 2019, 18; Fuchs 2014). In some cases, new media allow evangelical **gatekeepers**—that is, vocal authorities who nurture substantial reservoirs of cultural and theological capital and actively maintain a stake in defining the parameters of what counts as orthodox—to extend their influence and control online (Helland 2015, 10). Campbell documents in *Digital Creatives and the Rethinking of Religious Authority* (2020) that this new class of authority, mediating between laypeople and clergy, goes by the name **religious digital creatives** (RDCs). RDCs include digital and technological professionals of various sorts, including congregational webmasters, church or ministry bloggers, email LISTSERV managers, and social media specialists who have tech-based skills beyond traditional ministerial or theological training. Gatekeepers in the digital era, in other words, may look less like credentialed pastors and professional theologians and more like Instagram influencers, Twitter pastors, or theoblogians (Campbell and Garner 2016, 73–75). New media allow evangelicals to negotiate theological stances, cultivate and influence followers, act in resistance to oppositional gatekeepers, and appoint alternatives who will speak for their own interests.

The result of the difficult synthesis between media sincerity and promiscuity is that new media have become for evangelicals a double-edged sword. New media solve all sorts of problems by allowing for the expansion of a person's social network and increased access to valuable reservoirs of information. New media provide new domains for ministry and evangelistic outreach. But these new tools engender additional problems. Digital media have the potential to undermine traditional authority, promote and encourage **heterodoxy**, and construct ambiguous, fluid, and potentially dangerous communities that are not beholden to traditional standards of evangelical Protestant **orthodoxy** and authenticity.

Digital media serve as platforms to debate what counts as *evangelion*, the "good news," to begin with. Evangelicals take to the internet to dispute theology and address who is—or ought to be—authorized to teach, write, speak, and produce discourse. Deliberations over religious authority have been a constitutive part of Christianity since before the Reformation, but with the rise of new media, the crisis has escalated in visibility, participative access, and intensity.

The Digital Evangelicals documents the changes in communication that come about as evangelicals attempt to manage this crisis. One of this book's most significant findings is that media are reconfiguring the broader milieu of evangelical interactions. Ultimately, authenticity in the age of social media is different than the authenticity of the print era. This book offers an anthropological and media-centered study of the role that Facebook, Twitter, Instagram, Skype, WordPress, Blogger, Zoom, Teams, and podcast technologies play in shaping everyday evangelical standards of authenticity. Though the **media sincerity and promiscuity paradigms** shape evangelical social media adepts, emerging social media practices, working out a tenuous compromise between the two inherited models, also adapt and reinterpret the religious tradition in several subtle ways.

Predominantly Reformed evangelical gatekeepers, for instance, reinforce offline, in-person, and face-to-face communication as the gold standard of authenticity but take to Twitter and the blogosphere to denounce **heresy** and defend orthodoxy. More progressive communities deconstruct the standard of face-to-face speech and redefine authentic communication to include things like glitch-prone internet media. **Emerging evangelicals** are quick to point out that so-called authentic in-person communication can be awkward and less than direct. The Indianan Midwesterners I discuss in chapters 7 and 8, for example, see Skype mediation as consistent with the genuine messiness of everyday life and interpersonal back-and-forth. At the same time, they experience pandemic-derived Zoom church as an efficient, temporary stand-in for "real" congregational activity but lacking in the depth of authentic in-person gatherings. The prevalence of comment and feedback sections in the blogosphere means that some prominent writers, including Rachel Held Evans and Sarah Bessey, find the media more authentic in an interactive, **collaborative** sense. For these writers, **blogs** may offer more authenticity and directness than traditional media, such as polished, professionally edited books. In other contexts, Instagram shapes evangelical authenticity connoisseurs into altered devotional habitats and subtly modified ways of seeing the world. As various evangelical writers suggest, new media alter daily rituals at the everyday level. Seeking after and producing the authentic, evangelicals experiment with digital fasts, practice spiritual disciplines aimed at slowing down and unplugging, and establish new rules in domestic spaces to increase sociability and manage invasive forms of mobile tech. During the onset of Covid-19 in early 2020, congregations across the globe experimented with collaborative live-video applications, such as Zoom and Teams, striving again to imbue online ritual and practice with authenticity and meaning. Predictably, things got controversial as leaders debated about the authenticity of virtual baptism and digital communion. Over 2020 and 2021, communities grew tired of what they would describe as the thinness of Zoom-mediated sociality and longed to return to physical gatherings. Across these myriad deliberations, sincerity discourse comes repeatedly to the fore as the evangelicals attempt to manage both the benefits and the undesired side effects of promiscuous media.

BOUNDARIES, BUFFERED SELVES, PUBLICS

Rather than define evangelicals or evangelicalism as a singular theological or historical tradition, this book makes a definitional intervention in that it describes the collective in terms of its inherited and applied media paradigms. *The Digital Evangelicals* recognizes existing definitional strategies but approaches the matter from a media studies perspective. This research emphasizes that whatever evangelicalism as a socioreligious entity is, it emerges out of and is inextricably linked to its discursive media. Evangelicalism self-constitutes and self-maintains publicly and dialogically. Following Kristin Kobes Du Mez (2020), it is more accurate to speak of evangelical*isms* in the plural than of a unified, overarching movement. Through the producing, circulating, consuming, rejecting, and validating of texts of various sorts, cross-spectrum evangelicals engage in concerted strategies of **boundary maintenance.**

Social anthropologist Mary Douglas's (1966) dictum, "Where there is dirt there is system," applies to the evangelical boundaries that are increasingly under contestation in the digital era. Digital authority is subject to horizontalization, but identifications of **"dirt,"** "contagion," and "matter out of place," all hygienic **metaphors** for social order, according to Douglas, are also frequent in digital deliberations. This means that when heated exchanges occur online and things are deemed inauthentic, unorthodox, heretical, heterodox, or theologically other, these exchanges evidence some sort of evangelical system or systems at work. Evangelicals build college campuses and create powerful institutions but lack any sort of centralized Vatican. There is no Rome, but there are scores of evangelical institutional hotspots like, Springfield, Missouri, (home of the Assemblies of God and the Baptist Bible Fellowship International) Colorado Springs, Colorado (James Dobson's Focus on the Family), and Lynchburg, Virginia, (Jerry Falwell's Liberty University). No unified papal authority guides and determines ecclesial activities. No monolithic evangelical structure holds power. Instead, multiple denominational and parachurch communities, sometimes with divergent theological stances and distinct forms of authority, share certain concerns and communicate them with analogous subcollectives.[11] These evangelical systems, to be clear, do not perfectly align. And as this book demonstrates, the best place in which to identify, observe, and study systems under contestation is on the periphery, where bounds are debated and "dirt" identified. As Jenna Supp-Montgomerie (2021, 205) argues, to effectively study networks, we must look as much to disconnection and disassembly as we do to connection and assembly.

Like Du Mez's insistence on plurality, Christopher Cantwell (2018, 284) describes the matter in economic terms, writing that evangelicalism "has a kind of internal religious economy where rival 'brands' of evangelicalism compete to win a share of the Protestant market." Such formational conversations and dialogues between evangelical brands occur in print, radio, television, and digital media. All religious traditions deal in boundary maintenance, but evangelicalism's preference for decentralized denominational organization means that debating theological boundaries remains its primary means of self-constitution. Contention, debate, and dialogue are the means through which evangelicalism lives. Contestation is the very media of evangelicalism's existence.

Boundary maintenance is a social and anthropological process that correlates with what Charles Taylor (2007, 37–41) describes as the relatively modern emergence of **the buffered self**. In his magisterial *A Secular Age*, Taylor distinguished ontologically between "buffered" and "porous" types of selves. Medieval porous selves, he argued, experienced the world through more permeable boundaries between the self and other entities. Modern buffered selves delineate more rigid, rationally defined boundaries. Updating Taylor's concept for the new media era, I document the rise of the **digitally buffered self**. Taylor's buffered self is a rationalistic and **secular** being that rejects the permeability between religious people and the divine, angelic, or supernatural. But where Taylor saw the buffering process occurring primarily in a vertical direction (i.e., separating between the level of the human and the extrahuman) I use the term in a horizontal and social sense. Indeed, as Taylor (2008) describes the situation of the original buffered self, "a much firmer sense of the boundary between self and other" develops than in previous eras. With the rise of the digitally buffered self, this boundedness intensifies as digital media produce exposure to difference. Much of this book's task, then, is to observe and document how evangelicals react when they encounter difference, internal and external, to their **imagined** groups. One significant outcome of the book's research is that in its generation of difference the internet is altering how religious people construe **alterity**. Social media are changing how people conceive of themselves and perform their own identities against perceived registers of otherness. Digital exposure to difference throws into heightened relief contending theologies and divergent social stances. Attributions of dirt—that is, apostasy, heresy, and general difference—proliferate widely. As the following chapters suggest, new media are the primary facilitators of these spaces of exposure to (and discourse about) the other.

Consider three brief examples of digital boundary maintenance from my online fieldwork observations. First, a link and commentary posted to Facebook by an ethnographic interlocuter back in November 2015: "Through a FB post, I was alerted to this site: https://t.co/JQJ6hDIXmv. Now, I have a sick feeling in my stomach #Nausea #ThisIsNotChrist"

This Facebook comment, which links to a procapitalist guide for Christian consumption, uses emotive language ("I have a sick feeling") alongside hashtags (#Nausea) to express disdain for the capitalistic ideology implicit in *faithdrivenconsumer.com*. Boundary maintenance, in this case, dismisses procapitalist, consumerist Christians as anti-Christ. The digitally buffered self is here on full display as the commenter experiences something claiming to be Christian but that, to them, fails the criteria for Christlikeness. Difference is encountered and performatively rejected online. This performed rejection bolsters the identity of the rejecter. As this book will show, such practices of negation constitute identity work in the digital era.

Second, Jesuit priest Fr. James Martin's "A Prayer of Welcome," posted to multiple friends' social media accounts after its delivery at the 2020 Democratic National Convention (DNC), speaks directly to boundary maintenance. "Loving God," Martin intoned, "open our hearts to those most in need." Those in need, for this Christian, included unemployed parents, underpaid women, black people, immigrants, homeless people, LGBT[QIA+] teens, unborn children, and incarcerated inmates. "Help us to be a nation where every life is sacred, all people are loved, and all are welcome," he prayed.[12] Posted and reposted in the months following the death of George Floyd due to police violence and the ensuing Black Lives Matter protests in urban centers around the United States, the benediction distinguishes good from bad and authentic from inauthentic forms of Christianity. The prayer originated in American Catholicism, but as a promiscuous text, it aspires for a much broader audience. Authentic Christians, to read between the lines, are those for whom the prayer's supplications have come or are coming into fruition. Authentic Christians have open hearts. Christians (ought to) care for those whom society turns a blind eye. Beyond a simple prayer, a repost of this sort might be read as a performance of boundaries between progressive and conservative Christians, between people who care for the disenfranchised and supporters of a presidential regime that actively marginalizes the socially dispossessed. That this text was delivered at the 2020 DNC underscores its inherently politicized tenor. I do not mean, here, to diminish the devotional caliber of the text. Prayers, after all, are religious technologies. But in the view of many evangelicals at the heart of this study, prayers are about speaking truth to power.

When a Pentecostal visits a Baptist church

Figure I.2. An @EpicChristianMemes creation illustrating Protestant diversity.

Not all social media instances of boundary maintenance are critical and serious. Often boundary maintenance operates humorously. Just the other day, a Facebook friend and theologian at an evangelical university reposted a comical **meme** (fig. I.2), originating on a Christian meme generator that comments on the differences between styles of evangelicalism. Yet even silly memes of this sort, which juxtapose familiar popular culture imagery to heighten the impact of the contrast being applied, still addresses boundaries.

This meme's seemingly lighthearted take masks the fact there are Baptists who consider Pentecostals and other charismatic Christians heretics because of their lively pneumatology and practice of controversial rituals like glossolalia. Pentecostals make some Baptists uncomfortable. There are some Baptists hesitant to concede that Pentecostals are authentic Christians, just as some Pentecostals argue that Baptists haven't enjoyed the fullness of the Christian life, because they haven't experienced the baptism of the Holy Spirit accompanied by speaking in tongues. Again, the digitally buffered self is at work in this public display of discourse about theological and ecclesial difference.

To talk about evangelicalism, then, is to talk about contested theological boundaries and ideological and political diversity. Yet, there is a long history of attempts to shore up a precise designation. One influential effort identifies devotion to the Bible as authoritative; eager dedication to sharing the gospel; and focus on the doctrines of Christ's death and resurrection as constitutive of evangelicalism (Bebbington 1994, 365–367). But Bebbington's quadrilateral ultimately falls short. Although such a broadly defined "family resemblances" paradigm for identifying who counts as evangelical holds sway (Noll 2001, 13; Coleman and Hackett 2015, 12, 16), scholars have continued to produce definitions underscoring certain aspects or tensions over others (Noll 2001, 2; Brown 2004, 1; Worthen 2014, 6). Evangelicalism often refers to the subtradition of North American Protestants distinct from but falling somewhere between the theologically ultraconservative Fundamentalists on the one hand and the liberal mainline Protestants on the other (Wuthnow 1988, 140–142). The term is a Protestant-Enlightenment hybrid that in its American origins opposed itself to more traditional "churchly Protestant" forms (Gloege 2015, 5–7). Evangelicalism encompasses the eclectic Protestant subcultures following the rise of the "neo-Evangelicals" and correlating with the public ministry of Billy Graham, the establishment of the National Association of Evangelicals in 1942, and the rapid establishment of influential evangelical journalistic, informational, entertainment, and educational institutions in the decades to follow.

In a wide colloquial sense, an evangelical refers to someone who identifies as "born again" (Kidd 2020, 4) or who belongs to denominations ranging from the Adventists to the Assemblies of God, the Baptists to the Brethren (Noll 2001, 18–22, 31; Lynerd 2014, 19–23). Although oversimplified, as Du Mez (2020) notes, a shared public assumption is that evangelicals are people who "watch Fox News, consider themselves religious, and vote Republican." Yet even Catholics are evangelicals if we follow these loose criteria.[13] Due to these and other definitional slippages, some scholars have rightly questioned the category's productiveness by tracing a critical genealogy of the term's discursive origins and fluctuations through time and showing how the category has been partially invented by academics, journalists, and publishing houses (Hart 2004). Since the Reformation, the term has been constructed and reconstructed to mean contrasting things and bolster competing theological agendas (Altman 2019; Fisher 2016). Evangelicalism is a contested, imagined, fluid category, yet the designation in various ways continues to hold linguistic value. Evangelicalism is both a native and nonnative qualifier, a category of insider self-identification and outsider public discussion. The critical study of this diffuse and ambiguous thing we call evangelicalism, to channel Derrida (1976, via Poveda 2021, 472), is a science of the *sous rature* (i.e., the "under erasure") since evangelicalism as a term "is both inaccurate and, yet, for lack of a better word, necessary." I think Molly Worthen (2016, 3) puts the matter most succinctly: The term is highly problematic and "definition-defying," nonetheless, "we are stuck with it."

This book makes a definitional intervention by conceiving evangelicalism in light of its media paradigms rather than in terms of theology or ecclesiology. Instead of delineating yet another definition, *The Digital Evangelicals* is more interested in studying how the boundaries of evangelicalism are created, maintained, debated, and patrolled. I am not, in other words, concerned with normalizing a criterion for who is in and who is out. I do not intend to join the high stakes theological game of identifying real versus supposed evangelicals (Du Mez 2019). Evangelical, after all, is at times an insider's code word for "authentic Christianity," or shorthand for "the best kind of Christian" (Altman 2019, 78).[14] For our purposes, evangelical as a descriptor refers to predominantly white,[15] sometimes evangelizing Protestants (Harding 2000, xvi) who wrestle with the media sincerity and promiscuity conundrum. By virtue of centuries of historical development, proponents of media sincerity have secured a monopoly on defining and enforcing what counts as authentic.[16] Yet, rarely have evangelicals avoided promiscuous media. This book documents the existence of an evangelicalism that is not a coherently bounded religious unit or time-tested theological tradition but a mediated social process continually forming, reforming, and performing through dialogue and intent on identifying doctrinal and communicative authenticity. Evangelicalism constitutes a robust media ecology, communicative paradigm, and public.

Michael Warner's (2002) concept of **the public**, in fact, provides the most convincing explanation of the conundrum of evangelical authority—the enigma of decentralized evangelical power. Warner delineates several criteria that constitute publics and **counterpublics**. A public enables a certain reflexive togetherness through "the circulation of texts among strangers who become, by virtue of their reflexively circulating discourse, a social entity" (Warner 2002, 11–12). Most applicable for our interests, publics lack "any institutional being" and ultimately depend on **circulation** and uptake (88, 91, 97). Warner's publics, summarized by Alex Fattal (2014, 321), are "infinite, expanding, interrelated text-based communities that engage in struggles within and among themselves through the process of circulation." The evangelical entity that is the focus of this book, in other words, is by no means a typical institution. Rather, as historian Daniel Vaca (2019, 9) puts it, evangelicalism is best understood as "an expansive social public," which exists alongside and overlaps with evangelical institutions but has influence much further beyond them. Evangelicalism, again, is an imagined social-textual community with unclear boundaries that are perpetually under debate.

The public as a concept challenges definitions that fall back on the register of theological belief. Both insiders and outsiders alike can constitute a public. In fact, publics and counterpublics emerge through the dialogue and contestation among divergent parties—dialogue over shared texts ranging from books, to blog posts, to tweets, to videos, to Instagram images. For these reasons, I am as interested in post- and ex-evangelicals as I am in conservative Protestants hailing from card-carrying evangelical denominations. Building on Douglas's theories of margins, this book focuses primarily on what might be variously described as vocal minority groups: the Christian Left, evangelical progressives, and even, occasionally, ex- or postevangelical communities. Of course, the evangelical conservative mainstream is a key player in this story—see especially chapters 3 and 4—but it shows up in most chapters more implicitly as a contrasting backdrop for or foil to the dissenting voices showcased. The *digital evangelicals*, then, in this book refers to those involved on both sides of the various debates and controversies featured in the upcoming chapters. As will be clear by the end of the book, whatever evangelicalism is, it is a complexly networked public that emerges out of the tenuous, constantly shifting Protestant media crisis between sincerity and promiscuity.[17]

CONTRIBUTIONS AND CRITIQUES

The Digital Evangelicals picks up where existing scholarship on religion and new media leaves off and aims to bring the study of evangelicalism and its contested boundaries into the era of digital technologies and habitual social media. I focus on American evangelicals for several reasons. One is to bring the scholarly record on evangelicalism and new media up to speed. To be sure, scholars have been studying Christian communication for some time. Significant contributions to this field have examined the developing print and publishing culture of American evangelicals (Marty 1973; Hatch 1989; Brown 2004; Nord 2004; Vaca 2012; Haveman 2015; cf. Hedstrom 2013) and surveyed evangelical mass media implementations in the form of radio, book publishing, periodicals, music, and television programming (Schultze 1990; Woods Jr. 2013). Other studies have focused on the rise of **televangelism** and the operations of the "electronic church" in the age of mass broadcasting (Fore 1987; Schultze 1990; Apostolidis 2000) or traced out extensive histories of Christian media from the ancient origins of the tradition to the contemporary period (Horsfield 2015). More recent work continues to document the use of books, films, videos, and magazine publications for ministry, identity building, and entertainment (Hendershot 2004; Woods Jr. 2013), noting the broader implementations of various media during the early years of the internet or cyberspace (Schultze and Woods Jr. 2008; Brasher 2001; Wagner 2012).

In the long view, scholars have only just begun to scratch the surface of the study of the implications of digital media developments on community building, ecclesial authority and power, theology, and religiosity broadly conceived (Hoover 2016; Ward Sr., 2014; Howard 2011; Whitehead 2018, forthcoming; Campbell 2013; Woods Jr. 2013; Campbell and Garner 2016; Cheong et al. 2012).

The field of digital religion is a relatively young but rapidly growing subdiscipline. Brenda Brasher's *Give Me That Online Religion* (2001), Lorne Dawson and Douglas Cowan's *Religion Online: Finding Faith on the Internet* (2004), Morten Højsgaard and Margit Warburg's *Religion and Cyberspace* (2005), Heidi Campbell's *Exploring Religious Community Online: We Are One in the Network* (2005), and Rachel Wagner's *Godwired: Religion, Ritual and Virtual Reality* (2011) helped define and delineate the contours of this pioneering subfield that merged religious studies with technology and media studies. While these works waded headlong into the questions of shifting authority, digital sociality, power, ritual, practice, and authenticity, most predated the release of the first-generation iPhone in 2007. Christopher Helland's (2000; cf. 2005, 1) pioneering distinction between "religion-online" and "online-religion" was useful for analyzing pre-1999 website participation but is less applicable to the current habitual media turn. **Data phones** as habitual media devices that we carry everywhere had not quite become the norm. Domestic technologies, such as Google Home, Google Nest, and Amazon Echo, were still a decade out from production. Additionally, these early studies focused primarily on religion or Christianity, widely conceived, with specific forays into Catholicism, Buddhism, paganism, Judaism, Hinduism, Baha'i, Scientology, Wiccanism, and other global religious expressions. While Christianity was a recurring subject matter, few of these early book-length studies focused exclusively on evangelical forms of Christianity.

One exception is Robert Glenn Howard's *Digital Jesus: The Making of a New Christian Fundamentalist Community on the Internet* (2011). Howard's work, which offered a close reading of participative media and vernacular religiosity, focused on a group located within the evangelical universe. *Digital Jesus*, in fact, with its nuanced observations into how pre-2011 new media provided venues for religious community formation, was a model and inspiration for *The Digital Evangelicals*. But where *Digital Jesus* focused on internet-mediated fundamentalist discourses, I turn in these chapters to the opposite side of the evangelical world: the progressives. If Howard's pioneering study is of the Evangelical Right during an age of LISTSERV email chains, web pages, and blogs, this project showcases the small but vocal Evangelical Left in an era of habitual media and the **Internet of Things**, wherein the internet would literally break out of its existence out there somewhere on the cloud or online, pervade daily existence, and routinize the rituals of everyday life. At the time of finishing this book in 2021, **new media** as a category has become somewhat sloppy terminology. New media, simply put, are no longer new. They are banal, quotidian technologies that ought to be studied as such. Likewise, to quote digital religion scholar Christopher Helland (2015, 19), online religion "is not representative of some form of extraordinary activity—rather it shows 'ordinary' religious engagement in an amazing and extraordinary environment."

In another direction, I also focus on evangelicalism because evangelical America is itself central to the development and rise of new, digital, and social media. *The Digital Evangelicals* tells a story about evangelicalism, in a narrow sense, but its implications expand much further, encompassing American communication patterns. On the surface, the United States boasts a significant amount of religious diversity. But by and large, the most dominant religion in a genealogical sense is white evangelical Protestantism. Because of the high degree of influence the dual impulses of media sincerity and promiscuity have had on Western communication patterns, one cannot understand American media practices without first studying evangelical communication history. Much of the public discourse submitted about the rise of social media and new media's highly mobile, quotidian turn links implicitly back to or at least corresponds closely with reformed criticisms of ecclesial authority, Catholic ritual, and mediations of all sorts. The rise of American celebrity and consumer culture in an age of modern advertising, in fact, builds on and develops the evangelical-revivalist penchant for promiscuous media's widely circulating advertisements. The correlation between American popular culture and American evangelicalism remains strong over time. As I will suggest in chapter 2, the history of the internet in America is rife with evangelical rhetoric in its defiance of authority and aim to empower everyday people. Decidedly Protestant, anti-institutional rhetoric structures the thinking and provides key metaphors for the supposedly "secular" internet architects and Silicon Valley movers and shakers. In the United States, ground zero for the development of personal computers, the internet, and social media, such formational ideologies have deep roots in evangelical Protestant language. With the rise of internet-mediated communication, the evangelical tension between sincerity and promiscuity secularizes and genericizes far past its specifically Protestant origins.[18]

This book also proposes a corrective to a tradition of negative public commentary and insufficiently critical scholarship on technology that deals in essentialist terms. Commentators have tended either to reify the internet as a social savior, depicting it as democracy, free speech, or populism personified or, to the contrary, write new media off as a coercive tool of the cultural overlords, contributing to the demise of societal order, or just existing as technological innovation run amok. Intellectuals bemoan digital and mobile technologies in print and online media sources, perhaps overcorrelating between rising levels of reported depression and loneliness and the spread of mobile technology. Veering from one extreme to the other, sometimes influential cultural critics write off social media and internet communication as ephemeral and inconsequential. Leading technology scholars, in still another direction, depict new technologies as seductive, dangerous, and ultimately detrimental to human sociality.[19]

Informed by anthropological methods and media studies, this book contributes a more nuanced perspective that details how real people actually conceive of, theorize, and put internet media to use. Rather than levy yet another predisposed criticism against technology by reducing the internet and its increasing mediatization to "good" or "bad" or oversimplifying its social effects to either harm or benefit (Couldry and Hepp 2017, 12; Chun 2016), I follow emerging anthropological pioneers who are currently documenting the plasticity and relativity of technological uses in lived contexts across the globe (see esp. Gershon 2010a; Horst and Miller 2006; Miller 2011). *The Digital Evangelicals* builds on Ilana Gershon's (2010a; 2010b) contention that **media ideologies** directly shape everyday applications and experiences of technology. Local media practices, according to Gershon (2010a, 6), do not take place in a vacuum but adhere to established idioms of practice gleaned from the use of other media in combination with existing cultural norms and mores, acting structures of behavioral etiquette, and interpersonal morals.[20] New media uptake and application, in other words, is structured by existing social and cultural ideas and practices—and, of course, theologies. Technology influences people and may partially determine action, but people on the ground interpret and apply their new technologies in creative—and not always expected—ways.

HOW TO STUDY DIGITAL RELIGION

Digital anthropology is itself an unorthodox hodgepodge of methods and theories.[21] Digital anthropology is understandably heterodox within the broader discipline of anthropology because of anthropology's own built-in ideological and communicative biases that apotheosize face-to-face interaction (i.e., the **transport view**) as the gold standard of human communication (Pink et al. 2015). Anthropologists who contend that the ethnographic method is the discipline's sine qua non—and I include myself partly guilty under this self-reflexive critique—have often been blinded by what one writer calls, in a lovely turn of phrase, the "fantasy of unmediated address" (Briggs 2017, 44). Face-to-face speech may be one of the oldest forms of social discourse, but it no longer accurately defines the complex, hypermediated digital era. To take a more holistic approach to the study of culture, anthropology is increasingly requiring more flexible, nontraditional methods, such as **nonparticipative observation** (Abdel-Fadil 2016, 5; cf. Bernal

2014, 23–27), rather than traditional long-term fieldwork. Classically conceived ethnographic fieldwork in the digital era simply does not cover all the bases necessary for plumbing the depths of the density and complexity of **real-world** social networks. Following Victoria Bernal's (2014, 24) important work, this book engages in an eclectic form of **deterritorialized, viral ethnography** to study communities that defy the tired online/offline distinction.

Such methodological eclecticism is a necessary result of the dynamic and boundary-transgressing texture of digital communication.[22] This field of multisite approaches and blended scholarly paradigms is working to record and analyze some of the raw data currently being uploaded by users in vast droves. Big Data experts estimate that in the 2020s the volume of data being recorded through digital media might reach some forty zettabytes. "Just to put it in perspective," commentators explain, "if you were to add up every single grain of sand on the planet, and multiply that by 75, that would be 40 zettabytes of information" (Smolan 2016). Even a few years back, experts pointed out that humans did more data processing in 2015 and 2016 than in the previous three thousand years combined (Smolan 2016). Digital anthropology is strategizing to understand the changes that interaction in mediated domains produces at the level of everyday interactions and discourse. *The Digital Evangelicals* is likewise methodologically experimental and eclectic, blending online database analysis with multisite ethnographic research.[23]

Rapid technological advances paired with their widespread adoption are rendering previous understandings of mediation obsolete. Another way to put this is to underscore that to study digital religion is to study everyday livelihoods in spaces not traditionally considered "online" or "digital." With technologies becoming more habitually ingrained into everyday life, more ethnographic research is needed to thoroughly understand and analyze the effects of the digital turn. In keeping with Douglas's (1966) concern regarding marginal social groups and broader systems of power, I conducted several years of ethnographic research in a **progressive evangelical** community in the American Midwest to study these changes. Given the sheer amount of social data being uploaded daily, this ethnographic dimension—paired with online data analysis—was my attempt to narrow vast global data into something local and concrete.

To paint a thorough picture of the layered complexity of the ethnographic study of digital religion, then, consider the examples of Heather and Ewan. Heather, one of my Midwestern ethnographic interlocutors, is an attractive, brown-haired woman in her early thirties who makes the point of smiling and greeting me any time I run into her around town or during church community gatherings. Heather works part-time as a self-employed counselor but spends much of her energy raising two children alongside her husband. If I wanted to observe Heather's everyday media-related practices, how should I go about it? How best might a researcher get at this woman's ideas about authentic living and social media? Heather practices digital religiosity in multiple locations. Digital media span numerous domains, including data phone use, computer access, entertainment media, domestic technologies, family and kinship networks, and time spent on social media, among many other possibilities.

One method would be to observe Heather's digital interactions. I might talk to Heather in informal conversations or befriend her on social media to observe and interact with her online. A more invasive strategy of observation might entail hanging out with Heather in person, watching her activities of life in first-person as she scrolls social media feeds. The above methods are all plausible, but one might recall that Heather is not an isolated individual. In fact, she lives a life embedded within dense local networks and meaningful extralocal communities, and I want to get a feel for the stratified aspects of her networks.

A second cluster of possibilities involves studying these communities. I might focus on Heather's religious community by designing surveys and questionnaires to produce written reflections in response to questions having to do with mobile technology and social media. I might also conduct **participant observation** in her local church community and detail how the group's leaders speak officially about technology, the general presence of technology within the church, and the everyday uses of mobile technologies in people's homes, at picnics, potlucks, recreational events, and other places around the city. Observations of this qualified sort would supplement and contextualize survey data in which community members discuss social media idealistically and objectively. Yet, the fact that the church community is only one group among multiple others leads to still another required level in studying Heather's digital religiosity. Heather's church community, after all, is part of a nationwide and global evangelical public.

As a third option, and to get at this highest and most abstract level of religious organization, one might study the online bodies of interaction and communities of discourse that Heather herself engages in or at least pays attention to. The process might involve consulting self-help, philosophical, or theological manuals written by evangelical leaders with whom Heather and her community may be familiar. Heather, to be clear, is an evangelical, and evangelicalism is a nebulous religious entity that emerges out of its discursive interactions.

On this third level, let me also introduce Ewan. An avid hiker, photographer, and Instagrammer, Ewan is a member of Heather's community. Like Heather, Ewan is also active on social media. To get at these practices, I might read and compare some of the evangelical bloggers Ewan flips to on his phone during lunch breaks. I might follow bloggers on Twitter and take note of broader discussions going on in the Twittersphere. I might observe the Instagram communities Ewan interacts with. Because I'm interested in evangelical boundary maintenance strategies, I might also observe on Facebook how not only Heather and Ewan but also their entire community puts media to use to debate theology, politics, and social issues. Their nontraditional church community provides an invaluable glimpse into how digital media are influencing structures of evangelical power after the digital turn.

Research for *The Digital Evangelicals* proceeded on all three of the above levels. Because I'm interested in the complicated category of evangelicalism, traditional **ethnography** alone was not enough to get at this transspatial entity. In addition to ethnographic fieldwork (chaps. 7 and 8), I used corpus analysis melded with content, discourse, and visual analysis methods to sample evangelical boundary maintenance strategies on Twitter (chap. 4), via the blogosphere (chaps. 4 and 5), and by way of Instagram visuality (chap. 6). Beyond these online case studies, I also consulted what popular evangelical writers have contributed to the published record in terms of social media manuals or technology self-help literature (chap. 3). As mentioned, I conducted five years of direct ethnographic observation in a local Midwestern community, interacting with congregants such as Rachel and Ewan, gathering group-wide data on social media practices via surveys, and observing technology uses in real-time, both in congregational settings and sometimes in more intimate domestic spaces (chaps. 7 and 8). In total, the data for the book included thousands of tweets and Instagram images, hundreds of blog posts, and thousands of pages written on technology and social media uses. Finally, I spent over five years observing digital evangelical interlocutors in action as a non- or quasiparticipant observer in online social domains. These digital observations, mediated through my own data phone, tablet, and laptop, brought together informants both nearby and far away. Such is the magic of social media to create communities of spatially distant people organized around ideas, images, arguments, and discourse.

THE CHAPTERS

To study digital evangelicalism as the hybrid, dialogical, extralocal public that it is, I organized the book into three parts. Part I begins with a bird's-eye view of the Protestant Reformation and American evangelicalism from a historical perspective and then in a second chapter moves into a textual ethnography of evangelical books written about internet technologies. Chapter 1 argues that the history of evangelical communication is the struggle between the paradigms of media sincerity and media promiscuity. The standards of media sincerity, having origins in the Reformation's theological-, ecclesial-, and communication-centered revolutions and the values of sincerity, authenticity, and directness challenge American evangelicals' adoptions of new media across the centuries. The chapter traces the development of a second influential communication paradigm, media promiscuity, a model that makes proselytization more effective and aids the evangelical community in being more public and wide reaching. The final part of this preliminary history and theory chapter discusses the concept of **media ecology** and the question of technological cause and effect.

Chapter 2 traces American evangelical media history through multiple eras of development, focusing on the strategies by which evangelical revivalists, including George Whitefield, Charles Fuller, Billy Graham, and Benny Hinn, unified the sincerity and promiscuity impulses. Evangelical revivalists used print, radio, and television, reconfiguring theologies with each new turn. The chapter shows how evangelical forms of Christianity vied for power in American media history. In addition to narrating the migration of religious institutions to the new digital domains, the chapter's deeper historical work lays bare the fact a genericized form of evangelical media ideologies laid the groundwork for the internet and its continued crises of authority and authenticity. Contrary to the claim that the early internet was an exclusively secular, rational, religion-free place, I show how several key digital technology architects employed the language and rhetoric of Protestant, anti-institutional critique in the building of what would become the internet and **personal computer**.

Chapter 3 takes seriously the claim that evangelicals are "book people," as Daniel Vaca (2019, 12) suggests. Building on the claim that what authorized evangelical writers have published about new technologies is critical data for the analysis of evangelical media ideologies, this chapter theorizes evangelicalism as a translocal entity that exists through the circulation of its discursive texts. Observing and analyzing a highly networked, textual community of technology manuals written recently by evangelical authorities, I show that these theorists' positions on the matter are contested, ambiguous, and complex. Manual writers, like the evangelical revivalists featured in the prior chapter, struggle deeply with the tension between sincerity and promiscuity. These writers vary in their stances on new media but by and large seek to provide practical strategies for evangelical audiences to learn to guard against the ills of the internet. Resisting rather than adopting media promiscuity, these authors identify the problems of informational oversaturation, diminished authority, delegitimized authority, increased diversity, problematization of truth, and populist access to knowledge, among many other issues. Proposed solutions to these problems are also complex. Some writers attempt to marry sincerity and promiscuity by penning how-to guides for pastors and laypeople to better use internet technologies. As a body, however, the general tone of the writers' position is one of ambivalence. For these writers, the internet and social media become key sites in which to deliberate about authority, boundary maintenance, orthodoxy, authenticity, virtuosity, and meaningful living. Evangelicals in the age of electricity stretched and played with the contours of media sincerity, tempering and combining it with the counterparadigm of media promiscuity, effectively reconfiguring what sorts of communication counted as authentic. To the contrary, digital experts rein in their understandings of authenticity and chide predecessors for their unbridled optimism. In this discursive evangelical public of texts, writers reconfigure and theorize anew the relationship between sincerity and promiscuity.

Part II shifts from historical description and textual analysis to focus on language communities and discursive publics that form via interactions and engagements online. Such a shift is necessary to account for the linguistic and communicative data trails that evangelicals submit in numerous online domains. This section analyzes large corpuses of online commentary uploaded to Twitter, Instagram, and blog sites by evangelicals of many ideological stances and melds quantitative and qualitative approaches.

Chapter 4 examines theological debates about controversial evangelical writer Rob Bell, author of the polarizing *Love Wins*, which occur via **microblog** and blog discourses. I argue that besides unifying communities separated by physical space, as promiscuous media, Twitter and blog technologies have a contentious effect as they serve as platforms for orthodoxy debates. The chapter's findings demonstrate that the internet is not an ideological or theological free-for-all and confirm that powerful evangelicals extend their influence into the online discursive arena to mark certain individuals as dangerous and other. To arrive at this conclusion, the chapter analyzes a body of approximately fifteen hundred tweets and one hundred blog posts written about or in response to the dismissive #farewellrobbell **hashtag**, originated and circulated by powerful reformed opponents of Bell's writings between 2011 and 2015. After showing these publics and counterpublics at work, the chapter concludes with a brief reflection on the Rob Bell controversy's effect on the evangelical media ecology, narrating how some young evangelical publics are once again drawn to the sincerity paradigm.

Chapter 5 explores the counterview of the internet's affordances. If the internet allows religious powers the ability to extend their influence, might it also have the opposite effect? This chapter is a qualitative and comparative study of seven progressive Christian and feminist bloggers who make use of the internet to cultivate voices that confront the patriarchal, heteronormative traditions of power in American evangelicalism. After narrating how the feminist bloggers produce and circulate their criticisms of evangelicalism's harmful purity or modesty culture—a nefarious tradition the bloggers contend objectifies and sexualizes young women rather than protects their honor—I show how progressive evangelicals theorize the medium of the blog in light of their inherited ideologies, both theological and communicative. The bloggers capitalize on the promiscuous benefits of social and blog media for cultivating wide audiences but temper that ideology with authenticity standards that link to print culture dating back to the Reformation. The bloggers address new problems engendered by promiscuity, challenges such as the rise of **trolls** who seek to dominate conversational spaces. The chapter demonstrates that evangelical idioms of practice mark blogging as more ephemeral and less authoritative than print text but also creatively construct it as more direct, authentic, and interactive.

Shifting from a qualitative analysis of the blogosphere, chapter 6 moves away from Twitter, Blogger, and WordPress to focus on Instagram, one of the most popular image-based social media platforms on the internet. Chapter 6 bridges between the online corpus analysis case studies and the fieldwork-based reflections of the subsequent part of the book as it contextualizes and analyzes the sizable evangelical Socality collective. Founder Scott Bakken created the hybrid Instagram-mediated community to, as he puts it, bridge the online and offline worlds and facilitate authentic social bonds in a world that for many feels increasingly fragmented. Drawing on affect theory and the burgeoning field of Instagram studies, I argue that the image empowered Socality shapes its community members through a **haptic devotionality**, of sorts, via the repeated scrolling, viewing, and visualizing of the collective's online imagery. In this chapter I analyze more than twelve hundred of Socality's images uploaded to Instagram, the collective's entire corpus of image uploads at the time of research, discovering that a vast majority of the images have to do with nature, hiking, and the outdoors. Socality cultivates in its users a mode of evangelical visual piety that fashions nature through a romantic lens and gaze of sublimity and wonder. The chapter also juxtaposes Socality's desire to experience and communicate authentically with the collective's vocal online critics. Even as a hybrid online and offline community, Socality is, like broader evangelicalism, a contested discursive space. Not all evangelical observers interpret Socality's authenticity discourse as authentic. Critics such as @SocalityBarbie appeal back to the model of authenticity from the media sincerity paradigm to chastise what they view as the unavoidable thinness of media promiscuity. The subject of authentic actions online, the analysis suggests, maps directly onto discussion of boundary maintenance and theological criticism.

In part III, the book's final section, I turn from qualitative and quantitative online content analysis to report on over five years of ethnographic fieldwork in the American Midwest. As a primarily descriptive and taxonomic piece, chapter 7 discusses local congregational data phone use, church media, including projectors and screens, technological glitches and Skype difficulties, websites and internet presence, and community social media trends. In terms of findings, eight primary forms of social media use are arising among emerging evangelicals:

entertainment and leisure; extension and maintenance of kinship, friendship, and social ties; informational collection and consumption; commerce and shopping; professionalization and work-related communications; ritual or devotional engagement; ideological and discursive contestation; and identity-based microperformances. The chapter argues that the media sincerity paradigm survives in evangelicalism, particularly in the form of the discourses about authenticity and inauthenticity, and that these evangelicals seek to synthesize the models of media sincerity and promiscuity. An ethnographic vignette on a Skype session failure in a church service, for instance, shows how evangelical leaders are redefining the authentic based on interactions with new media. Evangelicals are **domesticating** technologies, theologizing them, and adopting them for their purposes. For these media users, misbehaving and glitch-prone technologies become *more* sincere, authentic, and reflective of real interpersonal communication rather than less. Social media are for these Midwesterners prime metaphors for theorizing about the authenticity of their interactions. The principal data for chapter 7 includes an extended period of ethnographic participant observation at Church on the Margins, a community in Bloomington, Indiana, a questionnaire on media use in daily life, and direct ethnographic observations on local media use (and talk about media) in everyday activities.

Chapter 8 takes a closer look at the discourses of new media adoption by Church on the Margins community members. This second ethnographic contribution and final chapter documents the strategies by which evangelicals struggle to find meaning and direction in a world they describe as being increasingly saturated in information, advertisements, and media—all undesired outcomes of media promiscuity. I discuss evangelical strategies for implementing digital Bible apps and distinguishing between authentic and inauthentic friendships in a post-Facebook social arena. Further, I examine evangelical uses of digital podcast media and the reconfigurations of pastoral power and authority that derive from the ability to outsource theological instruction. Most importantly, the decidedly eclectic religious community cultivates an ethos of authentic "messiness," which distinguishes both the church's identity and its technological implementations from problematic forms of evangelicalism, such as the **megachurch**. Lastly, a few practices of media restraint are arising that are intended to address such issues and construct meaningful living patterns in a fragmented and media-saturated world. Sermon discourse, ethnographic observations, and survey and interview data map out emerging evangelical suspicions regarding the problems of contemporary living and its increasingly mediated communications patterns all serve as data. As with previous chapters, this final contribution theorizes the uneven ways contemporary evangelicals inherit, resist, and adapt the remnants of the media sincerity paradigm, merging the model, to the best of their abilities, with the promiscuous media forms that have now integrated into the domains of everyday life.

The Digital Evangelicals concludes by thinking about digital, postpandemic, virtual forms of religion. Returning to the crisis of authority that permeates evangelicalism as an American phenomenon, the conclusion looks back at the various multisite case studies and reflects on the role the internet and social media have played in evangelical deliberations about authority and authenticity. The dueling tension between sincerity and promiscuity remains axiomatic in evangelical practices. This final chapter reiterates the contested nature of evangelical organization and summarizes both the problems and benefits the medium has supplied evangelicals. In brief ethnographic accounts about the uses of Zoom and Teams platforms for evangelical congregational life, I show how these dueling media ideologies are ever present, especially given the global pandemic. Controversies over authentic theology and authentic rituals continue with full force into the COVID-altered world. I focus on baptism and communion, two Protestant sacraments whose recent migration to the digital sphere has caused, as one might anticipate, a tremendous degree of controversy and debate. *The Digital Evangelicals* concludes by tracing the widespread globalization and exportation of sincerity and promiscuity as part of the fabric of the global digital system used by nations, cultures, and religions the world over. This tension might have roots in evangelical Protestantism, but because it interfaces with and embeds into cutting-edge, capitalistic, secular digital media, the ramifications of the powerful ecology influences even nonreligious groups and non-Christians. Evangelical media, to put it simply, have gone viral. The conclusion culminates in a methodological slant by summarizing several recent problematic works on new media and calling scholars of social media to study and analyze **negative media ideologies** rather than advance them.

But before getting to the digital evangelicals, we need to uncover what sorts of communicative paradigms shaped the genealogy leading to the birth of the internet and the evangelicals' accommodation of social media. The achievement of this task requires temporarily setting aside the newest of new media, leaving the United States, crossing the Atlantic, rolling back centuries of time, and reemerging in Old World Catholic Europe during a period of particularly feverish religio-political and media-based turmoil.

NOTES

1. Articles appear in *Forbes* (Priestly 2015), *New Yorker* (Konnikova 2013), *Huffington Post* (Neo 2015), *New York Times* (Roose 2017), *The Atlantic* (Twenge 2017), and *Washington Post* (Wang 2017), to name only a handful of writings published—ironically online—in this genre. In this book's conclusion, I discuss a few more book-length treatises of this insufficiently critical sort.

2. Criticisms of technological developments in the visual arts range across mediums such as digital collages, fine art photography, and mixed-media paintings. For a selection of online galleries and commentaries on critical works, see Design You Trust 2015; Geiger 2015; Pickersgill 2018; Jobson 2010; Saint Hoax 2015; Hooton 2014; and Chin 2016.

3. A brief note on reading this text. This book includes a glossary of key terms to aid inquisitive readers. Terms included in the glossary appear bolded in the body of the text.

4. Byung-Chul Han outlines the concept of the **shitstorm** in his pessimistic *In the Swarm: Digital Prospects* (2017). See the conclusion for more on the weaknesses of Han's approach.

5. On the structure of everyday interpersonal interactions and performances, see Goffman 1990. For Connor Wood, a postdoctoral researcher in religion and science at Boston University, such social decorum is under attack. See his aptly titled essay, "Social Media Is Toxic. Religious Studies Tells Us Why" (2016). For a critical rebuttal to Wood's piece, see Cooper 2017d and 2019a.

6. Or **online and on ground**, as some anthropologists prefer to mitigate this spatial difference (Fewkes 2019, 3, 13–14).

7. I'm not the first to apply promiscuity language to new media. Chun (2016, 51, 107) describes digital networks as "leaky" and "promiscuous," writing that "promiscuous exchanges of information" are a constant in online domains. Kenneth Cmiel and John Durham Peters (2020, 223) likewise describe the digital age as characterized by "promiscuous knowledge."

8. The tension has possibly existed since before the Reformation given that early Christianity formed around communities of circulating texts whose authenticities were under dispute (Horsfield 2015).

9. David Chidester (2005, ix, 9–10) identifies the question of authenticity as "the central problem of religion in American popular culture."

10. Molly Worthen (2014) traces the crisis in evangelical authority from a historian's perspective, but my book emphasizes a media studies, ethnographic approach and asks how particularly new media have escalated the crisis.

11. Shared concerns range from theological or doctrinal considerations to political affiliations, from ideologies of gender and sexuality to ethnic and racial norms (Bebbington 1994, 365–367; Noll 2001, 13; Coleman and Hackett 2015, 12, 16; Brown 2004, 1; Worthen 2014, 6; Wuthnow 1988, 140–142; Lynerd 2014, 19–23; and Hart 2004). That evangelicals share ideological interests does not mean that evangelical subgroups agree on these matters. The "-ism" attached to evangelical can in this sense be grossly misleading.

12. For the full video of the prayer and a brief commentary, see Martin 2020.

13. To make matters even more confusing, Catholics sometimes identify as evangelical on surveys and questionnaires (Noll 2007, 4–5).

14. As Harold J. Ockenga, the first president of the National Association of Evangelicals (NAE), established in 1942, argues, midcentury American Christianity was in danger of liberalization and thus required "a true revival of evangelical Christianity" (Lynerd 2014, 169).

15. Evangelicals as white conservative churchgoers, in the clever words of one journalist, "might be the best bad definition of an evangelical there is" (Brobst 2021). In most scholarship evangelicalism codes as white, either by wholesale ignoring or effectively erasing African American, Asian American, Native American, and Latinx evangelical groups. For important historical and cultural work in this direction, see Thomas 2021; Butler 2012; Wong 2018; Tarango 2014; Smith 2008; Sánchez Walsh 2003; Mathews 2017; Espinoza 2014; Hinojosa 2014; and Mulder, Ramos, and Martí 2017. For new work on race as a category of inquiry in religious studies, see Yukich and Edgell 2020 and Gin Lum and Harvey 2018. The evangelicals that appear

in this book are primarily (though not exclusively) white and middle-class, but more research needs to be done on the digital practices of nonwhite evangelicals.

16. From a religious standpoint, authentic communication is face-to-face, interpersonal communication (Radde-Antweiler 2013, 88–89). From a scholarly perspective, authenticity does not exist inherently or essentially. Rather, authenticity, as with authority, must be created, constructed, debated, maintained, monitored, and enforced. Authenticity is constantly mediated and performed and always subject to contestation (Enli 2015; Cobb 2014; Bruner 2005; Benjamin 1969; Goffman 1981, 1990; Martin 2012, 148–149; cf. Turkle 2011, 4). Gatekeepers who determine what counts as authentic enjoy a significant measure of religious power in the digital media age (Helland 2015; Hoover 2016, 5). On these terms, authenticity is always about control (Chidester 2005, 192–197).

17. Consider the fact the NAE, one of the most influential of the evangelical institutions in America, arose for the sole purpose of giving conservative Christians a foothold in the promiscuous media world of radio communication (Lynerd 2014, 168–169).

18. Just as Protestantism beget liberalism in the English context (Simpson 2019, 10) and paved the way for secular developments and consumer capitalism (Gregory 2012), the internet is the logical outcome of centuries of Protestant media deliberations.

19. For a smattering of the insufficiently critical language of the sort I have in mind, see Twenge 2017 (cf. Cavanagh 2017); Dean 2010, 7; Žižek 1999; Turkle 1997, 2011; and Han 2017. Occasionally commentators focus on a specific technology, such as texting. On the overstated negative rhetoric surrounding young people and text speak, see Crystal 2008.

20. Although perhaps using the category of belief too uncritically, Simone Natale and Diana Pasulka's argument in *Believing in Bits: Digital Media and the Supernatural* (2020, 2)—that "the question of what we believe, and of how our systems of belief inform our experience and interactions is inextricable from the question of how we perceive, employ, and actively shape digital media technologies and environments"—holds true here.

21. For a nonexhaustive list of digital anthropology and digital ethnography's methodological considerations, see Sanjek and Tratner 2016; Horst and Miller 2013; Pink et al. 2015; De Seta 2018; Cooper 2019a; and Fewkes 2019, 7–10.

22. Chun (2016) argues that the most pressing reasons the internet and its effects are so controversial are because of its propensity to blur dichotomies previously taken for granted, such as public versus private.

23. Additionally, the field sometimes makes supplemental use of quantitative **corpus analysis** (Bennett 2010: 2–3) through the lenses of **discourse** (Thurlow and Mroczek 2011; Myers 2009; Gumperz 1982) and **critical discourse analysis** (Fairclough 1989; Chouliaraki and Fairclough 2005; Heather 2000).

PART I

MEDIA AND MESSAGE

ONE

MEDIA SINCERITY AND PROMISCUITY
Origins

ON OCTOBER 31, 1517, A perturbed Augustinian monk marched to the castle church in the community of Wittenberg, in rural northeast Germany, and nailed to its doors a lengthy list of theological complaints. Commentators sometimes romanticize this event by painting a picture of a stalwart religious firebrand desecrating the physical structure of a Catholic church with a massive hammer and crucifix-worthy nails. But such was hardly the case. In fact, there were ninety-five theses, but these aphorisms were likely attached to the door among pamphlets, notifications, and academic information. As the entry to the parish church, this door served as the public bulletin board. Imagine Martin Luther's paradigm-shifting list—nearly as famous now as the Ten Commandments—stapled amid flyers for upcoming lectures and lists of disputation theses for public presentation and defense. A world-altering text among miscellanies.

Historians argue as to how widely Luther intended his theses to circulate. As he disclosed in a personal letter, he may have only wanted the attention of local theologians and other educated men. But according to Andrew Pettegree's *Brand Luther: How an Unheralded Monk Turned His Small Town into a Center of Publishing, Made Himself the Most Famous Man in Europe—and Started the Protestant Reformation*, over time Luther proved himself a shrewd businessman, celebrity brand, and author of popular texts who almost single-handedly drove not only the fracturing of Christendom but the European print revolution. As Pettegree (2015, 54, 73, 75) writes, "It was the printing press that made Luther's theses a public matter and would rapidly make of their author a controversial and notorious figure." Regardless of his initial intent, as Luther became cognizant of the untapped power of the printing press, he strove to give his work "the widest possible circulation." The Ninety-Five Theses, once authorities beyond Wittenberg caught whiff of them, went through an unprecedented three separate reprintings. Here, at the beginning of what was to become the great Protestant Reformation, we see hints of media promiscuity beginning to stir.

Many studies of evangelicalism take for granted the communication media at the crux of the debate, but this chapter foregrounds a reading of the proto-evangelical Protestant Reformation event "that is organized around its media," to adopt one religion scholar's apt phrasing (Ward 2014, 116). This chapter tells the curious story of the birth of the dueling impulses of media sincerity and promiscuity, which is to say, it narrates the story of the Reformation and its immediate aftermath. Out of the Reformation, in short, emerged two intertwined media paradigms that would not only engender a new religious movement but would structure the entire system of Western communication. After tracing the beginnings of this new media paradigm, the second part of this history- and theory-oriented chapter focuses in on the usefulness of the concept of media ecology for the study of evangelical publics and addresses the questions surrounding technological **determinism**, affordances, **uptake**, and media ideologies.

THE RISE OF MEDIA PROMISCUITY

To describe the birth of media promiscuity, the first of two roots of what by the end of this chapter I will define as the evangelical media ecology, I turn initially to the example of one of the key motivators behind the Protestant Reformation: Martin Luther (1483–1546). In this section I describe Luther's textual endeavors and the aftereffects of the Reformation's innovations on religious authority and power. Evangelical media promiscuity, it turns out, originated with the Reformation's emphasis on mass textual production and circulation.

When Luther came on the scene, the disgruntled Catholic monk did not so much invent a new media paradigm as he commandeered developments already underway in Catholic Europe. Bibles printed in vernacular languages had begun to enter the consumer market. Cheaply produced and easily distributed small media, such as pamphlets or tracts, had grown in circulation. New visual art and image duplication techniques were on the rise. Although the task sent him into bankruptcy, Johannes Gutenberg (1394–1468) had by this time developed the movable type printing press by tinkering with Chinese designs. Ten years before Luther posted his list of theological disputes more than two hundred European cities already had presses and had put some six million monographs into the quickly growing consumer market (Horsfield 2015, 188–191).

In Germany, however, the few presses up and running were devoted largely to the labor of printing Catholic documents not intended for mass circulation or vernacular reading practices, such as indulgences or dispositions. Luther's rapid and controversial rise to publicity owed much to the developing media currents. In fact, the production of texts and their unintended uptake by unexpected audiences played a leading role in bringing about the Reformation. In a letter to Pope Leo X, Luther claimed that he intended his theses for the community at Wittenberg only and not a wider audience. "I did not wish to have [the Ninety-Five Theses] widely circulated," Luther (1518 [1908], 23) worried at one point because he "only intended submitting them to a few learned men for examination.... But now they are being spread abroad and translated everywhere." His published complaint, he explained, "was made public in such a wise [sic] that I cannot believe it has become known to all men" (Horsfield 2015, 192; cf. Dillenberger 1962, xxi). From a media studies perspective, Luther, at least at first, intended his theses as **local media**, not **mass media**. Luther's theses were by intention **small media**.[1] But his experimental texts quickly got away from him. Promiscuous media tend to be unpredictable like that. Regarding new media, Chun (2016, 102) writes, "This impoverished privacy is a habit, a possibly dangerous habit that covers over the promiscuous nature of networks, their wonderful creepiness."

If Luther did not foresee the trouble his theses posting would cause, he would also not have anticipated how the mass dissemination of his critical message would alter the future of Christianity. Regardless of Luther's surprise, when confronted by the authorities, he refused to recant. Finding support in the Wittenberg community (and from printers in north Germany) and aided by his penchant for vernacular preaching and writing, Luther took advantage of the burgeoning promiscuity of the print media milieu and began to seek out and create wide reading publics. He had launched his disruptive career printing in Latin, the official language of the Catholic Church, but by 1523 converted almost entirely to the German vernacular. Luther's discursive output was impressive by any standard. At conservative estimates, publications during his lifetime alone may have exceeded some 3.1 million copies. Luther's successes in generating large audiences meant that the printing presses of his day vied competitively for his business (Horsfield 2015, 192–193). Thick theological tomes were expensive for printers and nowhere near cost-effective. There was no economy for this type of heady work beyond the needs of the Catholic institution. Luther solved the problem of revenue by writing rapidly and frequently, publishing mostly pamphlet-sized works written in languages that people outside of the academic and monastic centers could understand. Luther's highly lucrative status with the presses meant that between the years 1518 and 1519, he became the Continent's most published author and a celebrity writer in his own right (Pettegree 2015, 105, 108–109). The printing press enabled the Reformation, but the Reformation fueled and financed the development of the printing press into a business that was its own veritable economy.

Promiscuous media, as defined here, are media that have the potential to spread widely and indiscriminately, transgressing old boundaries and redefining new ones. Luther's equivocating about to whom he intended his early provocations is the paradigmatic illustration of this impulse. Promiscuous media, whether evangelical or not, are evangelizing media. Media of this sort clamor for the gaze of the viewer, constructing readership collectives simply due to the fact of the media's ease and speed of textual production, circulation, and uptake.[2] Sociality forms around ideas, and mass-produced texts became a medium for spreading and sharing ideas widely. Circulation intends for the mass exposure of the media's message. Yet, promiscuity often produces unanticipated results. Again, consider Luther's case. Because of the potential for promiscuous media to travel widely beyond immediate contexts of production and intended audiences, they tend to breed controversy. They are helpful yet unpredictable, productive yet dangerous. If we take Luther at his word, he did not originally plan on going to trial as a heretic before church magistrates. Sometimes new media transgress old communicative orders; sometimes they support and extend them. Promiscuous media may aid social powers, but they may also challenge them by forcing authorities into defensive strategies of containment. It is no wonder that when faced with the eruption of heretical Protestant textual media, the Catholic hierarchy resorted to a concerted program of defense that involved a very literal method for silencing audience-soliciting texts: book burning.[3] But how does one stop the spread of a viral, dangerous public? By reducing the textual media circulation to ash and smoke. But even extreme measures of this sort did little to quell the burgeoning Protestant public.

THE RISE OF MEDIA SINCERITY

Promiscuity was not the only impulse during this tumultuous period. Media ideologies are always partial and contested (Gershon 2010a and 2010b), so it follows that other influential paradigms were likewise at play during this era of religious upheaval. A second impulse, what I identify here as media sincerity, tethered to and challenged promiscuity from the very beginning. These two ideologies of communication overlapped and diverged in complex ways. In the case of the Reformation, neither impulse existed without the other.

Is it anachronistic to think of Luther as a sixteenth-century social media **influencer**? Print text is, after all, inevitably social as a media form. Perhaps this analogy is too much, but our task as scholars of religion, as theorist Jonathan Z. Smith (1982; 1990) suggests, is to tinker in the humanistic laboratory of comparison and contrast, bringing similar and disparate things together for the sake of elucidation and understanding. Luther understood the ability of sincere media to sway hearts and minds and create new communities based on the consumption of shared texts. He capitalized on the power of promiscuous media to solicit audiences and call out theological opponents. Like the transcontinental itinerant revivalists and the televangelists who would follow centuries later (chap. 2), not to mention the theoblogians, Twitter pastors, and Instagram influencers after them (chaps. 4, 5, and 6), Luther theologized print technology as a divinely ordained tool of communication. He circulated vast numbers of booklets and pamphlets because of their efficiency in production, transportation, and audience building. Whatever else he was, Luther was an influencer.

So far, the concept of promiscuity describes much of what happened. But what about sincerity? Luther's booklets were radically different than existing works of theology, often less than forty pages in length that could be read quickly. In addition to shorter writings, the reformer also published sermons and aids for biblical teaching and exposition. His early works, as Pettegree (2015, 5, 81) describes, were "honest," "unassuming," and reflected his "intuitive genius" as a vernacular authorial brand. "Luther in effect invented a new form of theological writing: short, clear, and direct, speaking not only to his professional peers but to the wider Christian people." This new form of writing, in a word, was sincere. Luther was a skilled orator as much as a writer, but even mediated through his texts, he embodied sincerity. His sentences, again, were "short and direct." Making the most of the affordances of promiscuous media, Luther carried out a fruitful mass propaganda campaign, literally moving the battle out of religious institutional bounds and into the growing marketplace of print texts and discourse. Luther bridged the oral and written divide, cultivating publics by entreating literate audiences to read his texts aloud to those who lacked the skill (Horsfield 2015, 193–194; Hillerbrand 1968, xxv–xxvi). Sincerity and promiscuity from the outset were two sides of the same coin.

To move beyond Luther and speak in terms of communication, theology, and authority, the reformed impulse of sincerity totally reconfigured the Christian **lifeworld**. Another way to put this is that Protestantism is not simply a theological tradition birthed during the Reformation's upheavals. Protestantism is an entire semiotic system that influences all life domains, interpersonal communication rituals included. Protestantism as a religious, political, social, cultural, economic, and communicative system aimed "to embed itself in everyday practices" (Keane 2002, 67). Responding to the directness of Luther and others, the mode of communication shifted into what anthropologist Webb Keane has described as the sincere speaker paradigm. I refer to this paradigm throughout the book in shorthand as media sincerity.

Simply put, the nascent Protestant paradigm rejected mediated Catholic rituals and materiality as false and ungodly, and in its corrective strategies of purification produced new communicative values (Keane 2007, 76–82; Latour 1993). Notwithstanding the promiscuity paradox, sincerity in speech became the most idealized value in the reformers' resistance to what they saw as the inauthentically mediated texture of Catholic ritual. Sincerity as a virtue emerged out of a specific Euro-Christian context but engineered the trifecta of global, modern ideals that (1) privileges the agency of the autonomous individual, (2) places importance on freedom and self-creation by people across the spectrum of socioreligious hierarchy, and in light of these reconfigurations, (3) devalues tradition for tradition's sake (Keane 2002, 68).

Luther's disenchantment with church tradition and his reifying of the importance of the individual, authentically interior relationship of each person directly with God (Pettegree 2015, 96) helped initiate the Reformation. Almost singlehandedly shaping the early modern era's new doctrine of the agential, individual person, the sincere-speech paradigm rejected tradition and ritual in its emphasis on the inward sovereignty and authenticity of the modern individual. Sincerity, to summarize, was in its earliest forms a discourse that sought to transcend the ritual carnality and materiality of the Catholic cosmos by severing authenticity and authority from the physical bodies of the penitents and the priests. For the reformers, authenticity did not lie in embodied rituals. Instead, the result was that the nonmaterial, spiritual, authentic interior took on religious value (Bialecki 2017, 123).

Sincerity had massive practical ramifications for both institutionally religious and everyday interpersonal communication. Sincere words were powerful words. In a matter of speaking, writes Keane, to be sincere as a communicator was to "utter words that can be taken primarily to express underlying beliefs or intentions" (Keane 2002, 74). Words existed as transparent indications of the speaker's interior state. Sincerity signified the mechanisms by which words map onto thoughts in close correspondence. Thoughts were not more ambiguous than the words that convey their meaning, and speakers operated in a self-aware, authoritative state to put words to work in accurate manners (Keane 2006a, 317).

Several practical examples from contemporary life illustrate how the paradigm of the sincere speaker works. Consider, briefly, marriage rites, prayer, and the proclamation of belief. One of the clearest examples of a sincere speaker paradigm is the model of Western marital rites in which the exchange of sincere speech acts—that is, the reciprocal "I do"—constitutes the marriage bond between two persons rather than an exclusive exchange of material goods, as practiced in, say, Melanesian culture (Robbins 2012, 41n1). And how exactly do prayer rituals embody sincerity's ideals? "Protestant prayers should come from the heart, spontaneous and truly felt," Keane explains. Prayers "should be sincere" and not memorized or recited (Keane 2002, 77; cf. 2006b, 443). Later in the evangelical time line, John Wesley's widely discussed claim to have felt his "heart strangely warmed" (Barbeau 2019, 14) offers further evidence of this paradigm's powerful ontology at work. The sincere-speaker model also relates to other types of speech and communication. Anthropologist James Bielo (2015, 70) summarizes, writing that sincerity "places a prime value on truth-telling, personal intention, individualism, and speech as a direct reflection of moral character, and favors spontaneity over rote formula." This ideology also maps onto select biblical texts, such as the Gospel admonition that "out of the abundance of the heart the mouth speaks" (Luke 6:45, New King James Version).

Ultimately, sincerity embedded itself in and expressed itself through Protestant denominational fracturing across centuries and spanning continents. Sincerity had a key role in structuring the very texture of modern and Western linguistic systems and communication forms. In this post-Protestant language ideology, meaning resides in the intention of speakers. Communication is contractual and transparent (Robbins 2012, 31). Speakers should mean what they say, and under ideal circumstances, listeners will successfully and accurately interpret speech acts. Even quintessentially American religious expression, what Winnifred Sullivan (2005, 8) describes as "private, voluntary, individual, textual, and believed," has its origins in the sincerity paradigm.

THE AFTERMATH

During the Reformation, media sincerity and promiscuity worked hand in hand and emerged within the selfsame context. An ideology of sincere communication minimalized mediation and a penchant for direct speech and writing fed on a system of promiscuously circulating, audience-building texts. In this early context, promiscuity took on dual form regarding authority. From the perspective of the Catholics, Protestant textual culture was promiscuously heterodox, seductive, and transgressive. From the position of the inchoate Protestant leadership, circulating textuality acted promiscuously by empowering laypeople and decentralizing religious authority in ways unanticipated by the early reforming authorities. For the Reformers, promiscuity was at first a positive rather than negative outcome, but from there it quickly cycled out of control.

Retrospectively, the Reformation's promiscuous media turn had massive effects on everyday Christian theology and practice. Through the combined efforts of Luther, Calvin, and others, an emphasis on the need for lay Christians to read and interpret scripture for themselves escalated. As post-Reformation Christianity became more text-mediated, liturgical structure decreased. Replacing the materiality of the liturgy, words became sacramental. Translation of the Old and New Testaments away from the Latin and into more quotidian European languages ensued. Protestant translation and publication practices increased the accessibility of the various texts, which led to an increase in reading publics and participative audiences.

Such initiatives shifted modes of textual production, circulation, and consumption. Departing from the Catholic consolidation of scriptural authority to the priestly and institutional ranks, top-down religious hierarchies diminished as communities took up smaller public reading rituals—events not always supervised by clergy. Individual reading and devotional practices in more private settings also took off alongside rising literacy rates. Although engaging the senses through the development of oral preaching styles and congregational singing, the Calvinists also tended to promote an ascetic and iconoclastic approach toward the highly visually and materially mediated practices of medieval Catholicism. Within promiscuous Protestant media activities survived persistent threads of antimaterialist, antimediation sincerity (Horsfield 2015, 198–201, 205; Bossy 1985, 102).

Promiscuous media, in short, circumvented Catholic authority and aided the construction of new Protestant communities. But in the decades following the Reformation, the **vernacularization** of biblical texts and corresponding reading rituals had severe repercussions for religious authority. Correlating with rampant vernacularization processes, promiscuous media created challenges for the decentralized Protestant authorities as well. Like the controversy over the intended audience of the the Ninety-Five Theses, promiscuous textuality empowered laity to a degree not anticipated by Luther and company. Luther came to regret his "priesthood of all believers" slogan and worried about an unregulated hermeneutical free for all (Pettegree 2015, 47; Simpson 2019). In this new era of personal Bible study outside of church walls, Luther and other Protestant leaders disseminated aids for reading and correct interpretation. Denominationalism spread and an authoritatively decentered Protestantism fractured in Europe, strands of which would later transplant to the New World. In Europe, and then North America, denominational leaders produced commentaries, scriptural expositions, devotional guides, and tools for biblical study, including concordances or other aids. Regardless of the Protestant claim to rely on the so-called plain-sense meaning of the biblical texts, such guides and manuals underscored the arbitrariness of interpretations on what constituted plain sense. This new genre of text aids served to rein in personal interpretations and establish the guidelines for correct interpretive practice. Translators and publishers often included commentaries and other reading aids directly in the biblical texts, whether they be in the form of instructive glosses, marginalia, illustrations, or doctrinal asides—strategies that continue even in twenty-first-century American Bible production.

Protestant models of authority contrasted with the hierarchy of the Catholic institutional structure, but Protestant authorities nevertheless sought to establish orthodox beliefs and practices. To put a finer point on the matter, questions of orthodoxy, correctness, authority, legitimacy, and power continued within the decentralized and vernacularized progression of the Protestant denominations out of Catholicism. Systems for boundary maintenance proliferated within the increased Protestant bodies. The contrast is telling. Instead of a top-down organization and institutionalized hierarchy of power, deliberations about authority for the new Christians existed in a discursive, decentered sense, both within the circulation of print materials and the more encompassing verbal or spoken dialogues about such texts (Horsfield 2015, 199–200, 214–216; cf. Brown 2004, 42–43). Protestant authorities now competed with one another in the growing market of textual circulation, a situation that would continue to define evangelicalism in the modern era and on an entirely new continent. In short, the Reformation would have massive global repercussions for both structures of religious authority and the growing consumer market. The Reformation would also lay the groundwork for religious pluralism and the spread of global capitalistic networks (Gregory 2012).

MEDIA ECOLOGY, DETERMINISM, AND IDEOLOGIES: A THEORETICAL TOOLKIT

This chapter's final section shifts from the history and aftermath of the Protestant Reformation to discuss several key media studies concepts central to *The Digital Evangelicals*. I have introduced concepts such as the public, but we still lack a vocabulary with which to accurately categorize and depict the activities covered in upcoming chapters.

To begin, what is media ecology? Like digital religion, media ecology is a field of study that takes on the name of its research subject matter. Media ecology is a scholarly paradigm, school, or discipline of study emerging out of the work of pioneering media studies figures, including Walter Ong, Neil Postman, and Marshall McLuhan, and headquartered originally at New York University and the University of Toronto. In 1970 Postman simply described media ecology as "the study of media as environments" (Strate 2004, 4). Following in the wake of this scholarship, media ecology has become a veritable intellectual tradition (Strate 2004; Lum 2014a) of which *The Digital Evangelicals* is certainly a descendent.

The tenets of the media ecology perspective apply directly. According to scholars, one of the overarching claims of the paradigm is that media are by no means objective, value-free carriers of information. Furthermore, each technology has its own unique configuration of characteristics, whether those characteristics be functional, structural, aesthetic, or symbolic. These predisposed, structural biases define how technologies function and may even go as far as to determine the nature of human communication via that media. Media ecologists argue that embedded within all technologies are implicit techniques or affordances for action and inherent limitations or "trade-offs" (Lum 2014a, 2014b). It is no wonder, then, that some scholars have interpreted media ecology as deterministic in terms of the social uses, applications, and uptake of various media. One scholar even answered the question of how to define this field of study with the following provocation. Media ecology, for insider Lance Strate (1999), "is technological determinism, hard and soft, and technological evolution." As Strate's comment suggests, there is ambiguity within media ecology about its level of determinism. McLuhan, for instance, famously theorized that "we shape our tools and thereafter our tools shape us" (Logan 2010, 67). Even if media ecology is to some degree deterministic, determinism is only one part of the equation. The media ecology perspective offers a limited, dialectical sort of determinism that accurately depicts how technologies interface with the social.

Other concepts within technology and media studies help us think beyond the impasse of technological determinism versus human agency. The concept of affordance, for instance, proposes that technologies by design have implicit, built-in rules for use (Hutchby 2001). Affordances are those things that a technology's features "allow or encourage you to do" (Tufecki 2017, 118). The rudimentary technology of a glass windowpane affords transparency. A car affords the transportation of bodies and things from point a to point b. A pencil affords the recording of text-based language. Things get more complex regarding digital and informational technologies because the digital often intentionally affords the bundling of multiple uses. An analog phone, for instance, affords the conveyance of sound over distance but a data phone affords video recording, file sharing, social media access, *and* audible communication across space. And what about specific digital apps? A central goal for mobile phone technology is interpersonal communication over distance, but each app has its own built-in preferences for use. Instagram, by design, affords imagery. YouTube prioritizes video. Twitter capitalizes on concise, text-based discourse. Facebook is a more hybrid medium that brings together text, video, imagery, and links to other websites and sources.

An anthropological perspective pushes back against hard determinism by first pointing out that design intent, including the existence of built-in affordances, does not always work out on the ground. People use technologies for unanticipated purposes. Twitter affords short bursts of textual comments, certainly, but that limitation has not stopped some users from writing entire novels via tweet (Crouch 2014). An anthropologist would, secondly, point out that technologies emerge within specific systems—never within cultural vacuums—and are thus always inevitably social to begin with. This is the first half of McLuhan's dictum: people shape technologies. In Daniel Miller's (2018) collaborative anthropological project, *Why We Post*, for instance, researchers found that social media use is far from uniform globally and that English social media differs strikingly from Italian, which differs from Chinese. Third, an anthropologist might also point out that over time use acts back upon and shapes the technologies at the level of design. Based on user feedback, Twitter eventually doubled its one-hundred-and-forty-character cap to two hundred and eighty. Product recalls, updates, and redesigns are an inevitable and regular component of late capitalist life. In short, technologies are profoundly and irrevocably socially constructed, even as they are to some degree determined (Schroeder 2018, 18–19).

An anthropological perspective does not deny the deterministic aspects of technology, per se, but it does challenge essentialist notions of how determinism works. An anthropological approach should focus on the **social shaping of technology** as it occurs during the development of technological forms—the very creating of the affordances to begin with—as well as later during the period of uptake (i.e., use and application). What this means is that we ought to identify and study media ideologies, what Ilana Gershon (2010a, 3) defines as "a set of beliefs about communicative technologies with which users and designers explain perceived media structure and meaning."

"That is to say," Gershon continues, "what people think about the media they use will shape the way they use media." Media ideologies are "culturally specific, nuanced understandings of how these media shape communication and what kinds of utterances are most appropriately stated through which media" (Gershon 2010b, 290; Natale and Pasulka 2020, 2). Affordances, again, are only part of the equation. Heidi Campbell (2006, 151–152) agrees by arguing that adopters of new technologies **domesticate** and normalize the technologies they take up, often doing so in culturally specific ways. We must locate and understand the design ideologies implemented to create technologies to begin with along with the ideologies of use and interpretation that users apply. The use of new technologies involves a complex process of mediatization wherein tech-mediated interactions take on layered levels of meaning, inevitably shaping social connections for good or for ill (Lundby 2009; Clark 2013, xi). Technology subtly alters the user at the level of perception, outlook, and being (Vial 2019). Using technology changes us psychologically, mentally, and cognitively (Hayles 2012).

The Digital Evangelicals is a media ecology project in that it poses the above questions about causality and agency to its subject matter, views media as having affordances, is sensitive to mediatization, and sees humans as being structured, at least in a flexible sense, by the technologies they employ. But it also adopts the "ecology" terminology as a productive way to label identifiable media paradigms that can be traced through history into the present. I introduced the concept of the loosely bounded, text-constituted public in the introduction. An evangelical public, I argued, is created by dialogue over shared texts of many kinds. To turn to this chapter's materials, Protestantism is a counterpublic opposed to the powerful institution of the Catholic Church. But until this section, we have still been lacking a terminology to describe not just the social entity but the encompassing media system, paradigm, and environment within which technologies emerge and people interact. There are Protestant and evangelical publics just as there are Protestant and evangelical ecologies within which the publics operate. To reach a definition, then, the Protestant media ecology is the total mediated environment and ecosphere shaped by the introduction of the moveable type printing press and enabled and constrained by the impulses of sincerity and promiscuity. But media ecologies are dynamic environments of ideas, things, and uses and are continually subject to change over time, as the next chapter will discuss.

CONCLUSION

This chapter has described a brief and selective genealogy of the Protestant Reformation and the cyclical relationship between the impulses of sincerity and promiscuity. Promiscuity, to summarize, aided Luther as he sought publicity from wide readerships and undermined the authority of the Catholic establishment. Sincerity, likewise, attacked religious mediations of all sort and pined after transparency, clarity, and authenticity. The second part of the chapter turned to media theory and commandeered the totalizing concept of the media ecology as a productive way to speak of the effects of new technologies, embedded in real social worlds, on their users. I argued that we cannot as scholars of the digital write off the question of determinism and affordances but neither can we ignore the social construction of technologies in both design and application. Media ideologies are always at play. With these concepts in mind, we are now prepared to turn to the long history of new media that leads up to the emergence of the internet in America, the subject of chapter 2.

The following chapter shifts continents entirely and jumps forward in time to trace the Protestant media ecology as it reconfigures into evangelical iterations in America after the late 1700s. I summarize evangelical applications of oral, print, radio, and television media, discussing the ways in which sincerity and promiscuity merged and split at various junctures. By the time we reach the internet, at the end of the chapter, the stage of Protestant evangelical media dominance in the United States will be set. The struggle for evangelicals is the continued synthesis of these dueling, interacting, co-constitutive paradigms. The next chapter narrates a media history of evangelical America.

NOTES

1. Debra Spitulnik's (1996) differentiation between **vertical** (mass mediated) and **lateral** (local, face-to-face) **communication** applies to Luther's situation as well.

2. Some scholars describe this situation of intensified speed and heightened emotion with regard to mediated interactions as *hypermediation* (Evolvi 2018; Scolari 2015).

3. On how Catholic book burning helped constitute and strengthen Protestant formation, see Daniel Vaca, "Book People: Evangelical Books and the Making of Contemporary Evangelicalism" (PhD diss., Columbia University, 2012), 11. Luther, too, engaged in his own book burning campaigns, torching books, treatises, and pamphlets from the "old church" system, which he found problematic (Pettegree 2015, 131–132).

TWO

EVANGELICAL MEDIA ECOLOGIES FROM PRINT TO THE INTERNET

THE ORIGINS OF THE EVANGELICAL media ecology—a mediated, mediating environment that encompasses technology, texts, objects, ideas, theologies, ideologies, practices, habits, customs, ways of being, and discourse—begin with the Reformation and the corresponding invention of the printing press. But in the eighteenth century, an influential wave of itinerant revivalists spanned the Old and New Worlds proclaiming a revitalized form of evangelical Protestantism that emphasized individual piety, conversion, and religious experience. Determined to bring the emotive, experiential theologies of both the "new birth" and having one's "heart strangely warmed" to the masses, John Wesley (1703–1791) and George Whitefield (1714–1770) were among the first international celebrities. The revivalist phenomenon placed a high emphasis on the process of individual conversion and personal responsibility. Revivalist preaching emphasized direct authoritative speech, physical presence, and sincerity.

These revivals were religious events, of course, but until relatively recently the mediated, mediatized nature of these happenings has been mostly overlooked. The revivalists inherited and adapted the Reformation's dueling media ideologies in strong measure. The revivalists' constitutive system of preaching and response organized directly around sincerity's principles. In this era, preaching occurred live and in person. Large congregations and crowds filled empty urban lots or farm plots in the country. Audiences pressed in as near as they could to the preacher. In Whitefield's case, revivalist media were both rudimentary and advanced. Beyond voice carried on airwaves, the most elementary and embodied of communication media, the preacher used a raised platform and a spoke through a cone to amplify his voice and project his message to those at the farthest reaches of the gathered body. The preacher's authoritative words conveyed truth to the willing listener.

At a direct, interior level, listeners ideally found themselves moved to penitential action because of the message communicated by the speaker.

For the revivalists, sincerity coupled in complicated ways with promiscuity. The revivalist impulse, in fact, is one of the most important historical events in the development of the evangelical media ecology. Revivalist preachers intended their speech acts to fall on as many ears as possible. Both the open-air model and the itinerant system of preaching aimed at cultivating mass public audiences. Having trained in theater before entering the ministry, Whitefield was a skilled rhetorician. His voice projected well in outdoor arenas and public settings. By the end of his career, Whitefield had delivered some eighteen thousand total sermons. At his prime, he spoke to audiences as large as twenty and thirty thousand at a time and spent up to forty or fifty hours per week in the pulpit. Wesley was also a skilled public speaker and dedicated itinerant, who traveled four to five thousand miles on horseback throughout Great Britain. At his busiest, Wesley traveled seventy or eighty miles and preached as many as four or five times in one day. Both preachers were skilled in soliciting emotive responses from gathered audiences.

Promiscuous media, to recall, breed controversy and contestation. The promiscuous, highly emotional revivalist programs met with a considerable amount of debate among traditional Protestant authorities. Preachers faced harsh criticism by religious opponents who resisted what they saw as the inauthenticity of the growing culture of celebrity and personality in Christendom and saw the wide-reaching messages and high emotionalism as threatening, unorthodox, and disorderly (Horsfield 2015, 224–226; Coffman 2017, 199; Stout 1991). Print's promiscuity served for Whitefield as a medium of subversion against authorities just as it had for Luther, the very first Protestant. Promiscuous religious media, sometimes inseparable from advertisement, aimed to spread information to the masses and reach the widest number of eyes and ears possible. Unsurprisingly, promiscuous media applications in revivalist settings often resulted in controversy. Promiscuous media are evangelical, I argued earlier, but they are also concertedly Protestant in their abilities to undermine—to protest—existing orders.

This chapter documents the evolution of the evangelical media ecology in the United States, beginning with the genre of print and ending with the digital turn. The first part of the chapter examines the clever combinations and syntheses evangelicals made in bringing the impulses of sincerity and promiscuity together in their adoptions of print media, radio, and then television.[1] The second part of the chapter focuses on how the evangelical media ecology became dominant—even hegemonic—in America and documents how Protestant media ideologies shaped the origins of the internet and the commercialization of personal computing practices. The third and final part of the chapter narrates the arrival of the digital evangelicals.

EVANGELICALS AND PRINT CULTURE

Open-air **oral media** were valuable venues of communication for the revivalists, but printed texts played an increasingly important role. The revivalist ministries of the First Great Awakening relied more and more on the growing industry of print, market of circulating texts, and advertising culture. The revivalists were fully aware of the power of media technologies to publicize their preaching schedules, advertise their messages, and establish new networks among disparate Protestant communities. The revivalists exploited promiscuous advertisement media, tapping into the growing consumer economy, all while repackaging sincerely held religious messages into competitive commodities that would fare successfully in cutthroat markets. Meanwhile, constituted by print advertisements and fueled by fervent religious activity, the consumer market continued to expand in the American colonies.

The revivalists made the most of the developing economies, jumping into the fray by putting commercial and advertising strategies to work for their own purposes. Whitefield routinely fed key newspaper outlets with preaching schedules and included statistical information on the crowds drawn to his events. The preacher not only paid for advertising in newspapers but expanded the reach of his oral messages by creating transcripts of his speeches and publishing full sermons and letters in the papers. In other words, Whitefield engaged knowingly and willingly in mass-market strategies. Much like Luther, Whitefield demonstrated shrewd business acumen. The revivalist's entrance into the market was a turning point for promiscuous media as preachers began to convert their messages into new media. In Whitefield's case, he went about, as Horsfield puts it, "remorselessly selecting, editing, publishing, and disseminating print." In sum, evangelical Revivalists extended Christianity into the consumer culture, cleverly adapting to the rising tides of industrialization and commodification (Horsfield 2015, 226–232, 248, 228; Stout 1991) even as they exploited the medium's revolutionary aptitudes. As with the spoken word, the word in print became a necessary ingredient for widespread promiscuous media. For Whitefield, as one historian (McAuley 2013, 37) writes, "print created opportunities for marginalized folk to collectively make noise; it was a revolutionary technology used to create space for the vocal subversion of traditional-imperialist power structures. Print enabled Whitefield to orchestrate (or simply advertise) a veritable chorus of resistance."

Revivalism was a key strand of the broader entity historians retrospectively describe as evangelicalism. Historian Candy Gunther Brown (2004, 41, 45) notes that in the late eighteenth- and nineteenth-century United States, the printing press served a number of important functions for broader American Protestants, including "facilitating rapid exchange of information, forming and preserving collective identity, educating adherents about core values and beliefs, responding to criticism by outsiders, and contending for controversial viewpoints." Acting squarely in the Protestant historical milieu, which valued direct speech and imbued words with efficacy—both spoken and written—evangelicals "felt deeply interested in language and optimistic about the creative power of words." Contrasting Catholic emphases on tradition or the authority of the Church as an institution, Brown argues that "evangelicals expressed a deeper commitment to both the literal and spiritual meanings of the Word and words." For evangelicals, she continues, "the Word *was* God, and the Holy Spirit really, not symbolically, operated through divine and human words in radically transformative ways." In short, "words became vehicles" through which God actively manifested and became present in the world. Words were direct and sincere. Inheritors of Reformation values, sincerely uttered words and texts functioned for the evangelicals as authentic and powerful sacraments.

Evangelicals used print culture to disseminate information, construct and maintain social and ecclesial boundaries, and deliberate about belief and theology. A growing ecology of textual circulation and consumption permeated evangelical culture in America. Evangelicalism became, as Brown (2004, 12, 14, 18) describes, "a textually defined community" in which the mere consumption of evangelical texts constituted membership and participation in what evangelicals idealized as the universal orthodox Christianity. Texts mediated everyday lives, accompanied life events, and extended the evangelical community. Texts circulated far beyond the walls of the local church building into the domestic, commercial, and broader religious and denominational spheres. Evangelical print culture provided the media platform by which distinct evangelical cultures, in Brown's phrasing, "competed for dominance." Evangelical print culture genres included Sunday school curricula, print sermons, fiction, advice literature, memoirs, devotionals, hymnals, denominational periodicals, and family almanacs, among additional genres.

The history of American magazine publication illustrates how print circulation altered evangelical structures of power. Heather Haveman (2015, 159–160), a historian of the periodical genre, writes that between 1740 and 1860 revivalist strategies and a national policy of ecclesial disestablishment contributed to an explosion of denominational formation and increase in overall religious participation. By some estimates, the number of congregations rose from 1,350 to 54,000. Discrete religious groups increased from 13 to 31.

During this era, schisms, fractures, and contentions characterized American religion. Magazines played a key role in social boundary maintenance and influenced patterns and practices of daily life. Magazines were central for Christian identity building and the maintaining of socioreligious boundaries. Haveman

(2015, 160, 161–162) identifies the circulation and consumption of religious magazines as the most important facilitators of changes in authority, power, and religious structures. Magazines expanded religious networks, sustained and linked local communities, and restructured authority. These magazines "built on a tradition established by the Puritans and reinvigorated by revivalist preachers: reading was central to the experience of religion in America, for Americans had always read the Bible themselves." As an evangelical print genre, magazines projected new theologies and identities, undermined previously established systems, competed with religious competitors, and sought out new converts. The production and circulation of magazines served as a primary tool for socioreligious world making.

Magazines and other print genres succeeded as mass religious media because the modes sought to extend or supplement direct, face-to-face communication, which was made difficult by the separation of isolated communities from each other due to difficult and expansive frontier. A lack of adequate religious leadership, either local or itinerant, also played a role. Because "people were spread thinly" (Haveman 2015, 169, 173), magazines served as a social glue for connecting these disparate communities. Print was an agent of ecclesial boundary maintenance, certainly, but editors also knowingly exploited the medium for its ability to "be deployed and to build community—both locally and translocally." Print allowed for socioreligious contestation among religious groups, but it also fostered social cohesion and mobilization. In historian Nathan Hatch's words, nineteenth-century magazines were "the grand engine of a burgeoning religious culture, the primary means of promotion for, and bond of union within, competing religious groups" (Hatch 1989, 125–126; cf. Haveman 2015, 18–19). Magazine circulations constituted a vital socioreligious fabric. Print was the initial medium of this burgeoning public's existence.

Fast-forward to the twentieth and twenty-first centuries, and print culture has continued to serve as a primary mode of evangelical sociality. In fact, as Daniel Vaca contends, the expanding market of evangelical book publication following the 1950s helped produce evangelicalism as a discursive label or "social public" recognized by outsiders and insiders alike (Vaca 2019; Warner 2002). Since the Reformation, the idea of layperson access to the Bible had been an evangelical imperative, but in the 1930s and 1940s, publishers such as William B. Eerdmans and Zondervan began to produce much more than just Bibles. At first Eerdmans and Zondervan saw little immediate success as publishing firms marketing beyond small reformed or fundamentalist audiences, but this all changed when the presses began to professionalize in the 1950s. The commercializing presses achieved further public success in the 1960s and 1970s, when Christian bookstores began to appear all over the nation in shopping malls and other public commercial outlets. By the 1980s, evangelicalism's visibility had ratcheted up to a degree that could not be ignored. Evangelicalism's commercial endeavors have continued to proliferate and have seen a high degree of specialization due to marketing strategies for various audiences (Longinow 2008; Hendershot 2004). Both shaping and adapting to the consumer market, Christian textual genres mirror the breadth of mainstream topics and range from self-help content, to children and young adult literature, to romance novels, to theological treatises, to general fiction, to devotional literature. Religious publishing in the United States currently exceeds a $1 billion annually.

According to the Evangelical Press Association, millions of readers still receive print periodicals and dozens of new print publications enter the market each year. The Billy Graham Association distributes its *Decision* periodical to some eight hundred thousand recipients. *World Vision* has a readership of five hundred thousand. *Relevant*, a contemporary magazine geared toward evangelical **millennials**, has eighty thousand print subscribers (and over one hundred thousand monthly visits to its online site). Other flagship magazines include *Christianity Today, World, Sojourners, Christian Chronicle*, and *Christian Examiner*, among others. More audience-specific publications address gendered readerships (*Today's Christian Woman, Christian Women Today, Just Between Us, SpiritLed Woman, Radiant, New Man*), sports and athletics (*Sports Spectrum* and *Christian Motorsports*), and child or adolescent audiences (*Clubhouse, Brio, Breakaway, Ignite Your Faith*) (Waters 2008, 71–72, 83). In the digital era, print magazines contend with digital reading habits but have far from died out.[2]

Rarely, if ever, do new communication technologies replace earlier ones entirely, but they do overlap and integrate with one another in different ways. Following such temporal overlap, this chapter's timeline is hardly neat or linear. Print, radio, and television have existed in tandem for some time now and continue to do so, even as the digital serves as a metamedia, of sorts, in that it colonizes and integrates older media by merging them into one platform, device, or network. Evangelical print culture continues to evolve after the invention and popularization of the radio. Evangelical media studios often broadcast in more than one genre. For instance, as we'll see below, Oral Roberts experimented with both radio and television. Like the ideas and ideologies that surround them, technologies themselves exist in complicated, overlapping relationships with older and newer media.

EVANGELICALS AND RADIO

More sensory than one-dimensional print, radio broadcasting technologies directly extend the capacity to project a speaker's voice to listening audiences.[3] The ramifications of radio technology for both sincerity and promiscuity are significant. The evangelical radio entrepreneurs I discuss below conceive of radio media as both sincere and authentic as well as wide reaching. Radio media were certainly promiscuous, but they projected the authority of the preacher's voice in novel, efficient ways.

The narrative of religious broadcasting in America is an account of eventual evangelical market saturation and control (Voskuil 1990, 69; Lynerd 2014, 168–169). According to scholar of religion and media Mark Ward, the 1920s were a chaotic time of trial and error when evangelicals experimented with radio broadcast technologies before government regulations applied to the nascent communication domain. The late 1920s to mid-1940s saw the rise of radio preachers who purchased airtime and rose to dominance, but between 1945 and 1969, the restricting of airtime for religious programming encouraged evangelicals to think strategically as entrepreneurs and construct their own radio infrastructures. The seventies and eighties were the golden age of conservative evangelical radio broadcasting as the total number of radio stations owned and operated by evangelicals reached around one-third of the total radio industry. Between 1999 and the present, several powerful evangelical media conglomerates have consolidated ownership of previously independent religious radio stations (Ward 2014, 123).

Although early evangelical radio entrepreneurs justified the medium as primarily a tool for evangelization, proselytization was only one of several functions. According to Quentin Schultze (1990, 188), "the 'ministry' stations with back-to-back preachers and Bible teachers were not evangelistic. For one thing, few nonevangelicals tuned in [to] the stations. For another, the programs were designed to attract evangelicals and to solicit contributions from them, not to lure unconverted radio listeners."

"Radio invoked the oral and musical qualities of worship," Horsfield (2015, 244) notes. Many activities migrated to the radio waves, activities including preaching, music services, teaching, and instruction. During the golden age of American radio broadcasting, evangelical churches and institutions extended their influence into the broader discursive milieu of the American nation.[4] According to revivalist Aimee Semple McPherson (Musa 2015, 97), radio was a "messenger of the gospel of God, speeding to the far lands, encircling the globe in one second! Harbinger of faith, and hope, and salvation traveling on the wings of the winds to one million listeners gathered in the Cathedral of God, which is the earth and all who dwell in it" (Lynerd 2014, 168). The National Evangelical Association (NAE) itself, one of the most powerful of historical evangelical institutions, formed for the sole purpose of aiding conservative evangelicals in gaining radio media dominance and expanding the global Cathedral of God.

Charles Fuller's *Old Fashioned Revival Hour*, one of the most successful mid-century radio programs, illustrates the attempted combination of sincerity and promiscuity in radio media. In the 1940s, Fuller's program boasted a regular audience of 20 million listeners and broadcast across four hundred radio stations. The radio show comprised what Ward (2014, 123) describes as "live media rituals," following the model of the typical revival service. The *Old Fashioned Revival Hour* had music and a live choir, a testimonial section in which Grace Fuller read from letters sent in by audience members, a sermon delivered live by Fuller himself, and a response period for decisions about conversions to be made by listeners (Ward 2014, 123–124; 2017, 62–74). Fuller solved the dilemma of the early itinerant revivalists constrained by space, time, and physical presence. Print had ameliorated these tensions, but radio appeared to solve them. Fuller perceived no mediated gap between preaching before a physical congregation and projecting an entire evangelistic service for people to experience hundreds of miles away. Promiscuous media served as a platform with which to convey and transmit authentic and direct experiences across physical distance. Radio media may have had the limitation of being nonimmediate in terms of audience participation, but audiences frequently worked to minimize this gap by sending in written testimonials to the ministry that were read on the air.

A media-centric account of evangelical history suggests that radio broadcasts produced discursive spaces that functioned as spaces of social integration, identification, and legitimization (Ward 2014, 119; Vance 2016; Wrench 2016). The technology structured evangelical lives at the everyday level. The radio became ubiquitous in many evangelicals' lives, with users often progressing through the grind of daily schedules by tuning in to favorite programming. As Ward (2014, 117) notes, "Christian radio gave the subculture everyday sustenance." Loyal to their favorite religious programs, evangelicals tuned in to their radios across domestic and occupational domains. As the radio became more functional, streamlined, and physically smaller with design improvements, bedrooms, kitchens, living rooms, bathrooms, offices, workplaces, cars, public transportation, and gymnasiums all became spaces occupied by radio. One could listen to religious programming while going about daily tasks. Radio had profound implications for evangelical habitudes, literally expanding the media ecology.

Consider one listener's comments on the expansive reach of Fuller's radio program:

> In thousands of saloons throughout the land would the gospel music be turned on, even men in their cups would not want to miss what they knew was from the Lord indeed, from whom they were trying to flee; automobiles crowding the lanes and highways of our land could tune in to this uplifting hour. Even people reclining on the beaches or in the mountain summer resorts, with small hand radios could let their souls bathe in this hour of spiritual lift. Hundreds of congregations without pastors, unable to secure the services of a local preacher, could gather together in a place of worship, or at a home, and listen to one of

the rarest hours of divine service that God has allowed any man to create in our generation. When a heavy blanket of snow confined millions of farmers to their homes, or rainstorms made roads impassable, the Lord's Day need not pass without such music as few church choirs can produce, and a message around which hours of prayer had gathered. (Smith 2014, 126)

In this evangelical's appreciative description, the radio was the solution to all sorts of previous issues. People listened to the program in their cars, while on vacation, or at home. When weather conditions would not permit rural laypeople to travel to church, radio extended the church to the context of the listener. This allowed working-class audiences the ability to tune into church services at a distance, perhaps even while doing other domestic or labor-related tasks.

Radio media, in summary, served as facilitators of religious cohesion and emotive experience. For evangelicals, radio media were still limited in that they did not afford for the authenticity and directness of a face-to-face interaction. But radio was the next best thing, and in tradition of evangelical radio entrepreneurs, the radio's promiscuity did not seem to diminish its sincerity of sensory experience.

EVANGELICALS AND TELEVISION

Television likewise reconfigured the media ecology of American evangelicals during and after the 1950s but did not supplant the earlier genres of print and radio. Sometimes radio entrepreneurs and television entrepreneurs were one and the same as when evangelical studios experimented with mass media broadcasting forms. But whereas radio projects voice in an auditory manner and privileges the sense of hearing, television technologies extend sight and invoke physical movement across vast domains of space. To some degree, television is a more holistic sensory medium than radio as it, in most cases, conjoins both sight and hearing and facilitates the experience of mobility and movement across distance without requiring actual physical movement. Television, in other words, can serve as an extension of ritual, ceremony, and religious affect into the public domain (Buonanno 2008 17–20; Rosenthal 2012).

Billy Graham (1918–2018) became one of the first celebrity televangelists in 1957 after media companies began to televise his meetings following a sixteen-week revival at New York City's Madison Square Garden (Balbier 2009, 71; Wacker 2014). Although Graham is the most iconic televangelist in American history, he is not the first to make use of the new medium. Two earlier mid-century television adopters were Rex Humbard (1919–2007) and Oral Roberts (1918–2009). Humbard was an entrepreneurial preacher from Akron, Ohio, who decided to broadcast his local weekly services to a broader audience. Roberts had already made extensive use of radio but eventually expanded his revivalist media platform to encompass more than sixteen television stations (Horsfield 2015, 251).

Revivalist entrepreneurs framed their technological adaptations in typical evangelical prose by describing television as an evangelization tool par excellence. But the revivalists' media experiments also transformed conceptions of community and sociality in the process. Graham's ministry, concerned first and foremost with proselytization, is a case in point. The use of the medium altered the modes by which evangelical discourse operated. Uta Balbier (2009, 77) writes that Graham's televangelistic efforts "changed evangelical processes of conversion and community formation and altered or even replaced traditional forms of religious life." As the audiences for Graham's message expanded incrementally so did the forms by which Graham communicated his message. Graham spoke for the audience at his revival meetings but also altered his address to include physically distant attendees connected through television media. Staring deeply into the lens of the camera, Graham communicated directly to his audiences. His was a form of charismatic, mediated intimacy projected via a mode unimaginable to entrepreneurial preachers like Luther.

In 1951, Graham's *Hour of Decision* broadcast received 178,000 letters from the audience—and double that amount in 1952 (Coffman 2017, 200). As letters received by Graham's ministry attest, television extended a new form of religious experience as "many eager followers had found their way to God right in front of their televisions" (Balbier 2009, 76–77; Wacker 2017, 2–4). Television reconfigured the revivalist space and brought religious experiences and rituals into the domestic sphere. When Graham first began using television, the black-and-white, fuzzy pictures appeared flattened. Historian Elesha Coffman (2017, 206) describes this situation, writing that "audience members could not help but be conscious of the layers of technology between them and the evangelist." But technologies improved rapidly so that "clearer radio signals brought Graham's alternately forceful and reassuring voice near, as if he were speaking directly to the listener." Improving on radio, sincere religious experiences could now be had in the privacy of the home, either on one's own or surrounded by friends and family. Television altered the space of evangelism, like radio before it, but this time provided a more holistic sensory event. In Graham's mind, television was unmediated communication. Television was for Graham a medium of untapped power (Coffman 2017, 206). It was, in his own words, "a medium of face to face communication. It's the most powerful medium we've ever known. And whether you're selling a bar of soap or whatever you're doing, television is the way to do it today" (Coffman 2017, 200). Graham reinforced the troubled marriage between media sincerity and promiscuity, theorizing television as direct, immediate, sensory, and thoroughly broadcastable.[5]

To be clear, not all Protestants embraced television media with the fervor of the evangelists. Not all Protestants preferred such a close relationship between sincerity and promiscuity. Mainline Protestants, for example, found televangelists too vulgar and anti-intellectual for their liking (Rosenthal 2007; cf. Coffman 2017). For these Protestants, television media were for entertainment and consumerist purposes and thus were not hospitable toward media sincerity. For them, television was not a proper media conduit. Mainline Protestants, for the most part, reject television at the levels of both media and message and in doing so provide an example of a Christian media ideology that in the context of television seeks to untether (rather than conjoin) the sincerity and promiscuity paradigms. Sometimes Christian liberals did use television to forward the causes of the Religious Left. Such was the case for Hollywood writer and producer Norman Lear, who used the popular sitcom genre to subtly preach the virtues of diversity, inclusion, and religious tolerance to the American public. Lear intended his work as a counter to the conservative televangelists (Rolsky 2019). Although there was some uptake among liberal Protestant cultural creators, this engagement was minimal compared to the Religious Right, among whom evangelicals were a constitutive part.

Evangelical television adoptions, especially in the revivalist and Pentecostal-Charismatic veins of theological expression, illustrate how technological development integrates in a complicated manner with religious development. In the charismatic televangelist domains, Kenneth Copeland, Billy Joe Daugherty, Kenneth Hagin Jr., Jesse Duplantis, Jerry Savelle, Creflo Dollar, Marilyn Hickey, Kathryn Kuhlman, Paul and Jan Crouch, Pat Robertson, and Benny Hinn all cultivated public programming ministries. Oral Roberts, Robert Schuller, Jimmy Swaggart, Rex Humbard, Jerry Falwell, Jim Bakker, James Robinson, and Pat Robertson ran some of the most sizable television programs during the 1980s. Conservative estimates of audiences in this era put viewership for these preachers at 85 percent of religious television watchers. Some quantitative studies estimated that upward of as many as 60 million Americans tuned into the above programming over a thirty-day period. Televangelism and the Religious Right dominated the airwaves (Frankl 1998; Rosenthal 2007).

Charismatic revivalist Benny Hinn, as another example of the combination of sincerity and promiscuity, is emblematic of other eager evangelical adopters of television in his concerted theological deliberations about and ultimate apotheosis of the medium. Hinn theologizes television, conceiving of telecommunication as a fluid, highly connective, metaphysical format. For Hinn, television was a divine gift bestowed upon Christians to spread the good news, convey teaching, and facilitate embodied healing practices (Cooper 2014).

Billy Graham's viewers faced the television and knelt on the floor of their living rooms to pray the Sinner's Prayer in their mediated conversion acts, but

Hinn's audiences decades later claimed to experience the power of the Holy Spirit imparted to them via the metaphysically fluid and permeable medium of the television screen (Balbier 2009, 77; Cooper 2014, 12–13). Television augments for the revivalist more than the senses of sight and sound. For Hinn, the medium transfers or extends physical presence and touch. In his television programming, the preacher encourages his viewers to extend their hands toward their screens so that he could impart divine healing through presence. Viewers take Hinn up on his offer. "I watch your program every day," a viewer from St. Louis wrote in a letter to his ministry. "I laid my hands on the television screen and I received my healing of a stomach problem" (Hinn 1999, 162–163; Cooper 2014, 13). Television is a conduit whose mediations appear to matter little for experimental revivalists. The media affordance for the dissemination of presence is even more efficient for these preachers than radio or open-air preaching.

Like other televangelists, Hinn uses television to extend Pentecostal **sensational forms** and convey physical touch, including the laying on of hands and proximal intercessory prayer (Meyer 2007; Brown et al. 2010; Hendershot 2004, 3). Hinn's televised endeavors offer one of the clearest examples of the revivalist synthesis between the dual operations of sincerity and promiscuity. He imbues television media with religious, theological, and experiential value. Like the early Protestant's high valuation of words as the material of the divine, television for Graham and Hinn becomes a divinely ordained medium. Communication media and technology have for evangelicals profound theological, ontological, and pragmatic necessity.

Televangelism created implications for new modes beyond proselytization and religious experience. During the second half of the twentieth century, an entire evangelical media empire arose via television broadcasting networks. Like radio, these new methods altered evangelical modes of interaction, including theological instruction and discipleship, community formation, entertainment, and boundary maintenance. In 1967, as Horsfield (2015, 251) describes the process, Oral Roberts "closed down his television program and began redesigning it, reopening two years later with a new variety show format featuring well-known guests and performers and a message delivered by Roberts in a much smoother, 'cooler' style." Likewise, Pat Robertson pioneered the televised *The 700 Club*, a parachurch, lifestyle-based organization, to provide evangelical publics with information beyond preaching and teaching resources for discipleship and theological exhortation. *The 700 Club* offered the evangelical equivalent of secular talk shows, interviews with public figures, cooking segments, health-and-wellness features, daily news programming, and other popular television genres (Cooper 2013). At present, evangelical television conglomerates, such as the Trinity Broadcasting Network, offer viewers evangelical versions of reality television, travel shows, children's programing, fictional dramas, and other visual entertainment subgenres (Wagner 2016). Yet, such genres are not solely educational, instructive, devotional, or entertainment based and like evangelical radio are engaged in boundary maintenance strategies and insider/outsider discourse (cf. Ward 2014, 125).

As with radio, evangelicals domesticated television and theologized it, molding the medium to fit their purposes and interests. For evangelicals, these media created new viewing, listening, and reading publics that extended their interests and influences into broader American society and linked communities across the previously unsurmountable abyss of physical distance. Most importantly, from the perspective of the televangelists, the impulses of sincerity and promiscuity remain mutual yet conflicted. In the case of television, the medium affords copresence and direct authoritative speech to be delivered on a mass scale. Television allows for the effective exchange of ritual words between parties, if in a compounded and more mediated sense, and for the partial extension of the body's aptitudes, functions, and senses. Television as mass broadcasting media, in this case, is key. As a promiscuous media form, evangelical television defied any sort of sacred versus secular divide and permeated the broader marketplace of American visuality.

EVANGELICAL AMERICAN MEDIA DOMINANCE

Whether or not America is a "Christian nation" is a complex and loaded question, but scholars of American history agree that Protestant Christianity has played a strong causal role in shaping American institutions. Tracey Fessenden (2007, 5–6) writes of a "Protestant establishment," which created a formidable "consensus" or "center," constituting the "unmarked category" of the American religious milieu, much like the category of **whiteness** in a racial sense. Employing a fitting technological metaphor, Catherine Brekus and W. Clark Gilpin (2011, 1) contend that "Christianity—like electricity—is simultaneously omnipresent and invisible in the modern United States." Christianity "so permeates American sensibilities about space and time, right and wrong," Brekus and Gilpin continue, that it operates by way of a "pervasive invisibility." Tisa Wenger (2009, 4) likewise describes a situation in which Christianity enjoys a monopoly on defining what counts as legitimate religion. Most recently, historians and sociologists have begun to trace the roles that racial identity and whiteness have played in Christian dominance in America.[6] Khyati Joshi's *White Christian Privilege: The Illusion of Religious Equality in America* (2020) examines how Christianity—in particularly white Protestant forms—came to be taken as the American norm, and Anthea Butler's *White Evangelical Racism: The Politics of Morality in America* (2021) is a survey of the social, cultural, and religious mechanisms by which white conservative evangelicals in America, from the nineteenth century onward, cultivated their institutionally hegemonic status by privileging whiteness at the expense of minority groups. But how does a **hegemony** of this sort translate into the overarching media ecology?[7]

One key argument of this book is that out of a slew of conflicting media ideologies, evangelical Protestantism had one of the strongest hands in shaping the American media ecology. Historical data supports this claim. American mass media originated with early-nineteenth-century printing presses ran by Bible societies intent on disseminating religious literature (Nord 2004). As an illustration of religion's influence on the early market, note that in 1740, 30 percent of works printed in colonial America were either written by Whitefield himself, the evangelical revivalist par excellence, or were commentaries about him (Coffman 2017, 199). Between 1741 and 1860, religious magazines constituted the most popular genre of periodicals in the United States—a genre that tended to stay in print longer than competing nonreligious subgenres and accounted for some 36 percent of yearly observations on magazines (Haveman 2015, 160). American print culture, in other words, has a rich Protestant genealogy. All of this reflects a longer historic precedent for the relationship between technology and religion as well. The Protestant Reformation, even further back, was the largest single causal force behind the printing press's development as a technology, economy, and industry (Pettegree 2015).

Conservative evangelicalism had its public image tarnished after the 1925 Scopes Trial, but radio media helped to reverse the trend, ultimately aiding the evangelicals in regaining public legitimacy due to its popular programming (Carpenter 1997, 139; Ward 2014, 124; cf. Bebbington 2005). In terms of broader American culture, evangelicals after the 1930s shifted from the status of religious outsiders to religious insiders (Voskuil 1990, 69–70). One of the main goals of the influential American Family Radio conglomerate and its network sponsor, the American Family Association, was to shape the contours of American morality to an evangelical standard nationwide (Wrench 2016, 181). The goal was widespread cultural influence, and radio, as Ward (2014, 124) puts it, "provided the means to disseminate an Evangelical subculture" to the broader American public.

The post-Scopes Trial dominion enjoyed by mainline Protestants eventually eroded as they for the most part, rejected and resisted what they saw as the vulgarity of mass mediatized television (Rosenthal 2007). The evangelicals increased their televised endeavors and taking up arms against the liberal Federal Council of Churches secured media dominance in the American milieu. As the twentieth century progressed, an evangelical media hegemony steadily spread and formalized, dominating the broader American media ecology (Attanasi and Young 2012; Apostolidis 2000). As the cases of print, radio, and television corroborate, by midcentury evangelicals began to enjoy success by way of sheer telecommunication market saturation.[8] Televangelists based primarily in the United States continue to control large segments of international airtime, as their influence has spread far beyond American national boundaries, colonizing the airwaves of the global north and south.

Protestant media ideologies, then, shaped American ones. But a crucial point to underscore is that within complex, pluralistic societies, the influence among competitive media ideologies is multidirectional. Evangelical experiments with new media shaped emerging communication technologies, and the use of the technologies acted back upon evangelicals in subtle ways. **Mediatization** of this sort is reflexive, dialectical, and circuitous. New technological implementation and media shifts always have unanticipated side effects. In the case of the evangelicals, new media adoption exposed the religious community to commercial markets and other secular domains and decentralized religious authority in a horizontal market of consumer goods. Other outcomes included a relativizing of evangelicalism in its contact with and categorization alongside myriad competing ideologies, including alternate forms of Christianity, non-Christian religious traditions, and nonreligious ideologies.

Without losing sight of the dual direction of influence, however, I do want to emphasize evangelical media's influence on the broader American media culture. This is a conversation that in internet studies and histories of technology often goes unnoticed. As with the Reformation's influence on the rise of the printing press, evangelical media postures had strong causal roles in influencing the development of internet technologies in a mainstream American sense. To restate for clarity, evangelical Protestant media ideologies had a powerful hand in shaping secular American ideologies about media and the consumer market. This should not come as a surprise. Historians of the Protestant Reformation and its aftermath, after all, have traced growing religious pluralism and the rise of consumer society and global capitalism back to this religious and economic rupture (Gregory 2012). Indeed, even in America, Protestantism was a key player in the production of the secular (Modern 2011; McCrary and Wheatley 2016; Cooper 2019).[9] The story of American media is the story of the genericizing of evangelical modes of communication. It is the story of evangelizing media.

These claims deserve some unpacking, especially given the fact other influential narratives, both evangelical and nonevangelical, appear to contradict evangelical media dominance. One story, for instance, involves persecution rhetoric and declension narratives. Christians have, since the Early Church, constituted their social identities as different from and alien to mainstream societies, often adopting the language of the marginalized, persecuted, and minority outsider to do so (Moss 2014). In the contemporary United States, evangelical subgroups use the language of "Christian America" or "Christian nation" to spin out a declension story that plots America's religious past as a golden age under attack by godlessness, liberalism, chaos, and disorder (Smith 2014; Connable 2016). Persecution rhetoric is alive and well in some conservative corners of evangelical America. In certain contexts, contemporary evangelical media work overtime to construct and affiliate with persecuted Christian publics (Duerringer 2016; Smith 1998).

A second perspective identifies evangelicals as the losers of the culture wars and quasisecular religious liberals as the winners. Historian of American religion Matthew Hedstrom (2013) suggests that a liberal form of public quasireligiosity gained influence in the twentieth century—and not by bringing in new converts or numerically expanding liberal Protestant congregations. Instead, liberalism saturated American public culture by extracting itself from denominational specificity and naturalizing in terms of a vague, therapeutic spirituality.[10] Regardless of whether liberalism won out in the public sphere or evangelicals truly lost the culture wars, scholarly attention to liberal dominance, taken together with evangelical folk discourses about persecution, draws attention away from the implicit, near-hegemonic role that an evolved form of evangelicalism has had in shaping American media currents. A genealogy of American technology cannot ignore what Finbarr Curtis (2012, 366) calls "the hegemonic quality of American liberal inclusion," but neither should it fail to pay attention to underlying and less visible media ideologies.[11]

The surface-level message of public American religiosity may be liberal, and discourses in therapeutic spirituality, inclusiveness, and intellectualism abound. But the medium is evangelical. By the time of personal computing and the rise of the internet, the American media ecology had inherited a genericized version of the evangelical's tradition of dueling media ideologies. American new media, especially television and the internet, became **cultural carriers** of the evangelicals' tenuous balance between sincerity and promiscuity. A nonspecific, secularized variety of evangelical media, extracted from and then taken far beyond the restraints of its specific theological and ecclesial origins, pervades the American (and the global) milieu.[12] Discourses that began with a crisis of authority and mediation in Christian Europe transplanted to America and then popularized, mutated, developed, and spread to entirely new realms of application. To document this rise to dominance, I turn now to the introduction of digital media, an event some commentators describe as the **Second Reformation** (Rouse 1999).[13]

THE PERSONAL COMPUTER AND THE INTERNET: SINCERITY AND PROMISCUITY 2.0

The invention of the personal computer (PC) and the internet as influential communicative technologies is not the exclusive story of evangelicals or Protestants (or Christians in general). The internet came into existence within a motley field of ideological contention, both religious and nonreligious. Although competing ideologies and rival discourses structured the internet's emergence (Dick 2011, 155; van Dijck 2013, 22; Turner 2006; cf. Noble 1997 and Robinson 2013), I borrow José van Dijck's (2013, 21) language to argue that the "cultural logic," which informed the rise of the internet's mass accessibility, was thoroughly infused with the language of institutional critique. Criticism of institutional power has a long and complex global history; for this book's purposes, it begins with the Reformation, continuing through the Renaissance and Enlightenment. In addition to evangelical ideologies, the latter two political and cultural movements each contributed to the contested American media ecology. Antiauthoritarian and countercultural discourse of different forms transplanted to the United States, solidifying doubt and skepticism of religious authority as an American virtue as early as the late eighteenth-century (Porterfield 2012, 5).

The internet, to be clear, is neither a religious nor nonreligious entity. Thousands of ideologically diverse designers, programmers, and technicians have had a hand in creating online worlds and the tools by which communicators access them. As Wendy Chun (2016) argues, to reduce the internet to one thing is to misunderstand the multiple divergent structures that shape and define it. After all, the internet itself emerged as a synthesis of its own dueling tensions, namely elitist, military-grade technological developments on the one hand and the humanistic communalism and digital utopianism of Russell Brand's *Whole Earth Catalog* on the other (Turner 2006). But I want to emphasize that the ideological origins of the internet and the PC are infused with media ideologies as old as the Protestant Reformation. Too often, commentators have misconstrued *countercultural* as a synonym for *antireligious*. The internet, to the contrary, is a cultural carrier of evangelical media tendencies.[14] Although a full analysis of the technical history of the PC and a comprehensive study of the ideologies of all the internet's designers falls outside the scope of this book, I focus in the next several paragraphs on several formational texts in the social history of the internet authored by Ted Nelson, John Perry Barlow, and Vincent Cerf. My intent is to trace the adaptation of the tension between sincerity and promiscuity into the digital era and show how evangelical forms were accommodated by top designers and influencers in the tech industry.

Consider first, "Computer Lib: You Can and Must Understand Computers Now," a 1974 manifesto published by Ted Nelson, a hacker, computer programmer, and creator of hypertext—a foundational component of internet infrastructure. Up until the mid-1970s, computer-mediated developments had taken place largely in closed systems, initially military, academic, and defense-oriented communities, then it was isolated in the hands of technology program engineers, designers, technicians, and specialists. The elitist origins of the communication technology took a **democratizing** turn in public discourse when Nelson released his counterculture technology manifesto (Segaller 1998, 129–135, 286–288; Turner 2006). Like the hypertext model he founded, "Computer Lib" is a provocative, nonlinear, rambling booklet comprised of typed text, hand-scrawled subheadings, and loads of comical illustrations and diagrams to elucidate dense technical points. Full of quips such as "computer power to the people," "the computer priesthood," or "down with cybercrud," the self-published, 132-page document is an overwhelmingly positive and bleeding-heart media ideology if ever one existed.

Large swathes of "Computer Lib" walk the reader through pages and pages of tech speak on how the underlying systems of computer media work. But the thesis of Nelson's manifesto is that "everybody should understand computers" and computers should become tools of everyday use. Predating Apple Computer's famous television advertisement that drew on Orwell's dystopian *1984* in order to position the company as antiauthoritarian and democratic, "Computer Lib" wishes to free computers from the systems of power and privilege where they originated and shape them into objects of populist expression. In Nelson's own words, "The chasm between laymen and computer people widens fast and dangerously." Nelson desires for computers to become affordable populist tools to improve and organize daily lives. Unfortunately, the author laments, "Man has created the myth of 'the computer' in his own image, or one of them: cold, immaculate, sterile, 'scientific,' oppressive." Computers ought not to be elitist tools but "versatile gizmos which may be turned to any purpose, in any style."

Nelson's populist document reads like an anti-Catholic, Protestant diatribe. Almost Nietzschean in its antiauthoritarian aversion to the institutional elite, Nelson is firm in his view that "knowledge is power and so it tends to be hoarded." According to the programmer, "The use of computers is *dominated by a priesthood*." The power of the computer, he warns, was at that time shored up under the control of scientific and academic authorities (Nelson 1974, 2, 9, emphasis added). Nelson's language is not specifically religious, but he draws on a genericized Protestant lexicon to underscore his antielitist activism. What is important for the purposes of this book is that the rhetoric of effective institutional critique is largely Protestant.[15]

The intent of the booklet is to humanize and domesticate computers, which must have appeared to readers in the 1970s as ominous, frightening devices with their computational skill and mysterious abilities to connect with distant others and store and process vast amounts of information. Nelson predicts the "New Era" of the computer in which the device will become so integrated into human systems that it will become "invisible" in its simplicity of use and efficiency of function. In sum, "Computer Lib" sought to make the computer familiar and compel readers to take interest in how the inchoate systems functioned (Nelson 1974, 2, 4, 12). Nelson's antiauthoritarian media ideology overlaps and corresponds with evangelical discourses on sincerity and promiscuity. Like Luther's concerted textual activity, Nelson advocates for media promiscuity. With its call to abolish the "priestly" mediations of new technologies and vernacularize computing media, Nelson's manifesto carries on and corroborates with evangelical media impulses. Nelson takes the Protestant attack on religious institutions to an unimagined extreme.

Second, note the discursive work accomplished by John Perry Barlow's impassioned 1996 text, "A Declaration for Independence on Cyberspace." Responding to worries about free expression abuse, particularly in relation to issues of pornography and other concerns about virtual anonymity and excess, Congress passed the Communication Decency Act (or Telecommunication Reform Act) earlier that year (Segaller 1998, 269). Where Nelson's manifesto was lengthy, self-referential, and replete with illustrations, directional arrows, and comical marginalia, Barlow's declaration is concise and readable. Consisting of sixteen aphoristic paragraphs, Barlow is reminiscent of Nelson's criticism of elite powers. "Governments of the Industrial World, you weary giants of flesh and steel," the melodramatic document opines. "I come from Cyberspace, the new home of Mind. On behalf of the future, I ask you of the past to leave us alone. You are not welcome among us. You have no sovereignty where we gather." Barlow, like his predecessors, professes the doctrines of independence, freedom, inclusivism, and equality: "We are creating a world that all may enter without privilege or prejudice accorded by race, economic power, military force, or station of birth.... We are creating a world where anyone, anywhere may express his or her beliefs, no matter how singular, without fear of being coerced into silence or conformity." Barlow, in short, repudiates authority and control. He renounces government manipulation, dismisses the Decency Act, and censures his imagined audience for infringing on the Constitution's affordance for freedom of personal expression.

A close reading of the document, however, picks up on other ideological and philosophical threads concerning the internet and cyberspace. In Barlow's (1996) view, cyberspace is a profoundly disembodied arena: "Our identities have no bodies," so unlike ruthless corporations and governments, "we cannot obtain order by physical coercion." "Cyberspace," he writes, "consists of transactions, relationships, and thought itself, arrayed like a standing wave in the web of our communication. Ours is a world that is both everywhere and nowhere, but it is not where bodies live." According to the tech activist's metaphysic, the online world is radically and wholly other in its nonmateriality. "Our world is different," Barlow emphasizes. Cyberspace is different. The internet is other. A careful reading picks up on a subtle mind-body dualism, a quasi-Protestant survival of antimaterialism that even in these early years worked to shape and form ideas about what the internet is and how it differs from life as it existed before. He contends that "we must declare our virtual selves immune to your sovereignty, even as we continue to consent to your rule over our bodies. We will spread ourselves across the Planet so that no one can arrest our thoughts." Mind is pervasive and flows easily through the infrastructure of the cyberworld. Body, in a physical sense, means less in the new era of virtual networking. Cyberspace, the world of the future, is "the new home of Mind" (Barlow 1996).

Unlike Nelson's manifesto, Barlow's internet immaterialism reiterates a Protestant undertone that makes sense given his Christian background and seminary training. The document is shot through with the metaphysics of a sincerity paradigm that places authenticity in the spiritual interior but marks material bodies with suspicion and distance. Barlow's metaphysic conceives of bodies as the provenance of governments and regulations whereas ideas and communication— things part and parcel to the immaterial, sacred, autonomous, authentic, and mindful life of the interior—reside in the new, purer cyberrealms. Barlow's individual ideology of sincerity marks materiality as lesser than thought and ideas. He joins the ranks of influential shapers of the internet in speaking up for unregulated freedom of expression. In doing so, he differentiates between the online and the offline, mind and body, and internet-mediated life and existence in the "real" world.

Third, Vincent Cerf's "The Internet Is for Everyone" memo, circulated in 2002, extends the populist agendas of the two previous foundational texts. Cerf, an architect of the internet, praised the network for its ability to "facilitate democratic practices in unexpected ways" (Cerf 2002, 1). He reflects warmly on the fact that at the turn of the century, the internet was already "becoming the repository of all we have accomplished as a society" and introduces a new populist campaign, the product of his involvement in an activist group called The Internet Society, "to facilitate access to and use of Internet everywhere." Cerf's is a democratic vision par excellence. He calls for making the internet free and available and the use of PCs more accessible for nonspecialists. Like Barlow and Nelson, Cerf decries government legislation and calls for popular access and everyday use. He anticipates the concern over privacy and user data that would rise incrementally over the course of the decade.

Cerf's official title for Google, where he currently serves as vice president, is "chief internet evangelist" (Google 2018a). In public, Cerf jokingly identifies as "*Geek* Orthodox." Cerf recognizes the powerful role religious institutions have had in structuring media domains and preserving information over time (Burningham 2016). He argues that in a thousand years, "Religion will still be with us. It has not departed from human culture within the last 20,000 years, and I see no reason why it would disappear in the next century. 'Truth' will still be debated" (*European* 2012). Like a father of the Reformation, Cerf conjoins religiosity with ideology, contention, and the impulse to censor online activities. He contextualizes the invention of the printing press as a catalyst for media revolution against what was the prevailing institution: the Catholic Church (Hutcheon 2007; Sawers 2013).

Cerf advances a media ideology that coincides closely with the perpetual evangelical tension between media sincerity and promiscuity. Note this statement from "The Internet Is for Everyone" memo: "The Internet is proving to be one of the most powerful amplifiers of speech ever invented. It offers a global megaphone for voices that might otherwise be heard only feebly, if at all. It invites and facilitates multiple points of view and dialog in ways unimplementable by the traditional, one-way, mass media" Cerf (2002, 1). Recalling the evangelical revivalists, Cerf claims that internet media extend the communicative aptitudes of voice and in doing so reinforce the value of media promiscuity in providing free expression and access to information to everyone.

In summary, these three influential voices issued a trenchant critique of institutions, elitism, and authoritarian control. One scholar claims that "the ethic of the Internet age is rooted in free expression, a breakdown of hierarchy, a sense of individual empowerment, and a distrust of central authority" (Robinson 2013, 12). While depictions of the internet as antiauthoritarian and anti-institutional are partly correct, they fail to name the rhetoric employed in expressing these sentiments. The very lexicon of critique used in these expressions is Protestant. In the formational years concentrated between the 1970s and the late 1990s, the internet came into existence in an increasingly populist media ecology that rejected its institutionalized, militaristic, and elitist roots and sought to wrestle burgeoning computer technologies out of the hands of the elite and into the hands of everyday people. Vocal preachers of communicative populism and vernacular access to information evangelized for the rise of PCs and the internet and sought to harmonize the paradigms of media sincerity and promiscuity. In the next section, I return to the evangelicals to discuss Protestant social media uses after the mass marketing of the PC for widespread use.

THE DIGITAL EVANGELICALS

In the 1980s, talk about religiosity via online bulletin boards gave way to experimental forums linked to specific offline congregations. Online groups began to form, organized around various traditional religions as well as new religious movements. Christian denominations started to send out newsletters by way of email. In the 1990s, the number of different types of religious expression online proliferated. The first virtual congregations appeared, and chat systems and message boards provided venues on which to discuss sermons and other instructional media, also disseminated online.[16] By the end of the 1990s, the number of Bible-study resources and interactive discipleship or study groups had grown exponentially. Blogs had existed since 1998, but in the 2000s the medium became more and more popular. Religious podcasting likewise grew at this time. Virtual congregations continued to experiment with online rituals. The emergence of the social and collaborative Web 2.0, including Facebook (2004) and Twitter (2006), provided further venues for evangelicals to discuss their faith, beliefs, convictions, and identities (Helland 2005, 2015; Campbell 2013c, 278–280, 2010a; Brasher 2001; Cheong and Ess 2012, 2; Ebersole 2013).

Robert Glenn Howard's *Digital Jesus: The Making of a New Christian Fundamentalist Community on the Internet*, published in 2011, offered one of the first book-length studies of Christian internet culture. *Digital Jesus* documented how across various internet-mediated platforms a network organized around discussions of end-time theologies emerged. Howard's ethnographic research suggested that not only did internet media encourage a novel form of vernacular activity, it also reconfigured authority structures by increasing access to diverse ideas and undermining the need for top-down institutional leadership. *Digital Jesus* is evidence of the internet's public-conjuring affordances for conjoined yet divergent communities, that is, both conservative and progressive evangelicals. At the end of the first decade of the new millennium, evangelicals across the spectrum had established entire discursive communities networked through internet media.

Yet the growth of increasingly mobile social technologies in the new millennium meant that the consumer demand for religious applications (or **apps**) for ritual practices, social connection, and entertainment also increased (Campbell 2013c, 280–281; Trammell 2016; Wagner 2012). Churches developed internet campuses, webcasting programs, and data phone apps for facilitating both church services and congregant interactions. Most of the time, evangelicals use applications intended for mainstream America. But in some cases, evangelicals submit their own versions of online services into the market, such as GodTube, the Christian equivalent of the video-focused YouTube (Einstein 2013), among a host of others (Trammell 2016). The 2000s also saw a rise in the number of manuals—see the next chapter—published in print, audio, and ebook form. Technology manuals of this sort instruct evangelical readers on how best to navigate the simultaneously dangerous and potentially helpful internet.

The evangelical media ecology again reconfigured after the rise of the PC, just as it had after the radio and television turns. On the one hand, evangelicals used the digital to extend their publics, increase sociality, congregate in new creative venues, and share information widely. But on the other hand, the inevitable process of mediatization means that evangelicals were also subtly altered through their uptake of these media. One such reconfiguration has to do with conceptions of temporality. As Zynep Tufecki (2017, 122) writes, digital media "affect how we experience space and time" and in doing so "alter the architecture of the world." The scholarly consensus is that digital media, and especially what are called **habitual** or **ubiquitous media** (Fewkes 2019, 6)—that is, widespread, integrated, everyday devices—are shifting perceptions and experience of the flow of time (Vial 2019). Popular discourses on technology, as we'll see, often describe time in the digital era in terms of loss and subtraction. As habitual media become more ubiquitous in everyday life, people report feeling even more pressed for time. Evangelicals comprise a significant percentage of those Americans who experience such a temporal deficiency and, as I'll show in upcoming chapters, design strategies and rituals to correct for the deficits of digital communication (Horsfield 2015, 264–265; cf. Honoré 2004; Menzies 2005). But evangelicals also began during these initial years of the digital turn to experience changes in the very modes and textures of their communication. These changes were so significant, in fact, that they began to pen how-to manuals about the best way to use digital media to their benefit and ward against the less beneficial outcomes of internet culture. Evangelicals had more access to information than ever before, but it quickly grew apparent that too much information—a barrage of data—was a detriment to healthy living rather than a boon.

CONCLUSION

At this very point, the entrance of evangelicals to the online domain—the rise of the digital evangelicals—the stage is set for the chapters that follow. Each of the upcoming chapters will observe, analyze, and theorize the relationship of evangelicals to the internet and digital media from a different vantage point and methodological perspective. Rather than simply narrating a history of evangelicals and technology from the Reformation to the present, this chapter has plotted a selective genealogy of evangelical media ideologies that informs the broader American media ecology.

The chapter issued several primary claims. Historically, evangelicals have influenced secular, public American media, contributing in vast droves to and inundating the consumer economy with their myriad communication artifacts. Evangelicals domesticate the technologies they adopt by "culturing" or "normalizing" new media, that is, theorizing them via their own ideological dispositions (Campbell 2006, 151–152; Matthewman 2011, 24). In the case of American evangelicals with dense roots in the media event horizon of the Reformation, new media use filters and processes through the dueling media ideologies of sincerity and promiscuity. Over time, evangelicals endeavored to shape print, radio, and television media as sincere, authentic, direct, powerful, effective, genuine, and meaningful. Revivalist evangelicals exploited promiscuous media to reach wide audiences and subsumed the new media into an ideology that placed high value on embodied presence and sensory immediacy. Finally, moving beyond their specifically religious origins, the ideologies of sincerity and promiscuity continue to inform the age of the internet, if in a genericized, secularized sense.

In the next chapter, I turn to one of the newest choruses of evangelical authorities as they strategize to make sense of the internet for Christian purposes. Evangelical media theorists and technology manual writers, like their predecessors working in radio and television, will debate over how best to put this newest media to use. Breaking with the media metaphysics of the evangelical revivalists, writers will revisit the defining evangelical tension between sincere and promiscuous media. Many writers will criticize their predecessors' quick adoptions of communication media as inauthentic and compromising for sincerity. Instead, some evangelical media theorists will argue for measured programs of restraint and separation from the secular information economy. Sincerity and promiscuity take on new understandings and the relationship between the two paradigms reconfigures in novel ways.

NOTES

1. The media discussed in this chapter are not the only technological environments of the modern era, but they may be the ones most central to the story of evangelical America. For a masterful study of religion in and around an older new media form and a kindred hybrid religious studies and media studies project, see Jenna Supp-Montgomerie's *When the Medium Was the Mission: The Atlantic Telegraph and the Religious Origins of Network Culture* (2021).

2. Contrary to worries about the death of print following the rise of digital media, some evangelical periodicals have hybridized, offering both traditionally printed magazines and digital versions in recent years. Cameron Strang, the founding editor of *Relevant* magazine and son of *Charisma* founder, Stephen Strang, has found that young evangelicals prefer both print and digital formats and that the latter is far from supplanting the prior (Strang 2017, 10–11; Waters 2008, 75–76). Print culture among some sectors of American millennials has undergone a recent resurgence steeped in a media ideology that idealizes the materiality of printed objects as meaningful ones and views the digital through a lens of suspicion (Strang 2017, 11; Chayka 2016).

3. In technical terms, radio is a form of wireless telephony in which a stretch of voice, vocal utterance, or other measurement of sound attaches to an amplitude- or frequency-altered continuous carrier wave that itself moves along a respective sideband of modulation (Sterling 2005, 633).

4. To this effect, radio, like print, also had a social boundary maintenance function. Carrying on in historic tradition, contemporary evangelical radio stations continue in the present to promote programming that "positions evangelicals as God's insiders" and fashions all sorts of religious and nonreligious others (Vance 2016, 45; cf. Wrench 2016).

5. Coffman (2017, 205) uses "sincerity" in a slightly different register, but her description of Graham applies equally well to the context of media sincerity: "Graham enjoyed copious and strongly favorable media coverage because he was sincere—and sincere in ways especially suited to a media-saturated culture."

6. Goetz (2012) offers a historical and regional account of how Christians constructed the category of race in early America. For a history of race and religion in the American South, see Harvey (2016). Emerson and Smith (2001) provide a wider sociological view on present-day racial issues in evangelicalism (cf. Hawkins and Sinitiere 2013; Tranby and Hartman 2008). Whiteness has been a dominant theme (if an undertheorized social category) in the history of American Christianity, but it is not the entire story. For historical accounts outside of the unmarked racial frame, see Johnson (2015) and Weisenfeld (2017). Jones (2016) documents the demise of Christian religious and racial hegemony. Kahn and Lloyd (2016) offer a multiperspective approach to the study of race and secularism in America.

7. By hegemony, in this context, I follow classic Gramscian critical theory to mean structures of power that have become so ingrained and pervasive that they have rendered themselves invisible.

8. Evangelicals also have a highly visible material culture—e.g., business signs and icons, church architecture, billboard advertisements, etc.—that is ubiquitous throughout the American heartland and present even in urban centers (Barton 2012). Media scholars have rightly pointed out that contemporary evangelicalism "has had a marked influence on both secular and religious American culture simply by the preponderance of popular culture materials and commodities they've injected into the media and retail marketplace" (Horsfield 2015, 253; Hendershot 2004).

9. Vincent Lloyd (2016, 4) argues that processes of secularism evoke "a religious domain that is managed by power and that is circumscribed by nonreligious forces."

10. For an account of how public religious auditory practices resisted liberal predilections toward individualized and privatized religiosity, see Weiner 2014.

11. As Daniel Miller (2014, 258) hypothesizes, if social media cosmologies shape religious and secular people across the board, then the study of those media ideologies that inform and structure contemporary media systems become all the more important to study.

12. Religious determination of global technology has historic precedent. As Supp-Montgomerie (2021, 3, 8) argues in her study of the early transatlantic telegraph system, "Religion—especially US Protestantism—forged an imaginary of networks as connective, so much so that we broadly define networks as systems of connection." Religion, she argues, is "at the origins of networks."

13. See Manovich (2001, 19) for a comparison between the printing press and the rise of the computer.

14. By cultural carrier, I mean that the internet and the PC emerge within a marketplace of media and communication patterns influenced by dominant evangelical media ideologies. For an account of how evangelistic and revivalist impulses shaped commercialized spirituality and American popular culture, see Lofton 2011. Dana Logan (2017, 604) similarly theorizes postindustrial practices of beauty and asceticism as "cultural carriers" of a Calvinist materialist restraint. For a longer history of how evangelical technologies subtly shaped so-called secular domains, see Modern 2011.

15. Notably, Byung-Chul Han's recent highly critical *In the Swarm: Digital Prospects* (2017), discussed in this book's conclusion, adopts Nelson's quasi-Protestant rhetoric. Even secular critiques of digital media are Protestant.

16. See Chidester (2005, 190–213) for a religious studies account of religious authenticity and virtual religions and Helland (2005) for a consideration of authentic participation in online religion.

THREE

EVANGELICAL THEORIES OF THE DIGITAL

THE TWO PREVIOUS CHAPTERS TRACED a genealogy of the evangelical media ideologies of sincerity and promiscuity from the beginnings of print culture to the digital era. Chapter 2 suggested that discourses emerging out of or corresponding closely to Protestant concerns saturated the birth of the internet. From the start, internet designers sought to vernacularize the PC away from its institutionalized and elitist origins in the government, scientific, and military sectors. This chapter focuses on the evangelical print market and the textual marketplace of ideas about technology after the turn into the digital era. Conceiving of evangelicalism as a community of discourse that exists both within and beyond the local, this chapter functions as an ethnography of circulating texts. I now turn to a select number of instructional monographs written by evangelical authors who prescribe meaningful ways of Christian living and adapting to new digital ecologies. Whereas revivalist predecessors interpreted sincerity and promiscuity as existing in a relationship of reciprocity and reinforcement, contemporary evangelicals problematize such a unity. These writers disagree about whether media promiscuity truly serves the interests of media sincerity. Recalling the rhetoric of the radio and television entrepreneurs, some evangelical technology theorists marry the ideologies and theologize new media as a divinely ordained ministry tool. But overall, most of the writers are wary to do so.

This chapter's key argument is that most writers view digital media with ambivalence and suspicion, denouncing digital communication as inauthentic and opposed to Christian theologies of the good life. Writers create descriptive generational taxonomies and address the issues of boundaries and authority in the age of Wikipedia, informational saturation, and the perennial problem of what counts as authentic. Out of this general ambivalence, three evangelical postures toward technology emerge, each offering a unique take on the sincerity/promiscuity conundrum. These are (1) critical/ascetic, (2) ambivalent/redemptive, and (3) optimistic/hopeful stances. Evangelicals prescribe strategies for best practices and create practical guides for adapting Christian ministry and sociality during the rise of habitual media.

At the same time, writers name and resist the ills of social media culture and call for periods of new media abstinence, or "digital fasts." Even the most hopeful endorsement of social media is aware of the problems that arise out of mediated interaction. According to the corpus of writers, social and dialogical contention, **hyperconnection, information overload**, disembodying effects, cheapening of so-called authentic social bonds, and the erosion of religious authority are all undesired effects of new technology use. Simply put, evangelicals fragment over the issue, and various camps debate about how sincerity and promiscuity ought to align. Indeed, as Ilana Gershon (2010b, 284) writes, "Media ideologies are multiple, locatable, partial, positioned, and contested." The framework of the dueling paradigms remains, but the relationship between sincerity and promiscuity is under increasing interpretive contention. In the rhetoric of these instructional manuals, one observes contrasting theologies and ideologies of media that aim to structure and shape a reader's outlook on what media are and how they ought to operate.

THE MANUALS

In the decentralized network of evangelical power and authority, the Protestant tendency is to produce and circulate dialogic, argumentative stretches of writing aimed at establishing order and maintaining orthodoxy. Again, this is a problem at least as old as Luther. Lay Christians need to be taught and admonished on how best to read the Bible. For an imagined community that emerges directly out of its textual activities, authority is constantly under fire. Because of the tenuousness of evangelical authority, an entire genre of evangelical self-help guides and manuals exists. These guides are the subject of this chapter. Legitimized by evangelical publishing firms and the consuming audiences who buy, read, talk about, and circulate such books, writers disseminate authoritative teachings to exhort, admonish, instruct, and normatively structure readerships.

Published guides, in short, engage in theological, doctrinal, and ecclesial **stancetaking**. As I will show, a strong predictive relationship holds between a manualist's tradition of theological upbringing and his or her media ideology. Authors ranging from pastors to scholars holding a variety of advanced degrees in history, theology, technology, and communication work to delineate the boundaries of evangelicalism and establish positions about correct forms of belief and practice. Reflecting a gendered imbalance that will come under fire in chapter 5, all but one of these authorized writers are men. In this explosive, male-dominated literary tradition, manuals range from subject matters like self-help and spiritual improvement, to biblical interpretation and theology, to politics and culture, to marriage and dating, to guides for Christian sexuality, to cookbooks. Rooted loosely within the categories of the evangelical how-to or self-improvement book written for a popular readership, but also appealing to the Protestant theological intelligentsia, a growing textual subgenre emerges. I describe this type of instructional work as the evangelical **technology manual**.

I identified fourteen manuals written between 2002 and 2015 on the various intersections of technology and Christian living (see table 3.1 below).[1] The books included critical theories on the effects of recent technological developments in both secular and Christian communication (Hipps 2005, 2009; Schultze 2009), evangelical investigations of social media platforms, like Facebook or Twitter (Rice 2009; Drescher 2011), theological justifications of virtually mediated church rituals (Estes 2009), and practical how-to manuals written for pastors and ministry leaders intimidated by the rapid rise of the digital (Crawford 2012; Bourgeois 2013; Smith 2013). Books published earlier during this time make predictable use of terms relative to the period. Schultze (2002) and Estes (2009) employ the somewhat dated language of the *cyber*, *virtual*, or *sim* (simulated or simulation) to refer to online, digital, internet-mediated religious rituals. Bourgeois (2013), Smith (2013), Wise (2014) and Challies (2015) prioritize currently vogue descriptors, such as *social*, *social media*, *digital*, and *digital media*. Although the manuals together reach diverging theological conclusions and conceive of technology in contrasting shades of appreciation, they do share one thing in common: he selected group of authors sets out to prescribe what authentic and virtuous Christian communication looks like in the age of the internet.

In the last two decades, a robust body of evangelical commentary on new media has entered the world. Overwhelmingly, the textual corpus advocates for the adoption of new technologies, but its optimism, on the whole, is tempered by a strong vein of what media scholars Rivka Ribak and Michele Rosenthal (2015) describe as **media ambivalence**, an applied form of technological resistance. In this section, I analyze the similarities and differences among the various evangelical media theorists, noting convergence and divergence in terms of both media ideologies and theological tradition. These texts tend to disagree as much as they agree; I intend to trace the contours of these contested terrains. To do so, I'll proceed thematically, beginning with the much discussed issue of generational contrast.

Table 3.1. Evangelical Technology Manuals Corpus

Number	Author	Date Published	Title	Publisher
1.	Schultze, Quentin J.	2002	Habits of the High-Tech Heart: Living Virtuously in the Information Age	Baker Academic
2.	Hipps, Shane	2005	The Hidden Power of Electronic Culture: How Media Shapes Faith, the Gospel, and Church	Zondervan
3.	Rice, Jesse	2009	The Church of Facebook: How the Hyperconnected Are Redefining Community	David C. Cook
4.	Estes, Douglas	2009	SimChurch: Being the Church in the Virtual World	Zondervan
5.	Hipps, Shane	2009	Flickering Pixels: How Technology Shapes Your Faith	Zondervan
6.	Drescher, Elizabeth	2011	Tweet If You ♥ Jesus: Practicing Church in the Digital Reformation	Morehouse
7.	Dyer, John	2011	From the Garden to the City: The Redeeming and Corrupting Power of Technology	Kregel
8.	Crawford, Terrace	2012	#GoingSocial: A Practical Guide on Social Media for Church Leaders	Beacon Hill
9.	Sweet, Leonard	2012	Viral: How Social Networking Is Poised to Ignite Revival	WaterBrook
10.	Detweiler, Craig	2013	iGods: How Technology Shapes Our Spiritual and Social Lives	Brazos (Baker)
11.	Bourgeois, David T.	2013	Ministry in the Digital Age: Strategies and Best Practices for a Post-Website World	IVP (InterVarsity)
12.	Smith, Nils	2013	Social Media Guide for Ministry	Group
13.	Wise, Justin	2014	The Social Church: A Theology of Digital Communication	Moody
14.	Challies, Tim	2015	The Next Story: Faith, Friends, Family and the Digital World	Zondervan

DIGITAL NATIVES VS. DIGITAL IMMIGRANTS

Multiple writers distinguish between **digital natives** and **digital immigrants**, terms that appear for the first time after the new millennium (Prensky 2001). Anthropologist Daniel Suslak (2009) suggests that distinctions based on temporal, generational difference are as equally important as registers of identity such as ethnicity, gender, and class. Institutional media, such as published books, work to define these categories. To put the matter another way, technology commentators often turn to age distinctions to explain how and why technological developments occur and how these developments get adopted into regular practice.

According to Tim Challies, a Reformed Christian, popular blogger, and author of *The Next Story: Faith, Friends, Family, and the Digital World*, digital natives "have never known a world apart from digital technology" (2015 [2011], 12, 55–56). Digital natives were born after the digital turn. They know nothing beyond this era since their world "has been (and always will be) digital." On the other hand, "older generations are now digital *immigrants*, having been forced to transition from the old world into the new." For younger generations, "digital technologies are like the air they breathe—a simple and unremarkable feature of the world they live in." But digital immigrants will always be playing catch-up with the natives, for whom perpetual technology upgrades are second nature. Challies dates the distinction: "If you were born after 1980, you are a digital native." A sizable difference in worldview occurs between these two generations in Challies's mind. For immigrants "there remains a sharp contrast between life *online* and life *offline*." But for the natives, those who live hybrid existences due to their increasingly mobile technologies, no such distinction makes sense.

By far, the digital natives and immigrants dichotomy is one of the most frequent taxonomies applied. Although before 2010 the terms had gained some traction (see Estes 2009, 245n34), they show up recurrently in the literature. Shane Hipps (2009, 134), a self-professed disciple of theorist Marshall McLuhan, employs the categories and essentializes immigrants as parents and natives as children. John Dyer (2011, 124) also applies the distinction, emphasizing that within any singular American household there exists significantly different cultures side by side. Elizabeth Drescher (2011, 45) does not deliberately apply the binary distinction but does identify a form of "native fluency" in technological language and expertise among children, a fluency that the author admits not enjoying herself. Leonard Sweet (2012), a cultural critic and historian, begins with this very distinction and then elaborates his own taxonomy of the Googlers and the Gutenbergers. The immigrant and native terms appear in Craig Detweiler's (2013, 96) manual, and Justin Wise (2014, 60–61) theorizes the immigrants and natives as conjoined by Generation Y. Authors who do not use the terms directly intend their books for an older generation for whom social media are foreign and strange (e.g., Crawford 2012; Smith 2013).

The use of this age-based distinction, to summarize, is a strategy of labeling that has real social purchase. Descriptively meaningful, the division between immigrants and natives explains how and why different groups of people come to embrace new technologies more naturally than others. For these writers, both the digital immigrants and the natives will need to learn strategies to flourish in this confusing new age of communication. But for these writers, the digital natives are more prone to the dangers of the internet, given that the perpetually online world is for them more natural than it is for the immigrants. For the natives, learning to resist the detriments of digital media will be significantly more difficult as these technologies are even more deeply ingrained in their everyday lives. The digital natives, after all, unlike the immigrants, cannot even conceive of a world without the internet and data phones.

POST-WIKIPEDIA BOUNDARY MAINTENANCE AND AUTHORITY

The narration of generational differences in approaches to technology provides the manualists with a shared descriptive language and the ability to address differences of experience and perspective. But even more pressing is the challenge to traditional forms of authority emerging after the rise of the **Information Age** and the digital turn. In his manifesto for virtual church communications, *SimChurch: Being the Church in the Virtual World*, college professor Douglas Estes (2009, 115–119) wrestles with the subject of online sacraments and rituals and makes a defense for the "symbolic" and "avatar-mediated virtual Communion" practiced regardless of a "lack of physical elements." As in so-called real-world practice, online rituals are both productive and problematic. Estes weighs this tension and envisions a "radical reformation occurring within the Christian faith in virtual worlds," a reformation that resists the problematic historical model of "entrenched power brokers" in Christian history. As he puts it, "The virtual world changes the authority game" and provides new venues for religious expression outside of traditional leadership forms (136, 137, 139).

Estes, however, is not entirely optimistic about the church's shedding of its "hierarchical shackles" by way of internet mediation. As with the tension between media sincerity and promiscuity as far back as the Reformation, newly found communicative freedom cuts both ways. Estes, although excited about the internet's opportunities for ecclesial development, ultimately warns church leaders of a potential "theological crisis," which may occur in the new experimental domains if existing authorities fail to pay heed to online developments.

Estes here names the problem of promiscuous media for church authority structures. "Heterodoxy has always been a huge problem for real-world churches," Estes admonishes, "and it looks as though it will be an even greater problem for virtual churches" (141, 147). Problems notwithstanding, Estes seeks to harness the affordances of the promiscuous media for the purposes of the church. He works to harmonize the impulses of sincerity and promiscuity. In chapter 4, I will clarify how evangelical gatekeepers have heeded Estes's call to move structures and discourses of authority and orthodoxy into new media domains. But not all manualists share Estes's tempered optimism.

In a McLuhanesque vein of criticism, and in one of the most complex of all the manuals, Dyer's (2011, 111) *From the Garden to the City: The Redeeming and Corrupting Power of Technology* makes frequent use of critical media theorists, Greek philosophy, virtue ethics, biblical studies, theology, media studies, communication history, and other theories of technology. As director of communication at a Protestant seminary, Dyer reflects on print media as a form of communication that "values exactness and precision" and produces "a sense of permanence and authority." Dyer's theologizing of media history comes to the fore as he suggests that in his wisdom God determined the era of written language and print technology with intention: "By choosing this technology, God was communicating that his Law did not contain optional truths or malleable commands. His Law was literally set in stone." Not necessarily a positive development—as digital media are for other writers, including Drescher and Wise—for Dyer the authoritative force of print text comes apart in the digital era of promiscuity, fluidity, source linking, and hypertext. As Detweiler (2013, 16) similarly narrates, "Our traditional sources of *authority* are shifting, from people to programs, from God to Google." Authority in the age of new media is up for grabs: "Who can we trust as an authority in a time of too many options?" Detweiler's *iGods: How Technology Shapes Our Spiritual and Social Lives* is a counter to Sweet's quasioptimistic *Viral: How Social Networking Is Poised to Ignite Revival*. The book also extends Schultze's and Hipp's suspicions. Detweiler (2013, 16) credits the rise of Google and other online search engines with the increasing erosion of traditional forms of authority. The ability of the internet to serve as an arbiter of knowledge is for Detweiler a worrying phenomenon. With its easy access to vast droves of information, the internet bears with it a "chaotic nature" and "decentralized authority," which is decidedly populist in orientation.

Reacting to pressures shared by some early Protestant entrepreneurs wrestling with the unanticipated effects of the explosion of print media, these critical theorists argue against media promiscuity. The internet, for Detweiler (2013, 108), is too democratic. That anyone can be an expert in this age of amplified voice and celebrity worship is a negative outcome. If the internet continues in the tradition of promiscuity that began in the Reformation, commentators such as Detweiler look to rein in the drive toward freedom of expression and the open circulation of information.

The most vocal critic of the antiauthoritative underpinnings of the internet comes by way of Challies's *The Next Story* (2015 [2011]). More than other writers, Challies emphasizes the dangerousness of new media's populism. In this author's history of technological development, he makes it adamantly clear that "technology shifts power." "In the digital world," Challies contends, "power has begun to shift from the old to the young. It is shifting from the expert to the amateur, from the printed word to the digital. Many of the old power structures are changing as an unintended consequence of digital technology." Challies recognizes the shift in the media ecology and marks it as dangerous. Internet and PC designers praised the democratic and populist underpinnings as virtues, but Challies laments the unintended effects of such freedoms on the authority of traditional church structures. "As Christians," he warns, "we are people who are subject to authority, and we must always take these changes in power and authority very seriously" (43, 44).

For Challies, Wikipedia as a digital platform is quintessential proof of the detriments of democratized knowledge. Challies devotes an entire chapter on the corrosion of authority by way of a scathing dismissal of Wikipedia as a crowd-sourced bastion of false knowledge. "Our understandings of truth and authority are changing in this digital world," he writes. "Wikipedia serves as a microcosm of that kind of change." The old-model standards of knowledge, such as *Encyclopedia Britannica*, were sources of what he calls "earned authority," which is that the truth of the encyclopedic entries rests on the ability of not only the experts who wrote them but the numerous fact-checkers who went about establishing the veracity of the experts' claims. Challies finds troubling that Wikipedia, on the other extreme, dismisses any value of earned expertise, knowledge, and ultimately, wisdom and truth. Wikipedia's consensus model of knowledge production, according to Challies, ignores authority. The **wiki model** "levels authority structures, assigning no value to age, experience, or education." "When editing an entry on justification that explains how God saves his people," Challies elaborates, "the ten-year-old child stands on equal footing with the most eminent theologian." Wikipedia compromises and undermines authority, redefines truth by consensus, and endorses a "radical egalitarianism seemingly at odds with biblical authority structures." Challies rejects the egalitarianism of promiscuous wiki models by calling for order and appealing to what he defines as the "proper" authoritative channels of the historic Christian church. Challies dismisses knowledge produced by crowdsourcing (what he refers to as "the cult of the amateur") and calls for a renewed appreciation of formal systematic theologies. In concluding his rant against Wikipedia, the author reiterates that Christians ought to live in resistance to "the great leveler," the internet (160, 166, 172, 173).

For a self-professed Reformed Christian, ironies abound. In sum, Challies repudiates the antiauthoritarianism that permeated his Protestant ancestors in their quest against the Catholic Church. As a Reformed Christian, he is fully aware of promiscuous media causing trouble for established structures of authority within Protestantism. But it is the rampant, taken-to-the-extreme aspect of promiscuous media that the author rejects. Challies (2015 [2011], 166) briefly confirms the theology of the **priesthood of all believers** but devotes much of his book to discussing what happens when such a theology extrapolates far beyond biblical intent. For Challies, promiscuous, internet-mediated new media are the primary source of problems for evangelical orthodoxy and a detriment to authentic standards of Christian living.

The issue of authority in the age of the digital is one of the most contentious points running through the literature. Evangelicals find themselves divided over the affordances and effects of the internet. Other writers view the promiscuous impulses and the medium's priesthood of all believer's agenda as thoroughly—even inherently—Christian. Consider Sweet (2012, 111, emphases added) on the matter of theology and democratization. "The *democratization* that is realized through Googler Culture is a reason for hope, action, and empowerment," he writes. In blatant opposition to Challies, Sweet contends that Christians should embrace such democratization "as a further elaboration of the Reformation doctrine of *the priesthood of all believers*." The digital turn, for Sweet, has similar effects as the original Reformation: "Just as the moveable-type revolution democratized Scripture by taking it out of the hands of the church, so the Google revolution is *democratizing* religion by taking it out of the hands of the gatekeepers and enabling more **open-source**, self-organizing connections with God." Challies rejects wiki paradigms. Sweet proclaims open-source technologies as gospel.

Sweet (2012, 55, 63, 111, 178–180) dedicates much of *Viral* to the task of theorizing the shift, in a more progressive evangelical stance, from the age of print to the age of the digital. But to be fair, note that even Sweet anticipates the possibilities of abuse within the paradigm of promiscuous media—what he calls "Googler Culture." The radically open-source platform of Wikipedia, he clarifies, "can be for good or ill." On the one hand, Sweet praises Twitter as "the ultimate medium for discipleship." On the other, he warns against the ease with which digital media might be exploited for authoritarian, propagandistic, and capitalist agendas. In Sweet's perspective, promiscuous media have multidirectional effects.

What Challies posits as vice and danger, Sweet and others envision as virtue and promise. Estes (2009, 195) proposes that internet-mediated ecclesial forms "have the means to tap into the exponential power of the priesthood of all believers because of the highly connective nature of the virtual world." Likewise, Drescher's (2011, 3, 126–127, 129) measured "digital optimism" endorses what she calls "distributed authority" or "digital leadership," which is "fluid, distributed, and more often than not, collective rather than individual." She praises the challenges of new media's collaborative authority issues against "practices anchored in top-down, institutionally sanctioned authority." Drescher's optimistic realism means that she admits the dangers of promiscuous media but contends the benefits outweigh the detractions. In Drescher's Bordieuan analysis, the new "habitus" of the digital era submits a radical "reconfiguration of authority." The rise of the digital continues in the Reformation tradition of dissent and protest against institutions (3, 134, 136).

Manual writers frequently take a mediating stance between theological and technological optimism and pessimism. On the issue of authority and power, Wise (2014, 13, 21) praises new media's reconfigurations of once dominant structures and is thankful that because of digital media "the gatekeepers are gone." Unfortunately, Wise gets the situation only half right. The internet's gatekeepers are not entirely gone. They are, in fact, the subject of chapter 4. But as a preview of that chapter's findings, note that although the internet has allowed for the leveling of authority, it also in some cases supports traditional religious authorities in extending their influences online. New media both support and undermine conventional religious authorities. Such are the paradoxes of the internet.

Wise (2014, 23, 24) romanticizes the Reformation and like Drescher positions social media as the most natural next stage of reformatory development. In Luther's day, Wise says, "Boundaries were shattered." The example of Luther's "heresies" resonates with the author on a technological level. According to Wise, Luther's story is an illustration of what Christian technological adepts can and should accomplish. "Becoming a social church," Wise continues, "means we need leaders who are willing to serve as heretics." Wise's heretic language is particularly telling. He is not endorsing theological heresy, per se, but a nontraditional approach to ministry and Christian living: "Not theological heretics, mind you. I mean to say we need men and women who are willing to challenge long-standing and widely beloved methods of communicating the gospel message." The "social church," as he puts it, is one that has adapted to the new media turn. Wise's heresy is media oriented, not doctrinal. Other manual writers will associate the promiscuous effects wrought by new media with an increasing "risk of heresy" (e.g. Bourgeois 2013, 41) but point to that label in a significantly less charitable direction than Wise. Do these writers forget that Luther, too, was deemed a heretic by the traditional religious authorities of his day? Unlike Wise's treatment, heresy discourse in this literature is typically a code for theological dangerousness and ecclesial disorder. Heresy equals heterodoxy.

In different ways, Challies and Dyer gesture nostalgically to the age of print and its affordances for authority structures. Although equally suspicious about technological adaptations and influence on religiosity, Hipps (2009, 133, 137, 138) does not reach the same conclusions as theologians working in Reformed theological paradigms. In Hipps's critical reading, media can be dangerous and distracting and engender toxic effects inclusive of narcissism, information overload, overemphasis on mechanist (or hyperlogical) rationality, and the threat of subliminal control by unseen powers. Hipps emphasizes the correlation between knowledge, information, and power, writing that "an elastic relationship between access to information and power" exists. "In the simplest terms, power is derived from information control." Changes in power structures correlate directly with shifting access to information. Hipps posits that the digital natives' increasing enjoyment of power and prestige "is the great reversal of the digital age." "When the parent becomes the child, cultural norms shift and reconfigure." (Note, again, his attention to the generational binary.) For Hipps, "the most alarming consequence is that young people are granted startling and unprecedented freedom." Countering Hipps, Wise celebrates new media's tearing down of boundaries, blatantly countering Hipps's claim that establishing boundaries "is of paramount importance."

INFORMATIONAL OVERLOAD, IGODS, AND AQUATIC METAPHORS

Promiscuous media, as I've argued, have unintended negative effects. As Hipps suggests, access to information correlates closely with power and authority. But a common theme that circulates throughout the literature is the idea that ease of access to an eternity of information online is causing problems rather than liberating the masses. Americans, in short, are "drowning in a sea of information" (Challies 2015 [2011], 207).

One product to emerge out of this body of technology manuals is an evangelical theory—or series of microtheories, rather—of meaningful knowledge. In dated technological language, Schultze (2002, 13, 26) narrates this transition. "Living in the age of cyberspace," he writes, "we have faith in the processes of collecting and distributing information. Words such as 'data,' 'knowledge,' and 'information' connote social progress and personal enlightenment." For Schultze, there is a disconnect between the claims that more information and more technology leads to social progress. Society is "succumbing to *informationism*, a nondiscerning, vacuous faith in the collection and dissemination of information as a route to social progress and personal happiness." Anticipating fake news rhetoric to come, the problem, he warns, is that if one fails to "take virtue seriously, the information explosion will become a plague of *misinformation*—endless volleys of nonsense, folly, and rumor masquerading as knowledge, wisdom, and even truth." The issue is not only too much information but an explosion of many types of informational excesses, ranging in degrees of usefulness, relevance, reliability, or value. In Schultze's words, the current era has succumbed to the "tyranny of the informationally urgent."

Relatedly, in his theorization of the "brilliant but imperfect technology" of Facebook as a social and ecclesial network, Jesse Rice (2009, 21, 101–112) describes an experience of "information overload," which results due to "hyper-connection," what we might annotate as an aftereffect of the rise of the digitally buffered self. And Detweiler (2013, 7, 15, 204) writes about media excess and abundance: "Never have so many people been able to create and distribute so many words and images. We are uploading our videos and updating our statuses in dizzying ways. We are inundated by too much information (of our own making). We desperately need a theology of abundance to figure out how to respond to this strange, new problem." Further, Detweiler worries about issues of privacy and corporate agendas in the age of information abundance, noting that "we solved the problem of too much information by giving a few key companies too much of our information." In his accusations against the "iGods," corporate Silicon Valley leaders, including the founders and CEOs of Amazon, Facebook, and Google, among others—the author contends that technology has "given us access to more—more knowledge, more content, more information." Such knowledges may or may not be better. In a decisively negative slant, Detweiler links information overload not only to addictive behaviors, like scrolling through news feeds and consuming bits and pieces of informational ephemera here and there, but to a pervasively dangerous form of "technological determinism" in which the media consumer falls prey to such **informationalism** without much say in the matter. Internet users may feel free and autonomous; they may have the impression that they are empowered social actors. But they are, in effect, blind to the invisible powers that structure their daily existences and social interactions.

As I have noted, Wise (2014, 86–88) does provide a romanticized view of the informational possibilities of the times. But even he questions the invasiveness of digital biotechnologies, including FitBits and FuelBands, and other fitness and data-trawling applications. These technologies literally layer devices onto the physical body via **wearable technology** and turn biodata measurements into information to be uploaded to social networks and the possession of corporations. Such developments are evidence of the increasingly habitual status of new media and these technologies' continual interest in shaping patterns of daily life and lived religion.

In his practical guide, Crawford (2012, 18, 26) describes information overload on various social media platforms as either "too much noise" or as "buzz" and provides helpful strategies for their reduction. Crawford's goal is to help readers use social media as "a powerful tool that God can use in your life and in your ministry," essentially cutting out the byproduct of informational buzz. Complete with hashtagged chapter titles, including "What Is #socialmedia?," "#Facebook," "#Twitter," "#Blogs," and "#YouTube," readers of Crawford's "reference or practical guide" receive step-by-step guidance on how to set up personal or group Facebook pages. Yet even Crawford's optimistic outlook on technology is tempered by the fact information embattles digital media adepts from all directions. As Sweet (2012, 126) claims, "The more we are 'information omnivores,' the more mindless is our devotion to facts over truths." Information overload, for these writers, is a serious problem. Too much information is source of severe stress and distraction from the good life.

Challies (2015 [2011], 12, 35, 107, emphases added) offers one of the most extended discussions of informational saturation. "We are now a digital culture," he writes—a culture so saturated in digital structures that technology now controls users rather than simply assisting, extending, or empowering them. "The digital revolution is global," Challies worries, "reaching to the farthest corners of the earth. It affects the way we see, what we hear, how we interact with the world around us, and how we communicate with others." Note the metaphors the author employs to make his point: "*Swimming in this digital sea*, we are caught up in *a torrent* of media, *striving to stay afloat* and make some headway against the rush of sounds, images, and words that seem *intent on drowning us out*." These commentators prefer aquatic metaphors in explaining the overwhelming nature of the Information Age. "Even those of us who live each day immersed in *the digital sea* have moments when we question what we are doing and what effect all of this is having on our lives," Challies suggests, equating information overload to drowning in an ocean of data. Similarly, Hipps (2009, 72, emphasis added) writes that "the *churning sea of information* never settles long enough to allow for the emergence of wisdom."

Returning to Challies's (2015 [2011], 50, 51–55, 89) history of technological development, the author locates the origins of information overload at the invention of the telegraph, noting that due to the new ability "to send information so quickly and so inexpensively, the new problem of information overload suddenly appeared." With the development of the telegraph, and quickly followed by the telephone and television, information became less immediate and local and more global and commodified. Challies theorizes media screens as devices of pervasive, capitalistic control that structure and determine human interactions more and more as time progresses. Life itself, he fears, "is mediated by the screen," and the inevitable "presence of media" dominates us by aquatic or fluid "saturation." Challies, too, employs metaphors of the aquatic sort.

But where do these metaphors come from? Like the digital immigrant and native binary, evangelicals may derive these negative aquatic metaphors from mainstream discourse on technology. Marshall McLuhan (1969, 5, 75) famously described preinternet humans as fish swimming in media seas. At the very least, the situation confirms that negative metaphors of the aquatic genre circulate throughout the American mainstream. Consider, for instance, tech designer Golden Krishna's (2015, 12) frustration with screens in *The Best Interface Is No Interface: The Simple Path to Brilliant Technology*. "I swipe right-to-left across the screen through *a sea of icons*," Krishna comments, "scanning their logos and the tiny type underneath, trying to find the app." Similarly, Jodi Dean (2010, 3, emphasis added), a critical theorist of social media and author of *Blog Theory: Feedback and Capture in the Circuits of Drive*, reproduces this exact sort of rhetoric by describing a near-biblical "*deluge* of images and announcements, enjoining us to react, to feel, to forward them to our friends, erodes critical-theoretical capacities." Media studies scholar John Durham Peters (2015, 107, 200, emphasis added) likewise describes the difficulties of "*navigating the swift-moving waters* of the Internet age." Aquatic metaphors are useful tropes for expressing the potentially detrimental effects of internet media. Such metaphors identify a feeling of overwhelming helplessness. If we take these commentators and the evangelical technology writers at their word, there is so much information bombarding people from every direction that they literally feel like they are drowning.

These worries are not unfounded. Challies's criticism correlates with what scholars (e.g., Gershon 2010a, 64–65; Campbell 2020a, 24–37) have described as the increased presence of algorithmic programs that structure online experiences, aiding users in seeking out data but also limiting their informational freedom in subtle but arguably productive ways. For other scholars, including historian Yuval Noah Harari (2017, 83–84, 87, 402), the algorithm is no less than a veritable artificial intelligence (AI) shaping human sociality and psychology for better or for worse (cf. van Dijck 2013, 12, 30, 50; Chun 2016, 120–122). Regardless of the long-term repercussions on human communication engendered by algorithmic effects, the evangelical manualists resonate deeply with digital media scholar Ganaele Langlois's (2014) claim that this is the age of the meaning-making machines. These ubiquitous apps, microprograms, and mini-AIs further complicate the mediated pattern of daily tasks and interactions. The meaning-making machines are subtle in their power even as they shape people's views of the world by controlling how and what sorts of information they access.

IN/AUTHENTICITY 2.0

Evangelical manual writers debate the benefits and drawbacks involved in new media use, and they argue about the increasing pervasiveness of their technologies in their daily lives. But one vital question at the heart of such ambivalence revolves around a distinction between **authenticity and inauthenticity**, a question that is at the heart of this book. Simply put, evangelical media theorists have a standard of authentic living—a paradigm of sincerity and directness, as I argued in chapter 1—that defies any easy categorical distinctions. The thesis shared by many of the writers is that promiscuous media breed inauthentic communication. Media promiscuity, for many of these manualists, is simply incompatible with media sincerity.

But authenticity refers to more than living meaningful and virtuous lives in an age of digital overstimulation and faux sociality. Authenticity certainly has to do with lifestyle patterns, interpersonal interactions, recreational practices, and consumer tastes, but discussions of communicative authenticity link implicitly back to theological or doctrinal judgments. Implied in these discussions, authenticity acts as a synonym for orthodoxy. The inauthentic, then, is the heterodox or heretical. Inauthenticity refers to social media newsfeed addictions and theologies, practices, or belief deemed suspect. Most of the manualists analyzed in this chapter deal in some manner with the issue of the authentic. Several writers go as far as to delimit entire taxonomies to establish barometers of truthfulness and meaning against digitally mediated artificiality.

As part of the internet's promiscuous affordances, digital media serve, according to Schultze (2002, 23) as "another means for individuals and organizations to communicate disingenuously." Schultze devotes an entire chapter of *Habits of the High-Tech Heart* to the question of authenticity. In short, cyberspace proves fertile ground for "hucksters" and "spin artists," who "fabricate both online and offline personas" and "contort our perceptions of reality." Schultze writes of authenticity as a quickly disappearing, in demand virtue. His is a last-ditch effort of desperation and admonition for readers to "live authentically." For this media theorist, the inverse of authenticity is artifice. People "fabricate human identities" and perceptions of those identities in online realms. They create and maintain "cyber-facades." Influenced by commentary on the internet in the early 2000s that worried about fake online personas and deceptive avatars, Schultze spends much of the chapter mourning the rapid increase of self-performativity, which he argues is one of the internet's most powerful affordances. Constituted in the domains of promiscuous media, identity is now malleable and constructible and given over to "false representations" and "deceptions" concerning identity, as religious studies scholar Deborah Whitehead (2015, 120) argues in the context of the blogosphere. Individualism and self-empowerment reign supreme (Schultze 2002, 23, 116–121).

In the gap of authority left in the wake of such identity constructionism, Schultze (2002, 116–130, 130–131) argues that internet-empowered "symbol brokers" become the new mythmakers and mediators in a symbolic sense. Unfortunately, the new myths propound the virtues of greed, corruption, and capital expansion in the name of self-empowerment and social connection. These symbol brokers and internet developers contribute significantly "to the unbinding of the world in many ways." But most pressing for Schultze is the symbol brokers' rejection of "the virtue of *authenticity*," which he defines simply as "saying what we mean and meaning what we say." Does a more pointed definition of media sincerity exist?

All this talk of authenticity—and failed authenticity—is the product of a Protestant media paradigm that has come under fire. This author's definition of the authentic corresponds directly to the entrenched Protestant semiotic ideology of sincerity identified by anthropologists of Christianity and outlined in chapter 1. In its clearest characterization, authenticity has to do with transparent, effective communication between parties. Authenticity is direct speech. Schultze goes on to delimit a threefold taxonomy of authenticity's component virtues—truthfulness, empathy, and integrity—and calls for less of a polished, professional veneer to communication. Only by resisting the pull of promiscuous media and cultivating these three virtues within the context of traditional Christianity will digital evangelicals guard against inauthenticity.

Concluding his authenticity chapter, Schultze (2002, 138–139) distinguishes between the media ideologies of sincerity and promiscuity. He calls for a return to the knowledges and habitudes of the revealed religions ("the Hebrew and Christian traditions") in an effort to stave off the human capacity "for self-delusion." "Authenticity discourse rightly challenges the power of secular empires, including informationalism," the author continues. "Most of all, the wisdom embedded in religious tradition, when let loose within society, can redirect us toward authenticity." Schultze's most pressing call is for the Christian to shore up his or her defenses against promiscuous media or in the writer's own words, "Against the winds of inauthentic propaganda and the waves of brokered consumer desires." The critic's message is clear. Not only is internet-mediated communication dangerously vice ridden, but the promiscuous medium is profoundly inauthentic and antithetical to a Christian habitude.

Manualists occasionally draw on psychological definitions to substantiate working definitions of the authentic. These critics also distinguish sincerity from promiscuity. Rice (2009, 28, 45), via psychologist Janet Surrey, defines authenticity in a relational sense. Authenticity is "the core of psychological wellbeing" and "the essential quality of growth-fostering and healthy relationships." In his account of Facebook, Rice points out various situations that lead to inauthentic relationships, digital problems such as "overchoice," "hyperconnection," and "disembodiment." Facebook's problem is that it provides networking and connection but only at a surface level rather than at the needed depth to qualify as authentic. Rice does suggest that Facebook interactions are important for certain levels of social "acceptance and affirmation," but the platform simply does not meet a person's hardwired social and relational needs. Authentic relationships require time, presence, commitment, and sacrificial dedication, whereas virtual relationships "*look* almost exactly like the 'real thing'" but fall dramatically short (83, 110, 113).

Still, Rice (2009, 163–166) is careful in his applications of the authentic/inauthentic pronouncement. He is less decided in his untethering of the sincerity and promiscuity paradigm. He counters Hipp's biting comment that if a church is virtual, "it ain't community," with blogger and theologian Scot McKnight's defense of online communication against face-to-face forms requiring physical presence and immediacy. Drawing on other progressive Christians, Rice theorizes the dangers of Facebook as a venue for communication but also seeks to expand the idea of social networking as an extension or supplement to more traditional forms. Reiterating Hipp's incarnational and Christological media ideologies, Rice considers Jesus as the ultimate guide for community building "rooted in authenticity." Jesus is the source of Christian communicative values and virtues, values that include "intentionality, humility, and authenticity," "genuine relationship" patterns, and freedom "from pretense and playacting" (185–187). Rice expands his definition of authenticity to include first "being real" or "not false or imitation" and second "living in accordance with one's true nature." One must continually resist Facebook's fracturing effects, which cause us to self-objectify or live as "splinters of our actual selves." Authenticity is acting out of deep and determined reservoirs of stable personal identity (202–207). Rice's book offers readers practical advice on how to cultivate authentic communication patterns on Facebook. Challies (2015 [2011], 86) also encourages readers to "be real," guard against the temptation to "fabricate," and minimize the gap between one's real-world and online identities or personas. In a **FOMO** world (more on that in chap. 6), being performatively true and realistic to oneself via social media is necessary to warding off the thinness of sociality on social media.

Contrasting Schultze's disapproval and Rice's cautious program of redemption, some writers conceive of promiscuous media's connecting people across distance as actually extending the potential for authentic and comfortable interchanges rather than undermining it. According to Estes (2009, 27, 33, 35, emphasis added), "For a growing number of people, especially individuals in the Millennial generation and beyond, virtual-world interactions can be far *more authentic* and less awkward than real-world relationships." Like his revivalist predecessors, sincerity and promiscuity are co-constitutive. Further, Estes rebuffs critics for proffering reductive accounts of the authentic, real, and genuine by suggesting even the subjective and perspective nature of such normative accounts. "Is a virtual church a real, authentic, and valid expression of the church of Jesus Christ?," the author inquires. The objective of the book is to delineate the opportunities and welcome affordances of the new medium but not without taking care to note the difficulties and pitfalls.

Most importantly, Estes's work conjoins the two levels of the authentic register that concern this chapter. Estes (2009, 32–33, 35, 66–67) discusses authenticity in a communicative sense—in terms of experiential realness and directness as well as the efficiency of the social exchange—but also in the same section correlates the issue of biblical orthodoxy and meaning. To engage in any evaluation of the authenticity of a virtual church, Estes continues, is to engage in ecclesiology. From this author's perspective, virtual church communities can be authentic. Online congregations can be "real, healthy communities," even when existing outside the literal physical presence. Even more so, virtual churches can in an authentic sense "proclaim an orthodox gospel." For Estes, authenticity refers both to effectiveness of communication and theological, doctrinal, and ecclesial registers.

Other writers, like Hipps (2002, 91, 114–115, 170), link considerations of authenticity with discussions of orthodoxy or slide into formulations of "realness" and "physical presence" as standards of judgment. "Authenticity means that we bring our grievances with an honesty of emotion and openness to correction," Hipps says, reproducing the ideology of media sincerity, much like Schultze before him. Inasmuch as Hipps assumes such honesty and openness take place in so-called real domains (the physical, real world, live, or nononline), Hipps and Estes are at diametric odds in their positions on sincerity and promiscuity. Still other writers reiterate Estes's stretching of conceptions of realness and authenticity. As Dyer (2011, 167) comments, "Our question then should not be 'Is it *real*?' because connecting online is just as 'real' as talking on the phone or sending a letter." Wise (2014, 31) confirms that digitally mediated congregational web pages count as "real ministry."

Barometers of authenticity and inauthenticity as well as realness and fakeness abound in the corpus of technology manuals. In his **netiquette** guide, Crawford (2012, 58, 77–78, 116, 143) encourages readers to engage social media **followers** and audiences regularly and with politeness and tact so that communicants "know there's a real person on the other end of the conversation." In one heuristic list, "Why Church Leaders Fail with Social Media," Crawford includes authorities "not living authentic lives" as a reason. This instructor encourages pastors to give up trying to portray a perfect or pristine online persona. "The truth is, nobody is perfect, and everyone knows it," the author warns. "If you act like everything is good all of the time, people will perceive you as inauthentic." In Crawford's view, authenticity is synonymous with transparency and sharing with others on a personal, even candid, level. Contrasting Hipps, Crawford suggests that social networks, because "two-way conversations" take place, qualify as "a real community." Even Challies (2015 [2011], 69) allows that for some people online networks can affect "deeper intimacy in relationships with people we have never seen than in people who can look us in the eyes."

Sweet (2012, 6, 22, 52, 79) brings up the issue of authenticity and realness frequently in *Viral*. He identifies the authentic as a register of normative critique by the Gutenbergers against the Googlers and like other writers argues that Jesus's example is the only true measure of the real, the transparent, and the authentic. In considering the ironic collapse between the local and the global within social media, Sweet acknowledges that critics often problematically reduce the authentic to the local. For that matter, not all evangelical media theorists agree that the local is the most authentic or the most meaningful. Smith (2013, 19), for instance, pushes for social media use in churches because, as he puts it, "We need to experience community in ways that we often cannot in local congregations." Social media may not be as physically direct as in-person conversation, but it does accentuate and extend communication in novel ways.

As a whole, the overwhelming number of manual writers appear to agree with Challies that the shift from the spoken word and in-person communicative context to the highly mediated world of social networks brought with it a diminished experiential authenticity. "The change in media brought about a vast shift," Challies (2015 [2011], 95, 97) narrates, a shift that altered "all of the ideas and ways of interpreting that were part and parcel of communication via the spoken word." The problem is that the mediated reconfiguration "cost us a certain element of richness, a depth that is available in face-to-face, immediate conversation." With the loss of physical context, nonverbal cues, and other elemental parts of in-person conversation, Challies views social media discourse as profoundly disembodied and disembodying. In his view, it is "real face-to-face contact that is best, that communicates most, and that builds true friendship, true intimacy." Detweiler (2013, 21) concurs. Friendship in the social media age is complicated and problematic. In short, these critical theorists of media evidence a media ideology of suspicion at play. Their negative ideology rejects promiscuity out of hand and contends for sincerity.

In no other manual is the link between communicative context and authenticity language so close. For Challies (2015 [2011], 96, 106, 112), the real, the true, and the authentic is none other than conversation done in close physical proximity with another person. Promiscuous media's electronic, digitally based discourse should never be, in his view, more than a supplement for so-called real communication. Digital media are "certainly not a suitable replacement for face-to-face contact." Challies submits that "the virtual church is *not* the real church" and that the "mediated community" of the online church "will span the limitation of space, but it must do so at the cost of immediacy, of true presence, [and] of the truest manifestations of love." Ultimately, in this author's theology of media, "God wants us to experience through the mess of real-world, flesh-and-blood, face-to-face relationships." In his rejection of promiscuity, Challies concludes that, for evangelicals, new media use should never be more than a supplement to the real, sincere, physical thing.

A TAXONOMY OF NEW MEDIA DISCOURSE

In this final section I pull back from the discursive fray of complexly networked evangelical book culture to submit some definitive conclusions about evangelical media ideologies. In short, I elaborate a sliding scale of evangelical theories of technology. I argue that out of the formational crisis between media sincerity and promiscuity in the evangelical ecology, three dominant evangelical responses have formalized.

On one pole lies a staunch, **Luddite** rejection of technology. The opposite pole is unbridled acceptance and implementation of developing technology and media forms. As the above survey of technology manuals demonstrates, evangelical technology experts rarely identify exclusively with either end of this continuum. Instead, most evangelical writers classify themselves somewhere along the middle of the spectrum. Not a single manual rejects technology use, and even the most critical among them distances from the Luddite extreme. Similarly, not even the most rose-colored endorsements of social media use for religious purposes fails to realize the dangers involved in digital communication. Three overlapping positions emerge in this middle ground of cautious use: (1) technological asceticism; (2) technological redemption; and (3) technological optimism. I will consider each of these positions in turn.

Technological Asceticism and the Neo-Luddites

Occasionally, evangelical theorists' writings appear Luddite, at least at first glance, in their demonization of promiscuity and apotheosis of sincerity. Yet even Schultze, a vocal critic of new technologies, does not quite qualify as one of the "haters of technology," which we might define as a **technophobe** (Vial 2019, 22). Schultze's (2002, 13, 24) goal, to recall, is not to reject technology but to "de-technologize" in order to integrate and cultivate more traditional religious virtues within new mediated rituals. Schultze engages in a program of virtuous subject formation, noting that although he is "sure that some readers of this book will label me as a modern-day Luddite," his intent, rather, "is not so much to discard database and messaging technologies as much as to adapt them to venerable ways of life anchored in age-old virtues." Hipps (2009, 18) is also aware of the Luddite qualification, but his is a program of media awareness and critical thinking rather than a no-holds-barred rejection. Dyer (2011, 149–150) spends a subsection of one of his chapters in *From the Garden to the City* contextualizing and historicizing the Luddite movement and its literal destruction of industrial machines in protest against capitalism. Dyer praises the Luddite valuation of human life over that of the machine. Challies (2015 [2011], 33–34) goes furthest in the Luddite direction, embracing Ned Ludd's perspective inasmuch as "technology is meant to serve humans, not the other way around." Again, none of the writers rejects technology across the board. The collective goal is to propose a theory of appropriate use. But several writers agree with the intent behind Ned Ludd's actions: To the extent that machines influence human lives for the worse, they ought to be rejected and resisted. In their writings and proposed strategies, these technology theorists anticipate what Cal Newport (2019) would later call **digital minimalism**.

Similar in practice to the Midwestern evangelicals I will describe in chapters 7 and 8, the media ascetics do not renounce technology or call for exclusive technological abstinence. But they do prescribe and make normative lists of restraints and limits for use, aiming to keep promiscuity controlled. The ascetics expound lists of virtues that they want to see extended into virtual worlds and social interaction online. They delineate netiquette lists for social media correspondence and warn against behaviors they predict will be unproductive in terms of building the kingdom of God. Gravitating toward ascetic strategies, the manualists spend many pages calling for periodic or temporary avoidance of technology use.

Challies (2015 [2011], 133–134) offers the most extensive program of abstinence in his cultivation of the virtue of solitude. Solace, he argues, "calls for simple digital solitude, digital silence. Seek times and places that are far removed from the digital." One must intentionally remove themselves for periods of time from the "beeps" and the "hustle" of contemporary life. One must obliterate "distraction." To do so, Challies suggests three specific types of abstinence. First, a person can take a short "digital fast:" "Set aside days in which you will fast from all digital media. On these days you will need to set aside your cell phone, turn off the television, put away the PlayStation, and leave the computer alone." Such a process will be difficult, he warns, as all virtue formation is hard. A fast of this first type may only last a day or two. A second type of fast—the most digitally minimalist of all the options—is the "digital vacation," in which one breaks from technology for one to several weeks. A third type of disciplinary restraint is less pronounced than the previous two. Writing on everyday life, Challies calls for

Christians to "carve out digital-free times" at specific intervals during the day in order to guard against pervasive bad habits, such as sleeping with a cellphone on the nightstand or falling asleep while scrolling through social media feeds. He suggests refraining from technology use after a workday to spend time with one's family or determining not to even look at one's data phone until one has read the Bible and spent some time in prayer. Challies even describes his own family's ritual of the "technology basket," a container removed from the home's central social spaces and into which each family member places their "most distracting" device for sanctioned periods of time in the evenings.

Similarly, Wise (2014, 149–150) praises secular initiatives, such as the National Day of Unplugging, and calls for readers to think about going on a "digital detox" or "social media fast" in order to rediscover "a place of stillness" and "connect with our Maker" outside of new media distractions. Rice (2009, 167–168, 212) encourages "Facebook fasts" and develops strategies for not losing sleep due to social media use and keeping up on daily devotionals. Dyer (2011, 177–178) recommends a disciplinary program of limitation, restraint, and boundary construction. Temporary periods of digital abstinence can help one to disconnect and realign with more important things.

In resistance to what they see as the pervasive and structuring ills of social media culture, some of the manualists appeal to the virtues of the contemporary **Slow Movement**. Although not an entity in an institutional sense, the Slow Movement is a minimalist lifestyle and subcultural philosophy meant to provide an alternative to the hectic and fast-pasted contemporary world. Carl Honoré (2004, 11), the poster child for the movement after the publication of *In Praise of Slowness: Challenging the Culture of Speed*, positions the slow philosophy against "this media-drenched, data-rich, channel-surging, computer-gaming age" in which Westerners "have lost the art of doing nothing, of shutting out the background noise and distractions." The author contends that people today suffer from "the orgy of acceleration" and "the curse of multi-tasking," not to mention overwork and "our obsession with doing everything more quickly." *In Praise of Slowness* is not a particularly religious work, though Honoré's language is thick with religious metaphors. He writes, for instance, of our contemporary "addiction" or "kind of idolatry" or "cult" of speed, in which "we invoke the go-faster gospel" (4, 6, 10, 11).

The Slow Movement finds varied expression not only in instructional books but in literary and poetic writings, conventions and meetings, the Slow Food movement, and hybrid print and digital journals, like *Kinfolk* magazine. This latter publication is a lifestyle quarterly that melds Slow Movement ideals with Wendell Berry's philosophies of the good life and a Waldenesque rejection of modernity. Nathan Williams founded the *Kinfolk* quarterly in 2011, but it has gained enormous traction with millennial artistic, craftsman, design, and foodie readerships, including some of my Midwestern informants. *Kinfolk* has produced an influential visual aesthetic that has, somewhat ironically, gained influence through social media, such as Instagram (see chap. 6). In both this corpus of evangelical writers and in lifestyle quarterlies such as *Kinfolk*, the goal is to return to simple, virtuous living, everyday rituality, and authentic social connections.

Technological ascetics, including Detweiler, envision the Slow Movement as the appropriate Christian context in which to resist the vices of the new media age. Like *Kinfolk* writers, Detweiler idealizes an escape to a wilderness free from data phones and WiFi. He endorses the writings of ethical ecologists, like Albert Borgmann and Wendell Berry. Ultimately, the manualist wants to transfer the virtues of the slow life back to the city, replete with its technology and bandwidths of digital connection. Within his program of sincerity and disciplined restraint, Detweiler (2013, 218–225) envisions a lifestyle where technology functions as a gift from the divine. Even in "an accelerated culture" the author calls for both "slow food and **slow church**." Detweiler is not alone in his convergence with Slow Movement ideals. Schultze's (2002, 13, 17, 24, 131) virtue ethics approach makes use of Wendell Berry's ecological writings. *Habits of the High-Tech Heart*, with its call to "slow down" and agenda for "de-technologizing" religious traditions and reinstating "the good life," reads quite similarly to Honoré's Slow Movement manifesto and Greek virtue ethics, as does sections of Dyer's *From the Garden to the City*. Influential evangelical publications inspired by the Slow Movement include Jonathan Wilson-Hartgrove's (2010) *The Wisdom of Stability: Rooting Faith in a Mobile Culture*, C. Christopher Smith and John Pattison's (2014) *Slow Church: Cultivating Community in the Patient Way of Jesus*, Shauna Niequist's (2016) *Present over Perfect: Leaving Behind Frantic for a Simpler, More Soulful Way of Living*, and Erin Loechner's (2016) *Chasing Slow: Courage to Journey Off the Beaten Path*. Alan Noble's (2018) *Disruptive Witness: Speaking Truth in a Distracted Age* continues in this genre. These books are not technology manuals per se, like those studied in this chapter, but they do include among other subjects advice on how to navigate the perilous worlds of data phones and social media. These writers are very much aware of and concerned with what scholar Kathryn Lofton (2017, 21–33) characterizes as **binge religion**, an outcome of the current era wherein people approach religion as they do mass entertainment media: as hyperindividuals and uber-consumers addicted to the cult of speed.

Technological Redemption

Most of the writers discussed in this chapter take a more measured stance in which sincerity and promiscuity remain in a loose relational correspondence. Rather than writing through heavy-handed technological suspicion, many of the manualists take full stock of the problems engendered by new media communications and then work to create redemptive programs of technology use. Although the redemptive category is the largest on the continuum, it is also the most complex and layered. When pressed on the matter, these critical writers confirm that the role of the dutiful Christian is to engage technology carefully for the purposes of cultural redemption and stewardship.

In this posture of redemption and renewal, evangelical media theorists do their best to provide structures and practical models for best practices. Such models are not simply strategies for exploiting promiscuous media's affordances for reaching the widest audiences or guides on how to blog effectively for mixed readerships; the structures proposed consider the human propensity toward sinfulness embedded within media systems and go on to extend authenticity and realness into mediated interactions. Digital media are communicatively flawed but should be engaged by Christians who take seriously the Christian initiative to spread the Good News. The majority of manualists examined in this chapter tend to fall into the centrist category of technological redemption, although several do fall into the domains of technological asceticism, as represented by Detweiler and Challies, examined earlier—or a third mediating category of optimism and hopefulness, as represented by Crawford and others in the following section.

Technological Optimism

The smallest section on the continuum is for the technological optimists, or those manual writers who are idealistic and explicitly hopeful about new media. Others in this camp hope to missionize older generations into new media use. Crawford (2012), Bourgeois (2013), and Smith (2013) are the clearest examples of this sort of media sanguinity.

Consider, briefly, the tone and purpose of Bourgeois's *Ministry in the Digital Age: Strategies and Best Practices for a Post-Website World*. Bourgeois (2013, 8) makes his appreciation of the internet age clear from the beginning of the book. "The Internet is the greatest communication tool ever invented by humans," he waxes positively, providing scholars with a prime example of "the ways in which people experience the 'newness' of new media" (Gershon 2010b, 290). Because "Christianity is fundamentally a communications event," Bourgeois continues, "it is imperative that Christians understand how to use the Internet well" (2013, 8, 20). The manualist theologizes the recent "wiring" of the world through the internet and World Wide Web: "Just as I believe the Roman roads existed two thousand years ago to allow Christianity to quickly take root, I believe that God planned for this digital infrastructure at the beginning of the twenty-first century for his purposes."

Reminiscent of the American evangelical entrepreneurs who had commended the promiscuity of radio and television broadcasting for their abilities to fulfill the Great Commission, Bourgeois (2013, 21–22) also translates the development of connective digital technologies through the biblical lens of Matthew 24. The author quotes Walt Wilson, an evangelical media mogul from Silicon Valley, to emphasize that "God has built this network to accomplish that very purpose within our lifetime. We are the first generation in all of human history to hold within our hands the technology to reach every man, woman, and child on earth by 2020 ... this is the tool to do it." Likewise, as Nils Smith (2013, 8) argues in his *Social Media Guide for Ministry: What It Is and How to Use It,* "Throughout history, I don't know if there has ever been a greater tool" to "share the love of Christ ... than the Internet and, specifically, social media." Like Charles Fuller, Billy Graham, Benny Hinn, among a host of other evangelical media tycoons, Bourgeois and Smith theologize and enculturate social media and digital communication.

If more moderately optimistic, other advocates of internet-mediated technologies also exist, including Estes's (2009) theology of virtual church, Drescher's (2011) proposed habitus for digital media communications, Sweet's (2012) theorization of social media as extensions for Christian communication, and Wise's (2014) theological support for new media's leveling effects. To be clear, none of these authors, no matter how pragmatic the manual, is ignorant of the potentially negative side of social media. But together this community of writers conceives of the internet as a flawed but necessary arena of human communication. Prepared with applied skills and best practice strategies, the optimists are excited about new media put to service for the Christian agenda.

MEDIA IDEOLOGIES AS THEOLOGICAL STANCES

In his claim that discussions of the usefulness of the internet for sociality and church building are really about ecclesiology and authority, Estes (2009, 35) conjoins two separate categories of influence: theological stance and media ideologies. In the case of the manual writers, their deliberations about technology or new media always reference or signpost to theological convictions. The findings uncovered from this chapter's close readings of the manuals confirm that theological stance and media ideologies are not discrete normative domains but operate instead as two sides of the same coin. In the context of evangelical communication patterns, the two registers work in a co-constitutive manner. Debates about theological orthodoxy are often operating just on top of standards of communication, such as the sincerity model—which prefers communication to be intimate, unmediated, and embodied. In the other direction, contestation about correct uses of various media expresses worry about the ability of traditional (i.e., offline) religious authorities to preserve their legitimacy. To rephrase the matter, theological stances and media ideologies exist in a causative relation with one another. Media ideologies proceed out of and reflexively inform the theological standpoints of every writer submitting some evaluative proposition about what media are and how they ought to work.

In other words, a strong and predictive correspondence exists between a manualist's tradition of theological upbringing and his or her location along the trifold scale of possible media ideologies: asceticism, redemption, and optimism. The most severe evangelical criticisms of technology and media tend to hail from the Reformed Protestant subtraditions, groups that reject the unbridled antiauthoritarianism of their Protestant heritage. Logically, perhaps, in their resistance to new media, these writers work to further sanction and sacralize the ecology of print culture, Protestantism's preferred communicative standard. Schultze, for instance, is a professor at Calvin College, a prestigious academic center in the Reformed tradition. Challies is a popular blogger, author, and speaker for Reformed Calvinist audiences. Endorsement blurbs for *The Next Story* come from Albert Mohler Jr., Michael Horton, and Justin Taylor—all influential figures in Reformed Christian circles. Justin Taylor, in fact—a contributor to *The Gospel Coalition*, an online blog community for the production and dissemination of **Reformed theology**—had an important hand in advancing boundary maintenance strategies against theological opponents, including progressive preacher and writer Rob Bell, the subject of the next chapter. Challies's blog will feature alongside many others in deliberations about Bell's status as an authentic and orthodox Christian.

The ascetics, in other words, resist promiscuous media because such media ideologies have foundations in theological worldviews that identify the total depravity of humankind and its propensity toward sinfulness. They imbue traditional print text, sanctioned by authoritative publishing houses, with even more value. The ascetics also write against what they see as the erosion of legitimate biblical and ecclesial authority by new forms of knowledge building by consensus, wiki formats, or crowdsourcing. As I will soon elaborate, internet-enabled microblogs, such as Twitter, do indeed provide an arena for nontraditional, progressive, or experimental figures to find a voice and garner audiences. In the sense of uncontrollable affordances and reception, the ascetics' worries find clear justification. At the same time, the analysis of Twitter orthodoxy debates will show how existing authorities, the Reformed or neo-Reformed tradition, exploit new media in effort to extend authority and control to digitally mediated domains. That upcoming discussion suggests that the internet's affordances for evangelicals dually challenge and reinforce authority rather than simply undermining tradition, as critics have worried.

An evident theological and ecclesial split emerges among the manual writers between those who adhere to Reformed doctrines and those who take more progressive positions, either through Protestant mainline traditions (e.g., Drescher 2011) or through an experimental, post- or quasievangelical collective loosely identified as the **emerging church movement (ECM)** (Cooper 2017c). Notably, Rice (2009) positively cites ECM-affiliated figures, such as Scot McKnight, and includes book-cover endorsements by Dan Kimball and Mark Scandrette, two leading writers connected to emerging evangelicalism. Estes (2009) thanks Andrew "Tall Skinny Kiwi" Jones, a formational ECM blogger, and Scot McKnight, another ECM figure, for influencing his book. Estes (2009, 17–18) also describes his own affinity with ECM conversations in the rhetoric he employs. Drescher (2011, ix, 91) acknowledges Chris Yaw's influence on her work and refers later in the study to a "Presbymergent" Facebook page, a prime example of the ECM's ecclesial boundary blurring, theological combination, and overall experimentation. Sweet, who's *Viral* is one of the most optimistic books toward new media considered in this chapter, is himself one of the seminal figures involved in the formational days of ECM in the 1990s (see Cooper 2017c).

CONCLUSION

This chapter has documented the tenuous relationship between media sincerity and promiscuity in evangelical print culture. Manualists, simply put, deliberate about authority. Some authors welcome the populist- and hierarchy-dissolving tendencies of new media; others decry the selfsame factors as antibiblical and anti-Christian. The writers, however, do converge on the issue of informational excess. Media theorists across the board agree that in the age of promiscuous media the problem is too much information. Evangelicals part ways, however, when it comes to authenticity, realness, and meaning; the debate about the merits and detractions of real communities versus online ones; and theorizations about Facebook-era "friendship." Some writers contend that new media communication can productively accentuate and extend traditional (i.e., in-person and embodied) correspondence. Others reject cyber, virtual, online, new media, or internet-enabled forms as authentic, real, and useful. As with the previous chapter, the discussion emerging among this networked corpus of texts is one that wrestles with its inherited paradigms of sincerity and promiscuity.

Most importantly, this chapter underscored the connection between discussions of communicative authenticity and doctrinal, theological, or ecclesial orthodoxy and suggested that evangelical media theorists fall along a continuum of media ideologies that include asceticism, redemption, or optimism. Through lists of best practices, prescriptions of new media fasts, and other stewardship strategies for internet use, evangelicals corporately seek to extend Christian virtues into online domains. Lastly, this chapter reflected on the interrelated relationship of correspondence between theological background and new media ideologies and found that scholars from Reformed traditions tend to reject the promiscuous implications of new media, while more progressive evangelical thinkers embrace the digital for its reconfiguration of authority and deconstruction of entrenched hierarchies. The next part of the book showcases studies from the front lines of digital evangelicalism, analyzing deliberations over authority and authenticity as they take place online. The upcoming chapter focuses on the question of Rob Bell's status as a heretic and mines the vast threads of thousands of Twitter interactions and blog posts, prime locations for these contentious debates.

NOTE

1. See appendix sections 1.1 and 1.2 for a discussion of the occupations and educational accomplishments of this group of writers and for more on the selection criteria and textual analysis methods that informed the chapter.

PART II

**AUTHENTICITY CONSTRUCTION
ACROSS NEW MEDIA**

Case Studies

FOUR

#FAREWELLROBBELL

Heresy Discourse and the
Horizontalization of Authority

ROB BELL MAY JUST BE the most controversial figure in evangelical America's recent history. His work, as one scholar puts it, provokes "visceral reactions that range from adoration to repulsion" (Wellman 2012, 9). Bell is best known for a series of experimental and provocative books on Christian thought and practice—including *Velvet Elvis: Repainting the Christian Faith* (2005), *Sex God: Exploring the Endless Connections between Sexuality and Spirituality* (2007), and *Jesus Wants to Save Christians: A Manifesto for the Church in Exile* (2008)—and a series of short instructional films on spirituality called *Nooma*. After publishing his most polarizing book to date, *Love Wins: A Book about Heaven, Hell, and the Fate of Every Person Who Ever Lived* (2011b), Bell drew more than ever the ire of conservative evangelicals. According to critics, *Love Wins* undermined historic Christian theologies of the afterlife. In 2011, the prolific writer, speaker, and pastor, having emerged out of a conservative Christian background and attended Wheaton College and Fuller Seminary, made it to the Time 100 list of most influential people around the globe. That same year, Bell left Mars Hill, the megachurch he'd steered from its inception, to serve as a celebrity pastor and influencer in Hollywood.

Evangelical opinions about Bell run the gamut. Many evangelicals do not appreciate Bell's experimental ministry and intentional obscuring of theological boundaries. Bell is a polarizing figure. Certain pastors describe Bell as "one of the most dangerous figures on the Christian landscape today," while others write him off "as a heretic or worse" (Wellman 2012, 10). Years after *Love Wins*, and following several more publications, Bell remains a lightning rod of controversy. Church on the Margins, the Midwestern community discussed in chapters 7 and 8, for instance, makes routine use of Bell's teachings, podcasts, and talks. The copastors draw on, and sometimes replicate, Bell's teachings in whole or in part. But recognizing Bell's divisive status, these pastors are hesitant to name the figure as an influence, at least in the context of public sermons. Yet, Bell remains an inspiration for these progressive evangelicals. Ben, an ethnographic collaborator I once attended an intimate David Bazan[1] house concert with, set out on a pilgrimage to southern California to take part in one of Bell's teaching seminars. According to Ben's report, the session included surfing with the writer, indulging in the sun and spray of SoCal beaches, and having philosophical one on ones with the postevangelical provocateur turned spiritual guru.

This chapter collects and analyzes the language and discourse used by evangelical opponents across promiscuous new media to denounce Bell and his ministry, degrade his work, and ultimately mark him as dangerous, heterodox, and theologically other. I am particularly interested in the ways traditional evangelicals engage in strategies of boundary maintenance in digital, online, participative, internet-enabled, and new media domains. The purpose of this chapter is to do a deep dive into the strategies and tactics such maintenance occurs online. Evangelicals have for a long time engaged in boundary maintenance strategies via written discourse. But in the case of promiscuous media, the affordances of the technology are such that the criteria for who gets to participate are far less restrictive. Some evangelicals argue that the internet enables anyone to act as a theologian (provided they have access to it). And as I argued in the previous chapter, evangelical authorities' concerns confirm and legitimate the populist digital affordances of promiscuous media.

For the theological powers that be, the internet is truly dangerous because it allows for the promiscuous spread of heterodox media. The Rob Bell controversy is one of the most explicit instances of such danger for theological conservatives. In this chapter, I focus on how evangelicals on Twitter and in the blogosphere are using new media for the purposes of boundary maintenance and theological deliberation. In contrast to some commentators' worries, I conclude that promiscuous media actually assist evangelical authorities in marking Bell as dangerous and aid them in putting online media to use to warn others about Bell's heterodoxy.

PROMISCUOUS MEDIA AND THE HORIZONTALIZATION EFFECT

Besides unifying believers across physical distance (Gelfgren 2012, 235), extending and facilitating community (Campbell 2013b), and providing novel forms of ritual mediation (Cheong 2012, 198; Cooper 2014), promiscuous new media also have a contentious or fragmentary effect in that they allow for users to criticize, denounce, mark as dangerous, and distance themselves from figures deemed suspect. Such activities are due to the rise of what I've described as the emergence of the digitally buffered self, in which one is exposed to greater degrees of difference in online milieus. In turning to blog and microblog platforms, evangelical theological factions struggle "for power, influence, and prominence" (Baab 2012, 287) as they construct and defend their identities. New media allow for the public identification of difference and alterity. But the question remains as to how novel these discourses are in new media compared to older forms.

Evangelicals have for centuries been using so-called new media for boundary maintenance. **Newness**, after all, is a temporally relative social construction (Gershon 2010b). Historically, evangelicals have fashioned their boundaries by debating in and through textual circulations of different types. Through printed sermons, religious journals, and magazine publications, evangelicals have long employed texts to span distance, construct evangelical reading publics, debate theology, and contend over what counts as orthodox or heterodox. Blog and microblog theology debates are in some ways simply the next logical stage in the evolution of evangelical communication media.

What the digital turn does offer in terms of novelty is a concerted reconfiguration of the manners in which religious powers negotiate authority. Media are the very stuff of sociocultural production. Nascent technologies alter existing media ecologies in profound ways. New media forms modify communication environments and adapt the logics of participants engaged in these reconfigurations of authority and power. Hoover (2012, xii) describes such authoritative renegotiations, writing that "the inventory of resources and practices through which religion and spirituality are known and done today is an increasingly 'horizontal' inventory, where the traditional sources exist alongside a range of other ones." Due to the horizontalizing effects of promiscuous new media, people now face a constant flow of information from a range of source materials. And due to the simultaneous possibilities of these developments, new media appear to be minimalizing the criteria for who has authorization to engage in public theological discussions. Debating theology on Twitter bypasses entirely the influencing of theological discussions at the level of the gatekeeper, editor, proofreader, and publisher. New media exploit the affordances of speed and immediacy.

In the following sections, after analyzing the corrosive rhetoric employed via Twitter and in blog posts and tracing the discursive life of one polarizing microtext as it reproduces in myriad forms across several years, I conclude with a consideration of evangelicalism's decentered and fragmented structures of authority, authority that plays out in a domain of loose media networks, publics, counterpublics, and circulating, dialogical texts. This study begins with one seemingly minor media event: the publishing of three short words compounded into a Twitter hashtag.

#FAREWELLROBBELL: ORIGINS AND CIRCULATION

Farewell Rob Bell. I first encountered the phrase while wrapping up an ethnographic fieldwork project in an evangelical community in Springfield, Missouri (Cooper 2011). At the time an ambivalently appreciated and somewhat polarizing writer among my interlocuters, Bell had just finished his newest book, *Love Wins* (2011b). The book's publisher, HarperCollins, posted a provocative video preview on February 22, just under a month before the book's official release (Bell 2011a). Four days later, a popular blogger writing for a theologically conservative evangelical group in the Reformed tradition, *The Gospel Coalition* (TGC), uploaded a response to the video titled "Rob Bell: Universalist?" (Taylor 2011).

Taylor's short theological critique of Bell's yet unpublished work pulled no punches. "It is unspeakably sad," the blogger chided, "when those called to be ministers of the Word distort the gospel and deceive the people of God with false doctrine." Identifying Bell with a theological camp considered by many evangelicals to be unorthodox or marginal (i.e., a universalist, or one holding the conviction that all persons will be redeemed in the afterlife, rather than some suffering eternal damnation), Taylor cited a biblical passage (2 Corinthians 11:14–15) to equate Bell with deception, falsification, and error. Heeding feedback on his post, Taylor later edited this section out of his blog, noting his desire to postpone the pronouncement of Bell's heterodoxy until having read the actual book. One journalist documented that Taylor's quick redacting included "deleting a reference to Cor. 11:14–15," a biblical passage that features Satan disguised as an angel of light (Bailey 2011). Taylor apparently thought that his satanic metaphor for Bell was too much considering the book had not been released yet.

Taylor's initial post embedded the *Love Wins* promotional video and thus effectively served as one of the earliest and most visited sources of commentary on the subject. One popular evangelical writer flirted with soteriological inclusivity. Another publicized and denounced said theological provocation. The conditions were ripe for an explosive media event and maelstrom of online discursive blogs, tweets, **retweets**, and Facebook posts.

Although Taylor's critical essay set the conditions for the discursive flurry, a subsequent tweet authored by a popular Reformed pastor and writer ignited the internet battle at the center of this chapter. On the same day as Taylor's blog post, February 26, 2011, John Piper—a prolific evangelical author with a sizable following—tweeted three words to his Twitter followers, appended by a link to Taylor's TGC post:

@JohnPiper: Farewell Rob Bell. http://dsr.gd/fZqmd8

Piper's instigation of this theological debate speaks to the horizontalizing effects of new media and the workings of the digitally buffered self as it encounters difference online. In short, Piper has gained a wide following and cultivated over time a reputation as a respected authority in the Christian world. Piper is a powerful Reformed writer and minister with a high degree of visibility and influence. His power derives from both his charismatic use of social media, like Twitter, but also his more traditional success in publishing instructive theological books for wide Christian audiences. But because Twitter at least partially horizontalizes discourse, Piper's comments appear online next to myriad other Twitter profiles with varying degrees of theological authority and credibility. As an evangelical authority, Piper extends his influence online, but it remains unclear what happens when the theologian's authoritative presence is juxtaposed with thousands of other microtexts, Twitter and blog discourses that may either confirm or collide with his own theological pronouncements.[2]

What is clear is that Piper's tweet resulted in what was an apparently unanticipated barrage of online discourse—promiscuity, again, at work. "'Rob Bell' was in the top 10 trending topics on Twitter Saturday," a journalist reported in 2011 for the flagship evangelical publication *Christianity Today*. "As of Saturday evening, about 12,000 people had recommended Taylor's blog post on Facebook" and around 650 people had left comments at the TGC site (Bailey 2011). "Social media did its work and soon tens of thousands and then hundreds of thousands of people were reading these comments and spreading them through their own networks; people were retweeting and liking and commenting and writing their own blog posts," another commentator noted (Challies 2011).[3] By the time of the initial research for this chapter in 2015, Piper's tweet had generated some 975 retweets and 221 unique Twitter users had favorited the post.

Scrutinizing Twitter as a domain of theological discourse, I trace the discursive life of Piper's text as Twitter theologians lift the message from its original context and broadcast it in the new environments of their own profiles, sometimes extending Piper's intent and other times undermining it. The goal is to analyze Twitter's affordances as a mechanism for theological stancetaking. The Farewell Rob Bell event spanned just under four-and-a-half years between February 2011 through the time of the initial drafting of this chapter in spring 2015. Thousands of posts via Twitter—which publishes some 500 million tweets per day, has 330 million monthly active users and 100 million daily active users, and boasts a total of 67 million American users (Aslam 2018; Cheong 2012, 191; Squires 2014, 44)—have been published on the subject of the Bell controversy. A substantial amount of commentary on the 2011 dispute has been submitted into the digital arena.

Using a combination of manual digital research methods via multiple online search engines and supplemented with Context Miner, a qualitative data-analysis program, I constructed a corpus of 1,431 tweets. Due to Twitter's inherent structural limitations in terms of the conciseness of information sharing in one instance (what was then a 140-character limit), the information generated by these tweets was also restricted. To make up for Twitter's communicative brevity, I also used Context Miner to put together a 102-item corpus of blog posts circulated between 2011 and 2015, all written about the Farewell Rob Bell debate.

The Twitter and blog post corpora provided ample data with which to record, describe, and analyze the ways that evangelicals employ language via new media to do important and overlapping social, cultural, ideological, theological, and ecclesial work. The Farewell Rob Bell media event, including myriad ensuing events and subsequent repostings, provides us with a clear entry point into the ways language on social media serves to establish, maintain, police, and reinforce social and ecclesial boundaries. Iterated via tweets and blogs, the theological controversy provides vital insight into the methods with which religious publics attempt to maintain boundaries by guarding against heterodox contagions.

RESEARCH OVERVIEW I: TWITTER DATA

Over the last several years, Rob Bell's status and identity as an evangelical and a Christian have come under heavy fire. Loud and influential voices online have not only denounced Bell and denied his evangelical status, but some have gone as far as to question his identity and standing as a Christian altogether. This section describes the mechanisms by which authoritative (or at least highly vocal) evangelical gatekeepers (Fairclough 1989, 47; cf. Tufecki 2017, 177) maintain evangelical boundaries by excluding Bell from "the fold," to commandeer a metaphor used by digital informants online. How, in other words, do people denounce Bell? Which words and expressions do they use to do so? Which sorts of lexical or syntactical forms? Which types of metaphors? Terminological binaries weighted with Christian historical significance come frequently to the fore on Twitter and in the blogs, but what other sorts of linguistic and textual patterns do these contending evangelicals make use of?

The original plan for the analysis was to code each singular tweet into one of three categories in light of the tweet's stancetaking on the issue of Bell's orthodoxy or nonorthodoxy: (1) denunciatory, oppositional, or negative; (2) neutral or disinterested; or (3) supportive or defensive. But such a method proved insufficient as I sorted through the data. In short, it became evident that I would need a fourth code to categorize the proliferation of tweets to capture the ambiguity or **opacity** of a very large section of the corpus. Adapting to this situation, I sought to account for the opacity of tweets and their theological stancetaking when a position was evident. The reasons for a prevalence of ambiguousness, one might hypothesize, stem largely from Twitter's program design and structured conciseness of information sharing. The 140-character limit does not provide an abundance of space to expound on doctrinal minutiae. But such concision does serve efficiently to pass on a short link to a blog post in which the Twitter user or another commentator expounds on doctrinal minutiae. On Twitter, stance is sometimes especially difficult to determine.

The retweet (RT), a function built into Twitter's operative structure, is an expedient way to pass information to one's followers. For analytic purposes, however, RTs are also inherently ambiguous. Often in the twittersphere people include a telling disclaimer on their profile pages: "RTs are not endorsements" or "RTs ≠ endorsements." It follows that a RT of a particular source, statement, text, article, or link does not always track with a positive evaluation. One cannot get into the mind of the tweeter, so to say, to gauge or determine the user's intention. One can look for clues, however—little textual add-ons or short emotive flurries that point to the user's interior convictions and stance—and these hints may or may not push the tweet closer to one of the categories outlined above.[4]

As table 4.1 illustrates, some 22.3 percent of tweets overtly or explicitly marked Bell as dangerous, heterodox, or other. A little more than half the number of denunciatory tweets collected, on the other hand, were overtly or explicitly in support or defense of Bell and his standing as an evangelical teacher and writer. By far the overwhelming number of tweets in the corpus fell into one of two categories that I've described as ambiguous or vague in their stancetaking; 52.4 percent of tweets were vague or opaque in meaning and intention, while 12.3 percent operated as standard nonvaluated RTs. What I mean by applying the ambiguous, opaque, or vague descriptor to a tweet, to be more precise, is that the decontextualized tweet does not immediately reveal its author's stance. Hypothetically, a Twitter user could RT Piper's post or use the #farewellrobbell hashtag and not necessarily wish to mark Bell as an apostate of the faith.

On the subject of a RT's characteristic opacity, keep in mind the common disclaimer circulated by journalists and academics online about RTs not being synonymous with endorsement. Such tensions pertain in evangelical online discourses as well. Consider, for instance, the following generic RT posted by Twitterer @rzhodgman:

@rzhodgman: RT @JohnPiper: Farewell Rob Bell. http://dsr.gd/fZqmd8

The tweet provides no explanation, posturing, or commentary and contains only four elements: (1) the RT header, the only new element added to the initial tweet; (2) the citation or handle of the original tweet; (3) the tweet content itself; and (4) the short link to the Taylor piece disseminated by John Piper's original tweet. Generic RTs of this sort are not exclusively (or entirely) negative gestures toward

Table 4.1. Twitter Stance on Rob Bell's Theological Orthodoxy (N=1,430)

Stance Category	Number of Tweets	Percentage of Tweets
Stancetaking		
(a) dismissive	319	22.3
(b) supportive	185	12.9
Nonstancetaking		
(c) ambiguous	750	52.4
(d) generic RTs	176	12.3

Bell, since one cannot discern the retweeter's intention from the repost alone. By the same token, interpreting all generic RTs as denunciatory would inflate the number of dismissive tweets, bringing the total to 495 discrete tweets or 34.6 percent of the corpus. In methodological terms, one inherent weakness of this sort of textual study applied to Twitter, to repeat, is that in decontextualized tweets, stances are unclear and undetermined. From a quantitative corpus-analysis perspective, Twitter data are ambiguous.

But rather than excluding the ambiguous tweets from my study sample, this characteristic opacity gives observers of new media an opportune moment to theorize. If, as quantitative social media analysts have argued, controversial information sharing generates largely **polarized crowds**, or "two distinct discussion groups that mostly do not interact with each other" (Smith et al. 2014), then interpreting vague RTs as denunciatory suggests that a larger number of dismissive tweets—again, upward of as many as 34.6 percent of the corpus I analyzed—is plausible. However, one must also be aware that polarized crowds serve as only one combination through which discourse online might take place. Another model that describes what religious groups experience is the **community cluster**, in which the sharing of information might "ignite multiple conversations, each cultivating its own audience and community" (Smith et al. 2014). Rather than two primarily separatist groups on Twitter, networked, informational hubs develop in a loosely interactive manner.

Either way, language and voice are highly complex human processes and become even more complex in new media domains. Rarely (if ever) do neutral utterances exist.[5] Perhaps a RT in this dialogic sense is tantamount to favorably quoting (i.e., endorsing, praising, or confirming) the source, in this case @JohnPiper. Although less than satisfying than determining outright if most tweets praised or denounced Bell, such overwhelming RT opacity is an interesting finding in and of itself. Circulating Twitter theologies are less than determined. Dialogical ambiguity abounds. Because Twitter is a promiscuous media form, one may not be able to anticipate or control how one's microtexts get interpreted online.

Opaque tweets aside, a total of 504 discrete tweets, or 45.2 percent of the total tweets collected, do come down clearly on either side of the issue by making evident whether their content supported or opposed Bell at the time. Typical tweets in the dismissive category include the following:

@ReformedRamblin: "@BurkParsons: Rob Bell says farewell http://bit.ly/p2jnOJ " going to spread heresy to a broader audience?

@mitcherator: Rob Bell says farewell - oh thank God Ive been waiting for heretical universalist Rob Bell to leave http://bit.ly/p2jnOJ

@shaunandrew: As Piper said "Farewell, Rob Bell." Rob, you must turn. I invite anyone to take some time to pray with me for Rob Bell today.

A selected sample of supportive tweets, on the other hand, include:

@All_4Given: I'm not a "farewell, Rob Bell" kind of person. I appreciate much of what he does. He . . . http://fb.me/1UF3g1dok

@StaceyPrickett: Happy to report that its not "farewell Rob Bell" he def knows that Jesus is the only way and that God is the only true god.

@RyanMiller: Rob Bell is putting out some killer stuff lately! The sad truth is that many will choose NOT to read it due to "farewell" junk.

Again, examples of an ambiguous tweet might include the following:

@NancyReece: RT @JohnPiper: Farewell Rob Bell. http://dsr.gd/fZqmd8>>What does this to do NOOMA videos?

@jacobrileyrush: @jakemcatee "Farewell Rob Bell"

@mollrob: If Rob Bell is leaving the evangelical fold, I hope evangelicals don't say "farewell" but instead offer to visit. http://buff.ly/1wn8UKf

The @mollrob tweet is less ambiguous than the @NancyReece and @jacobrileyrush tweets because it submits criticism against evangelicalism as a collective. But in terms of stancetaking, it is still not immediately clear whether the author of the statement agrees that Bell is indeed "leaving the evangelical fold."

Over time, the gap between the original **entextualization** by Piper in 2011 and its simultaneous extractions and repostings—carried out in the seemingly simple act of clicking the RT button and adding (or not adding) a few words of commentary—notably widens.[6] By 2015, and as I'll discuss in the coda to this chapter, the gap had broadened enough that tweets began to employ the phrase for humorous reasons or instances of resistance that supported rather than denounced Bell. Editing this chapter in 2019, the phrase continues to circulate online. But the most recent uses of the hashtag tend to be meta-analytical and criticize evangelicals' inclination to engage in heady public debates. Put simply, more recent instances of #FarewellRobBell in 2018 and 2019 do not mean the same thing Piper intended in 2011.

CONTENT ANALYSIS I: DISMISSIVE TWEETS

From the main corpus of tweets, I constructed a smaller subcorpus of sixty Twitter posts that I identified as overtly staking out in variable word or phrase constructions what the originators saw as the issue with Bell. These denunciations ranged from one- or two-word statements appended to RT links to longer explanatory sentences full of distancing metaphors and allusions. The following lists depict these snippets and phrases, analyzing the types of distancing mechanisms and negative stancetaking that occurs via Twitter.

One small but significant category in the dismissive subcorpus employs biblically derived animal and nonhuman metaphors in effort to mark Bell as theologically dangerous and other. Several notable examples include:

@daviswmorgan: Gotta watch out for wolves in sheep's clothing: RT @JohnPiper: Farewell Rob Bell. http://dsr.gd/fZqmd8 #tc #earnestlycontendforthetruth

@markmyles: RT @JohnPiper: Farewell Rob Bell. http://dsr.gd/ // Do not b fooled by wolves among sheep. My sermon next wk will address this Eph 4:14–16.

@andyoutcast: "@JohnPiper: Farewell Rob Bell. http://dsr.gd/fZqmd8" ... It's time to put an end to wolves in sheep's clothing.

@brianlusky: @LShallenberger I took it to mean, farewell, as Rob Bell has officially left orthodoxy. You don't let wolves play with the sheep.

The sheep/wolf analogy has biblical precedent and thus finds frequent implementation in discussions of Christian orthodoxy. Matthew 7:15 reads, "Beware of the false prophets, who come to you in sheep's clothing, but inwardly are ravenous wolves." Other passages that involve sheep and wolf metaphors include John 10:1–18, wherein the Good Shepherd discusses keeping dangerous wolves at bay. Twitter users playing with animal metaphors more than likely have biblical references in mind. Allusions to the Bible, with the Bible's central place in evangelical cultural and religious life, in fact, are the most powerful form of appeal to textual authority.

A higher percentage of tweets employs intentional theological jargon in their distancing maneuvers. A total of twenty-three out of sixty tweets (38.3 percent) make use of key religious (and particularly Christian) terms having to do with boundary maintenance. Thirteen of sixty (21.6 percent) explicitly use the term *heresy* and/or its cognates (*heretical, heretic,* etc.). Examples of typical tweets in this category include:

@AusMcCann: RT @JohnPiper: Farewell Rob Bell. http://dsr.gd/fZqmd8 it's about time the truth comes out about Rob Bell ... it's sad how he spreads heresy

@VinceStiffler: RT @JohnPiper: Farewell Rob Bell. http://dsr.gd/fZqmd8 // Important for us to distinguish heresy vs. truth.

@Lekrom: RT @JohnPiper: Farewell Rob Bell. http://dsr.gd/fZqmd8 - sooner or later, all the heretics will reveal themselves @juanvwyk @jacquesbornman

Where the preceding tweets invoke heresy to mark Bell as other, some—like the following—use theological jargon, employing words and phrases such as *false doctrine* and *idolatry, bad theology* and *blasphemy*. Occasionally tweets make note of what they consider to be Bell's fraught relationship with "orthodoxy," such as the last on the list.

@PastorHarv: This is sad. Another pastor falls prey to false doctrine and idolotry // RT @JohnPiper: Farewell Rob Bell. http://dsr.gd/fZqmd8 #fb

@jeremyhorton: "@JohnPiper:Farewell Rob Bell. http://dsr.gd/fZqmd8" // I won't lie, this makes me sad. Shows what baby steps of bad theology does over time

@SonKing: "Accepting, confessing, believing-those are things we DO ... How is any of that grace?"-Love Wins by Rob Bell Blindness or blasphemy. Farewell

@Fake_Andrew: @RyanECHamm "Farewell rob bell" was a hateful tweet? I can't imagine a kinder way to put someone leaving orthodoxy

Two twitter commentators go as far as to make a metacomparative statement about the pronunciation of heresy via Twitter contrasted with more historical and violent inquisitional forms:

@PaulKoopman: I don't know why Rob Bell fans are upset. In 1560, Piper wouldn't be tweeting "Farewell", he'd be handing Bell over to the executioners.

@tc_moore: Bell is beyond farewell. The Coalition will burn him at the stake for this!! #lightningrodbell

Another significant portion of this subcorpus makes use of spatial, landscape, and geographical metaphors to invoke an illustrative picture of Bell as moving away from traditional Christian ecclesial convictions.

@galsterm: I always thought he was a bit out there. Now I know why. RT @JohnPiper Farewell Rob Bell. http://dsr.gd/fZqmd8 #fb

@Biggzipp: RT @JohnPiper: Farewell Rob Bell. http://dsr.gd/fZqmd8 // talk about laying your cards on the table. Hate that he's this far off track #fb

@made2sing: RT @stovallweems: RT @JohnPiper: Farewell Rob Bell. http://dsr.gd/fZqmd8. // sad - but you could see he was going this direction

@ericwatt: RT @JohnPiper: Farewell Rob Bell. http://dsr.gd/fZqmd8 // a sad story of drifting away. Let's pray for a turn around

A total of eight out of sixty (13.3 percent) name Bell's theological inadequacies or excesses by implying the concepts of mapping or space, center and periphery, and near versus far. Thus, for @galsterm, Bell is "a bit out there," rather than *over here*, where (presumed) orthodoxy dwells, perhaps suggesting a crooked, lateral, or diagonal direction. For @made2sing, Bell is increasing his distance by moving in the spatial "direction" of unorthodoxy. This last tweet, in fact, is reminiscent in content to @jeremyhorton's above on "baby" steps away from orthodoxy. @ericwatt's tweet captures the plotting along spatial-theological continuums as well, noting that Bell is "drifting away" from some implied orthodox center and that to improve his standing, Bell ought to literally "turn around" or turn back toward what such critics construe as the truth.

Lastly, an eclectic fourth category embedded in the subcorpus of dismissive tweets qualifies Bell using negative terms or derivatives, including deception, distortion, danger, or even dirt or filth, reinforcing Douglas's (1966) theorization of social maintenance as hygienically concerned.

> **@stephalbright**: RT @JohnPiper Farewell Rob Bell. http://dsr.gd/fZqmd8 // finally. so frustrating. what a deceptive man. so sad
>
> **@brandoncrosby**: RT @JohnPiper Farewell Rob Bell. http://dsr.gd/fZqmd8 // Wow. That's both sad and a bit sickening to see the Gospel that distorted.
>
> **@infinitewisdom7**: John Piper's "Farewell Rob Bell" continues to echo. That man is in danger. #RobBell
>
> **@NotTommySmith**: @RoyBoi10 In the words of my friend John Piper, "farewell Rob Bell." Or, in other words, no I won't read that filth.

Although not working in specifically racial or ethnic registers, this last category offers an example of the digitally buffered self that verges on a form of **digital orientalism** in which critics mark Bell as other, that is, as "as sneaky or dirty, or savage, dangerous, and threatening" (Jamerson 2017, 123). In summary, such corrosive discourse intended against Bell is predominantly (though not entirely) figurative and metaphorical in a linguistic sense.[7]

RESEARCH OVERVIEW II: BLOG DATA

To supplement for Twitter's concision as a communicative genre, I also constructed and analyzed a corpus of 101 blog articles and short online essays published roughly over a four-year period between the posting of @JohnPiper's initial tweet and **reentextualizations** occurring in 2015.[8] In contrast with the Twitter data, the results in terms of denunciation and support is more even, split nearly down the middle (see table 4.2 below). Out of the negative blogs, some might border on being described as "abusive" or "bullying" (Baab 2012, 286). The blog

Table 4.2. Blog Stance on Rob Bell's Theological Orthodoxy (N=101)

Stance Category	Number of Blogs	Percentage of Blogs
Stancetaking		
(a) dismissive	30	29.7
(b) supportive	30	29.7
Nonstancetaking		
(c) ambiguous	41	41.0

and microblog genres have the potential to blur boundaries between laypersons and authoritative clergy (Fischer-Nielson and Gelfgren 2012, 300) but only to a degree (Campbell 2013a, 15; Teusner 2013).[9] The data below suggest that the online world is fairly evenly divided on the issue.

CONTENT ANALYSIS II: DISMISSIVE BLOG POSTS

Theological Jargon

Like the Twitter posts, blog criticisms fall into several overlapping, nondiscrete categories. The heresy tags, along with other theological terms, come up frequently. One blogger describes Bell as becoming "more and more overt in his long established heretical views" (Buettel 2011). Lindsey (2011) also marks Bell as having "strayed far enough from the gospel as to have fallen into heresy." Albert (2011) agrees that Bell's work is indeed "dangerous and heretical." Another blogger takes a pessimistic stance toward Bell's future contributions, fearing that he will only "spiral further into heresy" (Delight in Truth 2013).

Analogous theological jargon proliferates. By some accounts, Bell demonstrates an "obvious disdain and resentment for the historic orthodox Christian faith" (Buettel 2011) and exhibits a "doctrinal seduction" (Mohler 2011).[10] Bell "has rejected virtually every orthodox doctrine of the faith from eschatology ... to theology proper." His work is a progressive "ever-evolving ... away from Christian orthodoxy" (McDanell 2015). Ultimately, Watts (2015) writes that Bell is "not Christian in any orthodox sense of the word."

As a subset of blog discourse in this category, bloggers ascribe to Bell several negative (i.e., nonconservative) theological appellations intended to demonstrate his ecclesial marginality. For Buettel (2011), Bell is a "non-Christian theological liberal." For Kennedy (2011), Bell is the "resident paradoxical wildcard threat" to evangelical theological stability. For Silva (2011a, 2011b), Bell is a "neo-Gnostic," contemplative, spiritualist mystic who is part of a "sinfully ecumenical neoliberal cult" as well as a "postmodern" and "Emergent menace." For Watts (2015), amending Silva, Bell is a "Neo-Marcionite Gnostic." For Yawn (2014), Bell has not "been close to biblical Christianity for more than a decade."

Spatial, Center/Periphery, or Inward/Outward Metaphors

A number of bloggers employ metaphorical analogues in an effort to illustrate Bell's marginality. Such comments often invoke a sense of travel, movement, motion, or departure. According to Taylor (2011), Bell has been "moving farther and farther away from anything resembling biblical Christianity." Taylor's comment, quite similar to @made2sing's above tweet, depicts Bell as moving along a continuum away from an orthodox center and toward an unorthodox distance. Buettel (2011) uses more of a spatial metaphor (building on interior/exterior or inside/outside dichotomies), arguing that Bell resides "outside of the [Christian] camp." Kennedy (2011), quoting another source, mentions Bell's being "thrown out" by evangelical authorities. Note the pushing of Bell in an *outward* rather than *inward* direction. Path or route metaphors depict Bell as straying, deviating, or diverging. For Lindsey (2011), Bell has "strayed far enough from the gospel as to have fallen into heresy." For Silva (2011b), Bell is "heading in that direction" of unorthodoxy. For Challies (2011), Bell has "stepped outside Christian orthodoxy." For Vander Hart (2013), "Rob Bell is off the reservation. Rob Bell isn't even on the map." For Yawn (2013), Bell's "departure was merely the next step." Sometimes the spatial analogies take on a circular and upward/downward correspondence rather *than near/far or inside/outside* ones. One blogger, for instance, classifies Bell as undergoing a "spiritual downward spiral" and predicts that future work will only continue to be heretical (Delight in Truth 2013). Bryant (2014) encapsulates this category of spatial or travel mechanisms well, writing that Bell "took a road at the fork that put us on two different paths." Bell's "trajectory" is a false one (Bryant 2014) as his theology is "ever-evolving ... away from Christian orthodoxy" (McDanell 2015). As a last example of the type of distancing mechanism under question, Watts (2015) comments that Bell undergoes a "turn *from* Christian themes *to* something else."

Scathing Qualifiers

Another category of dismissal has to do with attributing overtly negative adjectives, adverbs, or qualifiers to Bell. Many of these sorts of accounts appear to go much further than a theological denunciation of Bell's writings and attribute personally negative characterizations of him. At times, such qualifiers can be metaphorical (e.g., Taylor (2011): "False teachers look like cuddly sheep and angels of light"), but they may also employ nonmetaphorical or more literal forms that have to do with perversion, distortion, fraudulency, dishonesty, or other nondesired characteristics. Buettel suggests that Bell is "perverting and confusing" the "plain meaning" of the Bible or that he has gone as far as "inventing" his own form of new gospel (2011). Further, for this blogger, Bell is "sneaky," only "pretending to be a Christian," and offers "vague, obscure, and foggy theology." Less frequently present in the smaller corpus of blog posts than the Twitter corpus, commentators sometimes put to use biblical allusions (via animalistic metaphors) to underscore not only Bell's deviance but also his secrecy or fraudulency. For Buettel, Bell dons a "sheep skin," under which, to draw on another blogger, exists a "fierce wolf" (Silva 2011a). Others continue the theme of inauthenticity. Albert (2011) says that Bell must be "exposed for the fraud that he is." Silva (2011b) claims that Bell's language is "twisted" and "rebellious." Bell operates in a "deluded state." Delight in Truth (2013) writes that Bell's doctrine—which he has the audacity to actually believe—is false. Bell's "fall," for these commentators, ultimately renders him as theologically and ecclesially different and other; what he posits is "a totally different gospel, and likely a totally different religion than Christianity." Bell "continues to mock the faith" (McDanell 2015).

CONTESTED BOUNDARIES AND NEW MEDIA CONTESTATIONS

So far in this chapter, I have evaluated the mediated ways evangelicals maintain boundaries, perform buffered selfhoods, and address the potential dangers, threats, or contagions that are replete in promiscuous media. At this point it would be beneficial to pull back to a broader perspective—to shift from the trees to the forest, so to say—and set these microblog and blog developments in the context of a more historical debate about evangelical authoritative, structural, and institutional forms. Evangelicalism, as a term, is equally problematic as both a meaningful category of self-identification and a secondary analytic construct potentially useful for scholars. Some scholars, pointing to the lack of existence of any centralized religious hierarchy and the eclectic grouping of conflicting theologies and practices under the term, have questioned the utility of the label altogether. This camp views the category as no more than an inflated umbrella term that serves no convincing purpose and fails to represent any sort of meaningful collective on the ground (e.g., Hart 2004; Olson 2016). Denominations and organizational structures exist, but these microcollectives (ranging from Pentecostals to charismatics to Southern Baptists) don't see eye to eye and don't concede each other's authenticity and orthodoxy. Nor do they report back to any legitimate center beyond that of the immediate denominational affiliation. As one *Atlantic* journalist and evangelical writer acknowledges, evangelical "is a tricky word" (Merritt 2011). For evangelical insiders and outsiders alike, evangelicalism is a contested concept. The collective's boundaries exist through disputation.

Issues of increased connectivity and new media exposure to other evangelical camps—all repercussions of promiscuous media—exacerbate such crises of authority, legitimation, and power. Cheong (2012, 203) argues that microblogging "can contribute to internet radicalization of a more malevolent kind," in which "extremist networked believers" may "tweet to spread radical views or instigate militant interpretations of faith." But this depiction downplays that the very microblogging technology itself, supplementing traditional books, sermons, and magazines, allows for the determination of scathing qualifiers such as *extremist*, *radical*, or in this chapter's case, *heretical*. Circulation of texts and discourse speaks collectives into existence not in some formal, centralized manner—as if a coherent and bounded evangelicalism actually exists as an observable, verifiable entity—but in an imagined and dialogical sense. As linguists confirm, social life is "discursively constituted, produced and reproduced in situated acts of speaking and other signifying practices" (Bauman 2004, 3). The same holds for the competitive evangelicalisms under scrutiny in this chapter, each promoting their own conflicting definitions of orthodoxy and heresy. Social media are not some superfluous arenas reduced to YouTube cat videos, humorous GIFs, or comical memes. Social media, to reiterate, are the very stuff of socioreligious boundary maintenance. To put the matter still another way, authorities can exploit the affordances of media promiscuity to defend against heterodoxy.

Overall, religious leaders feel social media and online technologies are becoming more integrated into their daily routines. One can engage in theological work on the subway commute home in the evening needing nothing but a data phone. Further, those online engagements do not stay online but filter into and affect the offline. As I discuss in chapters 7 and 8, research at Midwestern fieldwork sites didn't turn up one person who had not either observed online or heard through everyday conversation about the Farewell Rob Bell controversy. At least one blogger from the corpus also noted hearing the phrase in sermons given in churches immediately following Piper's infamous tweet. Because the internet is becoming "embedded in everyday life" and serves as a "routine appliance for communicating and being informed" (Hogan and Wellman 2012, 49), one might safely assume that theological skirmishes and orthodoxy debates occurring through blogging and microblogging work to shape and construct the realm of the so-called real world. It follows that tweets and blog posts are playing an important role in religious formation.[11]

CONCLUSION

Rather than creating an unstructured, democratic, laissez-faire domain for unprincipled self-expression, the internet complicates and compounds conflicts of religious authority. But the question remains: Do new media work by extending existing authoritative structures into the digital arena? The answer, as we've seen, is not simple.

This chapter has focused on the effects of promiscuous media. I analyzed corrosive discourse intended against one quasievangelical iconoclast and described the ways critics use metaphor-heavy terms (frequently employing, for example, linear, movement, spatial, and biblical metaphors) and noted key theological jargon employed in denouncing Bell and marking him heretical. Although significantly ambiguous, Twitter discourse tended to lean toward dismissive language. The blog data was more balanced, confirming the status of Twitter and the blogosphere as veritable arenas of debate wherein two sides come into direct conflict.

I also argued that these online skirmishes partly reinforce the claim that no unified evangelicalism exists and instead a number of overlapping and contrasting publics and counterpublics operate in hybrid online and offline worlds through the circulation of socially relevant and boundary-maintaining texts. By way of theological publics vying with one another for dominance online, religious boundaries and identities come into existence. An evangelical public may inundate the internet in order to denounce a particular individual, but it does so at the risk of legitimizing other potentially vocal counterpublics in constructing identities and circulating texts. As one blogger questioned with still another appropriation of @JohnPiper's tweet, "But doesn't all this exposure increase Bell's celebrity? As I say, hello, Rob Bell, I hadn't thought about you much before the allies said farewell" (Hart 2011). The danger of social media contestation is that one's utterances may indeed through horizontalization and dialogical exposure reify the very entities one seeks to mark as unorthodox. Promiscuous media are a double-edged sword.

CODA: HERESY REDEEMED AND THE
AFTERMATH OF #FAREWELLROBBELL

This chapter has focused on Twitter and the blogosphere as they have been transformed by writers into an arena for theological debate between the years of 2011 and 2015. A brief Twitter archival search of the #farewellrobbell hashtag after 2015 suggests that the debate is still ongoing but has slowed significantly. As time passes the phrase takes on ironic significance and does intend to dismiss Bell's orthodoxy. Rather, the hashtag negatively comments on the internecine combativeness of evangelical Christianity. In other words, the most recent uses of the hashtag operate meta-analytically as commentaries on commentary, or rather, countercommentaries, addressing in a critical light the original 2011 utterance. Consider this Twitter user's summary of the event:

@Steve_Sherwood: #IDontUnderstandChristians who become irate at the idea that God's grace might end up including everyone. #farewellrobbell

This tweet is emblematic of others that entered the archive after 2016. The hashtag is indexically dismissive of Piper's dismissiveness against Bell.

Bell himself remains a lightning rod of controversy. He continues to tour, speak publicly, and write. He published new books in 2017, namely *How to Be Here: A Guide to Creating a Life Worth Living* (2017a) and *What Is the Bible? How an Ancient Library of Poems, Letters, and Stories Can Transform the Way You Think and Feel About Everything* (2017b). By early 2018 he had a Bible commentary nearing release. One of his most recent endeavors is a semibiographical documentary movie on his life and ministry as a Christian iconoclast. The title of the film is *The Heretic*. The film's trailer features short snippets of condemnation by conservative evangelical leaders. Franklin Graham, the son of the late evangelist Billy Graham and vocal supporter of the Trump administration, says that "I believe the man is a false teacher; I believe he's a heretic." "Rob Bell should fear God," an unnamed street preacher opines, "because he's a liar and a heretic" (Untold 2018; cf. Relevant 2018a). The heretic label, however, is no mere negative descriptor. The film reemploys the title as a badge of honor, a sign that Bell's theological pot-stirring has hit the right chords and is affecting change within evangelical structures of power. Such a creative application of the term invokes the strategy of Justin Wise (2014), the evangelical technology manual writer discussed in chapter 3. In progressive evangelical camps, heresy takes on ironic, even positive, cultural capital.

Relevant Magazine, a publication geared toward millennial evangelical readers, has taken a neutral and slightly defensive stance with regard to Bell when offering commentary on the Farewell Rob Bell event (e.g., Carey 2014; Relevant 2014; Hurd 2017). One *Relevant* contributor aimed to take on the entire system of evangelical heresy accusations in an article titled "4 Bad Reasons Christians Call Each Other 'Heretics.'" One of the writer's reasons is that Christians simply love the thrill of the game of heresy naming. Christians enjoy "competitive evangelicalism," and "theological competition." To illustrate this point, the author draws on the 2011 Twitter event:

> When Rob Bell published Love Wins in 2011, John Piper sent out a now infamous tweet with only three words: "Farewell Rob Bell." I respect Piper and his ministry, but this tweet shows that anyone can fall into the trap of theological competition. Piper used a cheeky salute to push Bell out the door of competitive evangelicalism. He wasn't concerned with Bell's spiritual health or his ministry, he was just competing. It was one heavyweight theologian taunting another.... When God becomes a game, labels of heresy can be used like a knockout punch to the opponent. (Northcutt 2017)

The author does not address the affordances of the Twitter or blog platforms in this short feature, but clearly they see as unproductive (and even dangerous) the role promiscuous media serve for corrosive discourse. In a 2018 interview with a *Relevant* editor, musician Audrey Assad referred to Piper's tweet as an instance of social shaming that ought to be resisted by Christians (Henry 2018). One of the magazine's recent issues, a feature titled "10 People Who Changed the Faith Conversation" listed Bell as number three and credited him with teaching people "to stop being afraid of questions." The piece offers no criteria for the list, but according to its rationale, Bell's significance was greater than other public Protestants and Catholics, including Bryan Stevenson, Beth Moore, Stephen Colbert (Brehm 2019), Bono, Rachel Held Evans (see chap. 5), Bob Goff, and Judah Smith. These figures were numbers four through ten, respectively. The editors deemed only pastor and author Rick Warren (number one) and hip-hop musician Lecrae (number two) as more influential (Relevant 2018b).

As a prelude to upcoming chapters, I should note that some evangelicals emphasize sincerity over promiscuity in their embarrassment of the Piper versus Bell event. These evangelicals reject social media as an appropriate venue for theological debate. Another *Relevant* writer, Jesse Carey, in a netiquette guide titled "How to Know Your Facebook Post Is about to Go Very, Very Wrong," calls on evangelicals to engage with sensitivity, carefulness, and discernment online. Carey advises readers on the correct protocol for maintaining friendships and warns against alienating those in one's networks due to insensitive, outspoken rhetoric. Most importantly, the writer admonishes evangelicals to avoid posting on social media if the content of one's engagement "attempts to definitively decide if someone has become a heretic and should thereby be excommunicated" (Carey 2018, 83). The writer does not directly name the involved parties, but the undertone of the Bell/Piper controversy is unmistakable. As Carey clarifies, "Debating theology can be a fruitful exercise. But if a thread turns from a friendly discussion about an interesting book to a Spanish Inquisition-style determination of the eternal resting place of the soul of some blogger you've never met, things may be escalating a little too quickly" (2018, 83). The author recalls, in contrast, the more appropriately long and drawn-out process of fourth-century church councils that "featured weeks of debates between hundreds of the world's foremost bishops tasked with choosing writing to be canonized as holy Scripture" (2018, 83).

Carey's position on social media's use for theological and ecclesial debate is clear: *Social media is the wrong location for theological discourse.* Carey's media ideology of sincerity submits that such discussions must take place "in real, face-to-face conversation with people who see the world differently than you do." Shortly later, the writer again recalls the implications of the Bell/Piper engagement in the present. "In 2017, some rando with a Facebook account can declare a leading Christian pastor to be an irredeemable heretic because they didn't like a two-minute YouTube clip of a sermon," Carey complained. "Obviously, there's a problem here" (2018, 83). Following the highly contentious online milieu during and after the election of Donald Trump to the presidency—another discursive Twitter fiasco in and of itself—a growing segment of evangelicalism in 2018 appears to be growing weary of online theological debates. But as the next chapter suggests, such weariness is only one possible stance regarding internet discourse on orthodoxy and authenticity. For progressive evangelical feminists, the internet is a valuable tool for the projection of voice and resistance to traditional evangelical authorities.

NOTES

1. Similar to Rob Bell, Bazan (also known as "Pedro the Lion") is a provocative post-Christian and independent music artist popular with progressive evangelicals and hipster music aficionados alike. For more on Bazan's religious background and influence on the contemporary music scene, see Beaujon 2006.

2. Quite like the domain of partially decentralized evangelical authority, Twitter is certainly not *entirely* decentralized or horizontalized. The social media giant has developed a verified badge feature, which distinguishes some authors and public figures from others. According to Twitter, the verification "lets people know that an account of public interest is authentic." A white checkmark on a blue badge background, the certification appears next to the verified user's handle. What are the criteria for verification and Twitter-approved authenticity? "An account may be verified if it is determined to be an account of public interest," Twitter clarifies, without letting in on the specifics of what qualifies. "Typically this includes accounts maintained by users in music, acting, fashion, government, politics, religion, journalism, media, sports, business, and other key interest areas" (Twitter 2018).

3. This is the same Challies whose published commentaries on technology work features in the prior chapter.

4. Additionally, not all RTs are purely or exclusively RTs. Many RTs in the Bell controversy corpus are more accurately modified tweets or MTs, that is, RTs that have been modified through evaluation or slightly edited, though few are acknowledged as such. For the purposes of this chapter, I follow my digital informants' use of RTing to include both RTs and MTs.

5. I have in mind, here, Bakhtin's (1981 [1934–1935]) focus on the dialogic orientation of communication. Thinking with Bakhtin, one might interpret even generic RTs as a form of nondirect, even double-voiced language (293, 313, 325).

6. See Richard Bauman (2004, 7) on the **intertextual gap**. Such a broadening confirms what Lauren Squires (2014) describes as **indexical bleaching**, that is, the loss of direct semantic reference due to the increased instances of reposting and diffusion across time.

7. See George Lakoff's 1993 work on the metaphorical operations of human thought (i.e., crosscognitive domain mapping) and communication.

8. Although it falls outside of the parameters of this study, a comparative analysis of discourse on Bell's orthodoxy or heretical status in published media, such as magazine articles or books, would also be constructive.

9. For more on the implications of blogging for religious communities and authority structures, see Radde-Antweiler 2013, 98; Hutchings 2013, 166; Teusner 2013; and Johns 2013, 241–242; cf. Whitehead 2015, 2018.

10. Mohler, like Piper, is a recognized evangelical authority in both the online and offline worlds. I consider his blogging alongside all the others of this section in an effort to illustrate the ways the internet may be providing horizontalizing affordances (Hoover 2016). Mohler's writing is taken by many to be authoritative. But on the internet, he competes with thousands of other bloggers who may or may not share his theological convictions.

11. Action can also proceed in the opposite direction as congregants tweet sermon discourse they hear live. For more on technological integration into everyday life, see Cheong and Ess 2012, 16; Fischer-Nielsen 2012; Cheong 2012, 201.

FIVE

FEMINIST PUBLICS AND THE PROGRESSIVE EVANGELICAL BLOGOSPHERE

NOT TOO LONG AGO, A stealthy group of private-college girls escaped their dorm rooms one night and tiptoed, suppressing giggles, through wet Midwestern snow to the gazebo of a nearby park. One would not have known by looking but this was a concealed statement—a covert rebellion, an act of defiance. The group of young women united in a single cause as they daringly identified as feminists, or at least closet feminists. But the students also had something else in common. Although layered in tank tops, T-shirts, sweatshirts, and coats, none of them wore a certain article of undergarment. Once gathered in the park, the rituals proceeded awkwardly. Someone read a pithy selection of relevant literature, ceremoniously burning the lines in a trash can afterward. Then the collective burned their bras, or at least made the attempt, until the smoldering polyester ignited and violent flames shot up toward the roof of the gazebo. A student kicked the can out of the structure, avoiding danger for the moment. As the comic panic subsided, the women basked in the aura of their experience, for they had just taken part in a real-life bra burning—a frustrated one, perhaps, but a bra burning nonetheless. Failed or not, the experience constituted a twenty-first-century Christian feminist ritual (Maynard 2013e).

Blogger Emily Maynard, reflecting on her involvement as one of the primary instigators of the above event, describes the bra burning as "the most secret of social rebellions" (Maynard 2013e). She reflects on the contained and private nature of the gathering. "We didn't have protest signs," the blogger recalls. "We would only refer to that night in smirks across cafeteria tables, through layers of inside jokes on Facebook walls." Maynard mulls over the symbolism of the event admitting, "Nobody was actually burning their real bras. This was all symbolic ritual. Besides, we were too frugal to go around destroying clothes we actually needed.

We were in college. We were Feminists, not idiots" (Maynard 2013e). Having graduated college, Maynard was at the time of my research a seminary student and popular blogger. Her position as a feminist was no longer an undisclosed part of her identity. On her blog, *Emily Is Speaking Up*, she wrote about issues of gender and gender roles, feminism, modesty, popular culture, and religiosity. Maynard did not work alone. A host of other independent but networked evangelical bloggers also picked up the Christian feminist banner, challenging traditional gender constructs and giving voice to the growing cohort. Harnessing the promiscuous affordances of blog media, independent writers actively work to bring evangelical feminism from "the most secret of social rebellions," in Maynard's words, to a particularly visible, interconnected, and growing practice of resistance toward traditional theologies of sex and gender.

OVERVIEW AND ARGUMENTS

This chapter argues that prolific blog voices have, in effect, established Christian feminism as a networked rebellion and veritable counterpublic through their synthesis of the media paradigms of sincerity and promiscuity. These progressives marry the impulses of sincerity and promiscuity, conceiving of promiscuous blog technologies in some cases as more authentic, sincere, collaborative, and direct than book publishing itself. Christian feminism existed prior to the rise of new media, but social media offers a new seemingly populist and immediate platform of discourse. Part of documenting the rise of Christian feminism on the internet, the intent of this chapter is to understand how one subgroup of evangelicals socializes the blog technology by way of their media ideologies and document and observe how they shape the medium for their own ends. The bloggers establish communities of resistance through the circulation of texts in online economies of interactive reading.

This chapter demonstrates, further, that blog media are a contested form of communication. The blog is not inherently immediate and democratic but must be constructed, performed, and maintained as such. As I show below, bloggers regard blog texts both as more ephemeral than traditional print books but also as more direct and authentic in terms of audience interaction. Because media ideologies are always partial and contested, part of the task is to identify which other systems influence evangelical new media practices. Along such lines, I consider whether and to what degree blog media have shaped the evangelical media ecology along **neoliberal** parameters. Blogs do serve as tools to speak out against the injustices encountered at the hands of the patriarchy and misogyny. But by virtue of new technology uptake and application, evangelicals also find themselves shaped by the neoliberal impulses toward self-marketing and engage in cultivating and performing a unique persona, or brand, as a writer.

In addition to Maynard's *Emily Is Speaking Up*, the chapter draws on six other evangelical feminist blog sites: Sarah Bessey's *Sarah Bessey*; Mihee Kim-Kort's *miheekimkort.com*; Danielle Vermeer's *From Two to One: Reflections on Marriage, Faith, and Feminism*; Rachel Held Evans's *rachelheldevans.com*; Marian Williams's *Redbone Afropuff and Black GRITS*; and Dianna Anderson's *Faith and Feminism*. I describe and document through thick narrative and discourse analysis the use of blogs in contributing to feminist reform.[1] This chapter focuses on the efforts of the bloggers to cultivate loyal readerships and modify existing cultural codes in terms of clothing, modesty, gender, and inequality. As far as the content of these online engagements, the bloggers argue that the evangelical culture of modesty and purity perpetuates harmful, sexually objectifying theologies of women's bodies, conflates lust with natural attraction, creates a cult of virginity, enforces harmful and gendered double standards, reifies white privilege, strips women of sexual autonomy, and ultimately forces negative forms of embodiment on women. The bloggers propose a "redemptive teleology of the body," to employ Kathryn Lofton's (2011, 101) language from an analogous context. Making use of promiscuous blog media, which moves more toward traditional publishing opportunities, such as book deals, the feminists seek to address and counter these issues.

The previous chapter took a modified quantitative approach by studying over a thousand tweets and a hundred blog posts on a controversial theological subject. This chapter sacrifices quantity for quality by focusing on seven key figures and the content of their online interactions. The chapter has several parts. First, I provide an overview of the conflicted historical relationship between feminism and evangelicalism, highlighting the heated rhetoric surrounding recent adoptions of the term by some evangelical subgroups. Second, I reflect on the academic study of blogging and discuss the media ideologies that surround it. Third, I introduce the bloggers, touching briefly on the styles and discourses of the respective writers and noting thematic similarities and differences. Fourth, I analyze the content by which the writers problematize conservative evangelicalism and provide viable alternatives for embodiment, dress, sexuality, and purity. Lastly, I comment on the bloggers' status as an evangelical counterpublic, reflect on media ideologies of the blog, and consider the writers' perceptions of the blog as an effective discursive genre.

EVANGELICAL FEMINISM: A SHORT, TUMULTUOUS HISTORY

Maynard's bra-burning story paints the picture of an embattled evangelical feminism, an awkward feminism unsure of itself and under substantial duress. But how did evangelical feminism in America get to that point? According to conservative religious writers, individualism and social disconnection escalated in postwar America. Men returned to bread-winning duties following World War II, while women withdrew to domestic spheres. Societal upheavals rarely leave earlier structures intact. Soon suburbanization, economic growth, and increasing mobility in both geographic and socioeconomic senses began to challenge the traditional functions of marriage and kinship-based stability. For some commentators, these reconfigurations threatened society at its core. A new narrative of personal fulfillment accompanied the growing individualism. Building on the first-wave advances made by late-nineteenth and early twentieth-century suffragettes, a second wave of feminism coalesced. Integrating these discourses of personal fulfillment and self-autonomy, feminists called out the unequal treatment of American women and gained considerable momentum into the 1970s. Writers, such as Betty Friedan, furthered the cause by striving for gender equality through publication and institutional organization (Bartkowski 2001, 31).

Conservative Protestants fractured over these changes but collectively viewed the multiple waves of feminist mobilization suspiciously. Fundamentalists denounced feminism, but the controversy divided neoevangelical responses. One camp of evangelical gender traditionalism further developed theologies of gender complementarity and difference. The opposite end of the spectrum witnessed the birth of evangelical (i.e., biblical) feminism. Conflicts proliferated between conservative and progressive parties. Emboldened by the women's liberation movement, progressives organized the Evangelical Women's Caucus in 1973 to condemn sexism and inequality in Protestant orders. The caucus evolved into the influential Christians for Biblical Equality by 1988. The traditionalists responded in full force, undertaking an applied campaign to reject the association of any form of feminism as biblical. This program continues to the present. "So great is the perceived threat of evangelical feminists," writes sociologist John Bartkowski, that the traditionalists "mobilized to form an explicitly anti-biblical-feminist" organization, the Council on Biblical Manhood and Womanhood. This reactionary organization has been busy. By 1991, the council published *Recovering Biblical Manhood and Womanhood: A Response to Evangelical Feminism* a six-hundred-page treatise railing against egalitarianism.

Other antifeminist organizations were also at work. An influential Catholic and conservative activist, Phyllis Schlafly founded the Eagle Forum in the 1970s and published popular works through the 1980s that posited feminism's threat to religious, economic, and social systems and general family stability (Schlafly 2003). Christian antifeminist groups, including Schlafly's Eagle Forum, the Council on Biblical Manhood and Womanhood, and Beverly Lahaye's Concerned Women for America, employ what one scholar of religion describes as **chaos rhetoric**, or discourse intended to "persuade an audience by stressing an imminent threat to a beloved entity" (Smith 2014, 5). In this case, the beloved entity is the American nuclear family, the sacred social core for both religion and advanced capitalist economics. Profeminist groups, in addition, launched and maintain *counter*-counterresponses (Smith 2014, 32–33). Linked to Christian ontologies of gender, religious discourse on sexuality and reproduction continues to proliferate.

Contemporary debates do not appear to have lost any of their vitriolic, polarizing qualities. In 1984, LaHaye described feminism as a tentacle "of the octopus Humanism, which is attempting to destroy Christianity and Christian principles in America" (Smith 2014, 46). "Quite simply," dismisses traditionalist Stacy McDonald in her 2007 *Passionate Housewives Desperate for God*, "there is no such thing as 'Christian feminism'" (Chancey and McDonald 2007, 145). The traditionalist Vision Forum describes feminism as dangerous and marks it as "an enemy of God and of biblical truth" (Evans 2012a, 52).[2] As a counterexample, drawn from this chapter's data, blogger Sarah Bessey published her *Jesus Feminist: An Invitation to Revisit the Bible's View of Women* in 2013, complicating one scholar's suggestion that the interests of evangelicalism and feminism are "dyadic opposites" (Gardner 2011, 15). Recently, evangelical feminists launched the Junia Project (2014) website and blog, a project whose goal, in the group's own words, is to cultivate "a community of women and men advocating for the inclusion of women at all levels of leadership in the Christian church and for mutuality in marriage."

Embroiled in tension and conflict, evangelical feminists continue to face pressure from influential groups. The secrecy of Maynard's early feminist experimentation makes sense given such a contentious backdrop. But clearly feminist reform has also steadily infiltrated mainstream Christianity. Feminism has had a profound impact on evangelicals, sociologists note, as evangelical feminists have fought for women's rights, including advocating for church leadership and ordination, employing androgynous languages to describe God, and challenging the subordinated status of women in evangelical households. Most importantly, studies of mainstream evangelical literature suggest that a "pervasive postfeminist ideology" reveals "feminist influence on Christian ideals of family life as its most prominent feature" (Stacey and Gerard 1990, 98–117, esp. 98–104). By Maynard's time, many evangelicals continued to retain symbolic patriarchal traditions and structures, but under the surface evangelical groups were becoming generally more egalitarian as they practiced mutual submission, had dual-earner households, and engaged family management practices through teamwork (Griffith 1997; cf. Mahmood 2005 and Bucar 2011).[3] In terms of leadership, women in some cases negotiate for themselves positions of powerful public influence as the wives of megachurch pastors or ministers, teachers, speakers, and writers in their own right (Bowler 2020).

In short, this partial incorporation of feminist advances notwithstanding, heated rhetorical battles over gender continue. The question at the heart of this chapter revolves around whether promiscuous media alter evangelical feminism's visibility and power. At one time the evangelical feminist contingent, promoting theologies of **mutual submission**—the "'evangelicalized' version of equality"— clearly remained marginal yet vocal.[4] Third-wave feminist writers of the 1980s and 1990s simply garnered less public attention than antifeminist gatekeepers, such as James Dobson, Jerry Falwell, and Beverly LaHaye. The feminists' embattled position prompts some scholars to describe the nascent collective as "a group of marginalized yet significant women in the history of American religion" (Cochran 2005, 190; Smith 2014, 1–3, 46–50). As with other instances in evangelical media history, it follows that promiscuous media are challenging conceptions and experiences of marginality.

The relative invisibility of the progressives is changing with the introduction of social media, including microblogs like Facebook and Twitter, especially given the affordances of promiscuous media for sharing, spreading, and disseminating a message (cf. Jenkins et al. 2013). As promiscuous media, interactive blogs—which can operate entirely outside of the direct control of institutional religious leaders and organizations—appear to extend or amplify voice through public writing. As summarized above, the history of Christian feminism begins much earlier than the birth of the internet. But in a complex feedback loop, social media do serve as inchoate, hybrid domains in that they simultaneously shape, develop, and are shaped and developed by those interactions that occur external to them. Social media and the blogosphere do alter and influence social and religious orders by introducing new tools into existing media ecologies. As arguments over feminism rage on, the contestations move into what the bloggers consider to be the more visible and horizontalized fields of social networking and from there expand out into traditional models of print book publishing.

BLOG ORIGINS, MEDIA IDEOLOGIES, AND UPTAKE

As a new communication technology coming into existence after the year 2000, blogs are described by scholars as media-rich websites in which site-specific contents display in chronological order (Kenix 2009, 792; Schmidt 2007, 1409; cf. Huang and Lot 2012, 208). Blogs are like personal journals but are more complex in that they serve as "public diaries" of a sort (Campbell 2010b, 253; Gershon 2010a, 165–167, 168, 170; Whitehead 2015, 121, 124). The ability to comment or respond to author posts is also a typical part of the media form, classifying it as a "**participatory**," "new," "interactive," or "social" media genre. Because blogs "not only encourage but depend on user activity," scholars describe the medium as more "user-centered" than alternatives (Stavrositu and Sundar 2010, 370). Blogs bespeak the ideologies and agendas of Web 2.0 designers, endorsing the paradoxically "paired values of community and collectivity with the imperative of personal freedom and empowerment" (van Dijck 2013, 6, 9).[5] Due to the structures and affordances written into the design and programming of blog platforms, and because of the medium's use of hypertext, nested citations, and hyperlinks (Kenix 2009, 792), both creators and consumers conceive of the platform as significantly more interactive, democratic, antiauthoritarian, and individually empowering than traditional forms of communication, such as print. For our interests, promiscuous blog media's ability to challenge existing orders is now assumed and taken as given (Campbell 2010b, 251).

This book, however, resists interpretations of media that focus exclusively on technology designers' ideologies and intents. Regardless of structure, form, or ideal use, the applications (what media scholars call **uptake**) of new technologies on the ground is difficult to anticipate. People can put media to work for unanticipated and unintended purposes. The virtues of populism and voice are common media ideologies that influence but hardly determine how to use and experience new media. Media ideologies, and not just design intent, shape use.

Indeed, outcomes are more complex than the ideologies of personal empowerment allow. Although some studies positively correlate blogging with empowerment and increased agency for women, others suggest that blog interactions reinforce gendered biases in online domains (Stavrositu and Sundar 2009, 435–456). In terms of the implications of blogging for religious communities, scholars have demonstrated that blogging and microblogging might extend, reinforce, supplement, and empower entrenched religious authorities (Campbell 2010b; Cheong 2013, 72–87; 2014, 1–19; cf. Hoover 2016). My intent is to document how evangelical uses and conceptions of blog media map onto the interrelated sites of authority and authenticity, not to elaborate a particular media ideology of the blog platform. These bloggers advance a new understanding of religious and communicative authenticity, reinforcing Deborah Whitehead's (2015) findings in her research on **mommy blogs**. The following Christian feminist bloggers are using promiscuous media to reformulate the criteria for media sincerity and authenticity.

BLOG FEMINISM: THE EMERGENCE OF
PUBLIC EVANGELICAL PROGRESSIVES

In January 2011, Georgetown graduate Danielle Vermeer began her blog with a critical fervor. *From Two to One: Reflections on Marriage, Faith, and Feminism* identifies and denounces power structures embedded within evangelical culture.

"Any way of relating in terms of zero-sum power structures (winner-loser, master-slave, boss-employee, parent-child, leader-follower)," the author submits, "is not the Christian way of relating." From the beginning, *From Two to One* reflects a nuanced understanding of power dynamics. Vermeer's feminism deviates from hard-nosed secular versions. She argues that the focus of Christian feminism should not be on equality per se but "mutual submission" (Vermeer 2011, 2013a; cf. Griffith 2004; Bartkowski 2001; Cooper 2013). In this blogger's work, one observes an evangelicalized variation of feminism. The issues of gendered power dynamics and sexual biopolitics have a long and complex history in American Christianity (Griffith 2004; DeRogatis 2014; cf. Griffith 2017), a history that informs the discussions in the blog literature. *From Two to One* is from the outset a quick-fire resource of logically structured, forceful short posts on the issues of gender, power, feminism, dress and adornment, faith, marriage, and justice.

Sarah Bessey: *The Intersections of a Spirit-Filled Life* differs stylistically from Vermeer's effective logical rhetoric. Both bloggers write on similar themes but have contrasting aesthetics. Bessey's posts are aphoristic in form, short and literary in texture. Bessey's writing is quotidian in content and elucidates in descriptive, flowery prose her poetic and theology-infused reflections on motherhood, homemaking, and parenting. Beyond her household poetics, Bessey blogs about theology, social justice, gender roles, egalitarianism, and power dynamics within Christian institutions. Her popular blog, which began as *Emergent Mummy*, transitioned to *The Intersections of the Spirit-Filled Life*, and is currently *Sarah Bessey*, also caught the eye of publishers in the evangelical media empire. Bessey secured a contract with Howard Books and published her first book, *Jesus Feminist: An Invitation to Revisit the Bible's View of Women* in 2013. A second book, *Out of Sorts: Making Peace with an Evolving Faith*, came out in late 2015. Bessey's example illustrates the process by which publishing firms seek out bloggers with large readerships or in which bloggers cultivate successful writing brands in an effort to secure book contracts with publishers. Successful (i.e., heavily trafficked) blog projects can both launch and sustain successful public writing careers for even envelope-pushing feminists.

Rachel Held Evans has produced five books with established evangelical publishing firms. Evans's corpus includes *Evolving in Monkey Town: How a Girl Who Knew All the Answers Learned to Ask Questions* (2010a) and the more recent *A Year of Biblical Womanhood: How a Liberated Woman Found Herself Sitting on Her Roof, Covering Her Head, and Calling Her Husband "Master"* (2012). The second book acquired national news coverage and rose as high as number eighteen on the *New York Times* bestseller list (Evans 2012d); it also caused considerable controversy among gender traditionalist camps in the evangelical world. Her most recent books include a republication of her first, retitled *Faith Unraveled: How a*

Girl Who Knew All the Answers Learned to Ask Questions (2014), followed by two new works, *Searching for Sunday: Loving, Leaving, and Finding the Church* (2015) and *Inspired: Slaying Giants, Walking on Water, and Loving the Bible Again* (2018). *Inspired* was the final publication before Evans's unexpected death in 2019 due to medical complications, the significance of which I discuss below.

Evan's prose is straightforward and intended for a wide readership. Her writing reflects her background as a Christian and Southerner. Evans covers several themes, including hermeneutics, theology, gender roles, feminism, modesty, and social justice. Due partly to the controversial nature of her content (Evans 2011b), her blog sees especially heavy traffic. Besides her success as a blogger and published writer, Evans's writings have appeared on CNN's *Belief Blog* (Evans 2013). Her appointment to President Obama's Advisory Council on Faith-Based and Neighborhood Partnerships in 2016 reinforced her standing as a powerful religious writer in the public sphere.

Other writers analyzed in this chapter deal critically as feminists with issues of race, racism, and alternative sexual orientations. Dianna Anderson's blog (2016d; 2016g; 2016f; 2016b) locates her as "a pro-choice, feminist, bisexual theologian." In the blog she identifies and denounces rape culture and champions for racial justice against pervasive, unmarked whiteness and other ingrained sources of power and dominance. She documents her participation in Pride Marches and criticizes entrenched experts who lord elitism over others. Anderson has published two books, *Damaged Goods: New Perspectives on Christian Purity* (2015) and *Problematic: How Toxic Callout Culture Is Destroying Feminism* (2018). Her work blends critical gender studies approaches with progressive Christian theology in its criticisms of purity culture. Anderson's biography, like others, emerges directly out of a conservative evangelical upbringing.

As an anthropologist studying social categories and mediated language, I am interested in how categories come into dialogical existence. The last two bloggers, along such lines, are not evangelical in the sense of identifying with typical evangelical denominations or neoevangelical developments coming out of the 1940s and 1950s but hail from more mainline Protestant groups. Nonetheless, religious publics have discursively contested symbolic barriers, so I include Mariam Williams and Mihee Kim-Kort because their writing intentionally addresses and constitutes evangelicalism in a dialogical sense.

Williams began her blog, *Redbone Afropuff and Black GRITS*, in 2010 and posts on feminism, blackness, womanhood, sexuality, social justice, and growing up in the Black Church's purity culture. She advocates that a "desire for equality" must go "beyond gender" (Williams 2013e, 2012f). Williams organizes her online writing around the topics of "faith, feminism, [and] family." Writing from the vantage point of a Southern-raised African American girl, Williams grew up in the African Methodist Episcopal Church but now practices an eclectic faith informed by progressive Christianity, Catholicism, Black theology, and liberation theology.[6] Even more so than others, Williams, alongside Anderson below, writes frankly about sexuality from a progressive standpoint (Williams 2013i, 2012c, 2012a; Anderson 2015, 178–183).

Kim-Kort, a Princeton Theological Seminary-trained theologian, Presbyterian minister, author, and doctoral student, calls for a feminist habitude that goes beyond a "narrow group of women," who are typically "white, privileged, and beautiful." She has published or copublished several books, including *Making Paper Cranes: Toward an Asian American Feminist Theology* (2012) and *Yoked: Stories of a Clergy Couple in Marriage, Ministry, and Family* (2014a, cowritten with partner, Andy Kort). Kim-Kort edited *Streams Run Uphill: Conversations with Clergywomen of Color* (2014b) and most recently published *Outside the Lines: How Embracing Queerness Will Transform Your Faith* (2018). Her blog, like Bessey's, focuses on domestic life, theology, ministry, raising children, and social justice but addresses in a more applied manner the issues of race, racism, ethnicity, and marginality. Each of these writers contribute in different ways to an ambiguous but growing collective of progressive Christian feminists.

Before outlining the content of the bloggers' collective resistances, it is important to point out that the bloggers are acutely aware of the influences of powerful structures and traditions on forms of female embodiment. Frequent entries consider the ways in which the body ought to be appropriately carried, clothed, revealed, concealed, and presented. Conservative evangelicalism, the argument goes, has promoted a double standard of modesty to the detriment of women. Evangelicalism has established a culture of shame, the blog cohort argues, and has led to insecurity and negative self-conceptions in women, not to mention sexual dysfunction in both women and men. The bloggers operate on the battle lines of the modesty wars while their own bodies function as the very objects of conflict and anxiety due to surveillance by the self and others.[7] Scholars have noted the role of religious traditions in promoting social cohesion and group solidarity (Workman and Freeburg 2009, 61–62), but these bloggers make the case that heavily regulated systems can often work to the opposite effect. Progressive Christian feminists argue that religious norms, especially in relation to purity codes, can cause social incohesion and create psychological problems and emotional stress for women. Compromised female embodiment is the ultimate outcome.

CONTENT OVERVIEW: MODESTY WARS AND EMBATTLED BODIES

What exactly is this "modesty" thing that draws so much controversy? One scholar of fashion and dress defines the term's contested status aptly, writing that modesty is "an inhibitory impulse directed against either social or sexual forms of display. It is opposed both to the wearing of [too luxurious or] gorgeous clothes, and to the wearing of too few clothes. It aims on the one hand at the prevention of desire or satisfaction (social or sexual), and on the other at the prevention of disgust, shame, or disapproval" (Laver 1969, 13). The bloggers in question agree about modesty or purity culture as the source of negative embodiment, shame, and anxiety. For these feminists, modesty is an elusive, imaginary state that no person could completely attain. Definitional debates on the modesty question proliferate. Feminist bloggers hurl themselves into the fray, seeking not to eviscerate the ideal per se, but instead they attempt to identify the power structures at the base of the construct. The bloggers see their writings as working to implement a body-positive ontology for evangelical women.

One of the most pressing problems is that of the "Modesty Myth." Williams identifies evangelicalism as the root of purity or modesty culture and presents her form of feminism as a way to improve Christian traditions on the subjects of sexuality, self-presentation, self-esteem, and identity. Vermeer also has much to say about modesty, clothing, evangelical standards, and the problems that arise in their application. During summer breaks growing up, she attended a Midwestern evangelical summer camp that taught her and her fellow female campers, among other things, about "what it meant to be a 'biblical woman' (and presumably future godly wife and mother)."

"As part of this instruction," Vermeer wittily details, "my fellow campers and I learned how to reveal our gentle, feminine beauty while subduing our feminine wiles." Such engrained instruction, year after year, led Vermeer to identify what she describes as the idea "that women can prevent men from lusting after them and that the state of a woman's soul is partially determined by what she wears." The blogger delineates a short list of criteria for her Modesty Myth in her denunciation. Modesty is a "pseudo-barometer of salvation," a "weapon to shame and objectify young women," "a measure of a woman's worth," and "an excuse to justify sexual sin." Ultimately, modesty "dishonors women and distorts God's creation," and Vermeer envisions her blog as "a quiet rebellion against how some within the body of believers and in our larger sex-saturated culture continue to shame, demean, objectify, and harm women and girls." The blogger seeks not to depart from modesty but to purify the construct and redeem women's position within it. Vermeer's project serves to extract from modesty discourse its negative effects on women. The writer's aim is to restore modesty as a useful, instructive, and meaningful term (Vermeer 2012).

Related to modesty is the equally problematic concept of sexual lust. "It is easier to teach abstinence than temperance," Bessy writes of evangelicals beholden to the myth of modesty. "It is easier to say 'take that bikini off' than to talk about sexuality and modesty from God's perspective" (Bessey 2008). Several infrequent posts about sexuality culminate in a lengthy article on modesty that Bessey wrote in 2013 titled "I Am Damaged Goods" (Bessey 2013b). The post submits that the church has contributed to a culture of shame for women. Bessey writes, "I was nineteen years old and crazy in love with Jesus when that preacher told an auditorium I was 'damaged goods' because of my sexual past." She narrates the efforts of one "well intentioned" purity speaker who by way of an object lesson passed around a plastic cup of water and asked the young people in the crowd to spit in it. The moral of the lesson, one that Bessey conveys has scarred her and shaped her at a deep and unsettling level, is that having sex before marriage defiles the body and soul. Experimenting sexually before marriage is like asking one's future spouse to drink from a saliva-filled cup of water. "This is what you are like if you have sex before marriage," the speaker said, "you are asking your future husband or wife to drink this cup." Other nefarious object lessons of this sort abound in evangelicalism. Anderson, for instance, mentions a case in which young Christian women were instructed that "girls who lose their virginity before marriage are like chewed-up pieces of bubble gum that no one would want" (Anderson 2015, 109).

For Bessey (2013b, 2013c), the object lesson was not an isolated occurrence. The event blurred together in her mind with many other evangelical teachings on tainted, sexually compromised, and typically feminine bodies into a "common refrain" of shame: "You are damaged goods, Sarah." Bessey marks evangelicalism as a "sexually-dysfunctional culture." The message to her readers is controversial as it dismantles the quasisacred status of female virginity. "Virginity isn't a guarantee of healthy sexuality or marriage," Bessey says provocatively. "Morality tales and false identities aren't the stuff of a real marriage. Purity isn't judged by outward appearances and technicalities. The sheep and the goats are not divided on the basis of their virginity." Like Vermeer, Bessey criticizes evangelical culture for valuing women primarily for their sexuality, that is, for objectifying women's physicality.

How do the writers resist such pressures? One way is to aspire to a better world through action or by reifying one's thoughts and criticisms through the writing of blog posts and books. Whereas Bessey's above post is a rallying cry against ingrained evangelical sexism, Anderson's *Damaged Goods* builds off Bessey's phrasing to elaborate an entire book-length biblical and theological model. Anderson takes to task Joshua Harris's 1997 *I Kissed Dating Goodbye*, which she sees as an influential part of the purity movement's origins, resists the errors of biblical literalism, challenges the arbitrariness of evangelical accounts of sexual virginity, and spars in a discursive manner with not only familialist theologies, such as the Quiverfull movement, but with dominant gender essentialist groups, like *The Gospel Coalition*. Anderson's oppositional interlocutors include Douglas Wilson, Albert Mohler, Mark Driscoll, and John Piper (see the Twitter heresy wars discussion in chap. 4). Anderson's position, as she is fully aware, is controversial. Her argument not only revisits biblical teaching and theology but draws on gender studies and critical theory to argue for the performative (rather than rigid or determined) status of gender. *Damaged Goods* calls for healthy theologies of sexuality that allow for fluidity and complexity but in every manner denounce violence, force, and coercion.

Still another method of response is to redefine or reconfigure understandings of modesty itself. In "Modesty: I Don't Think It Means What You Think It Means," Evans (n.d.) comments on actress and entrepreneur Jessica Rey's release of a new line of high-coverage swimsuits. Rey's video on the evolution of the swimsuit—and criticism of seemingly skimpy or skin-showing ones—went viral in 2013 (Rey 2013). At first Evans speaks admiringly of Rey's initiatives and credits the businesswoman for having "generated renewed interest in the hot topic of modesty." Putting on her feminist hat, she then cuts to the chase, writing, "It's no secret that women today are bombarded with mixed messages about what it means to be a woman in a woman's body." By implication, even Rey's well-meaning swimsuit line is contributing to such confusion.

Evans (n.d.) depicts the situation on two extremes. On the one hand, popular culture suggests that women cultivate a strong sex appeal, dress seductively, and subjugate their bodies through rigorous fitness regimens into equally firm and curvy forms for male visual pleasure.[8] On the other hand, women face contradictory pressures. "We know what it feels like to have rulers slapped against our bare legs so our Sunday school teachers can measure the length of our skirts," she writes. "We know what it's like to be told over and over and over again by red-faced preachers that our legs, our breasts, our curves, our bodies have the bewitching power to 'make our brothers stumble.' So it is our responsibility to cover them up, to dress modestly to 'please our brothers' by keeping them on the path of righteousness." For Evans, the problem is not just the Janus-like paradox of moral codes. It is that women face undue pressure at the level of self-presentation and the dressed body. Social forces put the impetus on the woman "to accommodate her clothing or her body to the (varied and culturally relative) expectations of men." Women must unfairly "manage the sexual desires of men." Rejecting cultural and religious double standards, Evans concludes in a vein of personal deference that "biblical modesty isn't about managing the sexual impulses of other people; it's about cultivating humility, propriety and deference within ourselves."[9] Purity codes, she clarifies, are culturally and temporally relative anyway since "a man can choose to objectify a woman whether she's wearing a bikini or a burqa."

This blogger's advice on how to cultivate true and "healthy" modesty? "Don't dress for men; dress for yourself. It's not your responsibility to please men with either your sex appeal or your modesty; each man is different, so it would be a fool's errand anyway. Instead, prioritize strength, dignity and good deeds, and then dress accordingly" (Evans n.d.).[10] Likewise, Anderson (2015, 82, 140) resists purity culture's objectification of women's bodies as a thing that influences men. Like Evans, she rejects its forced socialization of women into their own "gatekeepers of sexuality" because of the pervasive male gaze.

Other responses include appeals to increased female agency. Maynard (2013h) discusses fashion, calls for increased power for women, and challenges caricatures of male and female sexuality. Intentionally breaking taboos, she reflects candidly on female visual attraction to male physicality and differentiates between "physical attraction" and "the sin of lust."

"I know it's counter-cultural inside and outside the church," the blogger points out, "but I propose we give women the same agency we give men to choose their clothes (on any part of the conservative-liberal dress scale) for personal and legitimate reasons." In her vocal critiques of modesty culture, Maynard finds especially troublesome the attempts by the "Modesty Police" to demonstrate the similarities between visual sexual lust after a woman's body and drug addiction. Maynard's argument about the biological determinism of such sexual urges finds supports in sociological studies of conservative gender ideologies and practices (Bartkowski 2001). According to evangelicals, the United States is a "sex saturated society," which bombards men from all directions (advertisements, the media, women's snugly fitting exercise wear, etc.). On the evangelical view, men are inherently visually and physically stimulated beings with bodies and souls "trapped and emasculated by their seemingly uncontrollable hormonal urges" (Gardner 2011, 2, 19). Contrastingly, women's sexuality in the conservative evangelical purview has more to do with emotionality and relationality and less to do with visual stimulation.

As *Every Young Man's Battle*, an evangelical sexuality manual popular in the early 2000s expressed, "Guys give emotions so they can get sex," whereas girls "give sex so they can get the emotions" (Arterburn and Stoker 2002, 208). According to Maynard (2013b), such biologically deterministic and therefore restrictive gender binaries "don't belong in the Church we're building, the Church we're inviting our children to build." Maynard looks to a better future in which gender-based oppressions dissolve, men are not reduced to rote biological sexual urges, and women act within fully agential statuses. Additionally, Anderson (2015, 142) argues that in fashioning women into sexual gatekeepers, society is both stripping them of agency and making them implicit in the "ignorance of their own bodies and behaviors." Ultimately, she contends, purity culture promotes "sexual dysfunction" across the genders.

Still another response is to move beyond the issue of gender and address other structures of inequality, such as race and racism. "Anecdotally and statistically," Kim-Kort expresses, "women experience violence, exploitation, belittling, silencing, and de-legitimizing because of gender at church, work, home, in the media, in public, private, and online." Not all groups "bear these wounds equally," since "women of color, queer women, abuse survivors, and others experience marginalization on multiple axes beyond gender." Due to issues of ingrained racial inequality, Kim-Kort says, "We cannot work for gender equality without also fighting white supremacy" (Kim-Kort 2014c). Williams also questions how perceptions of whiteness among Anglo-Americans will perpetuate inequality along gender lines. She urges feminists not to "ignore factors like race, class, or sexual orientation, because feminism should be intersectional." Because Williams herself is "living at the intersections of blackness, feminism and Christianity," she works to expand progressive feminist Christians past "alleged or perceived middle class whiteness" (Williams 2014a; 2013g; 2012e; 2013b; 2013c). Hailing from a white, Midwestern background, Anderson thinks reflexively about the power, prestige, and privilege her racial identity affords her (2016; 2016c).

In summary, the bloggers identify, characterize, and reject several highly problematic discursive fields. Purity and modesty culture (i.e., the Modesty Myth) promotes negative forms of embodiment for women and objectifies their bodies, obsesses over (female) virginity, and creates impossible standards for and then shames the women who fail to meet them. Orientalist, race-based rhetoric continues to shape subaltern groups, either by mythologizing them into "model minorities" or through alienation via subtle but persistent racial stereotyping (Kim-Kort, Rice, and Park 2014). Popular aspirations toward "Biblical Womanhood," the bloggers aver, are at base a set of concealed, antifeminist discourses that perpetuate American conservatism. The "Modesty Police" regulate and monitor women's bodies and sartorial choices even as more pervasive forms of biological determinism flatten out the complexity and beauty of healthy female and male sexualities. Collectively, the bloggers distance their versions of healthy Christianity from such specters in their most overt and insidious manifestations.

NETWORKED FEMINIST PUBLICS AND MEDIA IDEOLOGIES

Together these blog texts constitute a robust feminist public and evangelical counterpublic whose texts circulate widely and generate attention. As part of a public, these blogs intertextually interact with, allude to, dialogue with, reference, cite, and recall one another. Williams (2013f) blogs about Bessey's *Jesus Feminist* and adopts the term, applying it frequently to her own identity. Kim-Kort (2015a) also finds inspiration in *Jesus Feminist*, features prominently on Evans's blog, and speaks at conferences alongside her. Evans endorses Bessey's first book in multiple posts and cites Bessey in *A Year of Biblical Womanhood*. Bessey contributes guest posts, and her name appears regularly on Evans's blog. Evans writes the foreword to Bessey's *Jesus Feminist*, makes an appearance in *Out of Sorts*, and shows up all over Bessey's blog. Evans promotes Vermeer's writing on her own blog. Maynard endorses Bessey, quotes Vermeer, and writes highly about interacting with Evans in person and speaking on panels with Bessey. Anderson guest posts for Evans's "Ask a Feminist" blog series. Evans endorses Anderson's *Damaged Goods* on her blog, contributes a cover blurb for Anderson's book, and through her own networks, links to Anderson's online writings about rape culture. Evans likewise wrote a blurb for Kim-Kort's 2018 publication. Finally, both Williams and Maynard contribute entries to interreligious and ecumenical edited volumes in print, such as *Faithfully Feminist: Jewish, Christian, and Muslim Feminists on Why We Stay* (Messina-Dysert et al. 2015). The seven bloggers, in other words, constitute publics through online textual circulation—extending out through published books—and interact in densely networked, intertextual, and overlapping collectivities. The bloggers and their audiences do not make up discrete evangelical subgroups per se, but they organize their networks through the circulation of texts and discourses, establishing loosely organized publics.

Turning from content to media, how do feminists think about, conceive of, and write in reflexive and metapragmatic frames about the blogging process as a promiscuous communicative medium? How do they theorize and shape blog media in their use? Consider, first, Bessey's (2014) media ideologies. Her conceptualization of the blog maps onto and references back to other forms of communication, such as public speaking and preaching. Perhaps she has in mind the highly politicized and symbolic pulpit under so heated of debate in terms of evangelical gendered dynamics. Blogging, for self-described marginalized outsiders like Bessey, "is how we've been heard." Bessey understands blog media as radically democratic and populist. For Bessey, blogs have the affordance of leveling of social hierarchies. "When else in the history of the Church would anyone care what a happy-clappy bleeding-heart mum from western Canada thinks about anything?," she inquires. Her reply is optimistic: "Never. That's your answer." The blog "is a powerful medium for connection and for change." Although she underscores the existence of promiscuous preinternet media for giving voice to evangelical women, Bessey's is a decidedly optimistic ideology of media. Promiscuous media aid in the deconstructing of power structures. The writer here constructs the blog's newness and imbues the medium with power and value. Several tropes arise in the blog literature that evidence media ideologies and other logics at work. Consider, first, the mode of *voice*.

Voice Amplification and Speaking Up

Vermeer, Maynard, Williams, Bessey, and Anderson all write of the blog as an extension of voice. Voice as an aptitude of personal identity and mediation is paramount. To speak "in one's own voice," after all, is a requirement of participation in a public (Fraser 1990, 69). Vermeer's (2013a) description of evangelical feminism bespeaks the feminists' counterpublic status. "Feminists of faith are subversively changing the system from within," she writes. "They are intrapreneurs, subtly changing the norms and beliefs and language of their religious communities. They are bravely stepping out and speaking up about feminism, even if they use other terms so as to avoid confusion at first." Notice Vermeer's choice of language: "subversively," "intrapreneurs," and "subtly" but then transitioning to "bravely stepping out" and "speaking up." Part of Williams's (2016) "personal mission," in which blogging is one significant aspect, "is to help Black women and girls in my community discover the power and importance of their own voices by sharing my story and the histories of other Black women." Maynard, like Vermeer, engages a similar media ideology in which remediation to spoken voice in immediate and physical settings remains front and center. Her entire blog, *Emily Is Speaking Up*, gestures to the idea that blog media extend, project, and disseminate voice to listening audiences. Early in her writing career, Bessey (2009) imagined her blog in isolationist terms: "No one publishes my books. I have no podcast. I have no voice beyond this blog," but both her increased readerships and print publications in 2013 and 2015 have proved otherwise. Writing after Trump's inauguration, Anderson (2017b, 2017a) promises readers that she will lament the president's egomania and lust for power and control "until my voice goes hoarse and my hands can no longer type." She showcases a Madeleine Albright quote on her blog's home page: "It took me quite a long time to develop a voice, and now that I have it, I'm not going to be silent."

The amplification of voice, for these bloggers, is a clear outcome of promiscuous media. Voice is a mode of expression amplified in the digital era. These blogger's online outputs, on one level, legitimize traditional gatekeepers' concerns that Twitter theology debates, blog discourse, and Wikipedia-style crowdsourcing are ultimately detrimental to church authority structures (Challies 2015 [2011] and Wise 2014). On this point, the feminist bloggers and evangelical gatekeepers agree, yet they differ in response to the growing digital populism. Critics of evangelical feminism are almost entirely white, educated, Anglo-American men who are anxious about the effects unorthodox marginal voices might have. For such powers, promiscuous blog media are promiscuous in an adverse sense.

New media's power comes from its danger and potential for disorder. At the same time, this dangerousness is its power. The dual affordance of promiscuous media confirms my claim that promiscuous media for all its uses has unexpected consequences.

Branding as a Neoliberal Performance

Voice amplification is only one trope, albeit a positive one, applied to blog media. At times writers suggest that social media engagements are in some sense constraining rather than liberating. Bloggers across the board conceive of their online works as inevitably bound to the concepts of **platform** or **brand**. Concerned with book markets, the consumer economy, and blogging audiences, Evans (2011c; cf. 2010b, 2011d, and 2011f) argues that "trying to 'build a brand' can feel a bit manipulative and fake." But she then spends an entire post justifying the blogger's position within neoliberal marketing strategies. Evans appeals to a sense of personal betterment: "I'm convinced that if you build your platform by being yourself, it can not only help you snag a book deal and establish a writing career, it can help make you a better person!" To stay true to one's identity even in cutthroat writing markets, Evans exhorts, one ought to develop a clear and unique sense of voice. After reading publics acknowledge a writer's voice and begin to anticipate it and seek it out, that voice can then evolve into something like a brand. According to Evans, "platform" is "a favorite buzzword at writing conferences and an absolute necessity for writers hoping to bring their voice to the competitive marketplace of publishing." Bessey (2014), too, feels the neoliberal pressures between what she calls her "whole self" and the "ideologue" and "propaganda" impulses in branding. Williams (2012a; 2010b) writes of "defining my voice and brand" in "fighting sexism, racism and their resulting social injustices," conjoining the concepts of identity and brand. Struggling to "live up to my own brand" can be difficult, she writes. For both Kim-Kort (Kim-Kort 2015b, 2014d; Kim-Kort, Rice, and Park 2014) and Maynard (2013c, 2013g, 2014), the ability to broadcast one's voice from a platform is paramount. Platforms enable a writer to project to a public. They provide a person with powerful capacities for public ministry.

Voice, platform, and brand, to summarize, are frames for identity performance in a neoliberal age where every aspect of personhood and existence comes under the governance of the market. Voice is a stand-in for individual personhood and serves as a characteristic of the self that is both mediated while still considered authentic (Kunreuther 2014, 5). Further, bloggers' entrepreneurial strategies and struggles with self-branding evidence what Gershon (2011, 539) identifies as the workings of a **neoliberal self**, a "reflexive relationship in which every self is meant to contain a distance that enables a person to be literally their own business." Social media scholars agree that a hybrid form of **communicative capitalism** is at play (Dean 2010, 4). Forced to engage competitive neoliberal economies, the bloggers must constantly perform writing skills, hone marketable strategies of self-presentation, and cultivate voice.[11]

Blogs as Participatory and Flexible

Neoliberal subjectivities notwithstanding, media ideologies are contested and multiple. Rarely is a singular ideology at work. In other words, the bloggers use new media to reconfigure understandings of sincerity and authenticity in communication. They revise sincere media standards by reinforcing differences between communication genres, especially between blogs and books. Writers at times conceive of the process of blogging as raw, unprocessed, processual, immediate, and ongoing and thus malleable or provisional.[12] In short, bloggers don't consider blogs as final or as determined products like published books. The rationale is quite clear. Blog posts can be easily edited, rewritten, or removed altogether from the blogosphere, as is sometimes the case (Anderson 2015, 66).

On *Redbone Afropuff and Black GRITS*, Williams puts the sentiment clearly in her comment that blogging is sometimes "a lesser art" of communication. I have already established that bloggers conceive of their online writing as powerful and a threat to traditional authorities. So why do Williams and others demote the blog in terms of artistic credibility? Speaking to issues introduced back in chapter 4, Anderson here alludes to the horizontalizing effects of new media. "Anyone can throw up a blog," she replies, since the internet "isn't restricted to use for good or even mediocre writers only." On top of that, blogging is not always the best use of one's time and resources in Williams's mind. One could always be working on more important projects, "like my book, or finding an agent for it, or an essay I've been trying to finish for more than a year, or researching journals to submit it to."

"If I can make time to write every day," Williams (2013d) continues, "shouldn't I put that time and effort towards something other than blogging?" Anderson later narrates her own blogging process in light of other writing projects: "I have also been struggling to write, particularly in this [blog] space. I've got new work (that I'll be announcing soon-ish) and a new book to work on." In these bloggers' media ideologies, blogging is useful for putting one's words out into the world in an expedient and interactive manner, but blog texts have a different value than published monographs. In the hierarchies of media value, scales established in no small part due to the Protestant predilection for circulating texts, book publishing is the superior form of communication—a sign of having arrived as a legitimate writer. Even in the so-called digital era, the print ecology's effects are still present and active.

The participatory nature of blogs is not as much a structural given as it is an ideology of media that must be performed. As most of the bloggers attest, interactive media is both rewarding and involved and difficult. Reflecting about blogging on the day of her thousandth post in 2012, Evans (2012c) said, "The posts that mattered the most to me are the ones that were collaborative, the ones we created together." Many of the bloggers encourage and seek out guests and cowriters for posts, not only encouraging the voice projection of others through their own mediums but entreating strangers to join the uptake of their respective textual circulations (Evans 2011a). Because of the value and appreciation of reader interactions—not to mention the necessity of circulation for creating effective publics—bloggers vie competitively for readerships and compete for post comments, likes, retweets, and forwards. Bloggers invoke publics by strategically ending blog posts with open-ended or leading questions, thus shaping their online documents into active and living texts, stretches of writing partially constituted by reader response. Many of Evans's posts, for instance, end in a bolded question or series of questions to stimulate and initiate reader feedback. Other bloggers follow suit and mirror Evans's highly successful model for audience engagement. But what happens when in building one's reading public one encounters strangers who are not welcome, strangers who see it as their task to correct what they see as theological error?

Troll Management and Comment Sections

Bloggers, as I describe them, cultivate reading publics as collaborative domains. Many of these interactions occur in what is known, somewhat infamously now, as the dreaded comments section. But at the same time, blog comment sections are hardly the unstructured arena for free and civil discourse implied by populist media ideologies of internet 2.0 proponents. Bloggers exert substantial amounts of energy in monitoring the highly valued feedback section of their blog posts. The writers posit detailed rules for interactions and issue contracts for potential commenters. Consider Evans's (2011e) rules of engagement:

> Comment Policy: *Please stay positive with your comments. If your comment is rude, it gets deleted. If it is critical, please make it constructive. If you are constantly negative or a general ass, troll, or hater, you will get banned. The definition of terms is left solely up to us.*

This comment policy is a land mine for the identification of media ideologies in operation. Evans's policy is intentionally comedic. She correlates trolls with "asses" and "haters." But her own comical antagonism does not undermine the contract's seriousness. Not everything goes on social media. Not every speech act is permissible. Not every comment is fair play. Even in comment sections, blog readers must follow the rules. The identification of trolls, in fact, speaks to the media ideology at play. Maynard (2013d), like Evans, espouses the interactive virtues of "humility, tenderness, care, and whole-hearted truth-seeking" in her blog. Blog commenters are acceptable only when they engage in constructive and thoughtful interactions with both blog text materials and other readers and interactants. Commenters do not have to agree with the posts per se, but they must get along civilly with other readers and discussants. Repeat offenders—those trolls who slander the milieu of constructive and congenial criticism cultivated by the blog facilitators—get banned from participation (Evans 2011e).

Operating blogs as interactive documents defined by participative feedback loops is an exhausting process for some longtime bloggers. Because she receives anywhere between four hundred and seven hundred comments weekly on the blog, along with extended interactions on Twitter and Facebook, Evans (2011e, 2012b) elaborates detailed strategies for "keeping up with the pace of the blogosphere and subjecting myself to the criticism it incurs."

"No criticism seems constructive at first," as Evans (2012b) puts the matter, but the daunting task of sorting through long threads of comments gets easier when one learns to efficiently discern and quickly remove "troll activities." To be clear, the bloggers do have the choice of whether or not to keep the comments sections open. Most structural blog designs allow the site manager to opt out of feedback capabilities, if one so chooses. But to close the comments sections, which in exceptional circumstances does occur, is to the bloggers a breach of both the unwritten blog contract and media sincerity's call for direct, unscripted, honest dialogue.[13]

Of course, not all blogs serve the same function. Maynard and Williams, for instance, envision their platforms as spaces for the healing of metaphorical wounds rather than battlegrounds for theological sparring. But regardless, to encourage and manage comments and feedback requires a lot of work. These above considerations underscore the plasticity of the blog format and suggest that the media ideologies guiding the feminist writers' approaches to managing blog media are not final or given but must be worked at and maintained. A blog and its public must be cultivated.

Blog Ephemerality versus Durability

Finally, an influential ideology of print formality and durability, as opposed to the ephemerality and informality of blog media, is dominant among the blog cohort. In many cases, securing a book contract is a highly symbolic and legitimizing experience for the blogger wherein material things, such as print books, are more meaningful than digital texts. Yet, blogs and books interface with one another in complex ways. Evans, for instance, conceives of her blog as not only incubating ideas for book projects underway but as actually making up for the material limitations (i.e., the rigidity and finality) of print monographs. In other words,

FEMINIST PUBLICS AND THE EVANGELICAL BLOGOSPHERE   143

bloggers publishing a book may symbolize having made it in the Christian writing world, but books also have their weaknesses. Success as a popular Christian book writer has its limits, for one, if the content of one's theological writing is controversial. In Evans's case, she may have counted on some lists as one of the most influential public evangelicals, but her penchant for controversy also got her books banned from some leading Christian publishers, such as LifeWay (Du Mez 2020, 9–10).

But books have issues in terms of the materiality of media as well. To return to the tension between sincerity and promiscuity central to this book, blogging as a promiscuous communicative process may be more sincere, raw, direct, and immediate than formally printed books. Blogs can incubate ideas for book projects in the works. Additionally, blogs can host book contents postpublication. After reflecting on the experience of publishing her first book, Evans (2009) writes that she hopes to "incorporate more themes from the book" in upcoming blog posts and "foster a community-like atmosphere with more participation from readers." In Evans's perspective, print as a media format bears with it a sense of finality but loses a degree of dynamism and collaboration afforded by the blog. Blogs as media are certainly promiscuous, but they also meet the standards for sincerity in that they allow for experimentation, editing, and revision based on literal reader interactions and discursive feedback.[14] Blogs, in a sense, are more immediately direct in their publicness than books.

CONCLUSION

This chapter has analyzed the emergence of one loosely organized counterpublic against traditional evangelical hierarchies of power. This research has recorded the discourses of resistance by describing the textual content broadcasted online by promiscuous media. From various vantage points, the various bloggers together denounce essentialism, inequality, traditional church structures, white privilege, sexual double standards, modesty culture, rape culture, biological sexual determinism, the exoticization of female virginity, biblical literalism, Orientalist assumptions, and mixed messages sent to women about their bodies, clothing, and sexualities.

But the bloggers' work is not exclusively deconstructive and critical. In a positive, constructive sense, these feminists write into existence new standards of living that reflect visions of healthiness for women (and men). The writers ascribe women agency and advocate for genders, races, ethnicities, sexual orientations, and other subjectivities at the receiving end of the dominant groups' normative machinations. Promiscuous media aid these progressives in counteracting entrenched structures of religious power. Blog media affords for these writers a means by which to cultivate digital reading audiences and create counterpublics and publics.

Drawing on the concept of the media ideology, the chapter suggested that although the feminist bloggers conceive of their platform of choice as immediate, collaborative, direct, and sincere, it takes dedicated attention to make blogs work as such. Promiscuous media, by definition, breed unanticipated and potentially negative side effects. Feminist bloggers feel constrained by the neoliberal pressures of self-marketing and branding. Ideologies about the blog are multiple; blogs are democratic and interactive, constructively critical, and lending toward the exchange of ideas and the projection of voice, brand, and identity. Bloggers conceive of their media as ephemeral, editable, and nondurable but also interactive, authentic, direct, and sincere. This research submits that blogging is not entirely unstructured but as plastic media must be managed, performed, maintained, cultivated, and monitored.

Additionally, blogs are good for some things, while books are good for others. The latter, for instance, are signs of having arrived as an author. Books authorize the writer and reify his or her brand. At least to some degree, books legitimize the theological stances of their writers. At the same time, the writers' brands emerge through blogging and the constructing of publics. Blogs are more experimental. Blogs are in-process, collaborative, and messy and as such represent to some writers more authentic and direct forms of communication. Recalling media sincerity's focus on authenticity and embodied communication, blogs, more than print books, hearken directly back to in-person, direct speech.

It remains to be seen how and to what degree the counterpublic will affect changes in lived experience that occurs—if such an experience really exists—outside of words and letters, that is, in the so-called real world. Will these circulating discourses influence habitudes **IRL**?[15] Even a question such as this one stems out of a communicative ideology that privileges not only face-to-face speech as the gold-standard of human communication but one that fails to pay attention to the significant degree of blurring between any sort of online or offline distinction occurring in new increasingly habitual social media developments. Regardless, if circulating discourse and textuality, exposure and reading, and conflict and struggle can affect social and religious change, the feminists are off to a good start. As Warner (2002, 61, 89) writes, "Texts clamor at us. Images solicit our gaze. Look here! Listen! Hey!" Publics may be vague, less than empirically identifiable, loosely organized social formations but such ambiguity may work to their benefit. "By coming into range" of a text, Warner argues, "you fulfill the only entry condition demanded of a public." It makes sense, then, why authoritative evangelical gatekeepers mark feminist developments and burgeoning blog media as dangerous. Promiscuous media expand the range of circulation for dangerous heterodox texts.

At the same time, I want to underscore the loosely bounded, varied, and transitional characteristics of publics, including the feminist counterpublic theorized in this chapter. By the time I had finished researching and writing this chapter, several significant changes had taken place. In partial rejection to the neoliberal forces she experienced as a Christian blogger, Vermeer (2013b) transitioned her blogging skills into a different project. "I have outgrown this 'platform' and 'brand' I've created," she notes, "especially as a Christian and feminist." Maynard and Kim-Kort have eased away from regular blogging due to life changes and pursuing further education, respectively. The other bloggers continue to circulate texts, but even they are not immune to the ebbs and flows of public writing life and the energy it requires. Bessey has kept up blogging but with far less frequency. Evans's tragic death in 2019 at only thirty seven was a severe blow to the strength of the evangelical feminist counterpublic. But Evans's passing in no way detracts from her pioneering significance in the progressive blogosphere and the legacy she leaves behind. Inspired by popular bloggers like Evans and Bessey, many other feminist voices have entered the discussion through increased blog and microblog discourse. A feminist counterpublic, in other words, is still emerging through discourse, contestation, deliberation, and interaction. One relatively recent *Relevant Magazine* article (Micah 2016) pronounced that "Christian millennial women and men are joining efforts and strongly advocating for gender equality inside the evangelical Church." The article, which emerged out of a panel consisting of Evans, Bessey, and others, concluded that "the conversation is getting loud enough for the most traditional churches to hear." Note the familiar trope of voice amplification. This article's title was "The Rise of Evangelical Feminism."

To conclude, media conversations continue to be guided by media ideologies. In the progressive evangelical blogosphere, the tension-ridden relationship between the impulses of sincerity and promiscuity remains as pervasive as ever. As the chapter has observed, media promiscuity does not negate but rather encourages new hybrids of sincerity and authenticity. The use of promiscuous media shifts and alters previous conceptions of sincerity. The next chapter moves attention away from words and toward imagery. The text-dominant blogosphere has played an important role in evangelical theological development and debates about authenticity, but what about a more seemingly entertainment-based and visual platform like Instagram?

NOTES

1. Please consult the appendix for more on this chapter's methodology for data identification and analysis.
2. For an account of the leading women of the religious right, see Johnson 2019.

3. On "soft-patriarchy," "symbolic headship," the rise of the "New Man," and shifting evangelical masculinities, see Wilcox 2004, 9, 13–14; Bartkowski 2007, 156–158; and Cooper 2013, 115.

4. Credit for this phrasing goes to Kate Netzler Burch. See also Hunter 1987, 105.

5. For an account of the virtues of "collaboration, flexibility," and "the capacity to generate and share information" in early cyberculture discourses, see Dean 2010, 19–22, esp. 21.

6. On Williams's Protestant background and current discussions of her struggles with religiosity, see Williams 2014b, 2013d, 2015b, 2013h, and 2010a. At times Williams's language is evangelical in texture: "I read and study the Christian Bible because I'm a Christian and I believe my personal walk with Christ requires that I know what he said" (2012b). Growing up, she read evangelical books on dating and purity (2013a) and reads widely and writes about evangelicals even as she avidly criticizes "evangelical purity culture" (2012d, 2013i).

7. For a comparative account of modesty, piousness, and self-surveillance practices in Muslim dress and fashion, see Bucar 2017, 2–4. Like *The Digital Evangelicals*, Bucar focuses on the important role of social media, including blogs and Twitter dialogue, in modesty discourse about women's bodies in Islam.

8. See Mark Greif's chapter "Against Exercise" (2016) for an account of the gendered aspects of gym culture.

9. Evans here criticizes the refusal in evangelical sexual politics to limit sexuality to the liberal domain of individualist choice. For evangelicals, sexuality "has political, as well as moral and religious, implications" (Gardner 2011, 3–5). They pour their energies into strict sexual abstinence campaigns that have mixed results. See DeRogatis 2014, Griffith 2017, and Smith 2020a for studies of American Christian sexualities from multiple vantage points.

10. For sociological accounts of dress, sexuality, gendered double standards, and rape, see Entwistle 2000, 150, and Workman and Freeburg 2009, 108. As Anderson blogs, "The predilection toward rape is a learned behavior. It is learned through speech about how sex is 'scoring,' through the objectification of female bodies in media, through fathers excusing their sons' actions as a sin of drinking rather than a sin of seeing other people's bodies as belonging to him" (2016e; 2015, 147–169). See also Williams 2011 and Kim-Kort's 2015c respective analyses of rape culture.

11. The neoliberal subject, Kunreuther (2014, 176) argues, "remains always already distant from himself [or herself], always strategically managing his [or her] alliances, his [or her] presentation, and his [or her] social strategies in a reflexive manner."

12. Slavoj Žižek, for instance, leverages his own media ideology in the argument that words online lose their "binding power or performative efficacy" (Dean 2010, 7; cf. Žižek 1999).

13. Only a very small percentage of blogs omit comment sections (Kenix 2009, 792; Lenhart and Fox 2006, iv, 20).

14. From a historical perspective, this writer-audience correspondence and dual directionality of influence is by no means unique to the blog. In the print era, authors sometimes published a book's content serially via periodicals and then, taking into consideration feedback by letter correspondence, altered the content of upcoming chapters based on reader responses. Many thanks to Candy Brown for this valuable comparison. For an account of the relationship between eighteenth- and nineteenth-century novel writers and their readerships, see Mayer 2017, esp. 7–8.

15. In colloquial parlance, **IRL** stands for "in real life."

SIX

INSTAGRAM, AUTHENTICITY, AFFECT

THIS BOOK HAS SO FAR addressed contestations over text-based media platforms, including print books, Twitter, and the blogosphere. When people conceive of texts and then type out, publish, circulate online, consume, read, and react to them, texts have the power to conjure publics. But textuality is only one single mode of communication. Over the course of the twentieth century, text has found itself challenged by an increasingly formidable communicative opponent: the image. The advent of the PC and the **smartphone** ushered in a media sea change, to employ yet another aquatic metaphor. Stephen Apkon encapsulates the situation well in the title of his 2013 book, *The Age of the Image: Redefining Literacy in a World of Screens*. As contemporary, complexly mediated creatures, images are a key cultural currency.

A powerful institution of the image-saturated era, Instagram shapes and influences patterns of daily life. Even more so than blogging, Instagram is a habitual media par excellence that capitalizes on **autodocumentation** practices where users upload data from their everyday lives into online spaces. As a form of ubiquitous media, Instagram relies on the widespread use of mobile technologies. Researchers describe it as a platform through which "users produce data as they navigate their everyday lives, smartphones in hand" (Boy and Uitermark 2016, 1). Instagram focuses on the temporal present and its operations follow the philosophy that "every moment counts." Social media scholars characterize

---

Selections of this chapter—"Authenticity and Discontents" and parts of the concluding subsection—were originally published under the title "Media Ideologies, Contested Authenticities, and Socality Barbie," with the *Religious Studies Bulletin* and the University of Chicago Divinity School and Martin Marty Center's *Religion and Culture Web Forum* (see Cooper 2016).

Instagrammers as taking "countless pictures of everything imaginable, instantly sharing them over the Internet" (Hochman and Schwartz 2012, 6; Fisher 2016, 103–104). As a neologism, Instagram itself implies instantaneity, suggesting "speed, quick decision, and fast action" (Manovich 2016, 24). Twitter affords for speech and writing, but Instagram showcases the image. Instagram is built upon photography, but scholars of the medium argue that the platform exists as an entire "conduit for *communication* in the increasingly vast landscape of social media cultures" (Leaver, Highfield, and Abidin 2020, 1).

Instagram launched in 2010 as an iPhone-only app focused on location check-ins, not photography. A year later the app had broadcasted over 400 million pictures by some 15 million users (Leaver, Highfield, and Abidin 2020, 1, 9–11; Hochman and Schwartz 2012, 6). By 2013, the application had grown to a total of 150 million users posting 55 million images per day for a combined total of 16 billion photos uploaded globally (Hu, Manikonda, and Kambhampati 2014, 1). In 2015, the number of users reached 400 million worldwide (Russmann and Svensson 2016, 1). Having doubled its active users since 2012, Instagram boasts the highest user increase of any social media platform on the market, beating out even the more established Facebook, its eventual owner (Giannoulakis and Tsapatsoulis 2016, 115). Current statistical studies confirm that Instagram continues to be one of the most popular social media programs on the market (Pew Research Center 2018). Rates of use vary, but Instagrammers typically post a minimum of one image per week (Hu, Manikonda, and Kambhampati 2014, 1), pictures that upload sequentially and together create a comprehensive photographic grid or collage on an individual user's or organization's home page. The most recent statistical research shows that users share over 95 million photos on Instagram per day for a combined total of 40 billion images since the site's inception (Sebek 2019, xii). The platform currently boasts over a billion users (Leaver, Highfield, and Abidin 2020, 2).

Because its audiences include everyone from close friends and family members to complete strangers, Instagram constitutes publics according to Michael Warner's (2002, 74–87) criteria. Following the Twitter model, part of Instagram's infrastructure entails the use of textual hashtags for making creative interuser links and creating online communities based on shared interests and user-generated content. The hashtag, in short, is a form of textual categorization with a concerted social intent (Fisher 2016, 108; Hu, Manikonda, and Kambhampati 2014, 4). Hashtags accentuate Instagram's identity as a promiscuous media, as texts pinned to images aim to solicit global audiences and win followers.

In chapter 4, I argued that Rob Bell was likely the most controversial figure in contemporary evangelicalism. Next to Bell, the evangelical media trendsetter and Instagram influencer at the heart of this chapter is an evangelical poster child (in a doctrinal sense). Scott Bakken converted to Christianity at the age of sixteen, attended youth group regularly, volunteered on the music team, and following high school went on mission trips around the world. After marrying, he and his wife, Jessica, spent five years studying and living abroad as a part of Australia's Hillsong Church community. In 2010, the couple relocated to Calgary, Alberta, to put down roots and raise a family. Bakken would then begin to apply his photographic, digital media, and entrepreneurial skills to create a unique and growing evangelical collective called Socality (Bakken 2017).

Socality is an online, Instagram-mediated group that aims to foster community formation and social connection across both online social media and the domains of real life. The collective uses images marked with hashtags (e.g., #socality and #thisismycommunity) to create active publics on Instagram. Socality claims not to end at the digital. Individual Instagrammers who contribute imagery to the #socality public organize at the local level via more intimate Facebook groups (e.g., #socalitywashington or #socalityindiana), where the members plan excursions, social events, outings, and meetups in person to develop relationships beyond digital connections (Bakken 2017).

Previous chapters of this book have focused on the ways authenticity discourses enmesh with discussions of ecclesial orthodoxy. The chapter on tech manuals, for instance, illustrated how evangelical discussions of the authentic are part and parcel to deliberations about authority, power, and legitimacy. For most technology writers, promiscuous media are dangerously powerful tools that threaten to undermine orthodox theology. But dissenting evangelicals, including the feminist bloggers, Twitter gatekeepers, and theoblogians, applaud the internet because of those very dangers afforded by media promiscuity. Such contrasting perspectives illustrate that new technology practices, shaped by media ideologies, are profoundly plastic. Not everyone agrees about the best uses regarding theological implementations of new media. Further, although some evangelicals put blog and microblog technologies to use, others criticize new media for cheapening so-called real-world connections. The relationship between media promiscuity and sincerity reconfigures time and time again as evangelicals take up new media. In the case of young evangelical communities on Instagram, the specter of authenticity remains front and center.

This chapter focuses on one evangelical collective caught at the center of such heated contestation about the role and purpose of the internet in contemporary Christian living. Bakken is himself something of a folk social theorist, media philosopher, and social networking aficionado. Although a theological conservative, in contrast to the critics encountered earlier in the book, Bakken is a technological progressive.[1] Drawing on a growing body of scholarship on Instagram, affect theory, and American visual history, this chapter takes Bakken's Socality as one further case study in the annals of online evangelical authenticity construction. Like the chapter on the feminist blogosphere, this chapter documents how evangelicals online strive to preserve proximity and reciprocity between the impulses of sincerity and promiscuity. Theorizing Instagram as an affective, habitual, ubiquitous media, this chapter serves as a bridge between the prior online case studies and the ethnographically local, fieldwork-based section of the book to follow.

Contrary to popular discourse about promiscuous media's ephemerality and social thinness, this chapter contends that the Instagram-empowered Socality aims to bring sincerity to the new world of habitual media. Socality, in other words, has real social effects. I argue in the in this chapter that Socality shapes its community members into a mode of evangelical piety and constitutes a particularly romantic view of the natural world. I suggest that Socality uses Instagram to create inclusive socioreligious bonds and, with a nod to the ideology of sincerity, minimize the gap between online and offline social domains. But what about promiscuous media's unpredictable effects? How in this case do social media side effects provide unforeseen challenges? In Socality's case, evangelical theologies reconfigure as the group cultivates a public theological vagueness that downplays religious difference in its unification of users along shared visual and emotive photographic scripts. Socality plays a key role in online controversies over what counts as authentic modes of Christian living.

The following sections situate Socality's emergence and history before delving into the heart of the research, a visual content analysis of Socality's entire corpus of imagery uploaded between 2014 and 2017. Following a discussion of the data analysis, I contextualize Socality as an extension of theological **Romanticism** and draw on affect theory to identify the rise of a new form of online ritual engagement: haptic devotionality. The final sections of the chapter examine opposing claims as to what constitutes Christian authenticity, focusing on one particularly vocal critic of the Socality project: Darby Cisneros's @socalitybarbie Instagram phenomenon.

SOCALITY ORIGINS AND PURPOSE

Socality is a hybrid evangelical community that simply could not have existed prior to the digital era. One religious commentator (Craig 2015) describes it as "a social movement turning online connections into real life encounters for purpose." The idea for the experimental project came to Bakken after he and his wife moved to snowy Calgary after living for over five years in sunny Australia. The contrast for the Bakkens was jarring, socially and geographically. According to Bakken, "A big difference we found was that everyone in Australia is always out and having conversations and it's very lively, where in Calgary, everyone hibernates and stays home." Bakken had trouble making social connections and "noticed it was harder to find community" (Gillespie 2015). Feeling isolated, he "looked to connect into a community that was of similar mind." The entrepreneurial photographer quickly seized upon social media as a window "for not only local community, but global." He describes the collective as "a church without walls," of sorts, which caters to members of the global **digital creatives** (Gillespie 2015; cf. Manovich 2016, 24; Campbell 2020). Evangelicals have always communicated socially and religiously across physical distance by using new technologies. Like past evangelicals who organized their denominations through the circulation of print periodicals, newsletters, tracks, and sermons—that evolved to include radio, television, and eventually the internet—Socality exists as a discursive collective because of the affordances of digital media networks. Because of digital media's organization of social connections beyond physical and spatial limitations, Socality—as a "church" for millennials—fosters an inclusive ecclesial structure that is, in its founder's words, "without walls."

The idea for Socality emerged out of a number of factors, including Bakken's appreciation of outdoor adventure photography, the circulation of striking images on Instagram by way of an experiential, poetic design (Manovich 2016, 15, 24), a growing sense of social isolation, and the possibility of developing technologies to build connections beyond the digital. Evangelicals have historically put visual culture to work in the service of enhancing the spoken word (Morgan 2007, 218–219, 222; Brown 2004), but Instagram reverses the flow of mediation. Although valuable for networking and public expansion, the typed, textual labels, including hashtags, take second stage to the preeminent imagery. Consider Bakken's narration of Socality's origins:

> Social media was growing and I started to go out to the mountains and take pictures of these images created by God and post them on Instagram. I started to connect with other individuals taking beautiful photos and talking about their faith. And I thought it was interesting that I was alone in this space, but yet connecting with other people in such a different way. I'm connecting with them over my phone on Instagram. Then I thought I wonder if we could create a space where people could connect locally because I needed local community. How could I find people like me? I began connecting locally with others and started to find a community. I started finding my rhythm and finding my place. But then I also saw all these people connecting globally. I saw the global window evolving on social media. (Gillespie 2015)

Instagram's visuality became, for Bakken, a window into the global world, a node or link to social connectivity and belonging. Intent on capturing the wonder and majesty of creation, Socality focused largely on outdoor photography. The organization's purpose was to establish authentic community based on this shared photographic culture.

The cherished evangelical impulse of media sincerity shapes Bakken's endeavors. His language is thick with admonitions for "authenticity," "the authentic," "authentic living," "sincerity," "realness," and "meaning." Inasmuch as he writes optimistically in heavy evangelical colloquialisms, his appeal to the authentic carries a subtle but heavy-handed criticism. Unlike some technology critics, writers who denounce new media as a threat to orthodoxy, Bakken rarely names or identifies the inauthentic. His goal, after all, is to create social bonds and expand the definition of "church" in the digital era. But the challenge is always implicitly present. Taking seriously Bakken's criticisms, as an extension of media sincerity, interpreting Socality as a mere evangelical parachurch ministry would be a mistake. In Bakken's phrasing, Socality is a veritable ecclesial structure devoid of physical boundaries. Socality *is* a church. Bakken issues a serious reimagining of the possibilities of authentic religious community after the digital turn.

It follows that Bakken's philosophy of church and media alters conceptions of sincerity by questioning the importance of traditional, in-person church gatherings. Christianity used to follow what Bakken describes as a "come to us" mentality in which people were required, either on their own initiative or at the behest of the community, to physically attend church services. The idea of church as a discrete, physical, sacred space no longer makes sense in the digital age. According to Bakken, "People are looking for more than [church like] that now. They are looking for *authentic community*, they are looking for sincere conversations, and they are looking to belong" (Gillespie 2015). Counterintuitively, the evangelicalism undergirding the Socality movement is something of an incarnational and hyperlocalized expression: "I think what Socality says is instead of come to us and we'll put on a show for you, we are going to come to you. We're going to be in your space. We're going to be in your coffee shop, we're going to be on your phone, we're going to be wherever you live" (Gillespie 2015). Socality is evangelicalism for occupiers of social media spaces—evangelicalism for the digital creatives. Socality is evangelicalism for millennials, Christianity for the everyday.

For Socality, then, *inauthentic* religiosity is a showy, pretentious, Christianity-contained-in-weekly-church-services form. Inauthentic Christianity operates by way of a severe disconnect or separation between love experienced in one's immediate church community and the external, "the world around it" (Bakken 2017). Although his language is consistently polite and deferential, in Bakken's perspective inauthentic Christianity includes the defensive religiosity practiced by the gatekeepers on Twitter. "I came to realize the power to connect and build relationships that existed in the forum of social media ... the possibility for social media to be used as a weapon," he says. "The power to delete, block and unfollow has the ability to isolate and excommunicate." Bakken is fully aware of the weaponized potential of social media but urges authentic Christians not to engage in the gatekeeping activities of heretic calling (Bakken 2017). This evangelical leader realizes the multiple potentials of use for social media and marks contention and argumentation as anathema.

Bakken chides Christianity for its insularity and social exclusivism. He strategizes bringing the authentic Christian life to the quotidian realms. What better media by which to do this than the champion of everyday visual minutia and autodocumentation? As a habitual media, Instagram provides Bakken the tools for the production of authenticity. In one interview about how to increase one's Instagram followers, his most forceful piece of advice is to "be authentic, be real and be purposeful" (Craig 2015). For Bakken, Instagram's increased aptitudes for broadcasting inspiring imagery and diminished affordances for corrosive discourse works against the inauthentic. Instagram is less prone to contention and debate. Bakken synthesizes the promiscuous and the sincere, leveraging the paradigms' combined strengths against their weaknesses.

Bakken's media ideology is more progressive than his tech critic counterparts who hail from the traditional shores of evangelicalism. But this claim requires more nuance. Bakken certainly challenges old ecclesial and communication forms in his adoption of Instagram. Yet within his ideology of media and projections of authenticity remain survivals of pragmatism and instrumentalism. As Bakken theorizes in rich evangelical parlance, "If we could gather people from everywhere, we could take the message of love and make it loud . . . real loud! This movement could not only connect us all socially but also create moments in time that would allow us to gather physically and meet each other face-to-face. That would allow us to build true, authentic, lasting relationships! This would be a community committed to helping each other develop in ability and mobilize to serve the community for the sole purpose of sharing the message of love, which is anchored in the truth of the gospel!" (Bakken 2017).

First, note the use of auditory, amplification metaphors ("loud . . . real loud!"). Reiterating neoliberal rhetoric common to bloggers developing their brands, Bakken also views social media as a platform for voice amplification and brand development. Second, following the principles of media sincerity, Bakken reifies physical presence and face-to-face interaction as the gold standard of human communication, even after he challenges it. He conceives of Instagram as a mere tool with which to achieve more meaningful communication. Instagram is a means, not an end. Third, not only does Bakken normalize physical presence but he marks such meaningful and embodied presences as "true," "authentic," and "lasting." Fourth, as I have mentioned, Bakken's media ideology unfolds through the rhetoric of a vague, optimistic evangelicalism. He writes of sharing messages and communicating love, practices he views as grounded gospel truths. All these tensions come into play both through Socality's Instagram page and its webpage home.

The website Socality.org (2017) is a central hub of information for Bakken's network. The design is a minimalist, scroll-through aesthetic that showcases large banner photographs of groups of young people gathered on a West Coast beach. The website has several functions. Its primary task is to describe the history, purpose, and ethos of Socality as a movement. An "About" tab provides a brief overview of Socality's founding in 2014 and discloses the rationale for the Socality label, which turns out to be a somewhat complicated acronym. "The word was creatively inspired through our tagline," the site details. "We are a (SO) social (C) community (AL) all for eternity (ITY). Socality!" Embedded in the tab is a video of Bakken's most recent vision-casting keynote address and links to other informational and networking tabs. One of the hyperlinks leads to "The Socality Story," a page that provides a brief biographical sketch of the founder, describes the events leading up to Socality's founding, and outlines the collective's values and ethos. Other functions of the website include: giving guidance on how to join the community, explaining how to be involved online and offline, and providing a group blog or "Journal."[2]

In summary, Socality is a multimodal evangelical collective that uses social media to facilitate authentic connections beyond the digital. The main website both informs potential community members and provides them with guides for action via links for getting involved locally. Socality uses Facebook to organize its more intimate and local connections, but it exists publicly through Instagram and the implementation of the #socality hashtag. By 2015, Socality's Instagram account had reached some 144,000 followers. Writing this chapter in 2017, the account had grown to 194,000. The #socality hashtag has been used well over 1 million times (Craig 2015; Bakken 2015). Socality does appear to be a unique hybrid community. While there are scores of individual accounts ran by evangelical influencers and celebrity pastors in the visual space, Socality, to my knowledge, appears to be one of the few truly collaborative collectives.

VISUAL CONTENT ANALYSIS

To document Socality's online presence and activities, I analyzed the entire corpus of its Instagram contributions uploaded over a three-year period, beginning with its inception in January 2014 until February 2017. The method of descriptive, analytical cataloguing yielded an important taxonomy of the network, which speaks to the broader issues of evangelical theological and social development and other authenticity strategies. In this section, I summarize some of the key findings from the quantitative visual content analysis of the Socality Instagram page. Socality consists of images, and these images include scenes of people doing adventurous things in cities, at international tourist sites, and in the wilderness. Out of 1,211 Instagram images analyzed, by far the most dominant genre of imagery was nature, landscape, adventure, and outdoor photography. Images of the natural world and humans within panoramic nonurban expanses comprised an overwhelming 73 percent of Socality's total imagery output (see appendix section 3.4 for a full account of Socality's imagery genres).

One of the goals of this chapter is to find out what the dominance of these natural images means. Images are given to multiple interpretations and varied readings depending on context, viewer position, and ideologies. Indeed, imagery is powerful precisely because of its interpretive complexity (Morgan 2007, 250; Murray 2009, 5, 75). A photograph can do more than one thing at a time. Dense layers of meaning and significance surround images, making it difficult for the analyst to ascertain value in an objective manner. But one strength of a systematic visual analysis is that it allows the scholar to identify recurring visual frames and content matter. Because, as one scholar (Miles 1998, 167) argues, images "have concrete social effects," I am more interested in what pictures *do*—i.e., their religious functions and social purchase—than what they *say* in a representational sense. An image's meaning is always contingent (Barthes 1981, 34).

To start with, what exactly does Socality *look* like? I suggest readers break for a moment to scroll through the collective's Instagram page (instagram.com/socality/). What you will encounters is thousands of high-quality, moody, immersive, breathtakingly aesthetic photographs of people doing various things, usually set within vivid natural backdrops, such as deserts or mountaintops, forests or beaches. Even a cursory glance through Socality's Instagram suggests that most of the group's imagery is captured during the photographically sacred "golden" or "blue" hours, when either the light is at its most intense just before twilight, illuminating people and objects from behind in a bright golden haze, or when the sun has disappeared behind—or is about to appear on—the horizon, evidenced by a deep-blue, surreal twilight. Overall, Socality's sublime aesthetic is constituted by cool colors: blues and greens with occasionally earthy tans.

Scrolling through the Socality Instagram page, the viewer encounters people trekking through vast misty expanses, perched in canoes in the middle of glass-top lakes, walking on beaches at sunrise, holding glowing lanterns in darkening forests, ascending steep mountainous precipices, dirt biking in the dunes, exploring urban cityscapes, skateboarding on palm tree–lined Californian roads, huddling around blazing campfires, or road-tripping with friends. Taken together, a certain type of visual energy—what by the end of this chapter we will name as the sublime—characterizes these images. There is a subtle yet evocative emotion to Socality imagery that may make the viewer *feel* something or *desire* something.[3] These images are, to draw on Roland Barthes's (1981, 115) theorization of photography, a sort of shared, "temporal hallucination," in that they draw the viewer into the world of the photograph.[4] Beyond this affective gradient, which I'll discuss in detail below, several content-related features characterize the corpus of Socality's collective photography. First, the focal point of the frame is the human form. Second, the images capture that silhouette within the grandeur of the natural world. Third, the textual commentary that accompanies each image speaks to the religious function of Socality as a photographic collective. Some images quote biblical texts, such as Psalm 19:1, "The Heavens declare the glory of God." Inspirational biblical prose is a common feature of Socality imagery and discourse. Occasionally brief inspirational quotes by evangelical pastors and writers accompany the images.

As these examples and the visual content analysis confirm, most of Socality's imagery features people, alone or in groups, backdropped by awe-inducing natural terrain. For an evangelical collective, Socality does not include imagery content that, taken on its own, might characterize it as overtly religious. Instead, the collective showcases photography meant to affect, inspire, and engage the viewer. In the next section, I contextualize Socality within the longer tradition of American art history.

RELIGIOUS IMAGERY, NATURE, AND THEOLOGICAL ROMANTICISM

Socality's Instagram may include little explicitly religious imagery, but its visual output is by no means marginally or infrequently religious. As a historian of American religion and expert on images, David Morgan (2007, 199) attests that "religious leaders have long recognized the power of images to shape public perception." Not only is Socality an overtly evangelical infrastructure, but by circulating images of natural beauty and human activities within sublime expanses, it serves as an effective (and *affective*) tool for cultivating a certain type of moral person and constituting gazes or frames of penitential seeing. Some studies (e.g., Diehl and Zauberman 2016) have suggested that Instagram use enhances happiness and restructures how users think about and anticipate upcoming events. In some cases Instagram not only transforms patterns of everyday life but does so in an emotively positive way. A key finding of this chapter's research is that beyond facilitating relational networks that span digital and nondigital divides or altering moods, Socality creates patterns of emotional scripting and experience within smartphone users. Instagrammers who follow the Socality page and upload their own images to personal Instagram pages learn to conceive of and experience the natural world through experiential frames of sublimity and wonder, frames mediated both in and outside of screens.

When not viewing landscape imagery directly (i.e., offline, on ground, in-person), Socality members gaze upon other members who, in turn, model their presences in the natural world through embodied postures and facial expressions that bespeak penitential moods. In one image, for example, a young woman throws her head back, enraptured in the light of the golden hour as the sun begins its descent into the sea. The caption is a lyric from a Bethel Music worship song. Myriad images of seemingly enraptured worshippers and inspired observers of the natural world abound (@ianandrewnelson 2016; @mattzoeteman 2015). "His glory appears," one photographer captions a photo in which light cascades through trees and bathes a person in a soft, illuminated glow (@d.leong 2015). In another image, a figure silhouetted by a vivid sunset raises a hand in worship (@brightong 2016).

Socality functions in a ritual and devotional sense by shaping its image connoisseurs into what site facilitators call "authentic Christians." Authentic Christians are those persons who go outdoors—to the woods and mountains and on the shores of lakes and oceans—to experience the divine or witness the wonder of the divine's created world. Socality's digital-visual platform exists to create a certain type of image connoisseur as both consumer and producer. The authentic both surpasses and encompasses real embodied experiences. Walking through the mists of Canon Beach on the Oregon coast is certainly a worshipful experience. But viewing others' experiences—self- or autodocumented via smartphones and Instagram—direct, inspire, and turn users on to the performances of authenticity.

Instagram is a relatively new platform, but some of the visual scripts and framings that circulate it predate the medium by centuries. In their visual activities, these evangelicals harken back to dated and progressive American theological and philosophical traditions. Acting within Romantic or transcendentalist visual tropes, Socality calls into being appreciators of sublimity as manifested through the beauty of the natural world.[5] Socality users seek out and document the sublime and in doing so extend the dated tradition of American Romanticism into the present. Instagram's broadcasting of breathtaking, nature-based photography is a new form of communication possible only in the internet age, but the Romanticist "appeal of the sublime" has concerned American religious collectives since before John Muir's environmental preservationist movement of the 1860s (Morgan 2007, 232; Albanese 1990). In direct contrast to nature photographer Ansel Adam's "sublime evacuation of human presence from nature," this chapter's visual analysis shows that Socality photographers emphasize human presence *within* nature, however dwarfed or miniscule, to provide an audience for God's creation. Socality performs what Morgan calls a variety of the "mystical sublime" in its rejection of Adam's apotheosis of nature and exclusion of humans from his scenes due to their invasiveness, exploitation, and destruction. Rather, as Morgan (2007, 233) argues, a softer posture of American visual sublimity "hovers at the misty summit of self-transcendence and union with the divine." In the transcendentalist tradition, the effect is an Emersonian "mystical dissolution" of self or "mystic religiosity" (Morgan 2007, 233–234; Bebbington 1990, 14). For Morgan (2007, 234), "All forms of the sublime constitute ways of seeing that position viewers both beneath and above what they see, and therefore in some way outside of themselves, stretching or shrinking the psyche or surpassing it altogether." In posting pictures of themselves and fellow adventurers staring into vast misty expanses or mountainous, upward-veering planes, Socality members position themselves similarly. As an "aesthetic mode," Morgan continues, the sublime "serves as some form of antidote" and "head-clearing prescription" for modern people exhausted by the stresses and difficulties of the postindustrial era. Socality users' image captions and comments regularly discuss the inspiring nature of the photographs and how the images transported them emotively and spiritually.

Socality image data confirm that Instagrammers who post nature photographs and go on outdoor excursions likewise conceive of their hobbies as antidotes against the complexity and speed of modern, urban or semiurban life. "Where do you find peace?" a caption for an image of a person on a misty lake inquires (@dansmoe 2017). A photograph featuring a woman's outstretched legs on a hammock, foregrounded against a mountain and lake, reads, "Too blessed to be stressed" (@jguzmannn 2017). These photographers imbue their outdoor experiences with religious value and frame the imagery in evangelical language. Encountering nature's divine wonder and sublimity is both a worshipful experience and a therapeutic sensory practice.

On the therapeutic side, the Instagrammers' online activities are simultaneously devotional, recreational, and escapist. Morgan (2007, 234–236) suggests that the "significance of getting away, of going to an isolated place that has sequestered itself from the temptations and abuses of ordinary life, especially life in the city, is a pervasive pattern in American religious history." The theme of retreating or withdrawing to unspoiled wilderness is nothing short of a mythic pattern that runs from the Puritans' exploration of the New World to revivalist camp meetings to evangelical summer programs for youth and wilderness camps to the rich tradition of isolated retreats and utopian or intentional communities.[6] According to evangelicals, periodic solitude has therapeutic benefits for the body and soul. Devotional writers, including Ed Cyzewski in his *Why Evangelicals Need the Wilderness* (2018), claim that "a withdrawal into solitude has been a common response to times of compromise and unfaithfulness." But why is withdrawal a theological necessity? "The wilderness," Cyzewski explains, "melts away our distractions, breaks our attachments to our false selves, and develops a capacity to listen to God and other people." Not many Instagrammers leave their complex, semiurban lives to live in the woods, as did Henry David Thoreau in *Walden*, but Socality's focus on the sublimity of the natural world is one of the most recent iterations of the mythic American relationship to the wilderness.

The Socality network doesn't fall into nineteenth-century evangelical visual arts traditions, à la painter Thomas Cole, which portray the natural world as a function of divine wrath meant to purge the sinfulness of humans. Cole's portraits likewise dwarf human forms. Unlike Socality's visual ethos, Cole's human depictions are helpless, miniscule creatures fractured against imposing natural backdrops or swelling violent tempests. To the contrary, Instagram-mediated postures of sublimity are more akin to contemporary painter Thomas Kinkade's model of wilderness as "rural idyll." According to Morgan (2007, 260–261), for Kinkade, "The landscape's wilderness appears to mean something far more benevolent: the soothing and abiding proximity of divine goodness." Socality's natural imagery may convey wonder by way of human smallness, but nature is still God's handiwork. Sometimes the Kinkade-Socality connection is even more overt. A recent commenter, posting under an image reminiscent of one of Kinkade's rustic, illuminated wilderness cabins, pointed out this very association (@lennart 2017).

In terms of its visual scripting and photographic aesthetics, Socality draws, knowingly or unknowingly, on a long tradition of Romantic seekers after the sublime. Socality's nature visuals, however, do not remove the human or depict nature as an external force of divine wrath against frail and sin-ridden human forms. Many Socality images recall artistic productions from the moody and melancholic era of the nineteenth-century German Romanticist oil painters. One striking upload by @matt_kuma mirrors Caspar David Friedrich's famous *Wanderer above the Sea of Fog* (1817) in both content positioning and visual tone (see fig. 6.1).

Art historians note that Friedrich intended his landscape scenes to stir in viewers "a sense of longing for the beautiful and the ideal," "create a sense of devotion and mystery," and "elevate the soul." The nineteenth-century artist held a theology of general revelation and "painted in a Romantic style because he believed all creation displays certain truths about God" (Schmucker 2012). Like Friedrich's Romanticist infusing of his landscape paintings with "a sense of the divine" (van Prooyen 2004, 2), Socality photographers position people within natural expanses to evoke wonder and experience sublimity. One caption for a similar Socality image reads, "Above the sea of clouds" (@zmelhus 2016).

Figure 6.1. David Caspar Friedrich, "Wanderer above a Sea of Fog" (ca. 1817). Oil on canvas, 94.8 x 74.8 cm. bpk Bildagentur / The Foundation for the Promotion of the Hamburg Art Collections / Elke Walford / Art Resource, New York.

A comment in this image's feed makes the connection explicit: "Reminds me of that one painting by Caspar David Friedrich. Beautiful!"

In summary, Socality images fall closer in theological comparison to visuals by Friedrich (or even Kinkade) than by Adams or Cole. For these contemporary image makers, nature exists as a mystical realm distinct from human contrivances, but the natural world is also a place for humans to explore, appreciate, and experience as the handiwork of the divine. Socality calls into existence a public of people who, seeing the wonder captured and conveyed by high-quality digital photography, are inspired to go out into nature and experience the sublime for themselves. Aided by Instagram's affordances, Socality shapes its users through rituals of viewing and digital participation.

INSTAGRAM AND AFFECT

I have made some strong claims about the currency of images circulated via digital media. As a brief aside, in this section I turn to the implications of new media, such as Instagram, for social order. I provide some backing for the claim that Instagram as an affective, visual medium shapes its users. Drawing on affect theory, I show how Socality cultivates its followers and communicants devotionally, ritually, and emotively. The blur of colors, shapes, and forms that one observes on Socality's interface hardly appears, at first glance, as a tool of religious coercion or force. After all, Instagrammers arrive to the Socality collective on their own initiatives. Participation, at least in the online side of the social contract, is minimal. One has only to click the mouse on "Follow" to enter digital relations with the network. "Following" means that the user will then see all new posts by Socality in one's temporally sequential, ever-updating Instagram feed. To exit the online community, one need only unfollow the page. It is a matter of a simple click and exit (at least in theory). But to stop there would be to fail to understand the power and pull that habitual new media have on their users. Although often accused in the media as being superfluous, time-wasting, entertainment-based activities, social media are hardly such. As this chapter suggests, Instagram has the power to alter patterns of daily life, thought, and interaction.

Theories of affect suggest that Instagram communities, at least in the case of Socality, are semibinding on their constituents. The seemingly simple act of viewing and seeing imagery is also about power (Lindsey 2017, 7). Images are useful for institutions, organizations, and religious groups in accomplishing certain types of work (Russmann and Svensson 2016, 3; Morgan 2007). Further, the appropriately "religious" viewing of images is a "committed and trained labor of imagination" (Miles 1998, 168). Although imagery has had a key liturgical role since Christianity's inception, in the modern era, the presence and function of imagery has increased incrementally (Lindsey 2017; Miles 1998, 165–166; cf. Murray 2009). In fact, scholars point out that "pictures and videos have become the key social currencies online" (Hu et al. 2014, 1). Photographic imagery and accompanying rituals of beholding them have become, as religious studies scholar Rachel Lindsey (2017) argues, a generation's medium for thinking, conversing about, and relating to the world. Such visual currencies do not simply supply representational meaning or convey information, since imagery, cognition, consciousness, and action are intimately intertwined (Murray 2009, 6, 75). Barthes (1981, 87) provocatively theorizes that images are a sort of "prophecy in reverse." Indeed, as Birgit Meyer (2015, 333) writes, pictorial media "involve embodied practices of seeing that shape what and how people see." Images act on viewers, shaping and disposing them for future interactions. Images constitute the very social fabric of contemporary societies.

In short, images are not merely rhetorically and emotively persuasive artifacts; they are conveyors of what scholars of emotion and embodiment describe as **affect**. To put the matter more precisely, Instagram images, much like museum-grade German Romantic scenes, postexpressionist oil paintings, and late-capitalist advertising imageries, "produce and transmit affect" (*affect* comes from the Latin *affectus*, or "disposition"). Aristotle described affect as an "embodied force that influences the mind," one that disposes and conditions a person to act through mimesis and imitation. Theorist Henri Bergson would much later argue that affect and perception are bodily and cognitive processes that exist in an intimate, causative relationship. Perception of the world does not exist without the workings of affect. Fredric Jameson and Marshall McLuhan further theorized that reconfigurations in sociocultural arrangements have profound implications on affect and that developments in communication media would have similar power (Shepard 2004).

A key tenet of affect theory is that media shape human dispositions even if communicants are unaware of those changes at an objective level. As one scholar confirms, "Americans are usually unaware of the extent to which our own visual practice is trained" (Miles 1998, 168; cf. 170). Scholars suggest that with the emergence of internet-mediated technologies, the production and transmission of different affects becomes dense, complicated, contentious, and volatile (Shepard 2004). One might define affect, therefore, as "a gradient of bodily capacity," not unlike "force," which influences the ways people "feel, write, think, and act in different ways" (Seigworth and Gregg 2009, 2, 14). Affect theory emphasizes body and embodiment at least as constitutive as other registers of human activity, such as thought, writing, and reading (Schaefer 2015, 2019). Because affect operates "below the threshold of conscious awareness and meaning," it may exist prior to explicit thought and ideological strategization (Leys 2011, 437).

Although I would resist strong versions of affect theory, which see bodily and emotive capacities as more inherent than language or discourse, it elucidates how seemingly innocuous image-hosting platforms, like Instagram, maintain a compelling degree of cultural, social, and religious power. Instagram's "affective power" and "affective economy" influence "taste" and "**tastemaking**" (Fisher 2016, 102) and delineate the consumerist agendas of "taste regimes" (Arsel 2015; Arsel and Bean 2012). Instagram plays a role in stipulating and endorsing consumptive choices in the late-capitalist, postindustrialist era (Manovich 2016). One Instagram researcher (Fisher 2016, 102, 106) aptly describes the "hegemonic force" of "Instagram's buzz" by asking, "Who should I know? Where ought I be? What must I look at? The affects conveyed in Instagram posts hold the power to impact individuals who seek to be 'in touch', understand what is going on, see what is emergent, hear what is currently thought." Sociality functions hegemonically by summoning its users to types of practices and visually endorsing consumer products. But beyond product promotion and the encouragement of active social lifestyles, Instagram's "haptic affective register" involves the "capacity to tune in to ambiances and moods." In other words, as an affective technology, Instagram acts as a stimulus for certain types of outlooks, gazes, dispositions, and operations in the world.

Sociality's digital affectivity—Bakken's "church without walls"—produces a new set of visual aesthetics and related religious rituals along the lines of what we might describe as haptic devotionality, as discussed earlier. "Becoming in the worlds inhabited through Instagram pertains not only to rhythms of passage, but also to palpable power that is of a different order," Fisher says (2016, 106). Haptic devotionality is that different order. One does not scroll through pages and pages of attractive, inspiring images for mere entertainment or even escapist purposes, as critics of social media often suggest. In Sociality's case, images viewed in repetition and with ritual frequency act back upon viewers to shape them into ideal appreciators of nature. The "ritual" trope applies well to Instagram. Instagram is an everyday, vernacular form of photography (Linsey 2017, 6–10). Users do not simply engage Instagram feeds thoughtlessly and with predictable interactions by thumbing through waterfalls, deserts, mountains, and seascapes. Catherine Bell's (2009, 100) description of the kneeling ritual as not merely reflecting a deeper state of respect to an authority but cultivating or generating within the kneeler a sense of respect holds true in the case of Sociality. And as other scholars attest, social media data "do not simply reflect the activities" of their users but rather perform, constitute, delineate, and create practices (Boy and Uitermark 2016, 2).

Instagram, to summarize, is an affective medium par excellence. The application's affordances allow its participants to construct devotional and even penitential moods, ambiances, fields, and gazes rather than communicate logical information or narrate a sequential narrative (Manovich 2016, 7, 10–11, 15; Morgan 2007, 1). Socality promotes subtle visual theologies over overt textual ones. Socality cultivates a modified and hypereclectic evangelical sensibility given its incorporation of Romantic approaches to visualizing the natural world. It creates this sensibility not only by bringing into being connections beyond the digital but by instilling a visual-devotional intensity regarding the wonder and sublimity of creation. One cultivates his or her status as a penitent through the touching, seeing, skimming, viewing, and lingering involved in the haptics of Instagram use.[7]

AUTHENTICITY AND ITS DISCONTENTS

So far this chapter has introduced the Socality collective, outlined its agendas and evangelical texture, documented its place in the history of American nature imagery, and discussed the underlying forces of affect, which shape, constrain, and enable Instagrammers. Socality, to summarize, intends to bring about and inspire authentic social and spiritual connections and in doing so produces a mode of haptic devotionality. Socality is, after all, an evangelical collective. But because evangelicalism is more a loosely bounded public (i.e., the sum of its circulating texts and discourses) than an objective entity, not everyone within the evangelical realm would agree to or self-align with Socality's agendas or prescriptions for authentic Christianity. In an era of digitally buffered selves, where social difference becomes more visible and pronounced in horizontalized online venues, one would expect counternarratives to Socality's optimism to emerge. If evangelicalism is to a large degree a discursive and dialogically constituted collective, as this book argues, Socality should have its share of detractors.

As a case in point, take the example of @socalitybarbie (2017), an Instagram sensation with 1.1 million followers, up from seven thousand in September of 2015. Again, I suggest taking a moment to visit the Socality Barbie Instagram page and scrolling through its visual content (instagram.com/socalitybarbie/). The account is aesthetically similar to Socality in content and tone, save for the plasticity of the Barbie, which is a stand in for the human figures at the center of Socality. @socalitybarbie's anonymous curator, eventually revealed as lifestyle photographer Darby Cisneros, far exceeded the attention she expected to draw with her parodic and intentionally provocative Instagram account.

Mainstream journalists praised @socalitybarbie for addressing troubling social networking trends having to do with visual self-representation, conspicuous consumption, and the high editability (i.e., filterability) of images regarding one's lifestyle for various online publics. One tech journalist pronounced @socalitybarbie as "a fantastic Instagram account satirizing the great millennial adventurer trend in photography. It's an endless barrage of pensive selfies in exotic locales, arty snapshots of coffee, and just the right filter on everything" (Glascock 2015). *People* described Cisneros's Instagram as a "brilliant hipster Barbie account," which "makes fun of That Girl on social media who always manages to make you feel bad about yourself for a) not traveling enough, b) not having enough friends, let alone hip ones and c) not eating artisanal ice cream on a regular basis" (Yagoda 2015). As Merelli (2015) commented in the *Atlantic*, "Socality Barbie is here to show you, with just the right amount of irony, how clichéd the #liveauthentic aesthetic really is."

In her staged photographs of Barbies hiking, camping, exploring cities, and advertising curated consumer goods, Cisneros offers a layperson's retelling of theorist Jean Baudrillard's *Simulacra and Simulation* (1994). Baudrillard argued, to summarize, that in postmodern society people can no longer distinguish between image and reality (Deal and Beal 2004, 51–54; Baudrillard 1994). Cisneros falls into a long tradition of critics wary that certain types of imageries misrepresent reality and falsify how things actually are. On this suspicious view, an image, in effect, "can present a prettified and superficial representation, misleading the viewer" (Miles 1998, 166). Cisneros's visual parody confirms cultural critics' worries that the proliferation of images in the postindustrial era has aided the destabilization of social meaning and order. Cisneros, in other words, is the evangelical Baudrillard.

The photographer directed her witty, playful, and ironically iconoclastic diatribe against several opponents. Cisneros's data includes Instagrammers who employ the #socality, #liveauthentic, or #kinfolk hashtags, among others. As various news media attested, @socalitybarbie critically parodied hipsters, Instagrammers, iPhone photographers, nature and hiking imagery framed with inspirational quotations, and hypercurated strategies of visual self-representation on the subjects of travel, outdoor enthusiasm, foodie cooking tips and restaurant suggestions, high-quality coffee shops, and other artisanal consumer patterns.

Unfortunately, journalists too quickly glossed over, or completely ignored, the evangelical roots of @socalitybarbie's criticisms. Cisneros did take issue with hipsters and Instagrammers, but she directed the brunt of her ire toward the recent brand of aesthetically inclined evangelicals central to this chapter. The @socalitybarbie media event is itself both an evangelical discourse and an encompassing media ideology. Cisneros's authenticity contestation, as I discovered, operates hand in hand with discourses of religious orthodoxy.

Relevant, the leading print and online magazine for youngish evangelicals, interviewed Cisneros. "How much of your original intent was aimed at spoofing the Christian hipster thing specifically?" the editors inquired. "It's the big reason I started the account," Cisneros replied. "I know Socality is full of Jesus-loving people with good intentions, and I've had some good conversations with people in Socality. But I feel like their overall message was lost amongst the pretty landscape images, inspiring quotes and product promotions" (Relevant 2015). Cisneros does not attack Bakken personally, but she does seek to delegitimize Socality's authenticity.

Cisneros's Instagram parody used the same visual platform—the selfsame visual aesthetics, forms, and scripts—to attack the validity of Socality's appeals to and performances of authenticity. She thus employed promiscuous visual media to leverage her claim that Socality's promiscuous visual media was not sincere enough. Commentary from the *Relevant* interview tellingly pinpointed what she viewed as the problem with Socality's agenda. "One of the issues I wanted to address was the way many of us Christians were using social media," Cisneros clarified. Note the use of the identifying pronoun in the first-person plural. Here, the @socalitybarbie originator both engages in linguistic stancetaking, by critically distancing from the specific organization (Socality), but self-identified with the umbrella category (Christianity). An inundation of Socality-related hashtags on Instagram, in Cisneros's perspective, promotes "a shallow view of faith and could give off the wrong idea about what it's like to follow Jesus" (Relevant 2015). Cisneros marked Socality as potentially shallow and argued that the collective is guilty of theological and social superficiality and lack of depth. In her perspective, Socality's attempt to marry promiscuity and sincerity had failed.

Contrary to Socality's depiction of such a process, authentic Christian living involves much more than curating aesthetically pleasing pictures framed with Christian inspirational texts. Cisneros laid out the weaknesses of promiscuous visual media, opposing the highly curated practices of habitual Instagrammers who quite actively and "selectively represent their lifeworlds by showcasing images they feel are suited for circulation" (Boy and Uitermark 2016, 2). Living as "a follower of Jesus is hard work," she expresses, "and there are a lot of ugly and difficult things we encounter in our walks with Christ." Cisneros's suggestions for improvement included resistance to the pressure of "curating every image" and avoiding using the dubious #liveauthentic hashtag originated by Socality proponents. This critic rejected the rampant self-curation that appears part and parcel of social media, even as she simultaneously confirmed the power of hashtags to invoke communities. Contrary to Socality's appeal to authenticity, Cisneros argued that self-curation and autodocumentation are only selectively or partially representative of life in the real-world (i.e., nondigital, noninternet) and thus antithetical to genuineness or realness (cf. Boy and Uitermark 2016, 14).

Echoing the critical evangelical technology writers, Cisneros reproduced in her criticisms of Socality the sincerity paradigm. She counteracted Bakken's progressive adoption of promiscuous media by restipulating a media ideology that prefers face-to-face dialogue and physical presence over the complexity of communicative meditation involved in digital mediations. Following Jesus in the real world is hard work, Cisneros said. She problematized Socality users' haptic devotionality and quest for the visually sublime as too thin by appealing to the difficulty and hardships of discipleship. At the same time, Cisneros paradoxically put promiscuous media to work in advancing her own sincerity-based criticisms therefore reinforcing the value of media for some things (orthodoxy discourse) but not others (authentic sociality).

CONCLUSION: THE VARIETIES OF SOCIORELIGIOUS AUTHENTICITY

To conclude, let's think critically about the @socalitybarbie media event. Cisneros's parodic experiment does reject what scholars of media and consumption have described, extending anthropologist Pierre Bourdieu's writings on cultural capital and consumption, as a **taste regime** (Arsel 2015; Arsel and Bean 2012; Bourdieu 1984). A taste regime is a "set of discourses," which "tell us how to prop our lives, how to set a dinner table, what not to wear, and more importantly, where to hang that fake antler in our living rooms." Circulated through Instagram, pervasive visual ideologies "prescribe us ways to document our lives" (Arsel 2015). Both @socalitybarbie's images and the unabashed endorsements of her work by journalists fall squarely into the category of media ideology. Cisneros rejects both Socality's taste regime and its positive media ideology. For all parties involved—Bakken, Cisneros, and the mainstream journalists commenting on the @socalitybarbie event—arguments about the ways media ought to be correctly used present themselves in full force.

@socalitybarbie offers an embedded discourse, a criticism-within-a-criticism. Having formed in 2014, Socality postured itself as a more socially effective form of Christianity than the established alternatives. In doing so, it rejected existing predigital rituals and practices as insufficient. @socalitybarbie agrees with much of Socality's theological and ecclesial agenda, in theory, but sees the collective's applied online practices as a shallow attempt at a more genuine possibility of living. The contestation between Socality and Cisneros, in fact, is an insider's battle between emic claims concerning correct Christian deportments. What Cisneros vies for is an allegedly more authentic authenticity, a deeper way of following Christ and practicing social media. Cisneros's authenticity seeks to delegitimize Bakken's original claim of offering a more authentic Christianity. Authenticity discourse abounds in layers and directionalities.

Bakken eventually issued a response to the @socalitybarbie kerfuffle in the form of a blog post meant to appease anxious Socality members. His first strategy was to address the issue and distance his collective from the parody account.

"In recent days, we have received many inquiries due in part to a social media account with the user handle @socalitybarbie," Bakken wrote. "While this account bears the name Socality," he continued, "we have not given consent for our name to be used, and it is in no way affiliated with Socality." Next, Bakken admitted the comical nature of Cisneros's criticisms before resourcefully using the event as an opportunity to clarify Socality's goals, motivations, and accomplishments. "We believe it's important to be able to laugh at ourselves every once in a while," he clarifies, "but, at the same time we don't want to diminish the impact that we can collectively achieve. At the end of the day, the people connecting through Socality are gathering and connecting for a purpose." Bakken then reiterates the collective's modus operandi, arguing that "tools like Instagram and creative expressions like photography" are—or ought to be—social unifiers and connectors of otherwise isolated or lonely people. Employed correctly, such tools serve as platforms for "showcasing the creativity of our community" (Bakken 2015).

One result of the circulation of Instagram's imagery that Bakken (and certainly Cisneros) more than likely has in mind is what in folk terminology goes by the acronym FOMO, the "fear of missing out." As Instagram researchers describe the matter, FOMO and related anxieties stem from the possibility of being "out of touch" and "the compulsion to remain connected lest one fail to notice something exciting" (Fisher 2016, 103). Users influenced in such a negative way report feeling "exclusion, loneliness and depression." In Bakken's understanding, Socality is FOMO's antidote. The emotive images should not produce depression and anxiety but should aim instead at encouraging social media users to break out of isolation into welcoming, open-armed communities exploring the sublime wilds.

After listing several of the social enterprises Socality members have contributed toward, including initiatives to fight global hunger or work against sex trafficking in various parts of the world, Bakken ends his response with a characteristically warm and evangelistic welcome that invites new Instagrammers to join the Socality community. In sum, the letter was a measured response to one critic's challenge to his organization's authenticity and legitimacy. The founder was careful not to lash out against the comical caricatures of Socality's visual style, mood, or aesthetic, perhaps even enjoying a degree of humorously critical self-reflection. But he made it firmly clear that such criticism was unrepresentative and inaccurate of Socality's goals (Bakken 2015).

The @socalitybarbie debate is a gold mine for scholars of religion, discourse, and new media because it both elaborates and maintains a broad media ideology and reveals strategies and tactics for the management of evangelical registers of orthodoxy and correctness. Instagram may be a highly valuable and affective tool for shaping users, establishing devotional moods and postures, and performing subcultural identities (cf. Manovich 2016, 19–20), but the platform is no less a productive means of social and religious boundary maintenance on several discursive levels. Hashtags and textual captions accompanying images, this research suggests, operate simultaneously as microcommentaries, theological stances, and performances of sociocultural identities, aesthetics, and affiliations. Rejection of hashtag use, as in the case of Cisneros, is a rejection of a certain evangelical brand or identity. Both the application of and resistance to hashtags serve as rhetorical devices and distancing mechanisms (cf. Daer et al. 2014).

To summarize, a major percent of Socality's output consists of nature and landscape images evoking a quasi-Romantic search for sublimity and fixity of gaze. Socality, it follows, functions in a ritual, devotional, and formational sense in its shaping of authentic Christians who act as image connoisseurs—both consumers and producers. I suggested that Instagram communities are binding to their constituents due to the cultural value of the image and drew on affect theory to think about Instagram's subtle power. I argued that Socality's digital affectivity engenders a haptic devotionality by constructing a penitential gaze or mood through the touch- and sight-based interfaces of mobile screens. Finally, I narrated a recent rift in authenticity discourse and concluded that if evangelicalism is a dialogically constituted phenomenon, then both @socality and @socalitybarbie appeal to the paradigm of media sincerity even as they exploit promiscuous media to publicize their criticisms. Cisneros counteracts Bakken's technological progressivism by sacralizing face-to-face dialogue and physical presence over the complexity of social and digital media interactions. Bakken redeems digital spaces by integrating and hybridizing them with in-the-flesh meetups.

NOTES

1. By "progressive," I mean that in contrast to many of the evangelical technology-manual writers analyzed in chapter 3, Bakken is himself a digital native and optimist who enjoys and anticipates technological innovations. Bakken has staked his career on the claim that promiscuous media are a (potentially) good thing.
2. For more on the structure, function, and aesthetics of Socality.org, consult appendix section 3.1.
3. "Bearing the embodied nature of seeing in mind helps to register the spatial reality of seeing, that it takes place within a physical setting and always under the power of desire," David Morgan (2007, 2) argues. "That is where the promise of images comes in. They offer us something we seek."
4. Barthes (1981, 115) writes that the photograph "becomes a bizarre medium, a new form of hallucination: false on the level of perception, true on the level of time: a temporal hallucination, so to speak, a modest, shared hallucination ... a mad image, chafed by reality."
5. See appendix section 3.2 for an account of the tense relationship between evangelicalism, theological Romanticism, and transcendentalism in American religious history.
6. Some of these evangelicals align with what Maier (2010, 246–265) has described as **green evangelicals**, a progressive evangelical camp concerned with environmentalism.
7. Goldsmith (2016, 67) discusses the "materiality" and "physicality" of digital media screen haptics.

PART III

**LOCAL TECHNOLOGIES IN A
GLOBAL WORLD**

SEVEN

EMERGING MIDWESTERN EVANGELICALS AND DIGITAL MEDIA

EXCURSUS: FIELD NOTES, FALL 2015,
BLOOMINGTON, INDIANA

I stand in an elementary school gymnasium observing a ritual unfolding. I'm surrounded by people, but these people are neither exclusively elementary children nor athletes. The ceremony underway, which holds all our attention, requires congregants to exit their seats and proceed in a linear fashion down two aisles toward the front of the room. In the center of the expansive space lies the destination of the penitents: a table overlain with a gray cloth. On the cloth is a French baguette displayed on a platter. Near the platter sits the remaining ritual implements: two wooden goblets filled with grape juice. Behind the goblets are High Church iconographic images and a wood-hewn cross of the Protestant variety. Around the table, rows of chairs fan out toward the back of the room. I scan the space. Aside from the eucharistic elements, rows of chairs in meticulous alignment, and large media projector screen, the space is functionally an athletic one. Retracted bleachers lie flat against the west wall. Withdrawn upward, basketball hoops face the ceiling rafters at an angle, where pipes and air circulation vents lie exposed. On the ground run spatial demarcations for basketball games in myriad colors, arching this way and that. My chair rests somewhere near the three-point line for the south-wall basketball hoop and backboard. Blank digital scoreboards hang high on northeast and southwest walls. People stand up from their seats and head in an orderly fashion toward the communion table. The collective I am describing goes by the name of Church on the Margins,[1] but we are in the "Home of the Wildcats."

This is an eccentrically dialogical space in a semiotic sense, a space that corresponds with and complements the pervasive multimedia practices of the gathered evangelicals. In both the sociolinguistic and folk conceptions of the term, signs and information hang everywhere. By the bathroom on the west wall, just behind the congregation, is a detailed list of instructions for elementary students visiting the restroom. The instructions permit bathroom breaks but only "after the first 15 minutes of class." Students must "ask permission" and then "carry the pass along with them to the restroom." On the east wall, just to the right of a receded stage area, projects a poster about fitness: "Are you a Jedi Master? Master the test, do your best. 2 Days until ISTEP Part 1." On the south wall, a guide to healthy eating urges children to check nutritional labels before consuming foodstuffs: "READ IT before you EAT IT!" Colorful cutouts of athletic bodies also adorn the space, bringing to mind the crime scene markings traced around murder victims' corpses in the movies. Here, a skinny red basketball player spinning the ball on his finger. There, a pigtailed cheerleader in yellow with one leg and pom-pom raised high. Regardless of all the texts and images and words that clamor for one's attention, a group of emerging evangelical Christians occupies the space at this moment and appropriates it every Sunday. Religious media direct the gaze of those gathered onto the items of ritual importance. Directive signs, including the cross, icons, and eucharistic implements, work to sacralize the space and alter its purpose. This very moment, I'm standing not in a grade school gymnasium but in a place of worship and community.

Signs, images, and texts abound. All intend to direct or inform the bodies that move about and make use of the space for various reasons. Like other religious people, these evangelicals establish alternative maps of familiar spaces and locations that compete with intended models. Because place-making processes align closely with the construction of social identities, the eclectic semiotics of the gymnasium fit the congregation and its rituals well. This group is no traditional Protestant church by any stretch of the imagination.

From my seat at the back, I have a good view of the ritual action that occurs near the front. By now most attendees have progressed through the communion lines and have returned to their seats. A prayerful, penitential mood hangs in the air. Toward the front of the collective, standing before the table, one of the pastors holds a small and somewhat squirmy dinosaur. The pastor shifts—communion bread in one hand—revealing a very little person wearing what appears to be a lime-green dinosaur suit, complete with bony (i.e., soft and fuzzy fabric) plates projecting off the back of the outfit. The pastor serves the child the bread, now dripping with grape juice. Garrett whispers into the stegosaurus's ear, "This is the body of Christ. This the blood of Christ." The dinosaur squirms out of his dad's arms and chews on the "Jesus bread" as he scampers back toward his mother in the front row.[2] At the head of the gathering, behind the communion table, minimalist white song lyrics project off a black-screen background. Congregants sway, slightly, as they sing several final worship choruses, bringing the service to a close.[3] After the service, volunteers pack the sound system and media technologies, fold up the chairs, and stow away any religious artifacts in large plastic tote containers. Withdrawing the technologies and artifacts that temporarily transform the space into a church, the school gym rematerializes. Religious media disappear. With those features that focused and

EMERGING MIDWESTERN EVANGELICALS AND DIGITAL MEDIA 175

directed the congregation's gaze away from the quotidian aspects of the gym now missing, the space is no longer a religious one. Ritual media have done their job, but now that they are gone for the week, the clamoring elementary school media take over.

INTRODUCTION

Previous chapters of this book have focused on evangelicalism's online bodies of discourse and communities of debate, but this chapter contributes an ethnography of evangelical marginals, media uses, technological adoptions, and burgeoning communication patterns on the ground. The first two parts of the book have demonstrated that all evangelicals struggle in various ways with the tension between media sincerity and promiscuity. But largely missing from the picture has been any observation of new media use at the level of the local and immediate. As with previous case studies, local evangelicals face similar pressures and wrestle with their own inherited ideologies in creative ways. The elementary school gymnasium, in fact, is a prime metaphor for the eclectic media environments in which evangelicals strive to find their place.

Including various stages of ethnographic research, I lived, worked, and researched among a small body of emerging evangelical discontents for just over five years, including preliminary fieldwork between May 2012 and June 2017. These Christians include professional photographers, visual artists, and musicians; legal assistants, office managers, career-development specialists, and web designers; small-trades craftsman, ranchers, and hobbyists; undergraduate students, graduate students in quantitative linguistics, doctoral candidates in philosophy working on theory of knowledge, metaphysics, and epistemology, and PhD-holding university instructors with Ivy League credentials specializing in critical studies of race and history; university journal editors and career-service professionals; stay-at-home moms, stay-at-home dads, and part-time stay-at-home parents; nutritionists and foodies; speech therapists, registered nurses, and counselors; recreational vehicle salesmen; nonprofit organizers; college-ministry facilitators and missionaries on furlough; primary and secondary school teachers; retailers in hipster clothing stores and boutiques; property managers; and engineers of small-machine propulsion devices employed by regional science, technology, and defense institutes.

The diverse congregation shares an important point of commonality, however; these evangelicals are dissatisfied with two looming sources of discomfort: alienation and compromised living, constituting, as one anthropologist puts it, a "shifting from one form of Christianity" to a better one (Gershon and Manning 2006, 147). Congregants are transitioning from multiple Christian traditions of upbringing to a ritually reflexive variety that embraces and merges the various theological streams found in historic and contemporary Christianity. The first problem identified by these Christians is the specter of suburban, middle-class, white evangelicalism, the kind of Christianity that gets caricatured in news media and pop culture as emphatically bourgeois; politically Republican; consumerist; individualist; vying for American religious, cultural, economic, and militaristic dominion; and having a predilection for all things large, such as supermarkets, shopping malls, and megachurches. These dissenting Christians, on the other hand, might best be described as engaging in an ironic and self-critical form of reflexive evangelicalism (Schuurman 2019, xiii–xiv).

A second conundrum tethers to a related set of worries. These evangelicals find themselves living in a period characterized by mass media, incessant technological advancement, the birth and rise to dominance of social media empires, and the development of hypernetworks via social media that are so quintessential to life in the contemporary West. As this chapter will demonstrate, evangelicals put to frequent use social and communicative technologies, all the while fretting about these technologies' potentially antisocial effects. Like other sectors of the American public, these evangelicals preach media ideologies into existence *and* perform them. In effort to counter the ironies of social fragmentation in the age of highly promiscuous social media—what they in their own words describe as loss of true community and forfeiture of an authentic, communally oriented lifestyle—these evangelicals produce constant discursive metacommentary on their ambivalent relationship with technological forms.

I conducted an ethnographic study of the abovementioned evangelical **church plant**—or "planted church," as one of the pastors inverts—a religious collective that goes to great lengths to establish a sense of "appropriate local Christianity" as it ought to be conceived of and lived out in the right ways (Handman 2015, 7). Church on the Margins is one of many area plants, in fact, justifying an interlocutor's apt description of Bloomington's religious arena as rife with a "startup church mentality." At a subtle level, the community postures itself as an alternative church model or unconventional evangelical kinship (cf. Luhrmann 2012, 54) over and against other versions of American Christianity.

This chapter descriptively inventories the technological, digital, screen-mediated, and social media-focused practices in the American Midwest, documenting changing everyday evangelical communication patterns on the ground. In the next, I turn to the negative, ambivalent, or critical theorizations such evangelicals make about their own (and others') practices. But for the remainder of the present chapter, I focus on data phone and mobile technologies, church media—including projectors and screens—technological glitches and Skype difficulties, church websites and internet presence, and local social media trends.

This chapter submits, first, that like the evangelical bloggers discussed in chapter 5 and the Instagrammers in chapter 6, Midwestern evangelicals are exploring configurations of the sincerity/promiscuity tension that depart from inherited definitions of authenticity and orthodoxy. An example of technological failure like the "weirdness" of Skype prayer illustrates how the collective is creatively reimagining what counts as authentic. In short, these evangelicals are revising the media sincerity paradigm in light of the ubiquity of promiscuous media. Second, the chapter reports on eight primary forms of social media use that are arising among emerging evangelicals, beginning with the increasingly habitual status of mobile cell phone technology.

EVANGELICALS IN THE AMERICAN MIDWEST

This chapter and the following one operate together as an ethnographic study of Midwestern evangelicalism. In an anthropological sense, "Midwest" labels my ethnographic "regional expertise" and demarcates my geographic unit of focus and analysis (Gupta and Ferguson 1997, 8). The evangelical community I discuss in this chapter lives in a semiurban college town located in the American Midwest, an admittedly arbitrary, contested geographic area. Specifically, I carried out my observations in southwest Indiana. But developing technologies, in terms of communication and transportation, increase mobility and networking between cities and states thus rendering regional specifications in the United States as less distinctive than they may have been in the past.[4] Regardless of rising mobility patterns, Americans often understand their identities as related to their regional surroundings. In public discourse, the Midwest is nothing more than a derogatory label or caricatured synonym for "nonurban," "nonrefined," "fly-over," "Red America," or any place located between the seemingly cultured urban enclaves of the liberal and intellectualist coasts. Church on the Margins actively resists such essentialization and is the clear product of having emerged in an ideologically eclectic college town, one characterized by religious, political, and ideological diversity. Calling to mind Diana Eck's (2001, 368) claim that religious diversity reflects "the new reality of the American Midwest," progressive-leaning informants occasionally emphasize Bloomington's ideological and political distinction by describing the city as a small island of blue surrounded by a sea of red. Pop culture savvy locals have nicknamed Bloomington "Bloomlandia." Indeed, multiple informants described the hipster friendly city as "the Portland of the Midwest," or like Seattle but surrounded by cornfields and forests.

This chapter's ethnographic data comes from one local evangelical community embedded in one region of the United States, but how does this *local* qualification map onto broader networks? Robert Orsi (2005, 167–168) argues that "religious cultures are local and to study religion is to study local worlds." Anthropologists tend to study particular regions, or cultural groups within particular regions, so I partially agree with Orsi's claim that social and cultural realities are "histories of people working on their worlds in specific ways at specific times and places." Indeed, Orsi writes, "There is no such thing as a 'Methodist' or a 'Southern Baptist' who can be neatly summarized by an account of the denomination's history or theology." But there do exist "methodists in Tennessee in the 1930s struggling with particular realities of work and home, politics and gender, with children leaving, old people dying, work closing, and so on." There are also "Southern Baptists in Virginia suburbs in the 1970s, with certain political affiliations, racial attitudes, fears and hopes about work and family."

Anthropologist Jon Bialecki (2017, 65) echoes Orsi's attention to the local, writing that forms of religion placed in a locale, "such as Alabama or Idaho, that is saturated with a certain stamp of Protestantism, will be different from one in a place like Portland, OR, where Christianity is seen as odd and perhaps ethically and politically questionable." Following this attention to regional context, one might agree that no generic evangelicalism exists apart from conditional circumstances. But there are Midwestern evangelicals who reside in southern Indiana and struggle to live authentic existences in what they feel is, acknowledging the paradoxes involved, a socially and spiritually anemic yet increasingly interconnected world. Progressive evangelical communities also exist in the Bloomington municipality, communities where I lived, observed, and studied between 2012 and 2017. In the following pages, my references to these ethnographic collaborators as Midwesterners is an anthropological strategy of geographic specificity, realizing that evangelicalism operates within cultural milieus.

Yet, from the perspectives of globalization and technology studies, focusing on local religiosity has limitations. Processes of religious formation in a globalizing milieu, for instance, expand past ostensibly bounded locals.[5] Webb Keane challenges Orsi's localism, writing that in some respects "Christianity has no locality," since institutions, people, ideas, practices, and truth claims all circulate and proliferate through networks, media, exchange, missionization, and travel (Keane 2007, 45; Asad 1993). And Bialecki (2017, 7) is particularly attuned to this paradox when arguing that Christianity is "a universal creed that is at the same time territorially delineated, at once everywhere and yet found only in certain locales, for all believers and yet expressed only in local forms for the faithful remnant." Along such lines, this chapter is a product of studying *in* the Midwest—not studying *the* Midwest, to adapt Clifford Geertz's (1973) maxim on studying in villages versus studying the village itself. Christianity often and intentionally overrides the local. Digital media ratchet up the intensity of this overflow. When

I say, "Midwesterners," then, I realize that the digital practices I describe are not entirely unique or exclusive to Midwesterners only. In a way, these Midwestern informants' shifting praxes are in keeping with nationwide trends. Ultimately, I intend this close study of a local community as a means of exploring broader social and digital trends.[6]

As the previous case studies on Twitter, the blogosphere, and Instagram suggest, sometimes the greatest register of evangelical difference has less to do with locals, universals, or regions and more to do with the cultivation of distinction (Bourdieu 1994) in ecclesial and theological form. One might therefore expect to see contrasts in social media interaction and technological use between a small congregation like Church on the Margins and its ecclesial antithesis, the American megachurch. A recent statistical study of American megachurches suggested that innovative in-service technology (e.g., use of interactive social media during services) is on the rise. The study also found that 69 percent of megachurches surveyed have begun to offer services via "online campus" and that a large degree of them are considering offering interactive online service options if they do not already do so (Thumma and Bird 2015, 4–5). A digital-ethnographic analysis of the Hillsong network's social media strategies provides an additional point of contrast. According to Atish Sircar and Jennifer Rowley, although Hillsong's global megachurch system uses social media broadly, some of which mirrors Church on the Margins's own practices (e.g., sharing messages, facilitating connections, and publicizing information about events and services), there is an overt emphasis "on one-way communication and promotion rather than on communication with members and community building" (Sircar and Rowley 2016, 698). This means social media aren't always "social," in that they aren't always interactive and collaborative in the tradition of the Web 2.0 paradigm. The study concluded that church branding, product sales, and marketing strategies dominated Hillsong's social media patterns, reflecting a neoliberal Christianity opposed by Church on the Margin attendees.

Sircar and Rowley found that on Instagram community members could post content as long as uploaded materials met the qualifications for "high definition photos." But on other media channels, such as Twitter, content posting was done primarily by Hillsong tech managers and other hired religious digital creatives (RDCs) with significantly less interaction between leaders and congregants (Sircar and Rowley 2016, 698). Considering that megachurches aim at a high degree of technological professionalism, use cutting-edge communication technologies, and hire media pastors and RDCs to assist with services (Thumma and Travis 2007, esp. 16, 41, 228; cf. Elisha 2011), these findings evidence a polished, professionalized, mediated seamlessness against which a congregation such as Church on the Margins will reject out of hand as inauthentic and insincere.

Church on the Margins identifies as part of the Vineyard Movement, an ecclesial collective ideologically diverse enough to include among its ranks both the deconstructive casualness of urban hipster churches and the high media professionalism of the megachurch. Vineyard churches tend to be ecclesially, ethnically, socioeconomically, theologically, and politically diverse and stratified (Bialecki 2017, xv; cf. Luhrmann 2012). The Vineyard is a diverse, decentralized evangelical movement that avoids the term *denomination* and prefers a more open-ended authoritative structure (Bialecki 2017, 19, 65). In light of the concepts central to this book, it is helpful to think of the Vineyard as more of an evangelical network than a rigid ecclesial system with a top-down structure of authority.

Much more quantitative and qualitative data for comparison and contrast is necessary for a full picture of nationwide evangelical media uses. But as with previous chapters, I reiterate here that "there are recurrent patterns in exchange, semiotics and speech, temporalities, and subjectivities for Christian groups" and such religious and communicative systems have the ability to transplant geographically (Bialecki 2017, xvii, 65). After all, local communicative values and idioms of practice certainly do shape media ideologies and therefore their use (Gershon 2010a; cf. Miller 2011; Leonardi et al. 2006). For the purposes of this chapter, I focus on the local practices that map onto, resist, or are ultimately restructured by the growing amount of information online in the form of podcasts, blog posts, church websites, and social media pages. I observe one community on the margins of evangelicalism because, as clarified earlier, one of the most effective ways to study ambiguous socioreligious entities is to study the activities occurring at their boundaries (Cooper 2017c; Bialecki 2017, 7; Douglas 1966).

MOBILE, SCREEN-MEDIATED, SOCIAL TECHNOLOGIES: A TAXONOMY OF PRACTICE

Like most Americans, Midwesterners engage in frequent technology- and media-related activities. My ethnographic field notes are chock full of hundreds of conversations about or direct uses of social media and mobile tech. To borrow a popular media ecology metaphor, Americans swim in media like fish in water (McLuhan 1969, 5, 75). They put technologies to use in all spheres and institutions, ranging from school, to home, to the workplace, to leisure and recreation, to restaurants and cafés, to stores and markets, to church. In both popular and technical discourse about contemporary technologies, local language often focuses on the various media screens or human-machine interfaces that permeate postindustrial life (Evans 2015, 14; Turkle 1997; Berners-Lee 2000, 6; Krishna 2015).

For the Midwesterners with whom I lived and observed, screens mediate contemporary existence. People sport small digital computers, iWatches, and Fitbits on wrists to measure and record personal biomedical metrics and keep track of time, communication, and daily schedules. Newer automobiles have navigational touch screens both to mediate personal communication while driving and navigate in a spatial or mapping sense. Like college classrooms, churches use large media screens attached to projectors and computers to convey information, visuals, song lyrics, and other data to attendees. A high percentage of this predominantly postindustrial, middle-class, white congregation spends most of its eight-hour working day inputting information into or downloading information from PCs. At home, people relax by watching television (on smart TVs) or thumbing through social media feeds on various media artifacts. Devices include wide-screen televisions, personal tablets, or smaller iPhone or Android data phone screens, which users also carry about with them, usually on their bodies or in bags kept near their bodies, and on average check multiple times per hour. At the tail end of my research, Americans have also just begun to integrate digital home-assistant programs into the domestic sphere, including Google Home and Amazon Echo.

This section constructs an initial taxonomy of such uses by a young Midwestern community as it strives to theorize and theologize such increasing technological presences in their lives in effort to construct what they feel are authentic communities. I list and describe the various uses of digital technologies by congregants at Church on the Margins. In addition to five years of ethnographic participant observation in the church and surrounding community, the primary data for this chapter include an online questionnaire disseminated to the community in 2017, long-form, supplemental interviews with key informants, and digital ethnographic observations from years of online interactions among Church on the Margins social media users.

DATA PHONE USE

Smartphones are hybrid technologies. Smartphones are complex metadevices that organize several previously disparate tasks, tools, and communicative channels under one convenient interface. In the United States, the cell phone has become a social fact due to its nearly ubiquitous presence in daily life. My research among emerging evangelicals reflects these patterns. To supplement ethnographic observations in the field, I disseminated a questionnaire about technology to Church on the Margins. Comprising fifty lengthy written responses—a high percentage of the church's core group—the survey documented that 98 percent of congregants own an internet-enabled mobile telephone, data phone, or smartphone. Among survey respondents, only 14 percent, seven total congregants, still use landlines at home. A mere one person owns a basic cellular phone (i.e., not a "smart" phone) with no internet or data abilities. Most Midwesterners

I encountered carry their cell phones with them at all times and use the device for daily tasks. Aside from making phone calls and texting with family members, friends, and colleagues, they create grocery lists and daily to-do itineraries, plan schedules, retrieve information online, browse and interact on social media feeds, read or skim news media, listen to podcasts, engage in religious or devotional activities, and read scripture or devotional materials, to list only a few of the hundreds of types of activities.

One cannot overemphasize how widespread data phone use has become. "This is an idol," Garrett joked during one sermon, holding his smartphone up for the congregation to see. Mobile technologies organize and structure daily life to store pertinent information needed for occupational tasks. In terms of the congregation as a whole, a total of 40 percent of informants report checking their phone multiple times per day for notifications. Some 32 percent check their device at least once per hour, while 22 percent report checking for notifications multiple times per hour. As many as 68 percent of my informants document that they take their data phone to bed with them and use the device as an alarm clock. These numbers correlate loosely with data from national surveys that report that 67 percent of Americans (twenty-five to thirty-four years old) look at their phones between twenty-six and fifty times per day. The percentage of Americans who recorded checking phones directly before going to bed and upon getting up in the morning tallied at 89 and 81 percent, respectively (Deloitte 2017, 2, 3). Seventy percent of informants use their phone to access Bible applications and reading programs online. These Midwestern informants use their data phones so habitually, in fact, that an entire discourse about addiction and information overload has begun to circulate, ranging from colloquial folk discourse and conversational asides to authorized sermon data.

Church services and community gatherings are no exception. Progressive evangelicals, including some people who attend Church on the Margins, do not, statistically speaking, carry a hard copy of the Bible. During one sermon, Pastor Jonathan launched into what was to be a short, biting, and rhetorically compelling aside on how mobile technologies and digital media were making it difficult to live meaningful lives. He emphasized that data phones were everywhere these days and explained how computing machines that once filled entire rooms now compacted efficiently into our palms and pockets. The preacher pointed out that mobile tech was causing stress in relationships due to the devices' inclination toward distraction. He riffed passionately about communication technologies oversaturating society with such an illicit deluge of information that people did not know how to process so much raw data, be it through the news, advertisements, or social media posts about everyday life. All this technology, which he admitted was powerful and convenient, brought untold negative consequences. In my field notes on this day, I observed the high irony of the moment. As Jonathan criticized digital media, congregants about the room took notes or accessed the liturgical readings via their smartphones. Jonathan at one point had even urged congregants to use their phones to read aloud Bible passages. A significant portion of these emerging evangelicals leave print versions of the Bible at home for private devotional use during the week and access digital Bibles on their iPhones and Samsung Galaxies when with the church community in public. As many as 70 percent of Church on the Margins attendees use digital Bible applications at various times throughout the week.

Although the social protocol and rules surrounding cell phone use in Western societies are still under development, several identifiable public restrictions are beginning to emerge. Acknowledging the harmful effects of promiscuous media, a vein of technological ambivalence, informed by the paradigm of media sincerity, is beginning to take hold among these middle-class Midwesterners. As urbanites, these evangelicals ironically qualify as some of the new technology's most prolific users (cf. Pew Research Center 2015a). In short, although used habitually and sometimes addictively, data phones have, through culturing and socializing processes, come to be marked as at least partially and circumstantially antisocial, isolating, and distracting devices. Because Church on the Margins strives to create and maintain what it prescribes as a meaningful and authentically messy community, data phones take on symbolic meaning of the societal ills against which the community is defending. Socially acceptable and inacceptable places for data phone uses exist.

Given Garrett and Jonathan's sermon topics, it follows that the data phone has an ambivalent place in their church services. Occasionally service attendees and facilitators themselves use iPhones to read prayers, check their sermon notes while speaking, record sermon notes from the audience, or access biblical texts from the lectionary schedule. For the most part, congregants strive to keep their devices stowed away in purses, bags, pockets, or under chairs. Devices occasionally interrupt the sacred space with their beeps, rings, buzzes, and vibrations, affecting in the device owner a moment of apologetic embarrassment. In my ethnographic observations, events such as this became predictable in their sequencing. A phone manifests its presence via ringtone or buzzing. People glance about wildly. Who forgot to put their phone on silent? Who had the gall to leave the ringer on? Although infrequent occurrences at Church on the Margins, these instances demonstrate the prescriptive and prohibitive rules that are congealing around the subject of public communication device use.

Examples of the ambiguous place of smartphones in church services abound. During one informal summer-service gathering that met in a ballet school dance parlor, a service leader read a list of speaking points off her cell phone note app but took pains to legitimize the appropriateness of device use in that circumstance. "I promise I'm not texting!" she exclaimed to the small gathering, which responded with laughter at her defense. In this situation, Shannon's reaction highlighted the data phone's quotidian use for texting. Because cell phones are hybrid devices that conceal their immediate functions to everyone but the person using them, Shannon felt the need to clarify how she had put her device to use in that public situation.

Congregants evidence similar tensions in other contexts. At the same summer location, the dance studio, service facilitators ran intentionally minimalist, low-tech, and pared-down services. That summer the congregation used the ballet hall for their gatherings. In previous summers, the congregation divided into smaller experimental house church groups and then reconvened in a larger gathering when undergraduates arrived back in town at the opening of the fall semester. But at the ballet parlor, the musicians led music with no electrical accompaniment, often singing choruses a cappella or with a lone guitar as accompaniment. To cultivate less mediated, screenless services, no Power Point or media screen projected lyrics for congregants. Embodying the values of the media sincerity paradigm, the pared-down service structure did appear to feel more authentic for congregants in its informality and directness.

Yet, occasionally congregants had trouble recalling lyrics to songs whose words typically manifested on the screen at the center of the room in front of them. During one particular shortage of song-lyric memory, the music leader reflected positively on the awkwardness of the moment, urging the group to take delight in the fact that "this is community." Real community, the musician urged, is messy, raw, and spontaneous. *Rawness* and *messiness* have at Church on the Margins become virtues synonymous with organic, collaborative, democratic, and authentic community formation. These discourses reflect the model of media sincerity, in which improvisational, heartfelt, direct conversation between face-to-face parties is ideal. In the situation of the song-lyric memory void, eventually one of the pastors' wives, Kelly, brought up an iPhone after having googled the correct lyrics. She then led the congregation verse by verse with the intended words of the chorus. Notably, the music leader teased Kelly from the front, explaining that he had been wondering if she was looking up lyrics for him or "just texting."

Because media ideologies are partial and contested, Church on the Margins does not always mark texting as a negative activity. In several instances during my early years of fieldwork, I noticed pastors and speakers—in an effort to inspire and solicit congregant interactions directly within service structures—actually enjoining and encouraging service attendees to text questions, inquiries, counterarguments, and even points of criticism at any time during or after the spoken message. Such a collaborative give-and-take of information and inquiries, the pastors explained, represents an ideal community. Mobile phone technologies are one partially effective, simultaneous way to help facilitate such interaction.

Community interactions outside of church services were equally ambiguous contexts for data phone use. During my years of fieldwork, I attended countless social gatherings, sometimes multiple events per week during busy stretches. As with their Protestant forebearers, emerging evangelicals center their gatherings around the food rituals of cooking, eating, and serving one another (Sack 2000). Home dinner groups, backyard barbeques, bonfires, and gatherings at local cafés, pubs, and restaurants served as frequent contexts of interaction. As with the church services, and because evangelicals have marked data phones as partially distracting, these informal settings were not hospitable toward data phone use. I paid close attention to congregant habits as they related to their habitual media devices. Rarely, over five years, did the devices see the light of day at these gatherings. Surfing Facebook on one's iPhone or Galaxy was something one did at work or home but seldom in the presence of one's gathered community of friends. Sometimes people pulled their phones out to snap pictures and autodocument some meaningful moment, access one's schedule for planning purposes, or look up some other elusive piece of information. And very occasionally, during moments of obvious social awkwardness, I observed how parties reverted to data phone access to fill uncomfortable voids of silence or discomfort. For the most part, interaction with the distracting technologies was kept to a minimum during social gatherings and one-on-one exchanges.

CHURCH MEDIA: PCS, PROJECTORS, AND SCREENS

Having met in a restaurant or catering venue, shared space with an aging American Baptist church, leased the gymnasium of an elementary school, gathered in an expansive urban warehouse, experimented with various house church configurations, and having met periodically in a dance-instruction hall, Church on the Margins is the definition of a **mobile church**. When this chapter was written, the church had leased and remodeled a storefront space on Bloomington's commercial west side, just south and west of some of the city's oldest and most socioeconomically impoverished residential sectors, nestled snugly between a local pizza joint and a sandwich shop. Later the church would rent out a Boys & Girls Clubs location on Sundays. Although the community's physical locations have evolved over the years, because of technological and media requirements, the gathering's interior spatial layout has remained the same.

Following Protestant tradition, rows and columns of chairs arrange outward and away from the central space of the head or the room. Within this central area,

Church on the Margins challenges evangelical Protestant traditions by drawing on and actively embracing more liturgical service formats. The altar, or display table for the eucharistic elements, is the theological center and focal point of the service. The lectern stands somewhat to the side and behind the altar. To the back of the podium and altar lies a bramble of musical equipment with various instruments and jungle vines of electrical cables and cords. Foregrounding the guitars, lectern, and altar, however, a white rectangular object rises against the wall and draws the eyes. Behold the ever-present media projector screen, the structurer-of-services and dispenser-of-crucial-information. In evangelical media ideologies, the screen is a blessing and a curse. It is perhaps the most necessary tool in the entire church service; at the same time, the screen as a black mirror, of sorts, proves itself a theological thorn in the flesh as it vies with the communion table for visual focal point of the worship space. The screen displays crucial information but later it distracts.

Several ethnographic vignettes illustrate the tensions at hand. I've already discussed the low-tech and less screen-centered service format at the ballet studio and some of the awkwardness that resulted from such technological gaps due to information that is typically mediated on screens and made available to congregants. Another summer planning section took place between the church's residence in the shared space of the Baptist church and its move to the elementary school gymnasium. The discussion session revealed the high degree of deliberation that surrounds even such seemingly simple arrangements as where to put the projector screen in a new worship space.

Garrett, one of the copastors, repeatedly stressed his concern that the media screen serves even subconsciously as the focal point of the worship service. In planning the new spatial arrangements for the upcoming venue, Garrett reiterated time and time again that the screen ought not to be the location where one's eye is immediately drawn. The media screen, he stressed in a functionalist vein, is only an aid. The screen should not be the center of the experience; it should not be the focal point. In Garrett's formulation, the media screen is only an informational and aesthetic extension. To grant the screen more power than that is to fall prey to technological determinism. Instead, Garrett proposed that several of the community's artists in residence create vivid paintings to serve as the backdrop to the communion table, canvases that tracked visually with the Christian liturgical calendar's progression through the seasons.[7] At the community's first location, the pub-like catering center with wooden floors and a full bar, the issue of the screen's prominence had been solved through the use of two separate, smaller television screens located on either side of the room. These screens doubled as media projectors and thus displayed key prayers, song lyrics, and Power Point slides of the sermon, as necessary. The divided screens were offset from the center of the room. The room's focal point belonged to the eucharistic altar and speaker's podium, not the media screens. Such a configuration would no longer work, however, in the new gymnasium location. In the gym, Garrett worried, the massive wall screen might dominate and overpower the space.

Media screen placement has been, and continues to be, a significant issue of deliberation for community leaders. But regardless of the hidden effects of media and projectors screens, the technology continues to see ubiquitous use. At the far back corner of the storefront space, behind the seating segments, café tables, and coffee bar, lies the audio-visual station. The station is a massive countertop spread of knobs, levers, cords, outlets, and other instrument panels that control the audio and visual output congregants experience at the front of the room via the projections of the looming media screen, microphones, and musical instruments.

TECHNOLOGICAL FAILURE: THE AUTHENTICITY OF DIGITAL GLITCHES

For the most part, technology within church services works so efficiently that it is invisible. Inevitably, however, tech experiences occasional glitches, ruptures, disconnections, and failures where its previously invisible status becomes glaringly and obscenely visible and apparent. Several pertinent examples range from microphone battery failures, to compromised lyrics on projector screens, to missing Power Point slides, to malfunctioning laptops. These instances of technological disjuncture provide direct insight into the way practitioners conceive of, theorize, and think about technologies that are typically running automatically in the background. These manifest gaps also provide situations for evangelicals to revisit the co-constitutive dueling tensions of media promiscuity and sincerity.

Consider one instance of unstable WiFi connectivity during a Skype session with a missionary couple living across the Atlantic Ocean. The following Skype illustration is perhaps the clearest example of a technology's occasional propensity to reveal gaps in its structuring of user experience. Colin and Audrey are a missionary couple in South Sudan, Africa, who consider Church on the Margins their home community back in the States. The couple had been a vital part of the community since my preliminary fieldwork began back in 2012 but had recently finished their furlough season and fundraising in the Midwest and returned to Africa. In an effort to stay in close contact with their home group, Colin and Audrey coproduced a public journal-type blog for readers at home and abroad and also periodically Skyped with church services to share short messages, give ministry or family updates, and offer and receive corporate prayer (more *directly* corporate than through individual email letters, FaceTime talks, blog comments, or phone calls). In other words, the missionaries made use of promiscuous media to sustain social connections with their home communities.

In January of 2015, Colin and Audrey Skyped with Church on the Margins during the service. For most of the service, Colin and Audrey each gave heartfelt narrations about their time in South Sudan. Audrey reported on ministry strategies, the unpredictability of daily work among economically disenfranchised populations, and the resilience of the still thriving South Sudanese people living in a war-torn, impoverished region. Colin reflected on the frustration of acclimating to new cultures under duress and reflected on their ability to develop reservoirs of love in ministering to people despite hardship. Church on the Margins congregants appeared to thoroughly enjoy the experience, even though at certain points, as experienced Skype, Zoom, and Teams users have grown accustomed to, brief and haphazard moments of digital and visual freezing occurred. More than once, the projected video of Colin and Audrey blurred and fragmented into a pixelated patchwork. After several awkward instances of disconnection and blurring, the pastors brought the Skype-mediated service to a close. Garrett offered to pray for the missionary couple but warned, laughing, that "Skype prayer is weird." Following the prayer, Garret thanked Colin and Audrey for allowing Church on the Margins "to be a part of their story, even from thousands of miles away." Then he made one last comment about the difficulty of technologically mediated conversation, comparing the awkwardness of ending everyday phone call conversations with that of the glitch-replete Skype.

Several aspects of this vignette are crucial to understanding how these evangelicals theorize and employ fallible new media. First, consider the use of the promiscuous media itself. Evangelicals use Skype to extend mission networks and maintain social ties. They acknowledge the wonders of internet-mediated visual technologies to aid in communication across geographic and temporal distance. In this case, communicants link together in the present—visually, vocally, and audibly—across some seven thousand miles between the American Heartland and sub-Saharan Africa.

Second, use notwithstanding, communicants are quite upfront and objective about the limitations of the media. Skype is glitchy. Conversation on the medium inevitably fragments. Faces break down into pixelated smudges and mosaic color-fields spread across the screen. Freezing and blurring of ideally dynamic imagery occurs more than one would like. The rate of partial communication failure is high, whether the situation involves missing a word or a sentence or misreading nonverbal communication cues due to the ill-behaving, pixelated image transfers of complex facial expressions. As part of Skyping, these Midwesterners expect and anticipate communicative awkwardness. Partial communication failure is normal and much more so than one would imagine in the alternative megachurch setting of media professionalism (Cooper 2010; cf. Elisha 2013).

A third point came to the fore after the Skype session proper ended, when Garrett commented on the experience to the community gathered back in Bloomington. Moments such as these, when leaders provide metapragmatic, ideological commentary on technological forms and media communication, are the most valuable data for scholars of religion and media. In these types of situations, communicants revisit the second media imperative common to their tradition: media sincerity. Garrett spent several minutes reiterating both how meaningful an experience Skyping with Colin and Audrey had been and how frustrating technological glitches can be. Church on the Margins views its modus operandi to be the construction of authentic, meaningful, and nonartificial community. One might expect these evangelicals to reject Skype's mode of promiscuous communication as inauthentic, cheap, or as only a shadow of the real thing (i.e., face-to-face or embodied conversation in the tradition of the sincerity model). But this is not the case. On the contrary, Garrett took several minutes to explain how Skype, though far from perfect, actually maps onto, reflects, and mimics so-called real life. He challenges the standard of sincerity and authenticity, pointing out that everyday life is full of disjuncture, miscommunication, fragmentation, and gaps. People frequently fail to communicate effectively with spouses, children, or colleagues. Married people suffer miscommunication episodes and must learn to navigate such difficulties with sensitivity and care. Deconstructing the sincerity paradigm, the pastor challenges romantic notions of in-person talk and embodied conversation. In Garrett's formulation, Skype is an inherently fallible but altogether accurate metaphor for real life. For Garrett, Skype's fragmented texture is an authentic rather than inauthentic effect. In the case of Skype, promiscuous affordance can aid sincere communication.

To summarize, mediated gaps occur, and they offer brief moments of clarity into the social and discursive maneuvers through which practitioners make sense of technologies and their uses. In these gaps, evangelicals synthesize the conflicting media paradigms of sincerity and promiscuity, rounding out the harder edges of the media ideologies to make them less conflicting and more amenable. At the ballet studio, congregants stumbled over song lyrics from memory in the absence of the screen. Because the projector screen in church serves to some degree as an outsourced reservoir of human memories, I observed iPhone-enabled Google searches for lyrics coming to the rescue in some situations. These congregants both resist promiscuous media's negative effects and use promiscuous media to solve problems. During the Skype session with the missionaries, fluctuating WiFi connectivity made for a not entirely seamless communicative experience but opened an opportunity for Garrett to generate normative discourse about technology. Throughout fieldwork observations, I noticed other small instances of technological gaps. Occasionally missing Power Point slides generated short windows of embarrassment while service leaders waited patiently for a liturgical prayer to load so they could recite it off the screen. Sometimes a missing slide meant that congregants had to recite it from memory (or make the attempt to do so). In other instances, as soon as the missing slide appeared, the service continued as planned. In another situation, a digital glitch ran down a slide that in the moment displayed the scriptural text of John 16:19–33. In all these situations of technological failure or mediatized difficulty, the presence of the technology comes immediately to the fore. The fault betrays technology's previously enjoyed invisibility of mediation (cf. Young and Åkerström 2016, 8).

Like the Skype experience, however, service leaders often apologetically used these moments of technological inefficiency to reinforce Church on the Margin's realness, rawness, and authenticity. As I suggest in the following chapter, casualness or informality marks authenticity for community members. The inverse model—that is, perfectly organized and efficient service orders, what congregants often dismissed as the megachurch model—serves as the discursive antithesis of the real and authentic. Massive megachurch congregations have the resources to hire professionals to run their communications, but small churches, like Church on the Margins, can only function because of volunteer service (cf. Bialecki 2017, 27, 29).

INTERNET PRESENCE AND IDENTITY ACROSS ONLINE PLATFORMS

If a church doesn't have a website, is it even a real church? For millennials, churches are as good as nonexistent if the group does not maintain some sort of online presence. In my ethnographic observations, I paid close attention to congregant discourse about their group's online activities. Over the course of several years, around six or seven couples and larger family groups joined Church on the Margins. Because Bloomington is a college town, nearly all new kinship groups discovered the church community by doing online searches. Such a situation would not be the case for larger and more established congregations that often put advertisements in local news media, pay for large billboards that share location and service time information, or use extended time and resources to extend their brand online (Sircar and Rowley 2016, 698). Church leadership was in turn sensitive to the importance of Google searches in researching potential church homes, and thus for leaders, online interaction and portrayal of the church was a subject of necessity and importance.

When meeting first-time visitors or newcomers to church services or broader community events, pastoral staff routinely inquired about how that person,

EMERGING MIDWESTERN EVANGELICALS AND DIGITAL MEDIA   191

couple, or family had heard about the community. With few exceptions, new members acknowledged using Google or Google Maps to identify and locate interesting churches in the area through websites. One visitor mentioned inputting a Google search for "missional" churches and having Church on the Margins show up in the results. The pastors later joked during planning sessions about this qualification since at the time *missional*—which further ties the community to progressive, emerging churches or postevangelical conversations going on at the fringes of conservative Protestantism—showed up only once on the entire website. Another visitor, whose family over the years became part of the core community, praised the pastors for the website design and noted that it was the pastors' short biography pages that sold them on visiting Church on the Margins in the first place. The biographical descriptions characterized the nontraditional format of the church leadership as divided among three shared, bivocational pastoral roles.[8] To some degree the biographies classified the personalities and theological proclivities of each of the three pastors, going as far as listing each pastor's favorite or most influential theological books. At least three or four visitors confirmed to me personally over my years of research that they were attracted to the church because of keyword search results online and via Google.

In short, and although leaders would resist the megachurch commodification of their community into a brand to be advertised, the internet is an increasingly important means of advertisement for young and emerging churches. Community leaders expressed worry about how online descriptions might limit, pigeonhole, or constrain the identity of the church, which they felt was fluid, experiential, and nonbounded. Leaders thus took great care to manage the website, church descriptions, and pastor biographies and recognized the performative nature of such online depictions. Pastor Garrett expressed with passion during one planning session that community is much deeper and richer than what can be portrayed on a two-dimensional, text-based web page and that the community ought to resist simplification or reduction of their identity.

In addition to the church website—a WordPress site maintained by volunteer designers within the church—Church on the Margins made use of several online and social media–oriented platforms for different purposes. Throughout my ethnographic interim, pastors and guest speakers uploaded sermons and events to MP3 podcasts available for free to the public on iTunes, thus shaping their spoken, discursive, and theologically instructive texts into **spreadable media** available for anyone with an internet connection (Jenkins et al. 2013; cf. Lofton 2017, 29). Church on the Margins used a Facebook group and email LISTSERV (and with lesser frequency Twitter and Instagram accounts) to keep community members up-to-date on information about services, special events, and outreach initiatives. A second private (local) Facebook group, "Church on the Margins Check-In," served as a bulletin for prayer requests, members' life events, praise reports, practical requests for assistance—such as to get a ride to the airport in Indianapolis or ask for help in moving—or other various activities. Lastly, at the close of my ethnographic research, the group was experimenting with its Instagram page and had made several calls to get community members to submit photographs with the appropriately hashtagged labels to link back to the church community. To summarize, Church on the Margins managed its identity across several online and social media–based platforms. The congregation used internet-enabled media primarily for informational and networking purposes but with the closed-community Facebook group also engaged in ritual or devotional practices in online domains.

COMMUNITY MEMBER SOCIAL MEDIA USE

Individual congregants manage their own identities online via myriad social media pages. In this section, I synthesize key survey findings into five tables organized around primary media platforms (table 7.1), frequency of Facebook access per day (table 7.2), Instagram access per day (table 7.3), and total daily time spent on Facebook and Instagram (tables 7.4 and 7.5, respectively). Consider first, via table 7.1, the primary social media platforms used by congregants.

Facebook and Instagram are the two most popular social media among congregants. One hundred percent of congregants surveyed used Facebook, compared to the national Facebook user average of 68 percent (Pew Research Center 2018). Congregants reported both frequency of access (the number of times they signed on or checked in to the social media site) and estimated hours spent per

Table 7.1. Top Social Media Platforms (N=50)

Media Platform	Number of Respondent Users	Percentage of Respondents
(1) Facebook	50	100
(2) Instagram	32	64
(3) LinkedIn	21	42
(4) Snapchat	19	38
(5) Twitter	16	32
(6) WordPress	11	22
(7) Tumblr	4	8
(8) Pinterest	2	4
(9) Nextdoor	1	2
(10) WhatsApp	1	2

Table 7.2. Facebook Access Frequency (N=50)

Access Frequency	Number of Respondents	Percentage of Users
1 time per day	4	8
2 times per day	10	20
3 times per day	10	20
4 times per day	4	8
5 times per day	6	12
6 times per day	1	2
7 times per day	2	4
8 times per day	3	6
10+ times per day	9	18

Table 7.3. Instagram Access Frequency (N=32)

Access Frequency	Number of Respondents	Percentage of Users
1 time per day	11	34.3
2 times per day	7	21.8
3 times per day	1	3.1
4 times per day	5	15.6
5 times per day	2	6.2
6 times per day	3	9.3
7 times per day	1	3.1
8 times per day	1	3.1

platform. In terms of Facebook, as table 7.5 reports, a majority of congregants accessed the social media platform either two, three, or ten separate times each day. These findings are comparable to broader national uses by Americans, where 51 percent of Facebook users access the site multiple times per day and 23 percent once per day (Pew Research Center 2018). Only four congregants reported going onto Facebook only once per day. And sixteen individuals recorded checking Facebook somewhere between four and eight different times per day.

Instagram check-in frequency is significantly less. Only twelve people recorded accessing Instagram between four and eight times per day. The largest category of respondents, eleven individuals, claimed to go on Instagram only once per day.

In terms of total time spent per day on the top-two social media platforms, Facebook again wins. Ten total people reported spending more than an hour

Table 7.4. Total Time Spent on Facebook (N=50)

Time Allotments	Number of Respondents	Percentage of Users
Less than once weekly	1	2
< 15 minutes per day	7	14
15–30 minutes per day	14	28
30 minutes–1 hour per day	12	24
1 hour–2 hours per day	8	16
2+ hours per day	2	4

Table 7.5. Total Time Spent on Instagram (N=32)

Time Allotments	Number of Respondents	Percentage of Respondents
Less than once weekly	8	25
< 15 minutes per day	9	28.1
15–30 minutes per day	5	15.6
30 minutes–1 hour per day	2	6.2
1 hour–2 hours per day	1	3.1
2+ hours per day	1	3.1

per day on Facebook, whereas only two people reported spending more than an hour on Instagram.

Although self-reporting via surveys is a notoriously difficult manner of producing reliable, accurate measurements (Wuthnow 2015; Chaves 2011), the method does have the benefit of generating data from which to predict trends or commonalities among even small groups. Self-reporting on surveys is also productive in the sense that it produces discursively idealized answers, as opposed to numerically accurate facts (Chaves 2011, 42–45). Similar to national survey instruments that inquire how many times a week congregants attend church, I expect that the answers submitted about social media use reflect idealized or overly optimistic answers. Because I am interested in discourses about social media and technology, such survey-based responses about media use are, to some degree, more useful at getting at certain questions than observing activities on the ground.[9]

Like estimated frequency of access and total time spent, the uses of social media show a significantly high degree of variance among even the relatively small corpus of survey respondents at Church on the Margins. In the remainder of this section, I draw both on survey response data and firsthand digital ethnographic observation among Church on the Margins community member interactions in online domains. What follows is a provisional inventory of social media practices, both as self-described by community members and supplemented by observations in the digital field.[10]

Before getting to this initial taxonomy, however, a few disclaimers about social media use are required. As an emerging mode of social interaction, new media serve as platforms for several strikingly different genres of communicative intent. In other words, social media showcase a bewilderingly diverse set of tailored uses. Users engage social media for different purposes. Some people use media such as Facebook for both professionalization and entertainment, sometimes within the very same temporal stretches of use. Social media may thus collapse a person's multiple social spheres, which may previously have been differentiated. Occasionally users prefer different media platforms for different purposes. An example is the claim that Facebook serves well for keeping up-to-date with friends and family, while Twitter works better for following celebrities, professionals, writers, or figures one does not know personally.

The crucial point is that none of these uses are set in stone. Platforms such as Instagram and Facebook do possess their own internal algorithmic structures, codes of use, and affordances for input and output of information, but such uses are highly malleable, plastic, and customizable in practice (Langlois 2014; Gershon 2010a; Miller 2011). Social media adepts can use these technologies for purposes not intended by program designers. In short, social media provide a highly illustrative venue for the study of interpersonal communication's socially constructed dimensions. As nascent communicative technologies, social media in their plasticity serve as an opportune arena in which to study how technologies come to be layered with social, cultural, and religious meaning.

This evangelical congregation uses social media for eight primary reasons:

1. Entertainment and leisure
2. Extension and maintenance of kinship, friendship, and social ties
3. Informational collection and consumption
4. Commerce and shopping
5. Professionalization and work-related communication
6. Ritual and devotional engagement
7. Ideological and discursive contestation
8. Identity-based microperformances

The eight categories are by no means discrete, exclusive, or present in every person's experience. Often, the categories blur into one another. One respondent, for instance, said, "I only use Facebook as a social media platform. I keep up with current news, major life events, prayer requests, and extended family chat." Such a response falls equally into category three, *information* ("I keep up with current news"), category two, *kinship and sociality* ("I keep up with ... major life events ...

extended family chat"), and category six, *ritual* ("prayer requests"). But regardless of this categorical slippage, the eightfold taxonomy does name different sectors of communication that constitute the stratified, eclectic, and networked uses of social media for emerging Midwesterners.

Mere entertainment is one rationale for social media use. One congregant notes browsing social media feeds and "friends' posts and photos when I am bored or distracted." Another respondent prefers Instagram as her primary and most meaningful platform of use but does revert to Facebook "usually because I'm just bored." "Keeping up to date on friends' activities" is visually stimulating and helps people pass time at various points throughout the day by looking at and posting images of daily life or seeing the images uploaded by friends, family members, and colleagues. Others appreciate social media for the ability to post and consume comical materials. "I mostly post photos or funny articles on Facebook," one person describes. Entertainment is a significant part of social media use in everyday life. In discussions with people at social gatherings, they often conveyed to me that through sheer force of habit, they turn to social media throughout the day during down moments simply to pass the time and thumb through various feeds. Social media, however, are not foolproof venues for entertainment. As I explore in the next chapter, communicants sometimes express frustration with the content they peruse in their various media feeds. One respondent admits that his Facebook newsfeed "often gets boring and repetitive so I lose interest." Entertainment quickly lapses into ennui.

Second, the most cited use of social media capitalizes on the *social* factors of the appellation. As anthropologists of media and communication have noted, social media (and especially archplatforms, such as Facebook) work with extreme efficiency to "aggregate networks such as friendship and kinship" (Miller 2011, 121). In terms of classic media theory, social media are indeed communicative extensions since they function as supplemental facilitators of human sensory abilities (McLuhan 2001). Facebook, Instagram, and Twitter extend family- and friendship-based relations that structure the world beyond the digital and screen mediated. Social media are aggregate media in that they layer upon extradigital relationships and provide additional venues of extended interaction. Midwesterners use social media to "keep up with friends and family" and digest content "posted by friends." Instagram generates for one person "mini 'updates' of what my friends or acquaintances are doing with their day or things that they find cool and want to share." For a different person, Facebook helps to "stay up to date on people" and view "pictures of friends." Facebook generates "photos of peoples' kids" and "updates on their lives." "I use Facebook just about every day to see what friends are up to" and "how family are doing," another informant says. Online observation confirms that congregants post about anniversaries, birthdays, special family events, social get-togethers, and a range of other activities. In informal conversations about social media, I also observed that congregants are feeling more and more pressure to migrate public appreciation of loved ones into online domains. People express knowledge of social obligations arising about what one's online contacts expect or anticipate regarding posts to keep others abreast of life developments.

A third category of use clusters around the use of social media for informational collection, consumption, and sharing. Simply put, social media assist Americans in keeping "up with current news" and other sources or information or knowledge capital. Congregants employ social media to "gather" and "collect information" from trusted friends and associates to read later. One informant prefers Twitter to "access news, opinion pieces, and other more intellectually stimulating content." For a different person, Facebook, rather than Twitter, is for staying up-to-date on "what's in the world news." Another person also prefers Facebook to gather and then "read various social, political, and religious articles." Still another communicant narrates a shift in the Facebook interface over time. This particular informant feels her "use of Facebook has morphed from finding out status updates from my friends," perhaps something like five years ago, "to now just reading interesting articles or blog posts that they share." Even the types of information social media platforms allow for changes as it itself evolves and develops. Information can range from minutia about friends and family members' daily lives to news or journalistic sources from major news outlets that publish online articles, to articles or essays about other types of content that may even include religious or theological subjects or entertainment or cultural pieces.

Fourth, a less frequent mode of social media interaction involves engagement in ecommerce, business, trading, shopping, or bartering online. One stay-at-home parent uses social media to "look at stuff on sale within Yard Sale Groups" in her local neighborhood. An informant notes that Facebook serves as both a small business platform and a venue through which to make purchases. Still another community member explains how she has been experimenting with the new Facebook Market program—a system akin to the older Craigslist method—to locate local items for purchase. People post about items for sale or inquire as to which sorts of items others are trying to get rid of. The social media economy, in other words, expands past mere social connections into the world of capitalism, markets, commodity flows, and consumption of goods. I witnessed on multiple occasions informants advocating positively for some product they were pleased with having purchased. On the flip side, social media also provided a venue for informants to complain about product disappointments, false adverting, and other capitalistic failures. Congregants frequently use Amazon to buy an array of items ranging from gifts to work supplies to books and media.

Professionalization is a fifth frequent use of social media by this group of Midwesterners. LinkedIn is like Facebook but for occupational and professional networking purposes, used "to stay professionally connected with folks," as one young professional within the community attests. Bloomington revolves around the massive educational institution of Indiana University. Indeed, many of Church on the Margins' attendees are either undergraduate or graduate students or affiliated faculty or staff. Digital ethnographic observation confirms that community members use platforms such as Facebook or Twitter to share articles and information directly pertinent to jobs or occupations. Scholars within the Church on the Margins social network post information, content, and links having to do with their research interests and academic endeavors. Photographers and other artists post links to their works and skill sets for sale or hire. Professionalization is a key function.

Sixth, ritual and devotional engagement via social media is important for American Christians. Congregants, in no particular order, use online Bible applications for daily or weekly reading purposes (e.g., YouVersion, Read Scripture, or The Bible Project) and share about Christ or their testimonies with friends through social media. Instagrammers based in the Bloomington area link up with Christian Instagram communities, such as Socality (the subject of the previous chapter). They listen to sermon or teaching podcasts and discuss matters of faith over Facebook Messenger. They conduct prayers over video media and collect and disseminate prayer requests and needs over distance through social media networks. Teachers in the community use internet-mediated platforms for "reading the lectionary online, using online translations" and locating "exegetical sources" and "religious articles," among other important sources of religious information. Frequency of ritual or devotional use for social media varies per person. For some, online activities of the devotional sort occur daily: "I access most of my religious/spiritual input (commentary, sermon, music, guided prayer) online." Other congregants resist the expansion of their religious activities to the domains of social media: "I don't like to engage with God via Facebook" or "I don't often engage in religion-based activities online."

Ideological and discursive contestation, the focus of the next chapter, is the seventh category of frequent social media use and the clearest indication of the digitally buffered self at work. The seventh group of activities blurs into other categories. For instance, discursive contestation can at times be profoundly or even primarily "religious." I separate between devotional activity and religious contestation because of the texture and intent of the activities. Both sorts are highly regular behaviors on social media. At times discursive contestation has to do directly with boundary maintenance, critique of existing church structures, and disagreements about matters of lifestyle, morality, and normativity. My informants' self-description of such activities makes use of words like *dialogue, conversation, engagement*, and *discussion* to characterize their activities online. "I have dialogues with people about issues of faith and practice," one person notes. People "engage in conversation regarding faith regularly" and have frequent discussions about theological or doctrinal matters. As an informant argues, Facebook is for "sharing articles and opinions/thoughts," which may lead to engaging discussions online. Another Facebook user makes use of the platform with the intent of "attempting productive public discourse." Occasionally, such normative metapragmatic discourse about how social media ought to be correctly used occurs. I will discuss this category of social media activity in more detail shortly but for now note that it exists as one of the primary forms of Midwestern new media interactions.

An eighth and final category of new media use arises not out of direct congregant reporting on the questionnaire or in conversations but by way of digital ethnographic observation. Simply put, social media—as extensions of nondigital social interactions in the world—extend, amplify, and transfer processes of quotidian identity building. People post frequently about entertainment media consumed, hobbies, intellectual subjects of interest, arts and culture points of fascination, athletic loyalties and teams' progress throughout seasons, and many other identity-related activities. Through social media engagement, digitally buffered selfhood constitutes identity and signifies identity-formation processes. Microcommentaries online are the very stuff of self-identity-construction and self-performance. Through posting and self-posturing online, a notable form of **performative individualism** arises within social domains (Horst and Miller 2006, 79; cf. Cottle 2006, 9; Miller 2011, 177; Lövheim 2013, 51; Cheong 2016, 85).

Social media expressions relate to self-cultivation along the lines of what Michel Foucault (1997, 177) has described as "technologies of the self." To push the Foucaultian analysis further, and summarizing many of my informants' worries, media function as a **panopticon** or **postpanopticon** in that one acts online knowing that someone is surveilling. Such surveillance-based observation of online activities might take place on behalf of one's immediate social network, broader religious community, government, or intelligent algorithms that monitor one's site visits and track consumption preferences (Marichal 2012, 75–76; Clark 2013, 41; Miller 2011, 179–180, 2014, 245–260; Hutchings 2015; Chun 2016, ix, 12, 94; Langlois 2014; Matthewman 2011, 60–66; Foucault 1977, 201–202). In linking articles, engaging in theology debates, arguing about politics, publicizing one's consumptive tastes, sharing prayer requests, posting approved podcasts, and self-monitoring one's etiquette and presentation to various publics, among myriad other online activities, social media users are engaging in subtle microperformances and strategies of self-construction. Microperformances like these address both individual identities and social affiliations (e.g., individuals as part of the Church on the Margins community). And as I have mentioned, Church on the Margins aims to cultivate an ethos of distinction over and against more mainstream evangelical communities in the area.

I observed hundreds, even thousands, of interactions online that link back to this eighth category of identity cultivation and mediated performance, but one key digital ethnographic vignette stands out, which speaks to these issues of identity performance and discourses of distinction. One evening I had been perusing my own social media feeds—hybrid networks that were sites for both personal recreational use and ethnographic domains for gathering data and observing interactions—when I happened upon a colorful post uploaded by one Church on the Margins congregant and Facebook friend.

Sharon, a young creative professional, posted a link to an online advent journal titled *Fuck This Shit: An Advent Devotional* (Rasche 2016).[11] As with most social media sharing of links to websites, Sharon provided a brief commentary along with the link. The *Fuck This Shit* devotional, Sharon clarified, was to be her advent reading for that particular season. Sharon's post occurred in an appreciative vein and was not intended, as outsiders to evangelicalism might expect, as a negative denunciation of a foul-worded devotional. Rather, Sharon described the devotional as "lovely and powerful and passionate" and encouraged her Facebook friends to follow the link and make use of the Lenten materials. "Give it a read if your soul is searching for comfort in this difficult and confusing time," Sharon posted. Beyond the seemingly simple act of uploading a link to Facebook, Sharon's *Fuck This Shit* endorsement and positive microcommentary acts as a socioreligious signal. The edginess of the material's rhetoric categorizes Sharon as part of a progressive religious community that defies the linguistic ideologies of traditional Christianity. Instances of this sort underscore social media's role in broadcasting identity performances of different sorts. Posts via social media are never just about the content. Social media users post knowing that their followers make judgments about who posts what and act knowing that what one posts reflects back upon the poster.

CONCLUSION

This chapter has submitted an account of emerging evangelical uses of digital, mobile, and screen-based technologies among one Midwestern church community. YouTube, Facebook, and Skype, alongside PCs, projectors, data phones, media screens, websites, Facebook, Instagram, and many other media forms, are integrating into the daily lives of evangelicals. Short gaps and brief technological failures provide insight into the tension between the media paradigms of sincerity and promiscuity, showing how these evangelicals are redefining their definitions of sincere and authentic communication in light of the advances of promiscuous media. For Church on the Margins, reflection on social media becomes an avenue for constructing and maintaining more robust forms of authentic communication. After confirming the high plasticity of evangelical media ideologies, the chapter concluded by noting eight categories of social media interaction. Although these evangelicals appear to be growing accustomed to habitual media, I have also pointed out how devices like data phones continue to be sources of ambiguity for religious groups. The next chapter examines in more detail the negative ideologies and discourses of ambivalence circulating and analyzes the intimate connection between authority and authenticity within progressive evangelicalism.

NOTES

1. To protect the confidentiality and preserve the anonymity of my informants and interlocutors, I have employed pseudonyms both for the church and all the community members mentioned. I take this title, however, from a planning meeting in which one of the pastors made it clear that "we are a church that leads from the margins," that is, a church for "the hurting, wounded, confused, and frustrated." "We want to lead from the margins," the pastor emphasized.

2. At a later date, I overhear a group of children—this one included—discuss who gets to eat the rest of the "Jesus bread" and drink the "Jesus juice" left over after a service.

3. For a more thorough description of Church on the Margins's musical rituals, see Cooper 2017b.

4. With regard to the statistical studies that exist on the subject of national internet and social media use, the urban/rural and generational differentials are far more significant than use between geographic regions of the United States (Pew Research Center 2018, 2015a; cf. U.S. Census 2010).

5. Anthropologists of non-American Christianity have often, in contradiction to Orsi, studied the formation as something "in opposition to local culture," not constitutive of it (Tomlinson and Engelke 2006, 19).

6. For a consideration of the tensions between the global and the local in terms of communication technologies, see Supp-Montgomerie (2021, 203–210).

7. Such a tension—melding the adoption of cutting-edge communications technologies with a posture in tune with ancient theologies of the temporal—confirms Church on the Margins as being in conversation with ECM conversations. One scholar's qualification of the ECM includes a paradoxical ancient-future standpoint (Bielo 2011, 10–16). At Church on the Margins, it is not strange to see both iPhones and icons in the same semiotic space.

8. A bivocational form of leadership refers to a situation in which "either by desire or necessity" pastors "work outside the church to support themselves and their families" (Bialecki 2017, 24).

9. On the difficulty of informant self-representation anthropologists face when doing ethnographic research of various sorts, including observations, interviews, and surveys, see Rabinow 2007, 119 and Bourdieu 1977, 18–19.

10. A brief word on citations and data. Stretches of quoted text with no source identification derives from the survey and questionnaire data. Quotations coming directly from social media observations are noted in text. Any discourse drawn directly from social media outlets and cited in the body of this chapter have been granted direct permission and consent by the Facebook comment or tweet's originator. Again, all names included are pseudonyms for the sake of protecting informants' and interlocutors' anonymity and confidentiality.

11. Tuhina Verma Rasche, the creator of the devotional, explains the origin and purpose of the journal: "When my fellow troublemaker and #FuckThisShit conspirator, Jason Chesnut, and I started talking about this devotional and its visceral nature, I had been filled with so much anger and so much rage because of police shootings, the destruction of black and brown bodies, and the racism and vitriol tied to the 2016 presidential election. These emotions fueled much of my writing and energies in the past months. I thought this anger and rage would keep me, in this body, fueled to write during the season of Advent, yearning for God's justice in the midst of so much that has gone wrong in this calendar year. As this devotion starts, I am weary, wanting now to keep that anger and rage at arm's length [sic], whispering 'Fuck' in the midst of a physical, emotional, and spiritual exhaustion that now gnaws at my bones. I come to this word of meditation and today's verse tired, weary, and so very much ready for Christ to come again" (Rasche 2016). Rasche's concerns mirror those of the evangelical feminists observed back in chapter 5. For a similar use of profane language in a religious, postevangelical context, see Wright 2018a and 2018b.

EIGHT

MEDIA AMBIVALENCE IN EMERGING EVANGELICALISM

THIS FINAL CHAPTER SUBMITS AN ethnographic account of emerging evangelical media ideologies. I have argued that evangelicals find themselves caught in a flux of competing ideological tensions involving media. Like the malfunctioning Skype call in the previous chapter, the tensions magnify when studying people on the ground. The tension between the authenticity of the sincerity model and the pull of convenient and efficient promiscuous media becomes even more evident.

On the one hand, Church on the Margins uses digital media to build community and promote appropriate forms of Christian living. I discuss, in the following, congregants as social media adepts who engage in online contestation about politics and theology. These evangelicals access scripture and use Bible apps to order their daily lives, worry about the thinness of post-Facebook "friendship," establish parameters for what counts as authentic relational ties, and outsource their own spiritual-formation practices by heavy podcast consumption. On the other hand, these evangelicals experience the negative implications of new media adoption to an acute degree, strategically accommodating new media by advancing nuanced media ideologies and discourses and practices of media ambivalence, suspicion, restraint, and resistance (Ribak and Rosenthal 2015; Syvertsen 2017). In response to a host of attendant problems, the digital adepts are aware of and keen on talking about the problems of sensory and informational overload. They frequently discuss and criticize the inauthenticity of Facebook friends, deconstruct the limitations of digital Bibles, and worry about the dangers of podcasting—at least when the media takes the place of robust, local, in-person community formation. In response to such concerns, emerging evangelicals apply varying degrees of restraint and quasiascetic disciplinary measures, sometimes undergoing extended periods of abstinence from their data phones and devices. This chapter concentrates on the synthesis evangelicals strive to create between their inherited media paradigms and focuses on the creative methods they employ to make promiscuous media use fit the parameters of sincerity and authenticity.

I argue that for Midwestern evangelicals, communicative sincerity takes on new forms. I contend that a third communicative and theological paradigm of **messiness**—be it theological, ecclesial, social, aesthetic, or practical—becomes for the congregation a strategy with which to manage between the levels of sincerity and promiscuity. Promiscuous media, for instance, may breed messiness in the form of exposure to a plurality of theologies at work but such messiness, my collaborators argue, more authentically reflects the standards of sincere media and embodied in-person communication. As a guiding trope, serving for the congregation as both an informal self-description and encompassing media ideology, messiness allows for these evangelicals to afford for many levels of difference, including internecine theological and political diversity, eclectic ritual modes, blending of contemporary media and ancient prayer forms, the casual nonprofessionalism of service formats, the double-sided effects of new media, and loosely defined socioreligious boundaries.

The following sections address these discussions of authenticity, inauthenticity, and power as they come into play in several different subtopics: new media and sensory overload, the use of social media for contestation and debate, the problem of digital Bibles, the thinness of post-Facebook "friendship," evolving patterns of authority within evangelicalism, the problem of podcast technologies, the radical nature of the Sunday-morning gathering, and a number of strategies for practicing digital asceticism. I conclude, briefly, by reflecting on the developments the sincerity paradigm undergoes in the age of ubiquitous promiscuous media.

SOCIAL MEDIA AS SENSORY OVERLOAD

I vividly recall my very first ethnographic foray into the field. The experience was lively and energetic, a thorough assault on the senses. Not having yet relocated to the elementary school gymnasium I described in the previous chapter, Church on the Margins was meeting in Al's Catering, a food-service and restaurant setting. With dark interiors, a corner bar, deep-red oak flooring, and tall bar stools, the space resembled a public house or food-and-drink establishment similar to the Irish Lion Restaurant and Pub, another occasional site for Church on the Margins–related meetings. The Irish Lion is a favorite hangout known by locals for its extensive list of scotch, bourbon, and whiskey, as well as the fleet of model ships that sails above the dining tables and bar suspended midair by strings. "Pub(lic) Theology," a small Church on the Margins group ran by a bright philosophy PhD student, met for a season during determined weekday nights at the Irish Lion. Having conducted participant observation with this subgroup, I can attest for emerging evangelicals' enjoyment of deep philosophical and theological discussion beside stout drinks.[1]

Back to my initial ethnographic foray. During the first few weeks of ethnographic observations I conducted at Church on the Margins meetings at Al's Catering, I took furious handwritten field notes on anything and everything I observed.[2] At first, all this recorded data was confusing.[3] I had a difficult time making sense of the various combinations and high degree of eclecticism of theological, ecclesial, and aesthetic styles in operation during church services. The music portion of the service was a stripped down, three-person folk band complete with the occasional ukulele.[4] Contemporary worship choruses took on a quasibrassy, folksy, and Americana texture (cf. Cooper 2017b, 80). The service itself involved several ritual and liturgical elements adapted from the Catholic mass, Eastern orthodoxy, and the High Church Christian liturgical calendar.[5] I discuss the ramifications of this adoption of modified liturgical forms and aesthetics for the sincerity paradigm at the close of the chapter but note, for now, the intentional religious eclecticism. Pastor Garrett resisted ecclesial pigeonholing, and in his sermon somehow managed to both lambast the excesses of old-school charismatic Pentecostal worship rituals, such as banner waving and running laps around the sanctuary, as well as denounce the reductions of cessationism on the other end of the Protestant continuum. The sermon was for the most part an appreciative discussion of John Wimber, the founder of Church on the Margins's own affiliation, the Vineyard Movement. Later in the service, just after I overheard a short delivery of tongues-speaking somewhere to my left, service leaders called for congregants to light candles, engage in introspective prayer, and meditate on several votive-lit icons at the back of the worship space. The folk worship group played to close out the service as the smell of incense and flickering candlelight filled the room.

I struggled with how to conceptualize and describe the theological and ecclesial status of a group that engaged in such blurry boundaries, aesthetics, and styles. Over the years of ethnographic observation, I grew accustomed to categorical resistance of this sort. Church on the Margins is a socially, ecclesially, and theologically inclusive collective that intentionally disregards boundaries in its adoption of various Christian traditions' practices and rituals. I later learned that Church on the Margins drew directly on six different historical "streams" of Christianity in an effort to provide a more authentic, robust, and holistic form of contemporary evangelical living.[6]

In the same way that I as an anthropologist of Christianity struggled at first with sensory overload and the inability to describe or classify the church within any easy ecclesial categories, Church on the Margins community members also experienced an increasingly severe onset of informational overload. Such surplus, the evangelicals argue, arises through the development of mobile technology, the exponential increase of media screens in daily life, and the advancement of neoliberal or late-capitalist advertising strategies through television, the internet, and personal social media networks. In the present section of this chapter, I look to sermon discourse to map out emerging evangelical suspicions about the problems of contemporary living and its increasingly mediated communication patterns.

One of the most problematic implications of social technologies, according to emerging evangelicals, is the media's penchant for inundating its users with vast swathes of information. Evangelicals feel the weight of informational excess and when discussing social media within the setting and genre of the sermon, this negative repercussion of informational saturation comes most frequently to the fore.[7]

In both clerical and lay talk, social media themselves become discursive entities and objects of direct discussion, criticism, and debate. From the pulpit, pastors question the merits of informational saturation, wonder about the sociotheological effects of online contestation, and challenge what they see as the broader culture's drive toward constant and incessant social connection and unlimited access to knowledge. In a 2012 sermon series, Pastor Garrett described how news feeds and newsreels dominate how people think about the world and often serve as a source of anxiety in their delivery of bad news. Seeing so much of the world's problems broadcasted in online news media, Garrett argued, can hamper Christian purpose in the world—that is, the call to love one's enemies and one's neighbors (rather than fear them). Instead, immersed in negative media reports and short clips about terrorist bombings, criminal acts, and an assortment of other evils, Christians increasingly experience "compassion fatigue." In Garrett's understanding, a person grows accustomed to the despair, violence, hunger, and evil in the world because one exposes oneself to these vices every time one signs on to Facebook or pulls one's data phone out of his or her pocket.

Through sermon discourse, focused studies of spiritual discipline or formation manuals (e.g., Calhoun 2005) and other strategies, Garrett and other leaders work to develop for the congregation robust spiritual and physical disciplines that will help one remain anchored and focused in an age of informational overload.[8] Garrett in particular urges the community under his watch to use social media with care and caution and remain locally focused in order to avoid being overwhelmed by the miasma of the external globalizing world. Garrett's worries confirm the ability of an embedded technological form to change the way humans both conceive of, exist through, and operate in the world. Facebook, for example, offers a new vantage into global life and new forms of self-discipline must be developed to deal with such exposure. For Church on the Margins, the global, at least in some sense, impinges on the stability of the local through social media.

Garrett's sermons also reflect what cultural commentators (e.g., Menzies 2005) describe as the increasingly stress-ridden lifestyles due to a "vast global network of digital machines." Modern life is anxious and disconnected even though more information circulates through various machine networks than any other time in world history.

Pastor Levi also expands on what he feels are the dark sides of social media connectivity. He names, in other words, the negative side effects of promiscuous media. In a 2015 sermon, he reflected on the role of social media in adding undue stress, pressure, and anxiety to already complicated lifestyles. Facebook and Twitter add to what he feels is the bewilderingly busy schedule of modern life by providing more data to sort through daily. In his typically comical approach,[9] Levi joked about how Pinterest was generating heaps of problems for stay-at-home moms by creating visual party-planning standards that are impossible to match. The combination of Instagram, other social media, social justice activism,[10] daily work, employment duties, children's schedules, school obligations, and other mounting pressures, including "all the unfriending and likes" going on online, added up to confusion and overstimulation. Levi argues that people are now experiencing "a lot of things kinda coming at us from all directions." Similarly, Garrett would later classify "2017 American culture" as constituted by "instantaneity," "speed," and "everything quick and immediate." Through the increase of technological presence embodied by promiscuous media, people claim to be losing even more time and not saving it as computer programmers in the 1980s and 1990s envisioned.[11]

According to Levi, with visual platforms such as Instagram, which portray aesthetically pleasing images of travel or interesting life events, we feel both anxiety and "a nagging sense of shame" or despair that we're not living as compelling or adventurous lives as those we encounter online.[12] For Levi, the complexities and multisource anxieties of modern lifestyles of connection and mediation are a wonder of technological progress. At the same time, these connections ramp up the speed and anxiety in which modern people feel trapped. Levi then turns to his expository text for the day, Colossians 2. He notes that learning from Paul can help to "cut out some of that stuff and get at what is simple and pure and to anchor ourselves there." In a subsequent sermon, Garrett would later employ Pauline agricultural metaphors to suggest an antidote lifestyle of meaning, slowness, and durability. Biblical teaching, along with other spiritual disciplines inculcated by Church on the Margins, intends to defend against the anxieties of informational excess and connective overload in the present. Yet, ironies abound. In the service mentioned above, for instance, Levi issued his criticisms and then urged the congregants to open either a Bible "or a Bible app" to access the texts relevant for that Sunday. Media ideologies and use in emerging communities are complex.

In the summer of 2016, while meeting in the dance studio, service leaders discussed the tragedies of the previous week's news items that they had encountered through online media. On one Sunday, congregants tearfully discussed a recent shooting in Dallas and the ongoing structural injustices helpfully exposed and publicized by the Black Lives Matter movement. "We mourn the emergence of these divisions," the service leader commented, reflecting on the increased exposure to such events and the resulting fear, sadness, and grief that the awareness extolled. Implied microcommentaries such as these get at another negative implication of social media use. Social media do not simply add stress by way of information excess to modern lives. In the lives of these Midwesterners, social media also exacerbate fragmentation and division. The answer to the growing tension is to gather directly together with people in diverse communities and pray and heal together. The service ended with a somber, interactive prayer refrain: "For the families of those killed and injured this week, Lord, hear our prayers."

Social media also serve as a platform for fragmentation and divisiveness within Christianity itself. In a 2017 sermon in the storefront location, Garrett preached on 1 Corinthians but spent a good portion of the sermon tying materials back to social media. "You can get in a lot of Facebook fights over stuff in 1 Corinthians," Garrett joked, and the congregation responded with laughter. But under the initial level of lighthearted comedy lies a weighted criticism against new media and Christian uses of it. Paul may have "just basically called them a bunch of babies," according to Garrett's narration of the passage concerning the apostle's accusations against the church at Corinth, but at least "he didn't tweet it."

The pastor then shifted focus, moving from the ancient Middle East to the Information Age. He mourned the amplified degree of Christian outrage that he observed in online realms and worried that social media publicize "a lot of correctives and rebukes" by Christians against lifestyles they do not approve of. Even here, biblical teaching—and indeed, Pauline models—may serve as antidotes to the increased tensions that people currently experience. What if Christians on social media mirrored "Paul's thankfulness and gratitude, even in and amidst rebuke?"

"The church has suffered greatly in the last year and the witness of the church has been damaged," Garrett continued, attributing social media as a primary cause of this damaged witness. "What if before voicing offense, we affirmed belovedness?" he inquired. "What if we voiced our thankfulness for the fact that we're allowed to have a Facebook account" because there are places in the world that do not have such availability? To conclude the service, Garrett led the congregation in a focused, embodied spiritual discipline activity that he called the "Breathe Prayer Exercise," a ritual involving taking note of one's breathing and reciting prayer segments on inward and outward breaths.[13] Such an experience intended to center the worshippers and ameliorate the ills of the social media–saturated "outrage culture." Behind me, I recorded in my field notes for the day, while kids in the back row entertained themselves with games on an iPad Mini. Later, during a follow-up sermon in the same series, Levi would confirm Garrett's worries about Christian divisiveness on social media. "Everywhere you look there is division," he pointed out. "Our communities are very divided." Differing Christian political allegiances and divisiveness online is doing little more than "dismembering" the Body of Christ.

SOCIAL MEDIA AS DISCURSIVE MEDIA

Congregant discourse about social media confirms the pastors' impressions of its effects as promiscuous media platforms. Facebook and Twitter serve as venues for divisiveness, fragmentation, and contestation. In this section, I draw on firsthand conversations, online fieldwork, and an extensive body of survey data to document congregant impressions about social media as a venue for both dialogue and confrontation. For these evangelicals, contestation is an attendant effect of promiscuous media. Operating as digitally buffered selves means that difference and disagreement is always just around the corner.

According to one community member, "My Facebook feed is constantly . . . full of politically charged comments and 'discussions.' I find that people (from all sides) say and post things that are downright mean." Another person notes, "I see a lot of arguments between Christians about differing theologies behind political policies as well." Facebook contestation among Christians, for another, is largely made up of "choir-preaching, followed by applause or outrage in response." For this evangelical, because most of their social media contacts fall to the ideological left, they witness primarily "left-leaning choir-preaching." Warren, a Facebook friend and Church on the Margins community member, once pointed out via the medium itself that he experiences "social media induced anxiety" because of the constant online contestation.

Subjects of discursive contestation run the gamut online. In no particular order, and in their own words, Church on the Margins congregants list "abortion," "bathrooms," "creation[ism]," "doctrine," "equal rights," "gays," "gay marriage," "guns," "liberal media," "presidents," "politics," "race," "Trump," "the moral failings of Christianity," "the moral failings of atheism," "women's rights," "world views," "theological topics, such as God's nature, sovereignty, character, etc.," "comments against the gay community," "nationalism," "progressive posts on religion," "religion," "Revelation . . . and the end of the world," "comments on alcohol," "bad theology," "the proper handling and interpretation of 'high profile Christian' books, persons, and ideas," and "the US ban on refugees," among other similar topics, as issues of constant social media debate.[14]

The above list includes topical contestations that Church on the Margins attendees have observed online among social networks. But emerging evangelicals, when asked to report their own immediate online deliberations with friends, family, and colleagues, report a highly diverse set of norms in terms of direct discursive engagement. As to the question of engagement in online contestation, activities are similarly plastic. Emerging evangelicals, simply put, do not agree over the merits or demerits of online argument and discursive dialogue.

On one side, a significant number of respondents submitted a curt negation, expressing that they engage in little to no direct contestations. Rationale varies. Some find the dialogical process "too exhausting" or claim that online argument "doesn't change anyone's mind." Others avoid deliberation "because it doesn't do much." Arguments via social media are simply ineffective. Some people do not reject theological or political dialogue or argument out of hand but riffing off thick media ideologies about authenticity, mark social media as "not the real platform for that" kind of interaction. Proper engagement ought to be conducted elsewhere. "If I want to engage, or someone tries to engage me, I take it to a private conversation. That sort of thing isn't for a forum," this respondent continues. Other people agree. They conclude that the internet is "a very bad place to have a serious, productive conversation." Language of this sort rejects the authenticity, legitimacy, and value of online discourse, refusing social media's status as an "appropriate venue" for dialogue. Operationalized media ideologies abound—in this case, discourses of negativity or ambivalence—causing some communicants to "refuse to engage in arguments online."

On the other side, a group of respondents do engage online. Sometimes they take to social media feeds themselves, noting the embedded ironies of their actions and calling for civil and open public conversation. One person occasionally posts thoughts "on either politics or spirituality, usually when a wider debate is happening publicly over a given topic." Congregants post out of an anger to the negativity they experience their fellow Christians spreading against gay friends and family. "I have a problem seeing people make posts damning people to hell without making a comment about that being wrong," this respondent notes. In other words, online engagement can serve the purpose of progressive Christian activism. Congregants post Instagram images of themselves in urban centers taking part in marches for women's rights and gender equality. Others advocate textually for refugees, calling out political authorities whose policies they view as putting marginalized people in danger. Another person notes that their criteria for engagement requires passion about the subject at hand. If this person reads something they feel strongly about, they will share and comment "in an attempt to promote fair-mindedness." Occasionally people play the role of devil's advocate or provocateur by questioning ideological opponents about "the reasons for their positions and unspoken assumptions." Engagements of this sort are not necessarily snarky but intend to generate quality discussion with people one does not ideologically, politically, or theologically align with.

Whether ideologically conservative or liberal, measured rationale and intentional restraint for engaging in discussion online appears to be the rule for this community. "Since I have a very conservative background (political and religious)," an informant writes, "I see lots of posts and comments I disagree with." But this communicant decides to engage only "when I think there's potential for real discussion," or in an activist slant, if they observe someone "treating others wrongly" online. Others "rarely engage in political or theological arguments online," "try to stay out of it for the most part," or engage only when they "think it's an important enough discussion to waste time (and emotional/social capital) on, which is no longer very often." Still others join online arguments and contestations "only very lightly [sic]," "not often," "very infrequently," or "not typically." Several people resist engaging in contestation and "try to stay out of it as much as possible" but still find themselves inevitably drawn in. More reticent social media users engage "only if I can be suckered into it" or "try to avoid engaging" but too easily "get sucked in."

Emerging evangelicals describe social media contestation as having several identifiable effects. Predictably, part of the effect of online dialogical contestation is negative or social fragmentation. "I've argued with and been blocked by two ultraconservative, Pentecostal cousins," one respondent admits, reflecting the congregation's broader uneasiness with traditional Pentecostalism, which circulates even within sermon discourse. Another person sees online argument as feeding into or legitimizing their non-Christian and international friends' notions "that Christians just love to fight about God." Others agree under the conviction that contestation engenders not much more than mutual judgment and disrespect. "I think these discussions rarely bear fruit on social media," one person worries. Engaging online compounds for others the feeling of growing "overwhelmed" or "weary." Social media engagements generate undue stress and anxiety.

Discourses among evangelicals about the appropriateness of social media for some tasks and not others sometimes develop into highly specific taxonomies of use. Two extended examples will suffice. First, consider the differentiation one of the pastors makes regarding the discursive uses of media like Facebook or Twitter:

> I feel as a pastor that it's important to share my pastoral voice when it might be beneficial or to take a stand for ideas that I think accurately represent Jesus's heart (as opposed to ways Jesus might typically be characterized by the church). At the same time, I often leave those conversations weary, wondering if

anyone changed at all from their preconceived positions. I don't think social media is a helpful platform for challenging/convicting messaging—that usually results in people just digging in on their previously held position. But I do think it's helpful for edifying those who already agree with similar ideas or are beginning to want to think about political or theological topics differently. (This is both good and bad as it eventually leads to a feedback loop.)

For this authority in the community, voice—recall the progressive feminist bloggers' use of this communicative and identity-related category—is crucial as it benefits others and publicizes correct theology and conviction. This pastor resists mainstream evangelical depictions of Jesus. He engages, selectively, but also experiences a weariness from online engagements. Finally, the pastor differentiates an evaluative typology of religious use. Social media fail at "challenging/convicting" but excel at "edifying."[15] Social media are a recurrent feedback loop of negativity and positivity.

Second, take note of a nonpastoral, lay typology of online contestation. For one particularly eloquent informant, social media contestations fall into one of two camps: "(1) Incendiary posts (usually political) meant to rally those who agree and aggravate those who disagree; these usually result in lots of useless angry energy and posturing from behind computer screens and (2) lively debates from a narrow contingent of friends on Facebook who, while rife with strongly held views, are informed, respectful, actually engaging with each other's thoughts and generally aware of argumentation principles."

Like the pastoral interpretation above, one observes evaluative typologies of "correct" and "incorrect" use arising around new media practices. For this person, the first category of **incendiary posts**—akin to what researchers have called online **flaming language** (e.g., Moor 2007)—is dismissed as a less productive form of dialogical communication. Note this respondent's wording and prose. Exploiting the promiscuous aspects of social media, incendiary posts "rally," "aggravate," and produce "useless angry energy and posturing." The second category, lively debates, also promotes "strongly held views" but does so in "informed," "respectful," and "actually engaging" postures rather than inflammatory ones. In both the pastoral and layperson's descriptive taxonomies of online interactions, one could observe and analyze social customs, rules, norms, and mores coming into existence as they reify through descriptive elaboration (and application). Promiscuous media have some ill-effects, but the results are not all bad. Normative typologies are beginning to establish the rules and social protocol for online engagement. Standards for authentic and inauthentic interactions are coming into existence not only regarding online contestation, in general, but also related to other social media tools and apps, such as digital Bibles.

DIGITAL BIBLES AND INAUTHENTICITY

One domain of contestation about new media and authenticity is the recent rise of digital Bibles. To a degree, these apps relate back to the promiscuous media paradigm of the Reformation in that they help to spread canonical texts widely. I have noted that pastors sometimes encourage congregants to use iPhones to access scriptural texts. My observations suggest that service leaders equivocate on the matter, encouraging data phone access of the lectionary readings by the audience but also railing against the onslaught of technologies from the pulpit. Beyond full acceptance of this new biblical medium, emerging evangelicals issue a wide range of opinions. Enveloped in rhetoric about digital scripture, media durability or ephemerality, and textual materiality, media ideologies shape and define how evangelicals feel technology ought to be used. Some evangelicals prefer print Bibles as material objects; others prefer digital versions for biblical studies and comparative translation reasons. As hyperpromiscuous media, digital Bibles take the original promiscuity of the print-and-bound text to an unimagined level.

As with social media contestations, users take contrasting stances here. Some evangelicals "almost always" use digital Bibles; others "rarely" or "never" do. Most respondents appear to engage in mixed or hybridized reading habits, putting to use both hard copy—a traditionally printed and bound Bible—and social Bible apps. Rationale for hybrid media use is decidedly pragmatic. "Each has advantages," one person explains. "I don't prefer one over the other. I use what I have at hand." One respondent prefers a digital Bible during "daily quiet time" but not necessarily in other contexts. Another informant details that they prefer a physical Bible "mostly at home" but use "digital on the go and for quick reference." Digital versions are convenient when one is traveling, "on the run," or "out of the house." The home versus away dichotomy does make practical sense. As one person comments, "I utilize the Bible app for on-the-go purposes, i.e. at church on Sunday. If I am studying scripture, I use a physical Bible." Aside from pragmatic considerations about "easy access," mobility, and convenience, several informants argue that digital Bibles are preferable over physical ones for the purposes of careful comparative study. Digital Bibles allow for the comparison of a wide range of Bible translations (and languages) in a matter of seconds. For informants who study scriptures in the original Hebrew and Greek, digital Bible apps provide a convenient platform for comparative scholarship. According to one congregant, "Digital versions are better because I can cross-reference views between different translations." Comments such as this one, replete with normative posturing (i.e., the digital being "better" than the material), stem from in-process media ideologies.

Confirming what one researcher (Hutchings 2015, 153) argues about YouVersion, one of the most popular social media and Bible reading apps available on the smartphone market, evangelicals put to use the "persuasive technology" of Bible apps because it reduces "the daunting task of developing a regular reading habit to a fixed daily routine of short, specified texts and allowing the reader to track their progress." Bible apps also serve as platforms for intergroup surveillance in that users may post devotional progress publicly and thus feel an obligation to meet their daily reading requirements because their activity is monitored semipublicly by their social networks (153, 154). "I do prefer a digital Bible for my current reading purposes," one Church on the Margins congregant notes. "I enjoy the 'plan' feature of the digital bible, which gives me an allotted amount to read every day." Another person confirms using the app "for a daily reading plan." "Having 'reading plans' is too nice," another person notes of the convenient structuredness of reading apps. Devotional Bible apps are reconfiguring both daily ritual practices and the ways the religious communities maintain boundaries through networked accountability.

Other congregants use digital Bibles only sparingly, noting that they "prefer to read a print version" over the digital. Looking closer at user rationale reveals the media ideologies and ideological hierarchies at play in these discussions about digital Bible apps. Why do over half of respondents (twenty-six respondents or 52 percent) opt for material over digital? "I prefer [a] physical Bible because I can write in it, it doesn't hurt my eyes after reading for a long time, I don't have to scroll to see the whole passage, and it just feels better to hold an actual Bible," one person submits. Another person waxes poetically about the medium of print: "I prefer a physical Bible. I am a 'book' person and love to be able to read from real books." This respondent, who falls in the forty-five to fifty-four age bracket, argues that "I like to be able to write in the margins, hold the book, turn the pages physically, and know that it is its own entity and not a small part of a billion other things on a smartphone."

In contrast to the worries of some of the evangelical technology writers discussed in chapter 3, respondent age, at least in the small sample size of the Church on the Margins congregation, does not appear to be a significant factor in terms of preferences toward print or digital. "I'm old enough that I'm more used to physical books," one respondent between the age of twenty-five and thirty-four explains. "I feel more connected to it when it's an actual book," she continues. "I find it easier to read a physical book than a digital one. I also think it's easier to flip around and go back and reread passages in a physical copy, and I also sometimes highlight or bookmark things in my Bible." Preferences for the tactility of a hard copy Bible emerge across the age brackets. A physical Bible, for those in their twenties and thirties as much as for those in their forties and fifties, is functionally "easier to hold" and is "more comfortable."[16] Others "like the feel of reading words on paper and turning pages" or enjoy "the feel of books" in their hands. Note the normative language at work in still another respondent's claim that "a real Bible feels better" than a digital one. Media preferences and evaluations link directly to discussions about the authentic and the inauthentic. "Feeling," "tactility," and other appeals to textual materiality loom large, but a hybridity of print and digital uses is common on the ground.

To put the matter succinctly, congregants are divided over the question of print versus digital. Some respondents can find scripture passages "a lot faster flipping through pages or using the index/concordance," but others categorically disagree, writing that it is "easier to find verses" on digital platforms complete with keyword search options. "Digital is quick" in terms of locating and inputting notes on passages. One might think that everyone would agree that data phones, in their portability, win out in terms of sheer convenience, but consensus is hardly the case. Occasionally congregants argue that physical Bibles are more convenient because they can be used "without charging or need for electricity to charge."

Antidigital language tends to coalesce around several points of concern: distraction, screen inundation, diminished reading retention, annotation and textual markup issues, attendant eye strain, length of reading duration, and interrupted flow. "I use a physical Bible because I find I am less likely to be distracted by other notifications if I were to use one on my phone/device," one person argues. The physical or print version for someone else "feels more intimate, and there are less distractions when you are focused on the reading material itself." "Despite my current habit, I do prefer a physical Bible. It doesn't have the thousands of built-in distractions my iPhone does." For this present group of negative responses, one "can make notes and highlight easier" in hard copy print form. "I retain information better with physical books," someone confirms. "I also like to annotate, which is much easier with a physical Bible." Physical Bibles for another person are better "because I can underline easier" and "it is less strain on my eyes." Some people "read more of the Bible with a physical copy than with a digital copy." As still others narrate, "I prefer a physical Bible for the same reason that I prefer print media in general: It is very hard for me to enter a focused, 'flow' reading state when the internet is at hand." Media ideologies and material preferences direct the ways users approach texts.

In sum, media ideologies transmitted both by broader Western reading habits and specific religious traditions shape the ways evangelicals interpret and make use of digital media technologies. Ideologies come clearly to the fore when one compares an older medium with a newer one. Congregants at Church on the Margins put digital Bibles to frequent use for various purposes. They describe digital media as convenient and helpful for specific tasks. At the same time, congregants also employ a hierarchy of media preference, and many appear to describe the material Bible in print form as more rewarding than digital apps.[17] The takeaway from this discussion is that new media ideologies (and their attendant applications in practice) are profoundly plastic and malleable. As the next section suggests, ideologies and practices about new media are also highly contentious and range from debates about the value of digital Bibles to the evolving sense of the term "friend."

EXPANSIONS AND DEGRADATIONS OF "FRIENDSHIP" IN THE SOCIAL MEDIA AGE

If Bible apps and involvement in social media contestation are important areas of concern for emerging evangelicals in the digital era, how are conceptions of sociality, community, and friendship changing? The average person can no longer separate as easily between "friends," "family," or "colleagues." One now has Facebook "friends" and Twitter and Instagram "followers." How are emerging evangelicals concerned with creating and maintaining authentic, close-knit communities responding to these reconfiguring modes of sociality? How are promiscuous media influencing social formation? In this section, I focus on discussions about the expanded sociolinguistic register of the "friend" category after Facebook's emergence.

Simply put, are Facebook friends *friends*? I posed this very question to congregants at Church on the Margins. The diverse replies proved insightful in documenting how emerging evangelicals are conceiving of friendship and community building both online and offline. In general, this tight-knit community replicates the Reformed Christian (and, by extension, Western) standard of media sincerity in which the face-to-face dimension is the gold standard for real, meaningful, or authentic communication.[18] In short, as I will discuss, Church on the Margins as a collective does not consider Facebook friends as friends. In other words, for congregants one negative effect of promiscuous media is a cheapening of social bonds. To be more precise, if social media friends are friends, they qualify as such only in a diminished, less valuable, more artificial sort of way. For the sake of analytical clarity, in this section I make a distinction between *Friends*^{1}, as so-called real-world friendships, and *Friends*^{2}, or those social connections, mediated online, which are reminiscent of but somehow less than traditional friendship.

Friends^2 are, as one informant puts it, "social friends," which are similar to Friends^1 but fail to meet the criteria of the "real-life encounter." Friends^2 are the kind of people that a person feels the need to "keep up with what they are doing in life but aren't necessarily close friends." "Meaningful conversations" must occur outside of Facebook. One response is relatively strict in terms of the face-to-face or embodied criteria. As this person argues, Facebook friends, in an ideal situation, ought to be "people that I've met at some point in my life." Embodied, physical, face-to-face presence is required by this definition.

A second respondent's comments, worth quoting at length, map closely with the strict differentiation between Friends[1] and Friends[2]: "I only follow and comment on friends' posts who I see on a somewhat regular basis. All others I don't follow, and if I see a post by them, I often don't bother to comment, as I don't see it worth my time. When I actually interact with human friends in real life, often what someone has posted comes up, and I appreciate having seen their post on Facebook, and I can contribute to the conversation."

Likewise, Friends[1] include those persons seen "on a somewhat regular basis." Friends[1] must map onto real-life experience. By implication, this second person does have online linkages of the Friends[2] category, but they do not necessarily follow their category two friends' online activities and "often don't bother to comment, as I don't see it worth my time." One observes in this example how users seeking after authentic online experiences conceive of social media as an extension of already existing social and friendship connections in the world. Communicants make other lesser connections, but such secondary connections are symbolically and relationally devalued. Friends[2] mean something to this informant but not nearly as much as Friends[1]. Evaluative hierarchies of social connection are arising as social media become ever more integrated into everyday life.

The concept of Facebook as socially supplemental, extensional, or aggregative of already existing social ties is for the most part shared among my respondents. "Facebook, I believe, is effective at facilitating communication in preexisting friendships, not necessarily facilitating friendships precluding an intimate, face-to-face context," a congregant submits, thus reifying the gold standard for human communication. In other words, Facebook extends and adapts but does not originate authentic friendship, at least not according to the standards of media sincerity. "I do find Facebook to be a useful form of communication between people who are already 'real friends' (i.e., scheduling times to meet up in person or sharing photos)," another person continues. "But I think if you are not already real friends, Facebook alone will not get you to that point." Another informant clarifies the matter: "Facebook isn't a platform I use to create new friends, but it can be a tool to help strengthen existing friendship." Lastly, another person puts the matter in an even finer point: "If you are already friends with a Facebook friend, [Facebook] can add connectivity." Facebook "helps facilitate friendships with those who are truly 'real world' friends, in that I'm able to stay updated on their life or engage with them in fun or supportive ways throughout the week."

In this vein of media ambivalence or even suspicion (Ribak and Rosenthal 2015), Facebook can only be supplemental and thus socially partial or incomplete. For some, Facebook is not much more than a "snapshot" of friends' lives.

To employ another useful analogy, Facebook is nothing more than "an expanded address book," which "facilitates" but "doesn't create friendship." Facebook "can be conducive to friendship but only if the friendship is or has previously been established in real-time interaction as well." One cultivates both Frindship[1] and Friendship[2] but a clear hierarchy of value is emerging to distinguish them. One sometimes adds or accepts online friendships but only out of social obligation or necessity. As one congregant argues, on Facebook one accepts friend requests to avoid hurting the friend requester's feelings by denying the acceptance.

Furthermore, Facebook may sometimes serve as a stimulating and generative platform that has the potential—albeit limited by many factors—to incubate Friendship[1]-level friendships. Friends[2] "are people that I consider people I like." Although "whether they have made it to being [Friends[1]] is up in the air," this person continues, "I have positive feelings toward them." Another evangelical argues to the affirmative that Facebook can "be used to facilitate friendship effectively" but clarifies that such transition in friendship levels is hard and strenuous work, writing that "in only 50 percent of my Facebook use would I say *real friendship* is being facilitated" (emphasis added). One congregant explains that Friends[2] social links are "better described as acquaintances" or as "interlocking virtual communities"—note the distancing work that both the "acquaintances" and "virtual" terms do—but admits that Friends[2] are assuming more and more agency as social media evolve. Facebook friends thus "perform certain social roles associated with friendship, such as celebrating, grieving, and supporting," roles traditionally "performed by one's community (neighbors, business associates)." For some informants, the gap between Friends[1] and Friends[2] may be shrinking.

Yet, the diminishment of value and authenticity that occurs in the shift from Friends[1] to Friends[2] is severe across the board. Friends[2] exist "just on the surface as far as friendships go." "Facebook friends only tend to be very surface-level friends with no real depth of connection." The people that informants "really care about" tend to fall into the Friends[1] category. On this view, Friends[1] are embodied and actual, not virtual. One sees them in person and builds relations with them in real life. One shares life with them in a way that includes but expands far past social linkages made and maintained online. Friends[2], on the contrary, bear with them a degree of removal and absence. Friends[2] are somewhat contrived and artificial—even if they are necessary and inevitable. In short, congregants deny that Facebook's "general friends list equates to real friendship." Friends[2] are "just acquaintances." Friends[2] lack authenticity, depth, presence, and value. Friends[2] "aren't real friends." In the shift from Friendship[1] to Friendship[2], social or interpersonal intimacy decreases as "friendship quality lessens." The authenticity of this node of sociality diminishes. Sincerity is difficult to achieve when social bonds are occurring over promiscuous media networks.

One must keep in mind that even though Friends[2] are comparatively devalued in terms of authenticity and worth, most users still maintain that Friends[2] are to some degree socially valuable. As one person contends, "Only Facebook friends who I speak to/see on a regular basis [i.e., Friends[1]] are 'real.' The others are friends [i.e., Friends[2]] in the sense that we share some common past, interest, or history." Be it acquaintances, colleagues, and high school classmates, fellow employees from past employment, informants enjoy the links and connections facilitated to some aspects of these peoples' lives, even if such relational-informational overload might be leading toward anxiety. As another person documents, "I have 1350 friends on Facebook, and there is no way I could maintain 'friendships' with that many people." Social overload leads to increases in discursive engagement, polarization, and frustration. Social media connections—complete with the broadening out of the linguistic category of the "friend"—"can make people appear harsh, legalistic, crazy, etc." For the most decisive of technology critics at Church on the Margins with social media, "All you are left with" is "blurbs and words." Friends[2] connections thus "tend toward assumption, judgment, frustration, misunderstanding, or annoyance" in that communicants "put each other in boxes and keep each other there because we don't have any *real-world* evidence to challenge that box" (emphasis added). These measured technological criticisms harbor complex and divergent philosophies of social media use that challenge mainstream journalism's frequent claims that most Americans are technology addicts.

AUTHENTICITY, AUTHORITY, AND THE PARADIGM OF MESSINESS

So far this chapter has discussed social media ambivalence as it relates to discourses about the authentic and inauthentic. But a still-unanswered question has to do with structures of power and authority in emerging evangelical communities and how such discussions link back to the authenticity discourse. As with the evangelical technology manuals in chapter 3, authenticity and authority are intimately conjoined concepts. The situation is similar for progressive evangelicals in the American Midwest. Pauline Hope Cheong (2013, 74–82) has identified two logics at play concerning the relationship of power and authority in digital arenas. A **logic of displacement and disjuncture** assumes that traditional structures of authority dissolve online due to affordances (what I would qualify as promiscuous affordances) of new media for democratic and populist activism. A second **logic of continuity and complementarity**, rather, assumes that religious institutions can accommodate and extend their authoritative domain to include and encompass the online. Both logics are in operation in the Midwest and either one may take precedent depending on the context and situation at hand. New media, after all, are demonstrably plastic media that shape and conform to not only designers' and platform architects' intentions but also users' divergent media ideologies and applied uses in everyday life. Promiscuous media, to put the matter differently, have multiple effects.

As a theologically eclectic and ecclesially progressive community, Church on the Margins is a unique case. In a word, Church on the Margins rejects out of hand traditional Protestant models of authority. For now I focus on ecclesial structures rather than communicative systems, but I will return to this latter topic at the end of the chapter. From the church's inception, communal or shared leadership strategies dominated over centralized headship models. To embody, model, and define the communally centered leadership structure, Church on the Margins began with three head pastors. These pastors cultivated different leadership and pastoral styles but made clear their intent to shift or mitigate typical church power structures by literally spreading out authority and leadership among the group. As Pastor Jonathan explained over several sermons in 2012, Church on the Margins aspires toward the organizational form of the "collaborative community" and "multiheaded" leadership model. Jonathan's goal was for Church on the Margins to fall, in his own words, somewhere between "totalitarianism and anarchy." His intent was an organizational and ecclesial middle way.

Shared-leadership models in combination with the evangelical theology (and influential media ideology) of the "priesthood of all believers" working in the background make for a lively experiment in authority and leadership. Pastors often posture themselves as humble; they intentionally project humility and fallibility as leaders. The pastors frequently claim no significant increase in access to reservoirs of theological and ecclesial power over their congregants. They promote a radically populist approach to ecclesiology that places the gift of everyday theological formation—"doing theology," as they put it—into the hands of the congregants and community. Leaders encourage congregant participation and interaction at every level of organization, call for and endorse frequent guest speakers from among congregant ranks, occasionally solicit in-service interactions and feedback via smartphone technologies, and seek volunteers to contribute to music activities, Bible studies, small groups, community gatherings, food-related events, and a wide range of other activities considered by the church pertinent to maintaining an authentic community.

In addition, as a group that self-identifies as a nontraditional church on the fringes of mainstream Christian practice, Church on the Margins is acutely aware of the processes of boundary maintenance, distancing mechanisms, and normative evaluations that take place as Christian subgroups attempt to create identities by establishing their differences to other Christian groups. Church on the Margins often described itself as a community that plays the role of "refuge" and "pathway." The definition of the latter term came under much deliberation and debate during my years of fieldwork in the community. Deliberations sometimes resulted in families leaving the community due to differences in opinion about how theological discipleship ought to take place. As a "refuge," however, Church on the Margins postured itself as a place of comfort, rest, and shelter for Christians (or otherwise) who had been burned by traditional evangelicalism and needed a safe space in which to heal and recoup theologically, spiritually, and psychologically.

One example illustrates the pastors' cultivation of the community—including its physical space—as a safe space. As Pastor Levi posted on Facebook directly after the election of Donald Trump as the president of the United States, Church on the Margins is a haven "of refuge and safety. If you need a place to pray and take a break from the newsfeed, I'll be here." In short, Church on the Margins aimed to serve as an inclusive ecclesial structure that is welcoming of anyone and everyone. Furthermore, the church adopted and sanctified the discourse of "messiness," referring to the casual organization and structure of their weekly services, the bricolage of the church's combined theological perspectives, and the process of living in so-called real and authentic communities. Life is messy and coming together in defiance of myriad levels of difference—organized under a love for Christ—became Church on the Margin's frequently repeated mantra.

Messiness is a congregational aesthetic and group "culture" (as community members put it), but it also, I argue, serves as an encompassing media ideology incorporated at the local level. One can think about messiness as a third paradigm added to the already existing tension between the media sincerity and promiscuity. Another way to think about the new paradigm, however, would be not as an exclusive third category but as the successful compromise or synthesis between the other two. Messiness, to be more precise, is for this congregation sincerity redefined through the lenses of promiscuity and promiscuity challenged and limited through the lenses of sincerity. Messiness allows for the possibility of ironing out the seeming incongruities between historical evangelical models of communication.

The ideology of messiness applies in multiple directions. Both social media and sermon discourse, for instance, often worked toward this inclusive, blurred boundary and thus "messy" effect. On one occasion, Pastor Levi took to Facebook directly following a Church on the Margins "Family Meeting" to write, "I looked around the room tonight and realized how awesome it is to have these people in our lives- other parents of kids at various ages, single people, empty-nesters, young couples, college students, liberals, conservatives, professionals, homeless, gay, straight, broken, healed, confident, insecure, etc. And it hit me (again): This is church. It's not convenient, easy, or a weekly one hour service. It's not like-minded friends. It's family. I love Church on the Margins."

On the subject of boundaries, during one sermon in 2017, Levi spent a good part of his discussion problematizing evangelical boundary maintenance strategies. Illustrating his claims via Venn diagrams on Power Point, Levi discussed two different models of social organization: the "bounded set" and the "centered set." In the bounded set, small discrete entities arise that are in competition with one another and identify everyone outside of the set's immediate periphery as exotic, other, and heterodox. Alternatively, in the centered set, the boundaries dissolve and the previously separate social entities merge haphazardly together, centered on a core identifying theme.[19] Such a centered set organizational model illustrates Church on the Margins's adherence to ecclesial inclusivism based on a Christocentric model. Christians can (and should) disagree politically, theologically, and socially, Levi taught, but dissention ought not to invalidate one's Christian identity in the eyes of others. In this manner, leaders conceived of the church as a theologically, ecclesially, socially, culturally, and politically diverse and eclectic space, organized loosely and messily around identity as Christ followers. Messiness became a theological and social value.

I pointed out earlier the church's affiliation with the Vineyard Movement or the Association of Vineyard Churches. Church on the Margins' association with this evangelical quasi- or antidenomination[20] corresponds closely with the congregation's nonhierarchical and shared leadership structure. As scholars of the movement attest, the Vineyard is itself a hybrid combination "of the nationally politically powerful Evangelical movement and the demographically diverse and globally powerful Pentecostal movement." The ecclesial entity is a diverse and institutionally decentralized "association of like-minded churches" or "movement" founded by John Wimber, a born-again Southern Californian (Bialecki 2017, xv). As an egalitarian charismatic movement, the Vineyard has historically sought to balance between biblical authority and the contemporary experience of the Holy Spirit, a "flexibility between the textual and experiential," as Bialecki puts it (6, 15, 25). The Vineyard in its early years was "an amalgam of the disparate landscape of late 1970s conservative Southern California Christianity" and "an odd mix of hippy-like Jesus people, middle-class evangelicals, and seminary-based Christian intellectuals" (16). The Vineyard's flexibility has meant that it has largely been open to new media developments and hospitable toward digital media as an extension of the church.

Made up of postindustrial, white-collar workers and Jesus followers, Church on the Margins, broadly conceived, continues in this eclectic evangelical tradition—even if this local instance switches out hippies for hipsters and seminarians with Research 1 university undergraduate and graduate students. Over lunch with Pastor Levi at Falafels Middle Eastern Grill in Bloomington's Fourth Street ethnic-foods district, he explained to me the process whereby the community had gone about researching denominations in an effort to locate an authoritative religious body to affiliate with. The goal was to find an evangelical structure that shared Church on the Margins's inchoate theological variety and appreciated its preference for innovative leadership styles. Levi explained that the Vineyard above all others, with its anti-institutional identity, loose organizational form, and decentered power structures, strongly appealed to the fledgling group of emerging evangelicals. The pastors then went through the process of pursuing and securing official affiliation as part of the Vineyard Churches. As Levi narrated to me, the goal was to find some sort of ecclesial form with which to hold their own actions and those of their new congregation accountable but at the same time become part of a system that would allow them to carry out their vision of appropriate Christianity.

The organizational multiplicity, diffused power, and theologically eclectic ideals of Church on the Margins bleed over into its ideologies of media and uses in everyday life. As one media scholar (Teusner 2013) discovered in his research on an Australian emerging church's blogging strategies, a church's online practices often mirror the structures of authority embedded in its offline social structure. But paradoxes also arise since although groups "challenge institutional structures and patterns of authority, they must also confront and adapt to these same patterns and structures online" (Teusner 2013, 188). Regarding the challenging of institutions, recall the highly deliberated arguments about online contestation engaged by Church on the Margins attendees. Some congregants use social media for activist purposes, not to mention theological, political, or social contestation. Such activities, whether congregants realize it or not, are boundary maintenance strategies for calling out error, addressing wrongdoing (or wrongheaded belief), and normative posturing. Even the most inclusive subcultural entities must engage in some form of boundary maintenance to survive (Cooper 2017c). Recalling Levi's illustrations, social media arguments about theology are akin to reinforcing bounded sets rather than centered Christocentric ones.

It is no wonder, then, that Church on the Margins's pastors in their sermons conceive of new media as at least partially divisive, socially corrosive, overwhelming, distracting, and dangerous to one's spiritual well-being. Such pastoral suspicions or ambivalence about social media are akin to Cheong's (2013) logic of continuity and complementarity in that leaders on the ground, regardless of how decentralized and collaborative they purport to be, extend their influences into online domains. Thus, as one leader contested on Facebook, "The conservative right does not get to lay exclusive claim to the beauty of the story and example of Jesus, who laid his life down for his enemies so the world could be healed and made whole again." The ability to mark entities as authentic or inauthentic, after all, is one of the clearest identifiers or signals of the possession of authority (Hoover 2016, 5).

But what about the logic of displacement and disjuncture (Cheong 2013), the claim "that digital media could act as a solvent to religious hierarchy, empowering individuals to form their own networks and practices, find new information, and evade official supervision" (Hutchings 2015, 143)? As authorities in a somewhat progressive community, Church on the Margins' leaders—as self-identifying evangelical marginals—embrace the potential of internet-mediated technologies to challenge entrenched or traditional or historical Protestant structures, norms, and mores. Again, irony abounds as evangelicals criticize technology even as they exploit that same technology for its very affordances. Social media, therefore, exist for Church on the Margins to at least some degree as a necessary arena of identity and social maintenance. Pastors and laypeople use social media to debate and contend with evangelical theological and sociopolitical others. They also use it to ameliorate the issues brought into existence by social media. As congregants explain the matter, the situation is "messy."

Discourses of authenticity and authority, then, work hand in hand with the paradigms of sincerity, promiscuity, and messiness. One pertinent example of this complex relationship concerns the use of podcasting technology to circulate Church on the Margins' sermons and the role of other podcasts as sources of authority in the everyday lives of Church on the Margins community members. Podcast media illustrate how intermeshed the discourses of authenticity and authority can be, even as they further confirm the advancement of mobile, habitual, quotidian media into everyday lives.

TWITTER PASTORS, PODCASTS, AND THE OUTSOURCING (AND UPLOADING) OF AUTHORITY

Before a guest speaker's sermon one fall service, Garrett and Levi explained to the congregation how they had met the visitor. The preacher for the day, a self-professed ex-fundamentalist and church planter, was among a list of religious authorities that Garrett and Levi endearingly described as their "Twitter pastors." Garrett and Levi noted the speaker's influence on them and expressed their gratefulness to be networked with him online and in person. By "Twitter pastors," these men meant a group of religious leaders, often public figures or ministers, in a local or national sense, connected via social media. Beyond this local church planter, the Twitter pastors of Church on the Margins included polarizing figures, such as Greg Boyd, Brian Zahnd, and Rob Bell (see chap. 4), who upload instructive content online via multiple platforms. "I ran across a YouTube preacher," Levi once said, commenting on his sermon preparation strategies for studying difficult biblical passages. Uploaded YouTube videos of sermons delivered in other states finds wide reception and uptake across the nation, including in congregations such as Church on the Margins. And Twitter, as I have argued, is one platform for people to disseminate links and engage in theological interchange and discourse. At least as disseminatable as YouTube videos and tweets, promiscuous podcast technologies are an evangelical media staple.

The emerging evangelicals I encountered consume podcasts voraciously, a practice common to their status as largely white, middle- and **creative-class** Americans. They listen to podcasts on morning and evening commutes to work or school or while lifting weights in the gym, at work or the office, in the mornings while preparing for work, doing domestic tasks and chores around the house, on road trips, when winding down in the evening, running or going for a walk, prepping food for the day, showering and dressing, or sitting on the bus. Throughout Protestant history, religious authorities have circulated sermon discourse widely via print, radio, television, and the internet. **Web 3.0** technologies (Campbell and Garner 2016, 44–48) are improving the ability of social web media to travel and embed in contexts separated by vast expanses of physical space. Podcasts are one of the latest, most cutting-edge genres for assisting the "spreadability" of and access to religious media (Lövheim 2013, 58; Jenkins et al. 2013). Podcast consumption does not make these evangelicals unique in America, but it does afford them with a means of outsourcing and uploading authority from extralocal sources.

Evangelicals consume podcasts from a wide number of sources. The most popular podcast genres for emerging Midwestern evangelicals, out of a total of eleven, include (1) religiosity, sermons, and teaching. Aside from Church on the Margins' own podcast, sources range from progressive pastors and writers, such as Science Mike, Greg Boyd, Brian Zahnd, and Rob Bell, to the boundary-defying experimental collective called The Liturgists, to the more traditional Christian apologetics of Tim Keller and Ravi Zacharias.[21] My analysis of the survey data generated a list of other popular podcast genres specifically among Church on the Margins attendees, including (2) news, journalism, and politics (NPR, *Fresh Air, Embedded, NPR Politics, The Pollsters,* and *Pod Save America*), (3) humor and comedy (*BBC Friday Night Comedy, Chap Traphouse, WTF with Marc Marion, You Made It Weird,* and *Wait Wait . . . Don't Tell Me*), (4) science, psychology, and technology (*Radiolab, Invisibilia, Partially Derivative,* and *Hidden Brain*), (5) business, economics, and entrepreneurship (*APM Marketplace, Freakonomics, Planet Money,* and *How I Built This, the Tim Ferriss show*), (6) culture and society (*This American Life, The Moth, Dinner Party Download,* and *Another Round*), (7) lifestyle, relationships, personalities, and advice (*The Minimalists, Anna Faris Is Unqualified, The Road Back to You, My Brother, My Brother and Me,* and *Urban Achiever*), (8) education and knowledge (*Stuff You Should Know, TED Radio Hour, Inside Study Abroad*), (9) music (*All Songs Considered, Piano Puzzler, Song*

Exploder), (10) travel and tourism (*Travel with Rick Steves*), (11) other religions and cultures (*See Something, Say Something, Radio Ambulante*), and a miscellaneous grouping of (12) folklore, crime, or fictional, magic realist, or regional news (*Lore, My Favorite Murder,* and *Welcome to Night Vale*). Similar to other social media forms, podcasts play an important, mixed-media role in the lives of emerging evangelicals in that they serve variously for the purposes of entertainment, to staying up on news and politics, to receiving religious instruction, to learning about science, philosophy, culture, art, society, and folklore.

To focus on the theological dimensions of podcasting technologies, for these evangelicals, podcasts afford for the spreading around, publicization, and consumption of correct teaching. Note, too, that Church on the Margins' definition of "correct teaching" does not align with, say, many of those technology experts analyzed back in chapter 3. (The promiscuity of podcast media, here, is key.) Podcasting and other digital technologies, after all, give this local congregation access and exposure to Rob Bell's teaching thus legitimating the fears of evangelical authorities who mark the internet as potentially dangerous. But if one interprets Bell as theologically beneficial and spiritually uplifting—and not heterodox and heretical—the internet's promiscuous effects are a positive affordance, not a negative one.

Even more than other social media, podcasts—as literally discursive oral media disseminated easily and with very few restrictions online—provide clear insight into how structures of authority are reconfiguring after the digital turn. Although religiosity and religious conversion in the United States has for a long time been about personal choice (Mullen 2017), podcasts increase the types of religiosities seekers have access and exposure to. Podcasting technologies allow local pastors to defer congregant theological and ritual instruction to online domains. Podcasts serve to expand discursive boundaries for local communities and project its ideologies and theologies to nonlocal individuals and ones.[22] During one 2016 sermon series titled "Simple Church in a Complex World," Garrett reflected both on the "wonders of technology," and its detrimental implications for everyday life. Not only do people surf multiple social networking platforms, chat with friends and loved ones, purchase goods, read news, and argue with others online, they also have the remarkable ability to listen to podcasts from anywhere in the world and learn under the authority of pastors, teachers, scholars, and ministers who are not geographically immediate to them. At first glance, we might expect Garrett to resist such mediations of evangelical authority as adding undue complexity and layering on even more information to our information-saturated lives. But instead, in this sermon Garrett condoned promiscuous podcast technologies as both highly convenient and theologically instructive before shifting focus to the role of the physical church in the digital age. With the rise of podcast technologies—conveyors of legitimate and authentic theological or doctrinal teachings—Garrett provoked, "What's the point of Sunday mornings? Why do we even gather?" His answer is complex and requires unpacking.

As I have already observed, Garrett views social media as sources of much daily anxiety and malaise. Facebook is pervasive. Trending stories are addictive clickbait. Advertisements, commercials, and consumerist social conditioning is omnipresent and omniscient. According to Garrett, "We are bombarded all day long with messages that are ultimately self-serving." Promiscuous images clamor incessantly to seduce people's gazes and command their attentions. Another speaker issued a similar wariness of neoliberalism's pervasiveness by noting that "the liturgy we grew up with" as American evangelicals is a "worldly liturgy of consumption" in which Americans are socialized into needing to constantly consume more, buy more, and experience more. Materialistic consumption has become so ingrained that "we don't even think about consuming" anymore. We do it blindly. Garrett reflects the language of laissez-faire economics in this pessimistic description of *homo economicus*. Quite simply, Garrett claims, for those of us living in the digital era, "we consume."

Garrett equivocates about the value of social media in a neoliberal era: "It's not all malicious." He acknowledges that social media do fulfill important functions, such as the podcast, that allow evangelicals to circulate discourse at will. Regardless, "every day we are being seduced" by ubiquitous advertising strategies and commercial agendas. We "ingest" information constantly and end up as slaves to ever-expanding informational economies. Yet, even in Garrett's most negative discourse against technology and media, one observes ambivalence. Technology is not all bad. Technology is helpful along some lines. Technology is virtue *and* vice. Promiscuity is helpful *and* distracting. As with many of the technology manuals from chapter 3, the goal is to be able to use technology with discernment and without unknowingly becoming slaves to the capitalist machine or the algorithm.

Garrett concludes his sermon by relegitimating the sacredness of gathering physically. The church service, Garrett contends, is now a radical, countercultural reorientation of values that defies promiscuous media by continuing to meet face-to-face. The community gathering is a slowing down, processual, and emotive and sensory event in which people join physically and socially (and as Garrett would argue, spiritually and metaphysically) with one another. The community gathering is itself a spiritual discipline, an act of unity to protest a world of social fragmentation and thin connection. In Church on the Margins' pointedly Christocentric, messy, and nonbounded social model, attending church is a weekly recentering of values and importance. Garrett's and others' words about slowness, craft, discipline, and focus track well with and directly recall the discourses of the Slow Church, an ecclesial stance that applies Slow Movement philosophies (Smith and Pattison 2014). Closing the service, congregants repeat a refrain: "We gather to / Reorient our hearts / Reset our minds / Center our lives on Jesus." In such a manner, community leaders reify the ideologies of media sincerity that privilege the face-to-face as the most authentic communicative mode but at the same time confirm the authenticity and legitimacy of promiscuous podcast technologies. A subtle program of digital restraint and restricted use appears to be solidifying in the evangelical Midwest.

FROM SLOW CHURCH TO DIGITAL RESTRAINT

One final strategy for decommercializing the church and guarding against the hyperconsumerist practices of American evangelical megachurches is to physically limit or place restraints upon technology use. Several examples of technological restraint are common in the Church on the Margins community. Notably, in the following instances, one observes the movement of media ideologies from the realm of the linguistic and discursive into the realm of custom and mores in everyday life with its attendant ebbs and flows of practice. Concerning data phone visibility and public use, children's screen time, and digital fasts, several ascetic practices are coming into practice. These practices aim to ameliorate some of the ills of promiscuous media.

As introduced in the prior chapter, one observation about technological asceticism has to do with the public presence of data phones in Church on the Margins services. In a word, community members conceive of mobile technologies as *disconnective* media within certain social parameters. Over the last several years, I've noticed during fieldwork observations that community members—while occasionally employing smartphones for ritual tasks, such as reciting the lectionary readings or accessing other service-relevant materials—typically keep their devices on silent and stowed away out of sight. These practices buy into the ideas circulating in both popular new media and sermon discourse that attention to one's personal media screen detracts from social presence and communicative immediacy in any given social environ. Communicants glued to their cellular, internet-enabled devices—"device bound" individuals, as Kenneth Goldsmith (2016, 57, 59) names them—are said by critics to be off "in their own world." "Like sleepwalkers, they're both present and absent," Goldsmith writes of common negative perceptions of public data phone users.

Burgeoning social media, then, reveal the methods by which the physical spaces of the church come to be marked off as special. Profane, distracting technologies do not under most circumstances have a welcome place in church services. The rules for mobile-technology use are certainly still being written—indeed, social rules are constantly changing and never entirely formalized—but at the time of composing this chapter in 2017, previously nebulous rules have formalized enough to transmute into something of a locally shared social protocol. Fieldwork evidence supports the claim. Regarding digital texts, one congregant confided that they had begun to only use hardcopy Bibles "when I'm in a group setting and don't want people to think I'm just on my phone." As we observed with the dance studio example and the jokes about texting versus looking up service-relevant details on one's iPhone, the importance lies in what one might describe as microperformances of **public-use differentiation**. Mobile technology use in church always runs the risk of being misjudged as inappropriate by fellow congregants. To observers, a person might very well be reading along with an online Bible app—or they might be surfing Facebook because they are bored. Which is it? The difference is hard to distinguish, and as ethnographic data suggest, must sometimes be made verbally clear. A person's technology use becomes the subject of direct public address.

A second observation has to do with children and technological restraint. How parents discuss methods for disciplining children with technology use is especially insightful as such talk frequently reveals parents' own media ideologies. In discussing children and technology use, parents distinguish between "screen time" activities and activities out in "the real world." One parent warns that too much screen time "has caused depression in my youngest daughter." Technology separates children from "real connections and the real world," this parent continues. "They shut themselves up in their room and do not get sun, exercise, or the real touch of people." Often, journalistic reports on scientific studies underwrite parents' negative ideologies about media: "Both research and my own experience indicate that too much screen time is detrimental." Another person evokes the power and authority of science, explaining that research "shows excess screen time is detrimental to a child's well-being." Technology use for children is "highly addictive." Endless screen time "makes for crabby children." Parents demonstrate evident worry about the influence of new technologies on their children.

To resist the negative repercussions of extended technology use, families strategize in different ways. Reflecting some of the language observed in the chapter on evangelical technology manuals, some families find that "limiting screen time helps with our kids' emotional stability and also requires us to be more involved and creative in our family interactions." What restrictions parents put into play do appear to be subject to both variety and change. Some families value technologies as educational aids but only within set parameters. Rarely do parents expand on what exactly those restrictions are, an ambivalence that may suggest a continued fluidity or elasticity, at least to the household's respective technology rules. One parent admits that "I should restrict more than I do" but then discloses that all phones and laptops are banned from bedrooms. "We don't have a set amount of time," one family confides but like the previous family does admit restricting use. "We don't have specific rules but do generally try to keep tabs on it," another family confirms. If extended screen time can become problematic, virtuous activities in the minds of these families correlate with physical movement, "exploring the environment," and "playing outside and being active." The virtuous or ideal, in these discussions, also reifies the dominance of face-to-face or in-person social interactions and experiences. We want our son "to spend time doing things outside, building things with his hands, and spending time with people," one family argues. Limiting or restraining technology use allows parents to "encourage healthy development of imagination, brain function, and social interaction." In this church's families' experiences, technological restraint, however variously applied, has a range of social and health benefits.

Finally, a third direction of restraint, **digital abstinence** or **fasting**, consists of periodic breaks from social media or other forms of technological use. Community members do report feeling addicted to and controlled by mobile technologies. "I think I am addicted to my phone in general," one person writes. "I check it all the time for notifications and new emails, and I think it really has a negative effect on me." For specific seasons in the church calendar, such as Lent, "I have deleted social media apps from my phone (the place where I do the majority of my social media browsing)," one person puts it. The reasons for the fast are multiple. Emerging evangelicals report experiencing "a storm of emotions," including, in their own words, anger, agitation, stress, exposure, distress, distraction, and dependence.

Digital fasts vary in length and outcome. Several people do fasts over the forty Lenten days. Others do modified fasts for an entire year. Still others do more impressionistic, customizable, media-specific, and less-strict fasts over the course of days, weeks, and months, whenever the informational overload becomes too much to bear. Several congregants do longer fasts but also apply specific regimens of restraint in their daily lives, prohibiting data phone or tablet use in bedrooms, putting their iPhone on "Do Not Disturb" for established times, or simply turning smartphones off "for several hours or a day per week." Predictably, fasts sometimes fail. But sometimes they're successful. Congregants who engage in digital fasting practices describe a completed fast as "a beneficial experience." After having "disengaged from social media" for around three weeks during the Trump election news cycles, as one person notes, "I felt relieved." Another community member feels that during moments of digital restraint it "was easier to see God's presence in my life." One person "felt less stressed and that I had more time" during and after the fast. Others note that during periods of abstinence, their social relationships had never been stronger. Another congregant replaced the time they would typically have spent on social media "with reading, learning new skills, and reconnecting more significantly with friends." Some respondents note that they have more direct control over their lives, writing, "It's been good for me to break the habit of constant use" or that they enjoy social media not "wasting my time" or "having to put up with unending banality." "I think I'm more engaged with my world," another person adds. Social media fasts for evangelicals can be "refreshing" and renewing.

Digital fasting is not an unanimously praised or endorsed ascetic ritual among emerging evangelicals. Even considering the negative repercussions of social media reported by Church on the Margins congregants, there are social deficiencies reported when one dislodges habitual media from their everyday lives and daily routines. One person misses "seeing my friends from different parts of the country." Another person argues that a technology fast has actually "not made me more productive" due to the fact they will inevitably fill the gap of social media use "with some other time-sucking mindless task." In reply to an inquiry about conducting a digital fast, another community member notes, "I haven't, and I don't really plan to. I have quite a lot of my day that is not social media involved. And I have that social connection because my entire family and a lot of my friends live very far away, and this is the best way for me to stay involved on a daily level." Such a response emphasizes the connective and socially facilitative affordances of new media under the parameters of correct, disciplined, careful use. Still others are required to use social media daily for work. Another person negates the utility of a fast for their circumstances, submitting that "technology is how I keep up on family life and connect to people who are not physically close." Disconnecting from social media sometimes results not in feelings of greater awareness, social connection, or presence but being "out of the loop and disconnected." In short, digital fasting has mixed results. Not all congregants in this Midwestern community agree that fasting, asceticism, or digital abstinence is the way to go.

SINCERITY AND PROMISCUITY EVOLVED

As I have narrated throughout *The Digital Evangelicals*, two highly influential Protestant models influence evangelical contentions about authority and authenticity. The media sincerity paradigm prioritizes directness and face-to-face conversation, prefers minimal mediation, and puts the value of authority and authenticity in close proximity. A second model of media promiscuity pushes for widespread dissemination of texts and discourse but breeds all sorts of unanticipated results, some positive and some negative. In this section, I clarify the emergence at the local level of a third communicative and theological paradigm, which combines the previous two models through a series of creative ideological merging: messiness.

Media ideologies, as I have argued, exist only in multiplicity and contestation. Never is one singular ideology at play. Depending on the context under consideration, occasionally one ideology comes to the fore while the others disappear momentarily into the background. More frequently, as we saw in the chapters' respective online case studies, communicants fuse together conflicting, co-constitutive paradigms to reconcile things for their purposes. Such multiplicity is also the case for emerging Midwestern evangelicals. Church on the Margins, for instance, has a conflicted charismatic background that brings with it all sorts of ideologies about authoritative speaking that provide a challenge to the more Reformed tradition of sincerity.

The congregation continues to wrestle with its charismatic survivals, but another development expands beyond speech and language patterns to include congregational aesthetics, rituals, and praxes. The invocation of messiness is a folk strategy and local communication paradigm aimed at describing and ordering congregational culture. As we've seen, Church on the Margins intentionally blends together and selectively adopts aspects of Roman Catholic liturgy, Orthodox visuality, and other forms of High Church practice. The congregation follows lectionary readings, performs a truncated version of the Catholic eucharistic mass every Sunday, and has experimented with iconography and votives. Church on the Margins practices *lectio divina*, an ancient Benedictine mode of experiential scripture reading, and *visio divina*, a related exercise that involves devotional meditation on an icon or image. Suffice it to say, overt adaptations of Catholic and Orthodox (non-Protestant) praxes—alongside its charismatic roots—complicate a straightforward reading of the relationship between Church on the Margins and the media sincerity model. At Church on the Margins, and indeed among other churches within emerging evangelicalism (Cooper 2017c), the partial return to a form of pre-Protestant materiality suggests a rupture within the forces of hegemonic Protestantism.

The messiness paradigm defines the church down to its service style and identity. Church on the Margins has consistently marketed itself as an ecclesially experiential and loosely bounded social space. Church leaders have embraced theological and ontological questions (rather than certainties) and have likewise challenged congregants to ask the hard questions about faith, life, and God. The church's mantras of messiness and authenticity, further, have remained central and have perhaps increased in focus over time. Throughout my years of fieldwork, I heard repeated time and time again the importance of questions and the necessity of ambiguity. Indeed, the congregation has strived to be a safe space for people who have questions, are hesitant about church as normal, and wrestle with doubt. Church on the Margins has been an exemplary model of in-process theology and ecclesiology. Although these sorts of uncertainties have certainly bled into the group's communicative milieu, I would argue that the messiness paradigm actively shapes, rather than simply reflects, the texture of its interpersonal connections. The church's deconstructive and eclectic practices are an attempt to peel away the layers of insincerity the community views as plaguing other evangelical churches in many different manifestations (e.g., rampant consumerism, conservative fundamentalism, cultural norms and mores, and religious pretension). Messiness appeals to sincerity as its standard but redefines sincerity to include ambiguity, mixture, and diversity. For Church on the Margins, authenticity is muddled, complex, and considerably less than direct. Like the glitchy-yet-authentic Skype session considered earlier, communication is not always characterized by clarity.

But how do the conjoined paradigms of sincerity, promiscuity, and messiness coalesce in the experiences of Midwestern evangelicals? Does digital connectivity in Church on the Margins work in service of or against sincerity? Like the internet itself, social media are hardly unified, single-use platforms. Rather, everyday social media practices on the ground are defined by the highly variegated social, cultural, religious, ethnic, national, political, and economic actors who comprise its user makeup (Miller 2011, 2018, Miller et al. 2016). Even in a small community like Church on the Margins, conflicting discourses about promiscuous media pertain. One stance marks digital media as the antithesis to sincerity and directness; another perspective appreciates and makes us of promiscuous media's allowance for direct access to instructive theological discourse online. In the latter case, the internet affords for highly efficient, instantaneous networking not possible in previous media eras.

The messiness paradigm thus seeks to make use of sincerity and promiscuity's strengths while minimizing their deficiencies. The internet affords for networking beyond the local in a way that allows for small volunteer-ran communities to thrive. Promiscuous social media help the congregation expand influence and project voice in a manner not possible without the digital. With a bit of conceptual tweaking and the ability to withstand a bit of messiness, promiscuous media also allow for and correspond to the sincerity paradigm. Messiness allows for this very convergence.

CONCLUSION

This chapter has studied emerging evangelical discourses about new media and mobile technologies in the American Midwest. Strikingly different interpretations are arising about the role of social media discourse and contestation, digital Bible apps, the meaning of digital friendship, the place podcasts have within authority structures, and the importance of digital asceticism to insulate against the malaise of the digital era. To summarize, several key findings deserve reiteration.

First, emerging evangelicals do attest to feeling increasingly anxious and stressed with the rise of new media technologies and their colonization of everyday life. Regardless of the dangers, almost all evangelicals use social media—for a wide range of activities. A vein of ironic criticism is common among congregants. Second, evangelicals disagree about the importance of online discourse. People resist engagement, take part in engagement sparingly, and develop and test protocol with which to decide how and when to engage with ideological opponents. Third, digital Bibles appear to be growing in popularity due to the sheer convenience of the mobile apps and the ability of internet media to provide a sophisticated platform for biblical research and study. At the same time, language about the materiality and functionality of physical Bibles confirms the hierarchy of media platforms that is in play. Fourth, a similar hierarchy is emerging in terms of an expanded definition of *friendship* after the rise and spread of social media, particularly Facebook. A dichotomy represented by Friends[1] and Friends[2] establishes a working folk taxonomy and like the digital/material Bible discussion applied the evaluation of the authentic and inauthentic binary. Fifth, regarding authority and new media, internet-enabled technologies (e.g., the podcast) both extend and displace structures of power and authority at different levels. Pastors can disseminate teachings easier than ever before, but entire communities can also engage in boundary maintenance work. Sixth, the habitual status of new media (technologies such as the podcast, digital Bibles, etc.) are moving even more persistently into the domains of the everyday and quotidian. But such an emergence requires new rules of public practice, and along these lines, performances of public-use differentiation, as I have called them, are sometimes important in the church setting. Seventh, hierarchies of friendship, dichotomies of authenticity/inauthenticity, and programs of digital asceticism appear for the most part to correspond to the emergence of a third localized communicative paradigm of messiness, which balances between the media sincerity and promiscuity models. Eighth, in keeping with circulating media ideologies of ambivalence, social protocol limiting the use of data phones in public gatherings does appear to be solidifying into loose scripts and flexible frames of contextual appropriateness and inappropriateness. Evangelicals put digital media to frequent use in the activities listed above but do so in a concerted mood of media ambivalence (Ribak and Rosenthal 2015) and sometimes resistance (Syvertsen 2017). To put a concluding point on the matter, one might identify the internet and digital media as both the source of these emerging evangelicals' problems and the solution to (some of) those issues.

NOTES

1. For more on the pub theology style of discipleship practiced by some Vineyard sectors, see Bielo 2011, 23, 66; Martí and Ganiel 2014, 77, 138.

2. My ethnographic activities hardly differentiated me from the evangelical audience I was observing. Note-taking on sermons and for devotional activities is a common evangelical practice (Bielo 2009). Later, I supplemented my note-taking strategies by taking digital notes on my data phone. Similarly, the use of data phones in congregational practices for accessing scriptural texts meant that my ethnographic presence blended in well with congregant activities.

3. I am reminded of anthropologist Anya Royce's (2002, 11) comments on the data-gathering practices of novice anthropologists. Royce writes that ethnographers early in their research tend to record "too much detail" with "too little context." Such an imbalance of data and contextual information was certainly my own case when beginning preliminary fieldwork among this emerging congregation. Over my years of research, I was able to fill in the context for the raw data.

4. Other musical configurations would showcase trumpets, violins, and harmonicas (Cooper 2017b, 80).

5. Similar to combinations between evangelicalism and other religions, such as Candomblé, I am interested in the ways that these seemingly oppositional expressions of Christianity are made to "converge and diverge" or "overlap and even intertwine" with others, to adopt Stephen Selka's (2010, 293) words applied to the Brazilian milieu.

6. An "Introduction to Church on the Margins" booklet delineates "Six Streams of Historic Christianity" and employs a diagram of a table in which each "stream" constitutes a single leg. The traditions include (1) holiness; (2) charismatic; (3) social justice; (4) contemplative; (5) incarnational; and (6) evangelical traditions. The booklet insightfully provides folk definitions of relevant terms, including streams or traditions, and underscores the community's extended Christ-centered approach: "Jesus gave us a complete picture of God, and demonstrated how we can experience fullness and vitality in our life with God. The historical Church, despite its divisions and differences, has upheld the core characteristics of Christ's life through what we now call traditions. We like to call them 'streams,' each flowing out of the river of Christ. Taken together, these traditions help us envision a balanced spiritual life." The booklet then offers a detailed taxonomy of each of the traditions, streams, or historic forms. See Mullen 2017 for an account of how the aptitude of choice has allowed American Christians to make sense of inherited religious and cultural paradigms.

7. For more on the sermon as a central oral-religious event within Christianity, see Tomlinson 2006, 129; Claridge and Wilson 2002; Coleman 2006; Hanks 1996; Bourdieu 1994.

8. For more on the interest of spiritual disciplines in the Vineyard and evangelicalism's tenuous relationship with Catholic praxis, see Bialecki 2017, 84.

9. Levi has developed his penchant for humor by taking stand-up comedy classes, adding comedy shows in local bars to the list of ethnographic locations of study for this project.

10. For more on this "new" attention by evangelicals to strategies of social justice and uplift, see Streensland and Goff 2014; Gasaway 2014; cf. Schwartz 2012.

11. Commentators have described the accelerated and compressed experience of modern time as the "maelstrom of twenty-first-century space-time" (Menzies 2005, 13). Additionally, the pastors' shared worries about social media reflect what one extensive anthropological study of Facebook use in Trinidad as akin to a "time-suck" (Miller 2011, 191–193).

12. Despair as an emotive outcome or affective mood emerging out of extended social media use is not unique to this small evangelical community. During a presentation given in 2016, a guest speaker from a nondenominational pregnancy crisis-care center also mentions a growing sense of "despair" or "general hopelessness" linked to digital media exposure. That social media exacerbate doubt and worry and other nonvirtues or emotions is a much broader media ideology.

13. Spiritual formation guides and historical accounts trace the origins of this prayer ritual to sixth-century Eastern and Russian Orthodox contexts. Historically, the method has been known as the "Jesus Prayer" or "Prayer of the Heart." See, for instance, Mathewes-Green 2009; Chumley 2011; Bacovcin 2003; DelBene et al. 1992. For an online guide to the contemplative prayer form, see Gravity 2018.

14. In response to an inquiry in the questionnaire about whether or not the user observes contestation in their personal social media feeds, answers are highly diverse and contradictory. Some respondents affirmed in all caps: "YES! ALL THE TIME!" Others affirmed by way of rhetorical snark: "You're kidding, right? This is a post-Trump world. Everyone argues about politics." Still others replied with a "yes, almost constantly," "constantly," or "often." Notably, however, a second group of respondents emerged. For this group, perhaps surprisingly, contestations online do not take place. The discourses one congregant witnesses on social media "are not argumentative." "Not really," another person weighed in. A mediating camp of respondents depicted social media contestations as occurring online but only "sometimes."

15. The feedback loop also accurately reflects what researchers have described as polarized crowds of online interactive dialogue and the community cluster (Smith et al. 2014).

16. Likewise, those respondents who prefer digital over physical Bibles hail from each of the age brackets.

17. Although not addressed specifically by Church on the Margins congregants, this preference for materiality also certainly falls into a long tradition of Christian material practices with regard to the Bible as a physical object. See McDannell 1998 and Bielo 2009 for more on the historic and cotemporary circumstances of biblical materiality.

18. This sort of linguistic paradigm also goes by the names of the **transport view** and **logocentrism** (Holmes 2005; Derrida 1976).

19. According to a book that strongly reiterates many of Church on the Margin's virtues and ideological stances, *Slow Church: Cultivating Community in the Patient Way of Jesus*, "Walls, borders and clear lines of demarcation give shape to the bounded set. The incarnational church, in contrast, is a 'centered set.' A centered set is defined by its core values. It sees people 'not ... as in or out, but as closer or further away from the center [which is in this case Christ]. In that sense, everyone is in and no one is out. Though some people are close to the center and others far from it, everyone is potentially part of the community in the broadest sense" (Smith and Pattison 2014, 34). Critics of the community—some dissenting families who no longer attend the church—suggest that Church on the Margins sacrifices the second of their theological foci, "pathway," in their overemphasis on "refuge."

This ecclesially inclusive maneuver has also gotten Church of the Margins in trouble with critics who find their modus operandi too focused on love and flexible boundaries and less on discerning sin and denouncing heterodoxy. The congregation's position on these matters also deepens its connection to the emerging church movement and postevangelical conversations (Cooper 2017c, 400; McKnight 2007, 6; Tomlinson 2003 [1995]; Schmelzer 2017). Although some Church on the Margins members consider themselves postevangelicals, the leadership does not appear to identify the congregation as such. Sermon data confirms that the pastors' desire is to redeem evangelicalism as a bearer of "Good News" and resist evangelicalism's public status as a producer of hellfire and damnation discourse. But the leaders do not aim to reject the movement outright. Church on the Margins seeks an authentic evangelicalism in which there is no room for Islamophobia, homophobia, and xenophobia.

20. See Bialecki (2017, 50–52) for an account of the movement's complicated relationship with rigid Protestant ecclesial structures, such as the denomination.

21. Other podcasts in the religious category include *Bad Christian, Ekklesia, Bridgetown—A Jesus Church, Pete Scazzero / Rich Villodas (New Life Fellowship), Phil Vischer, Relevant, Pray-as-You-Go, Inglorious Pasterds, City Church (Judah Smith), Pulpit Fiction, Nomad, Truth for Life—Alistair Begg, The Jordan B. Peterson Podcast,* and *The Graveyard Shift* (Scott Evans).

22. Occasionally the technology expands the community's social boundaries. One college student, and then young professional, who actively attended Church on the Margins for the duration of my fieldwork confided that she first learned about the community by listening to one of the pastors' sermon podcasts uploaded online by a friend.

CONCLUSION

Zoom Church, Cancel Culture, and the Exportation of Evangelical Media

THIS BOOK OPENED WITH AN unsettling image of a family around a dinner table praying to the internet. It ends with a discussion of equally disturbing imagery. Picture this: Winnie-the-Pooh, Tigger, and SpongeBob SquarePants attending a church service as a digital pastor baptizes an anime character in a virtual Japanese bathhouse. In 2019, a ten-minute YouTube upload of a live-capture virtual baptism went viral. The service culminated with the baptism of Drumsy, an online tech journalist and religious seeker persona, by D. J. Soto, founder and pastor of Virtual Church. In terms of avatar bodies, Drumsy was the pink-haired anime character. Soto's avatar was humanoid and more "regular" looking. Other service attendees included Winnie-the-Pooh, a friend of Drumsy, and later SpongeBob and Tigger, among others, who popped in and out of the service (Syrmor 2019).

The baptism was simple enough. Relocating from a dreamlike expanse of sky and mirror-top sea to a wood-slatted bathhouse, Soto spoke for a minute or two about the significance and meaning of baptism as steam arose around the avatars, now submerged up to their waists in digital water:

> Thanks for being a part of this spiritual moment. And it really is a spiritual moment. I think some people think of it maybe as a religious ritual, and that's fine, too, but this is something that has spiritual significance to it. There's a couple of things happening, Drumsy, when we're baptized. One of the things is that we're talking about being immersed in God's love. When you go underwater, that symbolizes that your spiritual cells are soaking in divine love, and new life, and forgiveness, and, you know, release of the old. So I think that's a beautiful, symbolic thing that that represents. When you are lowered into the water, that symbolizes that you're dying to the old Drumsy, the old attitudes, and the old things that have held you back. And maybe there's guilt, and regret,

and failure, and that stuff is dying. It's going to be buried there because God wants you to experience new life. That's what that represents when you come out of the water.... So just as Jesus was dead and buried and rose again to new life, that's what we're going to symbolize for you today.... Baptism is a declaration that you're going to walk in a new path, in a new direction, and have a new attitude and a new mindset. And that's a very beautiful thing. (Syrmor 2019)

Following these remarks, Soto asked Drumsy to immerse completely in the pool. Drumsy kneeled down until the entire avatar body submerged, save for the very top of their neon-pink ponytail. Reiterating to those gathered that baptism is about marking newness and change, a dying to old selves and being reborn into godliness, Soto uttered the sacramental rites: "Drumsy, I baptize you in the name of the Father, and of the Son, and of the Holy Spirit . . . Rise up, again, into new life." As Drumsy arose, anew, out of the water, Soto encouraged the congregants to celebrate the event. "Awesome, yay!" they respond. "Wohoo!" "Good job! So proud of you!" The attendees were happy for the newly baptized. Coming out of the water, Drumsy's posture was Pentecostal—hands raised high in ecstatic surrender. A banana with sunglasses and a grumpy black cat celebrated the baptism, raising their arms, waving their hands, and jumping into the pool to congratulate Drumsy (see fig. 9.1).

As if the above scene wasn't bizarre enough, something even more unexpected soon happened. The water suddenly disappeared, causing the avatars to drop to the bottom of the pool. "And the water's gone." Someone deduced. "Oh, there goes the water." The avatars looked about confusedly, finally spying the culprit. A SpongeBob avatar, who appeared at the tail end of the baptism, left as quick as he had come, beelining for the pool stairs with that typically mischievous smile splayed across his angular face. The waterlogged yellow sponge made his escape, signaling the end of this semiotically eclectic, theologically experimental, live digital baptism.

Assessing this newest example of virtual baptism—supposedly one of the very first instances of its kind in recorded human history—this concluding chapter rounds out this book's study of digital evangelicalism by focusing on how religious life is changing after the coronavirus pandemic of 2020 and the ensuing months of social distancing. If anything, COVID-19 has affirmed, accentuated, and accelerated the rise of digital religion, not out of choice but out of obligation to stay safe during the pandemic by working from home and ceasing in-person social gatherings, including church services. The following pages contextualize the digital baptism in terms of ongoing debates about evangelical authority and authenticity. Later in the chapter, I put my ethnographer hat back on to observe how Church on the Margins is responding to the pandemic through its use of Zoom to promote togetherness in a time of shelter-in-place orders. The final

Figure 9.1. Screenshot from "Real Pastor in Virtual Reality Baptizes an Anime Girl." Syrmor, YouTube, 2019 (https://youtu.be/N_88DBmdnNA).

portion of the conclusion addresses the most recent strategies of boundary maintenance and gatekeeping through the concept and lens of **cancel culture**—a particularly fraught digital phenomenon—identifies ramifications for the spread of evangelical media beyond evangelicalism, and calls for scholars to be more aware of their media ideologies.

VIRTUAL CHURCH'S NEW AUTHENTICITIES

D. J. Soto, whom I introduced at the beginning of this chapter, is a minister and self-described apostle of Virtual Church. In his descriptions of Virtual Church, Soto often emphasizes the novelty of these controversial online rituals, yet there have been previous attempts to do "online church," most of which have been highly experimental and short-lived as once cutting-edge platforms quickly grew outdated and were replaced by newer ones after the turn of the new millennium (Hutchings 2017; Helland 2005, 2015). Virtual Church represents the newest, most cutting-edge iteration of what an exclusively virtual congregation might look like. As still another example of an authenticity contestation, the church's creators consider it the first virtual congregation proper, and in a way they are correct, since wearable virtual reality (VR) devices have not been available for mass consumption until relatively recently. According to Soto, Virtual Church is the first church "to exist entirely in virtual reality" (Virtual Church 2020a). Virtual Church is a church made entirely digital, but with the rise of Facebook's

Oculus (Rift and Go), HTC Vive, and Samsung GearVR, critics can no longer claim that the online space is completely disembodied and untethered from so-called real life. With VR, the digital maps onto and extends the participant's body into the virtual space. Even more than the subtle haptics of Instagram use, VR further erases the gap between offline/online and real-world/digital spaces. VR puts the body of the user into the digital domain, merging the physical and the online. VR is about making the digital tangible, somatic, and three-dimensional (French 2018). Online and on ground spaces now overlap even more.

As with previous case studies, Virtual Church fully embraces promiscuous media, predictably reimagining again sincerity and authenticity in close correspondence. These impulses characterize Soto and others involved in the leadership of Virtual Church as progressives, in both technological but perhaps also theological senses. Soto, after all, is himself an ex-megachurch pastor with a theology degree who rejected megachurch evangelicalism to create something "radically inclusive and consistent with Christianity's long history of adapting to new forms of media" (Virtual Church 2020a). Soto intends Virtual Church, founded in May 2017, to attract people not beholden to traditional religion. He discusses with pride, for instance, how one of the first attendees of Virtual Church's first service was an atheist. Recalling the genericized evangelicalism of Scott Bakken's Socality network, Virtual Church keeps a minimalist "Beliefs" page on its website (Virtual Church 2020b; Syrmor 2019). "We believe God loves the world and wants everyone to know it" is one of its core doctrines. Theologically, the page gestures to the Apostle's Creed, a sort of lowest common denominator in terms of Christian doctrine. Is such theological flexibility a requirement for pastors willing to lead quasiserious experimental services where mischievous SpongeBobs and pant-less Winnie-the-Poohs are in attendance? Soto was happy to do Drumsy's baptism, for instance, even though Drumsy admitted to just being a little "Jesus curious," not a typical convert (Syrmor 2019).

As one might guess, Virtual Church is nothing if not controversial. Soto reports that after one teenage participant's mother found out about the experimental format, she forbade her son from participating (Syrmor 2019). Debates about the validity of VR congregations tend to focus on the legitimacy of VR sacraments. Critics worry that VR rituals are not real, that is, that they're inauthentic. "If a 'baptism' is only simulated in a virtual world, is it still real in any theological sense?" one tech writer asks (Au 2019). Thomas Kuster (2018), an administrator with the Christ in Media Institute ran by Bethel Lutheran College, classifies Soto as an evangelical for whom "baptism is merely a symbolic event reflecting the experience of a major life-change." Kuster's subtle boundary maintenance applies a **High Church vs. Low Church** binary between mainline Protestantism and more generic evangelicalism. "Among us, for whom baptism is a sacrament, not just symbolic but bringing the forgiveness of sins, and to be administered strictly according to our Lord's instruction (using real water)," Kuster distinguishes. "A virtual baptism would be more than problematic." He here refers to the evangelical contention against Catholicism that sacraments such as communion and baptism are symbolically charged moments. The bread and juice *represent* Christ's body and blood but are not the real thing. Immersion within and then coming up out of a body of water *depicts* entering new life. In traditional Protestantism, the sacraments are metaphorical events, not literal ones.

These digital matters are metaphorically fraught, revealing the tensions at the heart of evangelical deliberations. If Protestant theologies of communion sacralize the metaphor, wouldn't a metavirtual sacramental service be an extension of evangelical logics? Consistent with evangelical theological deliberation elsewhere, theologians disagree. Some leaders reject out of hand the implications of VR for performing sacraments, noting that although technologies of this sort are helpful for missionization and evangelization—spreading the Good News widely—they "should not be used to substitute important events in a believer's life" (Carlton 2018).

In conducting virtual rituals, Soto and others are extending these powerful sacramental metaphors into a new realm of representation that appears to be quite hospitable to the meta. We see evidence of Soto's emphasis on representation during the Drumsy baptism with his frequent repetitive mention of the symbolic registers of VR's affordances for religious ritual. Kneeling symbolizes immersion, he expresses. Immersion into and exit out of virtual water symbolize immersion and exit from physical water, which symbolizes leaving the old life and entering the new. Yet Soto refuses to equate such metaphorical mediative thickening with inauthenticity and heterodoxy. Soto and his entrepreneurial VR pastoral team are challenging and redefining the very parameters of sacramental authenticity and orthodoxy.

Soto's VR use reconfigures the authentic in three notable ways. First, Soto addresses one of critics' main concerns, the issue of avatars. As the Drumsy baptism suggested, the use of avatars drawn eclectically from across popular culture can cause disorientation for those who are expecting the decorum of the virtual space to mirror that found in, say, a formal church service, where people wear their Sunday best and put on their best behavior. Congregants as avatars (Winnie-the-Pooh, anime heroines, etc.) may be off-putting for traditionalists in that these icons bring with them worlds of their own interpretive contexts and meanings. Soto, however, emphasizes the anonymity that avatars bring as liberating for nontraditional potential attendees who are not looking for church as normal. During the Drumsy baptism, Soto used an avatar that mapped closely with his real-life appearance. But during other services, he has opted for an old-school, retro-style robot. According to the VR pastor, avatar anonymity means that the situation "can be more authentic" because the level of mediated distance brings some congregants comfort and sets them at ease. "Within that anonymity comes a sense of authenticity," he expresses. Soto further notes that some of his strongest most meaningful friendships are not in real life but "are in VR" (Syrmor 2019).

Second, Soto addresses head-on Protestant anthropologies of the body and being, filtering VR through standards of evangelical sincerity but also adapting them in imaginative ways. Soto dismantles romanticized notions of physicality offline, focusing on the mediative and mediating nature of the body. "Even in the physical world," he argues, "your body is just a shell of your spirit. I mean, your spirit is your person." Here, Soto reflects the Protestant rhetoric of the internet architects discussed in chapter 2, who envisioned the internet as the domain of the spiritually sincere core and the body itself as a mere container of the authentic interior. "The physical shell," although important, Soto clarifies, "is less important, you know, than what's inside the spirit and the attitude." Soto here channels Protestant sincerity in one of the purest expressions that we've observed in this entire book.

Third, the pop-culture iconography of VR avatars notwithstanding, VR paradoxically extends the body's sensations and emotions into the digital. When Soto baptized Drumsy, Drumsy really was kneeling in whatever room he was wearing his VR equipment. When Drumsy stood up after the long immersion under the digital waters, he really, authentically felt a sense of exhilaration as blood rushed back into the veins and arteries that had been pinched as he kneeled because he had been hunched over for a considerable amount of time. For VR users, this embodied aspect is part of the attractiveness of the experience and informs how users interpret and bring meaning to their actions and motions in the VR space. Drumsy struggled for the correct words to describe what he was feeling: "Wow, I got blood rushing to my head when I got up. I feel . . . I feel like I'm out of breath. I feel like . . . like I just had an experience." VR is embodied. Movements are real movements. Gestures are real gestures. The body is more present via VR than in previous tech forms.

Continuing the theme of the body, Soto argues that VR can engender *more* authentic experiences than in the so-called real, non-VR world. Soto gives the example of a disabled woman who was told directly in a traditional evangelical church that her being confined to a wheelchair meant that she didn't have enough faith in God (Syrmor 2019). Soto's evangelical emphasis on the authentic spiritual interior, together with his appreciation of the anonymous affordances of VR, means that for disabled people and others in similar circumstances, VR church can offer a more authentic, welcoming, and inclusive religious community than possible in real life, where people, as social beings, deal inevitably in constant microaggressions and judgements about people's bodies, racial identities, sexual orientations, and skin colors. Soto doesn't use these exact words himself, but his argument is that critics of virtual technologies are implicitly **ableist** in that they fail to acknowledge the limited benefits that experimental technologies bring to disabled and marginalized people (Alper 2017; Haller 2010).

POSTPANDEMIC CONGREGATIONAL LIFE
AND ZOOM CHURCH

By May 2019, the Virtual Church congregation, led by apostle D. J. Soto and his team, had attracted 100 to 150 congregants per Sunday. Service attendees hailed not only from the United States but also Great Britain, the Netherlands, Germany, and a few visitors from the regions of the Middle East, Africa, and South America (Au 2019). As VR technologies improve, sharpen, and popularize for a mass market over the next few years, it remains to be seen how this experimental young congregation, and others like it, will fare. But a world-changing event in early 2020 quickly brought what had remained a somewhat fringe concept—church online, religion made virtual and digital—from the margins to the mainstream.

The outbreak of coronavirus disease 2019 (abbreviated COVID-19) was first identified in December of 2019 but not declared as a pandemic until March 2020. Government-level responses in the United States and abroad included stay-at-home and shelter-in-place orders alongside directives for self-isolation and social distancing. As of the fall semester of 2020, experts estimate that there have been more than 37 million confirmed cases of the virus and more than 1 million deaths worldwide. Social distancing and shelter-in-place practices radically altered the daily social and occupational lives of Americans, upending the economy in what may be the most detrimental recession since the Great Depression. Many workplaces, at least those deemed nonessential, shifted into virtual and work-from-home formats. Universities canceled in-person classes midsemester and reverted to online. College instructors like myself experimented with synchronous and asynchronous methods, strategizing about how best to engage students over distance.

The COVID-19 pandemic changed everything. Even religion was not immune. Churches nationwide reeled from the disruption caused by the disease, provoking varieties of responses in different church bodies. It is true that some congregations ignored stay-at-home regulations, infecting congregants in their defiance of state orders, orders they interpreted as infringement of church-and-state separation and a broach of religious freedom. But such cases were mavericks. Overall, American Christians ranging from mainliners to evangelicals made the drastic but necessary shift from in-person services to online church. Heidi Campbell (2020b, 10), in a recently released collaborative e-book, *Religion in Quarantine*, drew on church consultancy research to show that in March and April of 2020, a majority of churches went online even as pastors noted feeling ill-equipped and unprepared to transition to streaming and other digital hosting methods. Campbell narrates the migration that occurred in 2020:

> Transferring church online involved simply broadcasting or livestreaming traditional worship services on the internet, trying to replicate the look and feel of weekly gatherings as closely as possible. Pastors and priests filmed themselves in empty sanctuaries or in front of home altars offering the same liturgical readings or sermons members would have encountered before the pandemic. Translating church online involves some innovation to worship rituals and spaces, such as turning the service into an informal talk-show style format where the pastor served as host and other members of the worship or music team as guests. Both instances show a very pragmatic response to this cultural shift—churches transferred or translated their worship services online in the quickest and most efficient way possible in order to fulfill what they see as their central mission, offering members a form of Sunday gathering.

Churches, then, tended toward pragmatic solutions and strategies of migration. As Campbell describes the matter, pastors were largely interested in translating the experience of the service event online, a "cultural shift," as she puts it, which required innovation and flexibility. To carry out these tasks, church leaders turned to existing media apps, such as Facebook Live, Google Meetings, Microsoft Teams, and Zoom, among other collaborative media options.

How has Church on the Margins fared during this season of disruption? With its paradigm of messiness, applied media ambivalence, and love-hate relationship with the digital, how has the group approached the task of maintaining authentic communal interactions? To answer these questions, I visited the church again as an ethnographic participant observer, this time connected with other congregants via a motley network of tablets, data phones, smart TVs, and PCs. The following pages report my findings regarding religion under quarantine as expressed in this one community. These developments, I suggest, show that by obligation digital evangelicalism is becoming a more apparent development during the pandemic. In 2020 and 2021, a biomedical rupture upended life as Church on the Margins congregants knew it, throwing into even greater relief the ways religious affiliation, theological contention, and community building occur in new experimental, hybrid domains.

VR equipment is still not entirely mainstream. It requires some effort and cost to purchase the relatively complicated wearable devices and learn how to operate them on digital networks. Zoom and Teams are less immersive, high-tech options for a qualified form of virtual religion and are currently much more accessible and affordable to use. Church on the Margins, in particular, began early during the pandemic experimenting with Facebook Live but soon migrated over to Zoom, a more efficient host for Sunday services. Like most American churches, Church on the Margins at first focused on the migration of their regular service components into a digital format. Facebook Live was the most straightforward option to host the service since the church already kept multiple Facebook pages, public and private, and therefore could simply stay in the platform. Aside from the fact one was now participating in church from the comfort of one's own home, the service itself was familiar, and notwithstanding the dearth of interpersonal social interactions that occur, say, before and after a formal in-person service, the structure of meeting together even digitally appeared to be comforting for this congregation.

As usual, the pastors co-led, taking turns delivering live sermons. Pastor Garret, whether he was speaking that day or not, typically took charge of hosting the service through his PC. Garrett often spoke from his home office, surrounded by theology books, sports paraphernalia, religious icons, and family photographs. Pastor Jonathan, during his turn, usually spoke from a couch in his basement in a room designated as the home music studio.

The online services proceeded as follows: A pastor would open the gathering, welcoming regulars and visitors. Congregants would join the service via a predistributed link but kept their videos and microphones on mute. Then the mediator would screen share to the designated music leader for the day, often Pastor Jonathan and his family, but sometimes another community member. After a song or two, another designee from a different family would read passages from the lectionary schedule. Then the speaker would deliver a short sermon, sometimes paired with a video clip or instructional media. At the end of the sermon, a pastor would lead a truncated version of the pre-eucharistic prayers and then everyone, alone together, would partake of communion in their own homes. The service would unofficially end with a familiar centering prayer and community announcements, but most weeks this was followed by more intimate breakout discussion and prayer groups. This format went on for several weeks into the pandemic during Spring 2020.

The pastors did their best to move the church's services online. Aside from minor digital glitches here and there, things went rather seamlessly. Glitchiness, as we've seen, combines well with the church's mantra of messiness. For a church that has met in restaurants, ballet studios, elementary schools, pubs, strip malls, and homes, congregants were well prepared for another experimental venue. But the reflexive community soon realized that the online format was not collaborative enough to measure up to the high authenticity standards of their ecclesiology and church culture. Even with small group discussions and guest scripture readers, musicians, and speakers, Church on the Margins still experienced a lack of connectivity in the purely online format. Simply put, people missed seeing each other in the flesh. To remedy the social thinness of digital church, the congregation began to experiment with basic format changes to facilitate a more robust sense of congregational togetherness. These simple changes largely had to do with the sacramental performances of digital communion.

Perhaps the simplest yet most profound adjustment the church made during 2020's upheavals was to encourage congregants to take communion live with their video cameras turned on so that they were visible to the entire church. Such a step made the most of Zoom's collaborative affordances, shifting congregant status from that of bystanders and observers to direct participants in the flow of the service. The service went from a mostly one-sided event in which attendees consumed the sermon and followed along with the liturgical media put before them to direct visual participation in the quasipublic meeting. Whereas before the pastor or speaker's screen dominated the congregation's view, it now fragmented into scores of little video frames, each containing the separate worlds of each family, couple, or individual. I felt during my observations that there was a bit of social magic in this collaborative shift from viewing to participating. During the few minutes in which parents and children, individuals and couples partook of breads and juices and wines of different sorts, one had what felt like a firsthand view into the domestic worlds of the community in its constituent parts. Some families took communion in their kitchens or at the dining table, huddled around their Zoom-hosting devices, perhaps mirroring Paweł Kuczyński's "Dinner" to an uncanny degree. Others did communion from the porch or deck, with fences, trees, yards, or hills as a backdrop. Still others participated from home offices, studies, and living rooms.

The creative anonymity of VR avatars provides some benefits, perhaps even allowing for authenticity in a counterintuitive way. But here we see a different sort of virtuality in which the digital avatars seen through the church's Zoom meeting map quite closely onto the real-life personas of the congregation. One is, after all, seeing live video of people one knows. All of these people together on one screen, in one digital space. That, from my perspective, was the most profound and useful aspect of digital church—the ability to bring together congregants who dearly miss each other's company into some sort of admittedly diminished but still quite social presence. During communion, before and after partaking of the elements, children giggle and smile, pointing out their friends from church on the laptop or TV screen and waving excitedly. Adults smile at each other, disseminating a strange sort of social warmth that seems almost palpable. For these progressive evangelicals, digital church isn't quite "real" church. For Church on the Margins, digital media doesn't yet allow for the rawness and realness of social existence experienced within communities on the ground. Using the tech at hand, employing what's available, it's still a somewhat quirky and frustrating mediated experience. It can be especially frustrating for those working from home and attending daily Zoom and Teams meetings. Church may feel like yet another meeting, another obligation to fulfill. Diminished sociality notwithstanding, this is a remarkable sort of visual realness that does seem to be making strides in its quest to map directly on to the real thing. But as Pastor Garret closed the gathering in March 2021, he worried that Zoom church "is not a full expression. It's not a full expression of a church community" nor a "legitimate way forward" for the congregation in the long term. Digital church, in some of its better moments, makes the pandemic endurable but only for the short term.

EVANGELICAL AUTHORITY IN THE AGE OF CANCEL CULTURE

Widening out from VR and Zoom church experiments, let's return to evangelicalism as a broader media ecology. What's the relationship of evangelicalism to promiscuous media in the current milieu? Because of its wide indiscriminate address, promiscuous media tend to get people into trouble. Promiscuous media made Martin Luther a celebrity heretic and continue to stir controversy for contemporary evangelical leaders in different ways. Following are two recent examples of how promiscuity, which is normally good for creating audiences and spreading influence, can quickly spiral out of control.

Just this year, a risqué Instagram image posted by Jerry Falwell Jr., heir to the evangelical Liberty University (LU) empire, helped to diminish his standing among what scholars have described as "court" (Fea 2020) or "establishment evangelicals" (Du Mez 2020, 8, 10), that is, powerful conservative evangelicals who hold a considerable amount of mainstream cultural capital and public sway. The image is difficult to decipher but involves unzipped pants, a woman who was not Falwell's wife, and what appears to be Falwell himself partaking in a strong drink—perhaps the greater of conservative evangelical taboos given that alcohol is prohibited in the LU handbook.[1] One bizarre image, of course, wasn't the sole cause of Falwell's fall from grace. But it did serve as the discursive battleground on which the wars over his guilt and grounds for dismissal from leadership waged. The controversy later deepened as journalists revealed that Falwell and his spouse had been engaged in what evangelical sexual norms deem as immorality. The situation involved a liaison between Falwell's wife and a hired worker. And did the memes fly. "HE LAYETH ME BESIDE POOL WATER," one meme suggested. "HIS ROD AND HIS STAFF COMFORT ME." The backdrop of this meme was a picture of a chiseled, shirtless young man in swimming trunks cleaning a pool. Over the image, a picture of Falwell Jr. in a suit and tie has been awkwardly and intentionally juxtaposed.

In another case of new media's promiscuous effects, a social media manager for a different evangelical empire, Hillsong Church, recently made a simple enough yet serious blunder. Forgetting to log out of the official Hillsong Twitter account and into their own, the account manager tweeted during the 2020 presidential candidate debate:

> **@Hillsong Church**: Can't they just mute Trump's microphone!! He is coming across as such a bully. No respect for him sorry. #PresidentialDebate2020

Religious digital creatives (RDCs) and influencers have increased power in the horizontalized digital age, but this example again shows how authority in contemporary life is tenuous and fragile. Progressive evangelical influencers praised the above Hillsong media manager's politics but worried about his or her job security after having made such a blunder during a politically volatile time.

For the evangelical powers that be, and those that are becoming—powers ranging from university presidents to RDCs and social media managers—promiscuous media can be both their making and their undoing. Digital media can promote and circulate ideas and language, bolstering a person's influence, but they can also serve as the means for their cancellation.

Digital media's horizontal affordances for direct address of celebrities and other powerful figures, in conjunction with its simultaneity, has led to an ongoing social phenomenon described as cancel culture. "Almost everyone worth knowing has been canceled by someone," Jonah Engel Bromwich (2018) explains for the *New York Times*. "Bill Gates is canceled. Gwen Stefani and Erykah Badu are canceled. Despite his relatively strong play in the World Cup, Cristiano Ronaldo has been canceled. Taylor Swift is canceled ... and, Wednesday, Antoni Porowski, a 'Queer Eye' fan favorite was also canceled. Needless to say, Kanye West is canceled, too. . . . In a recent interview . . . Kanye fretted extensively about being canceled, using some form of the word seven separate times. 'I'm canceled. I'm canceled because I didn't cancel Trump,' he said."

Cancel culture is sometimes described as a brand of antagonistic, shallow, #MeToo-era, liberal critique applied to any and every part of society deemed problematic by social justice warriors. But the phenomenon is much broader than that. Evangelicals, both conservative and liberal, are key actors within cancel culture. Jerry Falwell Jr., following the above incidents, has certainly been canceled from both the right and the left. Conservatives, for their part, have canceled public evangelicals who get divorced or come out as gay. Conservatives cancel controversial Netflix movies and then cancel Netflix when the streaming giant refuses to comply with conservative morals. After one of the most divisive presidential races in American history, some conservatives late in 2020 canceled Facebook and Twitter for canceling free speech and migrated, however momentarily, to Parler Free Speech Network, a fledgling Facebook alternative. Cancel culture is akin to heresy discourse. To cancel is a form of boycotting, a performative and applied boundary maintenance tailored for the social media age. Cancel culture is the product of the digitally buffered self and its heightened exposure to difference and contrast.

Commentators are split over whether cancel culture is good or bad for the church. Some writers see it as a dire problem and urge Christians to move beyond it—canceling cancel culture, as it were. Rachel Hewitt (2019) in a recent article for *Relevant* titled "A Way Out of Cancel Culture in the Church" urges readers to follow the gentle and forgiving way of Christ rather than being so quick to "cancel each other out." Hewitt understands the utility of cancel culture for calling to task those who have abused power from their platforms—those who have preyed on the weak and the vulnerable—but suggests that church cancel culture, rather, is "when individuals or groups deviate from a set of community rules resulting in immediate and mass redaction of community approval." In Hewitt's conception, cancel culture is not Christlike because Christ welcomes outsiders into inclusive community and does not exclude, isolate, or mark as dangerous other or different. Other writers see cancel culture as a useful tool for apologetics and defending the faith from its enemies. Jacob Haywood (2020), blogging for *LifeWay*, a major Christian publisher, which canceled Rachel Held Evans's controversial books, argues that cancel culture may be a good thing since it encourages Christians "to verbalize the gospel in their communities, even and especially when there's opposition." "Bible-believing churches," Haywood continues, "must be able to articulate why they believe biblical truth and morality are absolute and true descriptions of reality." Haywood, here, acts defensively toward cancel culture, wary that outsiders will cancel traditional Christian theologies that part ways with liberal society's political correctness. Yet, he conveniently ignores the role that the evangelicalism itself plays in driving cancel culture. Haywood misses the fact promiscuous media have always been useful tools of critique.

From a media ecology perspective, what are we to make of cancel culture? Cancel culture, I'd argue, is but a symptom of a more pervasive media development that I've observed and documented in *The Digital Evangelicals*. The argument that I've advanced throughout the chapters of this book is that new, digital, social, habitual, and participatory media—what I've described as promiscuous media, or those discursive technologies disposed toward wide distribution and indiscriminate connection—have for evangelicals multiple paradoxical effects. Technology is a double-edged-sword. Promiscuous media solve some problems but breed others. Social media, for evangelicals, are both the answer to their troubles and a primary cause of those problems to begin with. Two key findings of this research are that promiscuous media have empowered marginal evangelical counterpublics, and that in their digital endeavors, these evangelicals have reconfigured and adapted the paradigms of sincerity and authenticity for a new era. In the remainder of the conclusion, I discuss the ramifications of these recent shifts in the evangelical media ecology regarding authority, authenticity, and American evangelical identity. I also confirm that evangelical Protestant media ideologies are never far from the surface of debates about media, even in public, secular, and extra-Christian contexts of communication.

The Digital Evangelicals began with two interrelated questions: In the digital era, to reiterate, how will authority and order survive? And in an age of mediation, complexity, and distraction, will authentic interpersonal communication die out? These case studies on digital evangelicalism, spanning print, online, offline, and virtual domains, provide particularly contradictory replies to this dual inquiry. Within the parameters of translocal evangelicalism, postdigital authority has become more fragile, dispersed, and decentered. As many of the manual writers from chapter 3 and the antiheresy Twitter discourse from chapter 4 confirm, gatekeepers of the traditional evangelical variety now have at their disposal the tools with which to extend their dominance into online domains.[2] Reformed collectives, such as *The Gospel Coalition*, and a podcast-centered online community, *The White Horse Inn*, do not denounce the dangers and wonders of technology so much as they take up these new platforms in order to contend against heterodoxy run rampant within Christian circles. Progressive media ideologies meld in intriguing combination with traditional theologies. Christian versions of the *Onion* such as the *Babylon Bee* use what contributors defend as satirical humor to advance the ideologies of traditional evangelicalism. Cancel culture is at least partly an inevitable result of evangelical deliberations popularized into the secular sphere. Cancel culture is the direct result of horizontally empowered social media users seeking to project their authority and ideologies.

Yet, this is a decentered sort of authority because digital media are a seedbed for the emergence of the nontraditional, theologically progressive gatekeepers who rail against their predecessors' authoritarianism. Cancel culture, as I've said, belongs to the left *and* the right. For as many vocally conservative collectives that arise (e.g., *The Gospel Coalition*), there are progressive counterparts (*The Liturgists*). Authority is tenuous in these new ecologies because, as we saw with the cases of the feminist bloggers and hybrid Instagram communities, there is no source or center of evangelical authority. In the experiences of these multiple evangelical counterpublics, the internet appears to have a horizontalizing effect as it lessens the criteria required to rise to the level of public gatekeeper. It also appears to be minimizing the criteria required for laypeople to engage in theological deliberation. There are still questions of class, socioeconomics, and the affordability and accessibility of new media tools (e.g., data phones, PCs, internet service, WiFi access, VR devices) to be considered (Alper 2017), but for the most part, such horizontalization looks to be widespread. As the ethnographic studies in chapters 7 and 8 suggest, the internet aids marginalized communities in downloading and uploading content, linking extralocal streams of progressive thought and practice, and vocally resisting what is to them the hegemonic forces of traditional evangelicalism—that is, commercialized, patriarchal, middle-class, mainstream, white Christianity.

But as this research has confirmed, no study of evangelical authority is complete without examining its inverse: authenticity. Indeed, the perpetuation of authority itself in these contexts traces back to the question of who has the power to advance convincing claims about what sorts of utterances and practices count as authoritative and genuine. In many cases, to denounce a new media form as inauthentic is to mark it as deficient and heterodox. Recall, for instance, the long discussion among evangelical technology critics, back in chapter 3, over whether virtual community counts as authentic. These debates have been going on for decades but have ramped up again with the creation of Virtual Church, not to mention the demands of COVID-19.

Progressive evangelicals, on the whole, argued that new forms of authenticity, emerging out of the digital, were possible. Most Reformed and theologically conservative critics, those who had a narrower definition of media sincerity, negated this argument—even as they used new media to make their claims. Feminist bloggers and progressive Christians, confirming the fears of evangelical traditionalists, commandeered the blogosphere to circulate oppositional messages to reading publics. In doing so, the bloggers theorized blogging practices as more rather than less authentic and sincere. Scott Bakken and his Instagram cohort experimented with hybrid everyday rituals that turned the inauthentic qualification on its head. Evangelicals on Instagram applied the inauthentic evaluation back on traditional forms of religious life and against those vocal online gatekeepers calling out heresy. Midwestern evangelicals on the ground made ambivalent yet steady use of new media platforms. Emerging evangelicals theorized the digital as reflecting and expanding (not negating or diminishing) sincerity and directness regarding theological formation and interpersonal connection. As the final examples suggest, VR is providing new realms of social connectivity for nontraditional congregations, seekers who would never set foot in a traditional church setting. Zoom is aiding evangelical congregations in ameliorating the ills of social isolation during quarantine.

DIGITAL MEDIA AND THE END OF EVANGELICALISM

In new media domains, including the discursive territory shaped by the sincerity/promiscuity tension, the crisis of authenticity and authority has come to a head. The conversation over authenticity and authority has become more public, visible, and accessible to evangelical laypeople than ever before. I have aimed in this book to advance a more accurate understanding of evangelicalism as a social, cultural, political, ecclesial, and religious collective. In the next few paragraphs, I reapproach the evangelical designation from the perspective of this book's findings.

What exactly is evangelicalism and what does the term *evangelical* encompass? From various scholarly perspectives, one might consider evangelicalism as a historical tradition, religious genre, ecclesial pattern, religioscape, theological formation, social phenomenon, belief system, cultural logic, or shared habitus.[3] Although not discounting these approaches, I have argued for defining evangelicalism in terms of discursive publics and media ecologies. Back in the introduction, to set the bounds for this study, I argued that evangelicals are those Protestants who invest their time trying to solve the conundrum of media sincerity and promiscuity. That is, for the provisional interests of this book, evangelicals are those Protestants who experience anxiety about how media may shape the message and vice versa. A flexible definitional strategy like this one is necessary due to the highly discursive and fragmented nature of the collective. This book confirms that not all evangelicals see eye to eye or concede the opposition's standing as either authentically evangelical or legitimately Christian. But regardless of these contentions, the evangelicals do unite over certain questions and act within the same media milieus.

In terms of this ingrained tension about media and mediation, I have argued throughout these chapters that American evangelicals, both at present and throughout the centuries, have had to creatively adapt their ideologies of media and communication to carry on with their tradition of synthesis. The relationship between sincerity and promiscuity ebbs and flows. Sometimes, as with the critics in chapter 3, the standard of sincerity remains dominant. In other cases, such as the revivalist preachers in chapter 2, promiscuity plays the governing role. I have documented, further, that any adoption of promiscuous media brings unanticipated side effects. At a foundational level, a significant implication of the evangelical love-hate relationship with promiscuous media is that the collective's technology use alters the bounds of the collective. In this manner, and confirming critics' worries, promiscuous media have been too effective, too powerful in their abilities to expand address and generate audiences. Digital evangelicalism, with its rapid processes of pluralization and fragmentation, is the victim of its own success.

It may be the case that digital media's attendant leveling effects of horizontalization and exposure will contribute to the watering down of evangelicalism as a meaningful designation. For gatekeepers who have a traditional model of authenticity in mind, this may very well be the end of so-called authentic evangelicalism. Digitally buffered selves encounter other digitally buffered selves online. As some theological commentators have worried, the designation may include far too much under its definition (Hart 2004; Olson 2016; cf. Altman 2019). Given this exposure via online confrontation, evangelicalism as a term may be reaching a breaking point. Its inclusivity and wideness may render the term nonsensical. The term's elasticity may also suggest its meaningless. What these chapters suggest, rather, is that digital media aid conflicting theologies and ideologies in coming into existence. For this exact reason, for groups who feel their power becoming threatened, digital media are, indeed, dangerous. On the contrary, for the progressives, digital media—provided one can manage the side effects of informational saturation and overstimulation, social thinness, and neoliberal effects, among other attendant problems—are tools for nurturing thriving communities outside of the mainstream and nominal. Depending on one's stance, then, digital media may signal the end of evangelicalism as a coherent theological tradition. But keep in mind that for many evangelicals, especially some of the progressive voices featured in this book, the end of American evangelicalism as history currently knows it—evangelicalism as it codes white, republican, capitalist, and conservative—would be a welcome event.

None of these situations are new. Newness, again, is an arbitrary qualifier with an increasingly short shelf life. Evangelicalism as an ecclesial category typically has organized several converging and conflicting streams under its purview. But these tensions in the era of digital media have become heightened and emphasized in their visibility and publicness. Exposure to the varieties of evangelicalism increase. Evangelicalism has often been defined by the theological similarities and differences within its bounds, but now such distinctions are more glaringly present due to the ongoing operations of digitally buffered selfhood. Difference is only the click of a mouse or the swipe of a screen away. The horizontalizing affordances of digital media have brought about an extended sense of buffered self-reflexivity and boundary maintenance. Whereas the imagined "we" may have at one point in history been taken for granted, digital media put a magnifying glass on the cracks, ruptures, and fractures embedded within such a tenuous designation. Whoever these digital evangelicals are, and are becoming, they and their discursive media are many. And they don't often agree with one another.[4]

EVANGELICAL MEDIA BEYOND EVANGELICALISM

This book has been about American evangelicalism, but the implications of its findings regarding contemporary social media use expand much further than this one religious public. For one thing, evangelical social media users don't wrestle with the dueling tensions of media sincerity and promiscuity alone. Anyone with a data phone or a tablet—anyone who logs onto social media via any touch screen—inherits the ecology engendered by the struggle to meld the sincere and authentic with the wide reaching. Not even nonreligious social media users are immune to this tension, which emerged long ago out of heated religious contention and resistance to Christian institutions. In the following paragraphs, I issue two challenges to scholars of religion, digital culture, and global technologies.

One contributing logic informing the birth of the internet and the new media ecology was Protestant anti-institutional rhetoric. Internet architects adopted Protestant language and ideas in their experimentation with networking technologies, personal computers, and the World Wide Web. The sincerity/promiscuity conundrum structured the internet from its most inchoate years. But evangelical discourse was not the only ideology at play during this time of rapid technological development. Many figures in the tech world have been agnostic, atheist, spiritual-but-not-religious, or generally nonreligious by their own identifications and affiliations. Others have been influenced by ideologies outside of Christianity, whether it be secular humanism, Buddhism, or Unitarian Universalism. Steve Jobs, cofounder of Apple, practiced Zen Buddhism and applied the aesthetics of these practices to the very materiality of his institution's technological objects. As his biographer has noted, "Jobs's engagement with Eastern spirituality, and especially Zen Buddhism, was not just some passing fancy or youthful dabbling. He embraced it with his typical intensity, and it became deeply ingrained in his personality." Colleagues have drawn a direct line between Buddhism and Apple products' very design, with the "stark, minimalist aesthetics" Apple has become famous for (Isaacson 2011, 35). In addition to Jobs, Tim Berners-Lee (2000), credited with having invented the World Wide Web in the late 1980s, at first took a humanistic, antihierarchical approach to designing it. But he later gravitated toward Unitarian Universalism's theological minimalism, seeing it as the perfect spiritual fit for his philosophy of life and the internet.[5]

Both digital media tools and the internet itself are cultural carriers of multiple religious and nonreligious logics. This book has highlighted the specifically Protestant undertones of internet design and digital media affordances, but more work is needed to uncover how these and other diverse ideologies, converging and conflicting, mix together to inform not only the history of the internet as a network of networks but also the ways such eclectic ideas shape the affordances of internet-mediated apps, gadgets, and tools that follow. One challenge for scholars, then, is to better understand how digital technologies emerge within particular social and cultural systems and are then exported into or against other social and cultural systems.

A second challenge has to do with the complexity of promiscuous evangelical media in a networked world made up of more than just evangelicals. Questions of authenticity and orthodoxy do not belong to the evangelicals alone.

Evangelicalism does not corner the market of evangelical media. Some of the most successful and wide-reaching evangelical media, after all, are the pervasive capitalist advertisements that clog social media and other websites. To put this differently, evangelical media are not the sole terrain of evangelicalism, or Protestantism, or Christianity. Beyond global capitalism, global religious traditions are all struggling, in different ways, with the sincerity/promiscuity predicament. This is to say that in the reception and uptake of digital media, different traditions operate within different overlapping ecologies. The overlap comes from digital media's successful colonization of the global media sphere. The difference comes from how traditions draw on their own logics, media ideologies, and theologies of media to determine how best to put these tools to use. The balance between sincerity and promiscuity plays out in different ways. I've focused here on how American evangelicals wrestle with their theological baggage and media ideologies. But other groups use different theological and ideological tool belts to do so. Consider two brief examples.

In Buddhism, an evangelizing religion older than Christianity, teachers have drawn on the concept of *upaya*, or "skillful means for disseminating the teaching," which allows for "unorthodox practices in the name of strengthening the message of the Buddha" (Grieve and Veidlinger 2015, 3). In Buddhism, questions of authority and authenticity are never far from view. Are digital Buddhist practices "actually skillful means for disseminating real Buddhism, or just dharma dilution and commercialization?" These are questions scholars and practitioners of Buddhism must wrestle with, and this is evidence of the implicit sincerity/promiscuity impulses operating silently in the background of their own pronouncements. Skillful means is a concept foreign to Christianity, yet the shared terrain between that and evangelical revivalists' justification of new media for fulfilling the Great Commission is ripe for comparison. In Islam, as well, scholars note that structures of traditional authority are changing as the internet provides new realms of authoritative information, with websites and apps now granting fatwas and other authoritative advices on religious inquiries (Bunt 2018). Like evangelicalism in America, global Islam may also be facing reconfigurations in traditional structures of power and authority due to digital horizontalization and increased internet access and social media use.

What exactly, one might ask following these questions of authority and authenticity, are new media good for? In terms of human epochs, we're only at the beginning of this digital era, so it will take a much longer retrospective, historical view to determine the full ramifications of these new habitual digital technologies on everyday life. But as this book has shown, digital media are skilled at bringing into heightened relief things that in older media ecologies may have been taken for granted as fixed and final. Digital media both challenge and reinforce concepts like authority, authenticity, realness, sincerity, virtue, orthodoxy, and order. New media are good for reconfiguring social, cultural, and religious systems. New media are good for sharing. New media are good for thinking and arguing. New media are good for world building and for building up and tearing down social constellations of words, ideas, texts, and images. New media are good for constructing religious empires and toppling them.

New media explode the inherited barometers of social and religious authenticity and redefine the boundaries of the legitimate and real.

POSTSCRIPT: NEGATIVE MEDIA IDEOLOGIES
AND SHITSTORMS ARE DATA

Three recent books on digital media came into publication toward the end my research. Adam Greenfield's *Radical Technologies: The Design of Everyday Life* (2017), Byung-Chul Han's *In the Swarm: Digital Prospects* (2017), and James Bridle's *New Dark Age: Technology and the End of the Future* (2018) all addressed technology through varying degrees of negative commentary. These studies together provide an opportunity to theorize about the affordances of social media and the weaknesses of many approaches to the study of new media. As I suggested in chapter 2, the evangelical tension between sincerity and promiscuity is one that over time has genericized and influenced social formation far beyond the religious boundaries of the tension's origins. In this expanded sense, evangelical media deliberations are American ones.

In Greenfield's *Radical Technologies*, state and institutional surveillance and the storing and evaluation of all social activities as data take center stage. The book's central concern is that there is not at present, and certainly will not be in the future, a single dimension of life that can be experienced outside of digital and information technologies. Bridle's *New Dark Age* follows suit, focusing on the hidden environmental problems wrought by digital infrastructures. Thoroughly Heideggerian in his criticisms, Bridle worries about the pervasiveness of digital networks and the ability of technologies to conceal from view the full effects of its structures and outcomes. This writer's call for the careful and disciplined stewardship of new technologies, rather than rejecting them outright, could be a page out of an evangelical technology manual. I want to focus momentarily, however, on the third recent work mentioned above, penned by an unabashed critic of technology.

Han's concise yet philosophically dense *In the Swarm*, which makes the two prior works appear relatively balanced, leverages a blatantly negative media ideology from the text's opening pages. The crisis global humanity is facing in light of the rise of digital technologies, Han (2017, ix, 3–4) argues, "Follows from our blindness and stupefaction." This author focuses on what he describes as the shitstorm, what is for Han both a technical term and a nod to a colloquial description of online engagements. In his definition, the shitstorm is a situation arising in a digital networking culture where "respect is lacking and indiscretion prevails." For this philosopher, digital connectivity is impulsive, devoid of necessary hierarchy, and destructive of regimes of power. According to Han, "Shitstorms flourish where hierarchies have flattened out." *In the Swarm* advances a critical theory of *homo digitalis*. Together with *Radical Technologies* and *New Dark Age*—and in the tradition of Sherry Turkle's (2011) and Werner Herzog's (2016) critical work—the grim state of social media studies, on the whole, appears unable to envision alternate possibilities of the new media era outside of nightmarish Orwellian scenarios.

I want to suggest that evaluative descriptors such as *stupefaction, indiscretion, shitstorm, real, unreal, authentic, inauthentic, genuine, orthodox,* and *heterodox*—among myriad others—are firsthand, folk, colloquial, and, in a word, nonscholarly languages. New media do not require scholarly approval or disapproval but rather critical study. To employ such normative and ideologically loaded concepts is to fail to observe, identify, and scrutinize the quotidian valuations that informants deploy in their deliberations about communication. Best-selling books and news articles on the addictiveness of mobile technologies are as relevant for the scholar of technology as internecine theological and ecclesial debates by religious authorities on the authenticity and orthodoxy of online religion. Media ideologies are everywhere in operation.

The chapters thus far have been primarily descriptive rather than prescriptive, but I attempt, momentarily, a normative voice when I argue that scholars should study such ideologies but refrain from producing them. Encompassing claims about what the internet is—i.e., the End of Civilization, the Great Leveler, the Dearth of Interpersonal Politeness, the Anti-Christ, the Priesthood of All Believers, etc.—are all data for study. Any grand explanatory, totalizing, or decidedly normative stance about new media or digital religiosity is data for study, as Russell McCutcheon (2014, 56–57; 2002, 14, 18–19) argues about an analogous situation. Pure immunity to media ideologies is, of course, impossible, as are unqualified appeals to supposed scholarly objectivity or neutrality (Cooper 2017a; 2019b). But scholars' primary aim should be to redescribe and contextualize informant practices and not to contribute to chaos rhetoric.

Let me clarify. These critical works are valuable in that they turn attention to the negative ramifications of new media. We can learn much from Greenfield, Bridle, and Han even if we disagree with their overriding normative stances. I am not advocating that one study the internet and habitual media through rose-colored glasses or ignore the hypercapitalist, neoliberal, and panopticonic characteristics of new media. But ultimately, my concern is that these works run the risk of reinforcing the dominant social order by marking the digital as an arena of otherness, difference, and disorder. Criticisms of this sort, taken too far, can border an ableism and ignore the usefulness of digital media for marginal communities (Alper 2017; Haller 2010). Insufficiently critical works in this tradition ignore or are oblivious to the payoff of social media's affordances for creating and maintaining counterpublics against hegemonic structures.

Performing negative media ideologies rather than analyzing them, these books fail to realize how real-world people, often social marginals or disenfranchised subcultures of some sort, are putting these media to use for their own reasons. As my ethnographic case studies demonstrate, people are not blind adopters of digital media—mindless cultural drones, as Han sometimes tends to depict them—but shrewd users who are particularly attuned to and thoroughly calculative with regard to the costs, benefits, and detractions of new media uses. For these reasons, what the field of social media studies needs is not another critical media ideology levied against digital technologies but more ethnographic investigations that observe and analyze digital practices on the ground. *The Digital Evangelicals* joins a small cohort of scholarship moving in this direction, but there is still much work to do.

NOTES

1. See Smith 2020b on the gendered aspects of Falwell's fall from evangelical grace.
2. For a study of conservative fundamentalist Christian formations online, see Howard 2011.
3. The term *religioscape* builds off of Appadurai's classic (1991) list of "scapes" in the globalizing era. Tweed (2006) also employs the term in this manner. Tomlinson and Engelke (2006, 19) describe the religious category as a **cultural logic** of sorts. On evangelicalism as a shared habitus, see Ingersoll 2003, 13, and Martin 2012, 88. The texts that have considered evangelicalism as a historical, theological, and ecclesial designation are too numerous to list here. Although scholars have begun to study evangelicalism as a public or counterpublic of circulating discourses (Vaca 2019), to my knowledge, this book is unique in describing evangelicalism as a veritable media ecology.
4. Christopher Cantwell (2018, 282) confirms that "any portrayal of evangelicalism that emphasizes its commonalities will either downplay or obscure the internal diversity that may very well give the movement its energy and shape." New media reveal the range of diversity encapsulated under the category.
5. "[M]y wife and I came across Unitarian Universalism [UU]," Berners-Lee (2000, 207–208) writes. "Walking into a [UU] church more or less by chance felt like a breath of fresh air. Some of the association's basic philosophies very much match what I had been brought up to believe, and the objective I had in creating the Web." Berners-Lee mentions that people often inquire as to UU's impact on his pioneering web design work. Given that it was a later-in-life discovery, he answers that UU clearly "had no influence on the Web. But I can see how it could have, because I did indeed design the Web around universalist (with a lowercase u) principles."

APPENDIX

1. METHODOLOGICAL CONSIDERATIONS

One academic group, the Committee on the Anthropology of Science, Technology, and Computing (CASTAC), recently chose the platypus as the name, image, and totem for their updated and redesigned blog platform. Why the platypus, exactly? As the editors clarified, the platypus, a "rare endemic species from Australia," is "a symbol of bricolage" and synonym for eclecticism, combination, and strangeness. "Like the platypus with its duck-like bill, fur, webbed feet, venomous spurs, electroreception, lactation and oviparity," the editors explained, "CASTAC's membership is an eclectic collection of anthropologists who represent diverse areas of expertise and sets of skills" (Platypus 2019). Likewise, to describe the research methods that fueled a project like this as simply "hybrid" or "multi-site" would be an understatement. *The Digital Evangelicals*, methodologically, is a bit of a platypus itself.

This method-, theory-, and history-oriented appendix describes some of the behind-the-scenes work involved in a study of evangelical formations across both online and offline domains. In particular, the subsections below refer to chapter 3 (on the technology books) and chapter 5 (on the blogosphere). Finally, several sections refer to and extend parts of chapter 6 (on Instagram). As I described in the introduction, the methodological eclecticism required of digital anthropology and social media studies is not to its detriment. Such multimodal, mixed-method, and interdisciplinary approaches provide a more holistic picture of the increasingly complex worlds in which we live. The information below was not immediately central to each of the above chapters' respective narratives, but it is nonetheless valuable for clarifying procedure, methods, and in some cases, historical backdrops. I focus on the technology manuals (2), the blogosphere (3), Instagram (4), and negative media ideologies (5). The Instagram section also includes a brief history of theological Romanticism (4.2) and an in-depth consideration of the types of visual scripts and pictorial genres that the platform affords, both Instagram-wide (4.3) and Socality specific (4.4).

2. TECHNOLOGY MANUALS

2.1 Selection Criteria and Methods

How did I arrive at the corpus of books discussed in chapter 3? A brief word on the process by which I vetted possible candidates for study is required. The first strategy for selection is best characterized as a digital anthropology of online capitalism. Using the same online search engines consulted frequently by my informants in the nonvirtual field, I exploited Amazon and Google algorithms in my research. A series of online searches by way of several keyword combinations ("Christians and technology," "social media and religion," "religion and digital communication," "social media and the church," etc.) quickly yielded, thanks to sophisticated algorithmic customizations, a number of relevant books on subjects central to my interests. Authors I had heard discussed directly in my fieldwork (i.e., Sweet, Challies, and Detweiler) immediately stood out.

Once I had identified four or five pertinent books, the challenge became how to gauge whether the manual was sufficiently "evangelical." Again, one might point out the discursive slipperiness of this term as various Christian subgroups resist, adopt, and sometimes distance from the classification for a range of different reasons. To make the determination, I resorted to publishing firms. For instance, Zondervan, the most popular publisher for the selected corpus, is historically one of the most successful evangelical publishing companies. Similarly, other editorial firms, including WaterBrook, Moody, and David C. Cook, have consistently published content for mainstream evangelical and conservative Christian audiences.

After acquiring around half of the manuals, I consulted the authors' prefaces, acknowledgments, in-text citations, references, and endnotes, as well as bibliographies and works cited to determine which sources writers found influential. The process confirmed for me the densely networked nature and complex system of connections, links, positive and negative citations, allusions, references, endorsements, distancing strategies, and associations that constitute the public of evangelical words and letters. Recognizing the manuals as a body of interlinked and networked cotexts or intertexts (Silverstein and Urban 1996, 6), I acquired the rest of the corpus. To name an example of the authorial linkages, Detweiler (2013, viii) acknowledges Rice (2009), Drescher (2011), Estes (2009), Schultze

(2002), Hipps (2009), and Challies (2015 [2011]). He also draws on an earlier book by Sweet. Because Hipps is one of the most prominent evangelical theorists of media and technology, Rice (2009, 163–173), Dyer (2011, 128), Sweet (2012, 53, 169, 179–180, 183), and Bourgeois (2013, 7, 48–50) all make note of his work, either to appropriate or challenge it. Drescher (2011, 105) cites research by Schultz. Sweet (2012, 109, 183–184) and Detweiler (2013, 162–163) invoke Rice (2009). Wise (2014, 39, 103–104) references Bourgeois (2013) and Dyer (2011).

In the end, I uncovered a networked community of texts in constructive dialogue and contestation with one another. I did not intend to identify every work published along these lines but through combined textual analysis methods, including memoing, theoretical sampling (Bernard 2011, 435), and analytic coding (Matthews and Ross 2010, 400–401) sought to systematically analyze the body of works. I did not intend to be exhaustive but aimed to identify a representative set of texts. Between putting to use digital algorithms, consulting textual sources, and contextualizing the works in light of knowledge gathered in offline fieldwork, I achieved sufficient theoretical saturation (Bernard 2011, 435) in terms of content and argument.

2.2 Author Backgrounds, Occupations, and Training

The manual authors hail from a wide range of educational backgrounds. Ten have advanced ministry or counseling degrees, including Wise's master of divinity (MDiv), Rice's master of arts (MA) in counseling psychology, and Smith's MA in ministry leadership. Seven of the writers either hold or were working toward doctor of philosophy (PhD) degrees at the time the respective books came into print, including Shultz in communication, Estes and Dyer in theology, Drescher in Christian spirituality, Sweet in history, Bourgeois in information systems and technology, and Detwiler in theology and culture. In addition to his PhD in progress, Dyer held a master of theology (ThM). Sweet had completed both PhD and Mdiv degrees. Besides his PhD in theology and culture, Detweiler had earned not only an Mdiv but also master of fine arts (MFA), specializing in cinema and television. Supplementing his PhD in technology, Bourgeois had earned an MA in management science.

Occupationally, just under half of the writers (namely, Schultze, Estes, Drescher, Sweet, Bourgeois, and Detweiler) are college professors. Dyer, in addition, is director of communications and educational technology at a Protestant seminary. Others are worship leaders (Rice) and pastors and ministers (Rice, Estes, Hipps, Dyer, Smith, and Challies) or have worked as professionals in churches but in nonpastoral capacities (Wise). As educators or ministers, many of the authors (Rice, Hipps, Crawford, Sweet, and Challies, among others) travel as public speakers in addition to other occupational obligations. A significant minority of the writers also have employment outside of the academy or the church. Crawford identifies as a "social media consultant." Drescher does business management and consulting for organizational development. Bourgeois is an information systems analyst, computer programmer, and consultant in related fields. Wise identifies as a "social media strategist" and founder of a social marketing agency. In addition, he runs an initiative that consults for and trains church communications directors. Challies works as a web designer. Hipps has a pastoral background but also approaches technology criticism having had significant training in consumer anthropology under employment for large corporate advertising campaigns, including Porsche. He has also dabbled, on his own, in advertising and real estate. Related to but also expanding past his academic work, Detweiler is an award-winning filmmaker and "cultural commentator." Likewise, Sweet identifies not only as a semiotician, historian, and theologian in academic parlance but is also, in his own words, a "social critic and cultural observer." Finally, many of the figures considered in this chapter produce and maintain web presences, ranging from simple informational websites to regularly updated and heavily trafficked blogs. Challies, for example, self-describes as a "pioneer in the Christian blogosphere." Many of the others also produce regular content via Facebook, Twitter, and microblog and blog pages.

3. THE BLOGOSPHERE

Like the textual community discussed just above, I constructed the corpus of feminist blogs from chapter 4 in a circuitous manner. In the initial research stages back in 2012, and through a digital ethnographic a process called theoretical sampling, I identified a wide number of microblog and blog sites written on the topics of Christianity, feminism, and purity culture. To engage a focused number of bloggers through qualitative case study methods, I then narrowed the number of blogs to include those seven that were, at the time, contributing in the most sustained ways to the conversations about modesty, purity, clothing, sexuality, and the body.

Not all the writers identify positively with evangelicalism. As self-identifying progressives, several of the writers either defected from evangelicalism proper as an adult or write from a self-critical stance about their own tradition. I include these post-, quasi-, or extraevangelical voices in this chapter because I am interested in the discursive boundaries of this evangelical entity. All seven writers analyzed in this chapter are at the forefront of constructing, criticizing, or resisting the boundaries of evangelicalism.

After identifying blogs to study, I applied the discursive and textual analysis models of memoing, taking field notes on blog texts, and analytic coding—the documenting of recurring patterns, shared concepts, or common discursive strategies in the texts. My goal in conducting this series of case studies was not to exhaustively analyze the entire progressive feminist blogosphere but, as with the above textual corpus, to reach a point of theoretical saturation, an accounting for a good portion of recurring concepts and themes in a particular discourse or narrative field. Given my position as a social anthropologist studying digital media practices, my use of exemplary quotes from the respective blog pages was the most efficient way to demonstrate the complexly interrelated counterpublic's emergence through a body of co- or intertexts. For thorough descriptions of these discursive methods, see Bernard 2011, 435–438; Matthews and Ross 2010, 400–401; and Silverstein and Urban 1996, 6. For more on narrative analysis and the value of comparative case studies, see Wells 2011, 16–17.

4. INSTAGRAM AND SOCALITY

4.1 Socality.org: Functions and Purpose

Socality.org serves as a medium for connection. Beyond recording the group's history and values in an informative sense, it contains crucial information for those persons who wish to be part of the movement. A "Get Started" page delineates six steps for getting involved with the Socality collective: (1) connect globally; (2) connect locally; (3) connect with us; (4) engage digitally; (5) engage in person; and (6) spread the word. The six directives speak to Bakken's modus operandi. He wishes to span the digital/real-world divide and facilitate meaningful authentic connections of love, friendship, and goodwill. As the description for the first directive exhorts readers, "Start using #socality. This hashtag will help you discover and connect with people who are a part of this movement all over the globe. You don't have to use the hashtag in your own posts, but it will certainly help you meet new people." The second directive shifts away from international and global social connections mediated by Instagram and the #socality hashtag. Instead, it refocuses on the local, which is mediated by closed regional Facebook groups. These localized Facebook groups include microcollectives, such as #socalityseattle, #socalitywashington, or #socalityindiana, where members organize outings and get-togethers to meet, commune, and interact in person.

Still a third directive simply lists the icons of various platforms that one might interact with Socality as an organization: Instagram, Facebook, Twitter, Vimeo, and YouTube. The fourth directive parallels the first but provides more detail on community obligations and online interactions: "*Engage* with others and make yourself known. *Comment* and like other people's photos to get to know each other; you never know what amazing friendships could be formed." The fifth elaborates on the second: "Attend a meet-up, a community dinner or a conversation hosted in your local area. Check out your local hashtag for more." Members can also get involved through "Community Projects designed to bring us together as a community to make an impact." The sixth directive, "spread the word," tips its hat to Socality's evangelical identity. "Don't only engage with the current community, but actively pursue inviting new people. Everyone is invited!" Part of the loosely defined requirements for being a part of Socality requires active proselytization, not necessarily (or immediately) for the saving of souls but on behalf of the community itself. Socality's version of evangelicalism, with its emphasis on visual art and avoidance of overt doctrinal statements, blurs the distinction between proselytization and advertising. Such evangelical theological vagueness may also characterize the collective as operating in a nondenominational paradigm that downplays theological distinctions for the sake of unity and connection.[1]

Finally, a function of the website is to host a group blog or "Journal" page. Socality.org documents the collective's founding, values, steps for involvement, and links for various platform presences across the internet and the local chapters, but the page also serves as a platform through which users can write about a range of topics important to Socality as a whole. The journal showcases member interviews, brief biographical sketches, write-ups on recent regional gatherings, and appraisals of certain types of fair trade and antisweatshop products and goods important to the collective's love of outdoor life, adventure, and urban and nature exploration. The journal features with every post characteristically high-quality, glossy photography of people traveling or scenic landscapes that are so central to the collective's identity.

4.2 Romanticism and Evangelicalism: A Contentious History

Part of chapter 6's thesis is that there is something of a revival or renewal of theological Romanticism among Socality evangelicals. But the relationship, as I show in this section, has historically been strained.[2] In short, there is a historically fraught and complicated connection between nineteenth-century American evangelicals and the Romantics in terms of biblical authority and textuality (Brown 2004, 3, 44–45, 201). Regardless of the rift over biblical authority, however, evangelical trade publishers in this era began to realize the importance of making visual art "subservient to the advancement of piety" (162) by the pictorial or illustrated accompaniment of text-based works for increasing aesthetic beauty (64–78, 240), marketing books to children (105–106), instructing children visually about other cultures and nationalities (113), and competing in broader literature markets that demanded illustrations by woodcuts or other visual techniques (158, 164).

The historical and theological connection between evangelicalism and Romanticism is certainly complex. But to borrow Bebbington's (1990, 10, 11) phrasing, evangelicalism was indeed "modified by the Romantic influences." According to this historian, "During the course of the nineteenth century, in different fields at different stages, Evangelicalism came to terms in many ways with Romantic thought." Such a coming to terms had to do with the adoption by evangelicals of Romanticism's poetic sensibilities and an emphasis on feeling—an emotive turn that went as far as to structure the practices of evangelical musicians, such as revivalist Dwight L. Moody's song leader, Ira D. Sankey. Bebbington argues that the Romantic turn in evangelicalism magnified desires to interact directly with the supernatural and resisted the Enlightenment's reification of the individual by refocusing on the importance of the social (11–12).

Most importantly, for the purposes of this book, Bebbington (1990, 12) reflects on the reconfiguration that occurred within the evangelical "field of aesthetics." "Attention for the beautiful was a Romantic preoccupation which certainly affected the church," Bebbington notes. In this direction evangelical churches experienced a growing "concern with nature." The Romantic turn led to a decisive conservative and liberal split within evangelical camps, a split that came to a head during the fundamentalist-modernist controversy during the 1920s. Three factors of development within conservative camps proceeding directly out of Romanticism included premillennialist theologies, the doctrine of biblical inerrancy, and the higher life movement (13–14). In terms of evangelical liberalization and doctrinal change, Bebbington argues that Romanticism "created a preference for vaguer statements of belief" and that "aversion to dogma became general." In short, evangelicalism proved highly adaptable to broader religious, cultural, artistic, and aesthetic trends. Romanticism gave rise to a pervasive form of "mystic religiosity" within and without evangelicalism (14, 15).

Other scholars confirm Bebbington's claims. Chad Stutz (2009), in his "Christians, Critics, and Romantics: Aesthetic Discourse among Anglo-American Evangelicals, 1830–1900," shows that Romanticism influenced the evangelicals as early as the 1830s. Further, for Stutz, Romanticism "initiated a break with the Puritan aesthetic tradition that contributed to the growth of a modern aesthetic consciousness." Some evangelical watchdog groups even warn readers about the heterodox theologies found in writings by C. S. Lewis and J. R. R. Tolkien, influential writers and scholars who were, and continue to be, wildly popular with evangelical audiences. Gatekeepers historicize Lewis and Tolkien as constituting a "Revived" or "Christian" form of Romanticism (Nathan and Nathan 2006; Davidson n.d.).[3]

4.3 Instagram, Mimesis, and Visual Scripting

One subsequent confirmation of this research is that Instagram operates by way of visual scripts and imagery genres. Given the high editability of Instagram's photographys, the close connection between Friedrich's painting and @matt_kuma's photograph appears intentional. Other Socality images in the style or script of the pensive Friedrichian landscape, to name only a few, include @wildrecollection (2015), @griffinlamb (2015), @haleyswinth (2015), @dyerandjenkins (2015), @philipleclerc (2016b), @bethelredding (2016) and perhaps even @lennartpagel (2016) or @jamieout (2016).

In short, visual content scripts circulate via Instagram. Whether or not such visual scripts are replicated intentionally is another story. For a contemporary example that suggests visual imitation is purposeful, consider photographer Murad Osmann's "Follow Me To" Instagram project, which went viral back in 2013. Osmann's visual style—images that feature part of his own arm extending out to grasp the hand of Nataly, his (then) girlfriend (now wife), who faced away from Osmann's camera, appearing to lead him in their travels and explorations all over the world—quickly took off (see Osmann and Zakharova 2016). Some Socality users replicate Osmann's visual script exactly. Compare, for instance, @dirka (2016c) with @muradosmann (2017).

One could push this visual mimesis theory further. My research suggests that Instagrammers are replicating visual scripts they have been exposed to not only through popular Instagram accounts but by visiting art museums, taking undergraduate art history classes, engaging in popular culture through film, and so on. As with the case of the Instagram-mediated collective, *Kinfolk* magazine, readers draw on aesthetics observed in particular types of art house films (Manovich 2016, 10–16). Although not overtly evangelical like Socality, *Kinfolk* wrestles with its own religious backgrounds. The magazine's editorial board, in fact, emerged out of the progressive margins of contemporary Mormonism (Chayka 2016; Cooper 2018). Like *Kinfolk*, Socality intends to resist the social fragmentation and loss of time it perceives as rife in the new media era.

4.4 Socality Visual Analysis: Full Findings

The primary data corpus for chapter 6 included exactly 1,211 Instagram images produced and uploaded by Socality. I began my analysis aware that typical Instagram use across the globe falls into eight primary content categories, including (1) friends; (2) food and drink; (3) gadgets or tools; (4) captions, word texts, or memes; (5) pets (primarily cats and dogs); (6) indoor or outdoor activities and events or places or locations; (7) selfies; and (8) fashion, makeup, and accessories (Hu, Manikonda, and Kambhampati 2014, 3). The content analysis procedures I employed in this project, however, suggested that the eightfold model is too simple. A digitally ethnographic approach uncovered in Socality's visual output more complex categorical combinations than allowed for by the generic categories identified in previous studies. In place of the eight exclusive and seemingly distinct categories, I identified sixteen overlapping image genres. Stipulating coinciding or merging categories rather than exclusive or distinctive ones allowed for a more accurate documentation of the content of Socality's image corpus.

The sixteen overlapping Socality genres emerging out of my coding include the visual categories of (1) portrait; (2) group portrait; (3) person(s) in nature; (4) person(s) in city or urban setting; (5) landscape or nature; (6) cityscape; (7) building, architecture, or structure; (8) object or artifact; (9) technology, cell phone, or camera; (10) animal or pet; (11) food or drink; (12) restaurant or café; (13) Socality emblem, brand, or symbol; (14) meme, written information, or text; (15) religious, devotional, or iconographic imagery; and (16) church building, architecture, or interior.

A brief description of the subcategories lays the groundwork for the discussion of the frequency and overlapping aspects of the taxonomy. The (1) portrait grouping is perhaps the most straightforward and involves the presentation of some sort of human form as the main object of observation.[4] In other words, a human face or body must in a presentational sense serve as the image's primary subject. Portraits in this analysis are not identical to selfies or even self-portraits, contrary to previous studies' findings.[5] (2) Group portraits, in addition, include photographs whose primary content is two or more people. Although I included couples in the genre, typically group portraits include large gatherings of people together on a beach or outdoors.[6]

(3) Person(s) in nature is not a portrait, since the main object of visual focus is the natural setting, landscape, or panorama in which a person or a group is part. In this category, it is sometimes difficult to determine whether the landscape or the person is the primary visual focus.[7] Contrary to the human form within the landscape, (4) person(s) in city or urban setting showcase pedestrians with skyscraper backdrops or human silhouettes against various illuminated cityscapes.[8] When the human form is absent in the urban setting, the image falls into the (6) cityscape genre.[9]

Different than person in city and person in nature but similar to cityscape, (5) landscape and nature is devoid (or mostly devoid) of the human form. Occasionally, people are present but are difficult to spot as they are mere specks in the visually arresting mountainous terrain.[10] Whereas in the person-in-nature category both people and nature might constitute the primary content of the image, in landscape and nature, humans are either nonexistent or so miniature in scale that they do little to diminish the sense of natural grandeur conveyed by the image.[11]

(7) Building, architecture, or structure documents the frequent presence of bridges,[12] roadways,[13] train tracks,[14] docks,[15] and other sorts of built or architectural features[16] or backdrops of the Socality images. (8) object or artifact includes

a wide set of objects or materials, things ranging from blankets, to books, to consumer goods, to maps, to transportation vehicles of various sorts.[17] Similar to the previous genre, (9) technology includes pictures wherein smaller technologies, including tablets, laptops, and cell phones or cameras, made appearances.[18] Another visual designation includes (10) animals or pets as the primary focus.[19] And still another category encompasses not only generic objects or things, as per above, but (11) food or drinks or other consumable materials.[20] A small but significant number of the photographic corpus has a (12) restaurant, café, or coffee shop setting as the backdrop.[21]

Finally, the last four visual categories encompassing the Socality image corpus have to do with language, information, symbolism, and visual religion. The (13) Socality emblem grouping notes those instances wherein the Socality image—a clover-looking, circular symbol—appears as a brand on blankets and clothing or in wooden sculptural form as an object itself.[22] (14) Meme, written information, or text includes images on which Socality facilitators layer textual or linguistic information by means of short quotes, hashtagged materials, or other short written segments. Such informational bytes contained pertinent material about local community gatherings, inspirational discourses, fundraisers, or other social initiatives and were not part of the textual caption but included on the image itself.[23] The last two groupings included overt markers of (15) religious, devotional, or iconographic representation[24] or explicit imagery having to do with (16) church buildings, architecture, or interiors.[25]

Among the sixteen overlapping subject genres, those visual forms relating to nature and landscapes are by far the most dominant. Table A.1 details the content analysis findings in descending order.

Reinforcing findings that Instagram images are commonly posted along with geographic or locational information (Manikonda et al. 2014, 1; cf. Frith 2015),[26] by far the two highest groupings of Socality images are categories 3 and 5. Statistically, Socality's highest concentration of images showcase landscapes and natural settings. Nearly 38 percent of the Socality corpus features high-quality imagery of mountains, lakes, beaches, forests, rivers, deserts, and plains, among other topographic and geographic areas. More than a third (35.1 percent) of Socality's images also feature natural backdrops showcasing the human form, in some capacity, as part of its primary photographic subject content. Think, here, of majestic snowcapped mountains at the base of which climbs a miniscule person. Typically in this genre nature is grand, lofty, expansive, awe-inspiring, and even at times borders on imposing. Explorers, hikers, and adventurers, to the contrary, are small and isolated characters against nature's vast sublimity. Together, the nature images coded in categories 3 and 5 count for an overwhelming 73 percent of Socality's imagery.

APPENDIX   271

Table A.1. Breakdown of Socality Image Genres (N = 1,211)

Image Genre	Number of Images	Percentage of Images
(5) Landscape and Nature	460	37.9
(3) Person(s) in Nature	426	35.1
(1) Portrait	282	23.2
(7) Building, Architecture, or Structure	235	19.4
(8) Object or Artifact	204	16.8
(2) Group Portrait	143	11.8
(14) Meme, Written Information, or Text	94	7.7
(13) Socality Emblem	75	6.1
(4) Person(s) in City	49	4.0
(11) Food, Coffee, or Drink	47	3.8
(9) Technology	44	3.6
(6) Cityscape	40	3.3
(10) Animal or Pet	28	2.3
(15) Religious, Devotional, or Iconographic	24	1.9
(12) Restaurant or Café Setting	17	1.4
(16) Church Building or Architecture	11	0.9

After the frequent landscape shots, categories 1, 7, and 8 loom large. Two hundred and eighty-two (23.2 percent) images fall into the portrait category because they include close-ups of a person's face or body. Category 7's building structures feature prominently. Sometimes involving natural settings, this genre includes scenes like high train bridges in the forest, famous points of interest for hikers and outdoor aficionados, the underside of docks extending into bodies of water, close-ups of cobblestone pathways or human-made trails, abandoned industrial buildings, sleek modern and contemporary architectural forms, or isolated highways. Sometimes people stand in front of these buildings or face in the opposite direction, back toward the camera, centered on a roadway in the middle of the woods. In other scenes, couples walk hand in hand along tops of vertigo-inducing train bridges. A total of two hundred and thirty-five (19.4 percent) images include human-built structures or backdrops. One hundred and forty-three (or 11.8 percent) include category 2 portraits of couples or larger groups of people engaged in various activities.

Following these six most recurring image types, the ten additional genres of the Socality image corpus include subgroupings under one hundred but over ten occurrences, namely, between 7.7 and 0.9 percent. In other words, Socality site facilitators also upload images that include the subjects of informational text, organizational symbols, urban exploration, food, technology, animals, restaurants, or overt religious imagery or church architecture forms but in strikingly less frequency than the landscape or nature shots. A mere twenty-four pictures (1.9 percent) include overt religious imagery, for instance, and only eleven photos (0.9 percent) in the corpus clearly identify church building exteriors or interiors. The contrast between category 16's church architecture and category 12's restaurant or café setting—the two most infrequent image genres—is also telling. Whereas Socality features seventeen scenes of restaurant or food business imagery, it only includes eleven of actual churches.

NOTES

1. Such doctrinal generics further support my claim below that these evangelical Instagram users reproduce Romantic theologies and ascetic scripts with regard to nature. Bebbington (1990, 14), for instance, notes the liberal evangelical "aversion to dogma," which occurred after the Romantic turn. In short, writes one scholar of religion and technology, "Transcendentalists like Ralph Waldo Emerson and Henry David Thoreau believed that religious institutions corrupted individual purity, and so they sought a self-reliant spirituality divorced of creeds and dogmas" (Robinson 2013, 7). Relatedly, from the perspective of contemporary American religions and youth culture, sociologists have documented the rise of what they call a "Moral Therapeutic Deism," which downplays theological distinctiveness and emphasizes shared basics, such as love, goodness, happiness, unity, and so on (Smith and Denton 2005). The evangelicals studied herein do not appear to reject theology or doctrine outright, but they do downplay difference for the sake of cohesion.

2. Not all evangelical artists who viewed art as a way to convey wonder turned to Romanticism. John Russell, an avid evangelical and pastelist known for his highly detailed, cartographic renderings of the moon, also conceived of his artistic endeavors as acts of devotion to God. Russell saw his works as imbued with the sentiments of, in his own words, "wonder, love, and praise" (Hindmarsh 2018, 170–179).

3. For more on the tenuous relationship between religion and technology that is rooted directly in transcendentalist, anti-industrial thought, see Robinson 2013, 7.

4. For example, see @philipleclerc 2016a; @jonathanzoeteman 2016; or @naomi4nn 2016. A brief note on this style of parenthetical citation. I include in these citations of individual Instagram images the Instagram handle or name of the person who captured the image, not the agent or facilitator responsible for posting it to Socality. The date refers to the year the image was uploaded to Socality's Instagram.

APPENDIX 273

5. For a critical theological analysis of selfies and selfie culture from the perspective of one of the evangelical technology writers covered in chapter 3, see Detweiler's most recent publication, *Selfies: Searching for the Image of God in a Digital Age* (2018).
6. See @tannerwendell 2017 and @dirka 2016a.
7. See @fabiooliveira 2017 and @littlecoal 2017.
8. See @skylerwagoner 2017.
9. See @hankhazen 2016.
10. See @jkwinders 2017 and @amandaseeyoudarrr 2015.
11. See @temi.coker 2015; @dansmoe 2015; @mrvalography 2015; and @technopaul 2015a.
12. See @sindreglaso 2015; @ineverstoppedlooking 2015; @8thgod 2015; and @ownthelight 2015.
13. See @davey_gravey 2015 and @silassao 2015.
14. See @evan.boutte 2015 and @matteoewing 2015.
15. See @lance_asper 2015 and @erwnchow 2015.
16. See @jollejolle 2015 and @brandoneckroth 2015.
17. See @bertymandagie 2014; @mark_whail 2015; @jontaylorsweet 2014; @shopboutonne 2015; @bluegerri 2015; @winniestranero 2015; @dinelianoel 2015; @sawyerkey 2015; @justin_02 2015; and @dirka 2016b.
18. See, in particular, @technopaul 2015b; @anthaang 2015; @filmography 2015a; @jeremyklefeker 2015; @ianandrewnelson 2015; @bradleymountain 2015; and @philipleclerc 2015a. Contrary to other pervasive Instagram aesthetics or styles, such as the one cultivated by *Kinfolk* magazine, Socality imagery does not always conceal the technology used by photographers to capture images later to be edited and then uploaded (cf. Manovich 2016, 24). A small but significant number of Socality images, in fact, are metapragmatic in that they refer visually to the process of taking the photograph, the materiality of a print photo, or to cameras themselves. For example, a number of its Instagram uploads are photographs of photographs (@technopaul 2016) or images of photographers taking photographs in the outdoors or elsewhere (@scottcbakken 2017; @patrickjjohnson 2017). Other pictures involved shots as viewed a step behind a disembodied arm holding up a smartphone (@socality 2016). One views the image through the screen of one's media device but also through the screen portrayed in the image itself. Mediation, here, compounds in layers of complexity. Such metapragmatic visuals, I argue, encourage users even more strongly to view the world through particular gazes. For images such as @hipturelife's (2016), one learns literally to frame one's world by seeing landscape as something to be reified through photographic capture.
19. See @jonathanzoeteman 2015 and @ryan_field_ 2016.
20. See @loveinjustin 2016; @estherlecler 2016; and @_joshes 2015.
21. See @ajfernando 2015; @filmography 2015b; and @lidiagulyas 2014.
22. See @philipleclerc 2015b; @winnterfresh 2015; and @philipplitvin 2015. Socality's use of the emblem is a form of brand recognition employed even by previous evangelicals in the revivalist tradition, preachers including Billy Sunday, who put photographs and postcards to work for the purposes of social and religious formation (Morgan 2007, 207–207). Further, the cultivation of a visual brand also tracks with the sorts of strategies employed by the feminist bloggers back in chapter 5.
23. See @socality 2015; @mike_pgregregory 2015; @bradleymountain 2015; @socality 2015a; and @socality 2015b.
24. See @tarynstine 2016; @scottcbakken 2016; and @reachalana 2015.
25. See @brenton_clarke 2015; @lebackpacker 2016; and @andrewwilson 2015.

26. As a point of comparison, Twitter users share geolocational information but at a much lower capacity and frequency than Instagram users. Such a social media comparison also points to the plasticity of actual uses of technologies in the field over and against intended or anticipated ones. Structurally, for instance, Instagram's allowance for textual caption characters is unlimited. This is a striking difference in comparison to Twitter's inherent brevity of 280 characters. Regardless, Instagram remains a primarily visual, image-based form of communication and comment-character average is quite small even though the technology's structural affordance allows for more input (Manikonda et al. 2014, 5). Instagram exists primarily as a nontextual, visual platform; imagery is its most common mode of communication. Instagrammers are largely viewers and visual participators rather than readers, as they are on Twitter or Facebook (Russmann and Svensson 2016, 2–3; cf. Fisher 2016, 104).

GLOSSARY

ableism A tendency to discriminate, implicitly and explicitly, against bodies considered "abnormal" when compared against ideal, fully abled bodies—at least according to social norms. Ableist discourse occurs when critics discount new media as problematic (addictive, meaningless, superficial, disembodied, etc.) without considering the affordances for disability that new media may potentially provide. **Further Reading**: 1. James Cherney, *Ableist Rhetoric: How We Know, Value, and See Disability* (2019). 2. Meryl Alper, *Giving Voice: Mobile Communication, Disability, and Inequality* (2017).

affect An embodied force that influences—and in its strongest forms structures—how people feel, behave, think, or act in the world in various situations. Affect resides at the level of the body and influences emotion, mood, feeling, and disposition. Problematically so, affect theorists stress that it exists deeper than or is in operation prior to explicit discourse, language, or ideologies come into being. **Further Reading**: 1. Gregory Seigworth and Melissa Gregg, eds., *The Affect Theory Reader* (2009). 2. Ruth Leys, "The Turn to Affect: A Critique" (2011).

affordance Built-in, predisposed designs that shape, and perhaps determine, how a technology should be used. In shorthand, affordances are rules for use that are predetermined by the designer, creator, and engineer and reenforced by the physical features of the tool. *See also* media ecology; media ideology; mediatization; uptake. **Further Reading**: 1. Ian Hutchby, "Technologies, Texts, and Affordances" (2001). 2. Zynep Tufecki, *Twitter and Tear Gas: The Power and Fragility of Networked Protest* (2017).

algorithm A list of programmed technical instructions built into digital computing and internet protocols to assist the user in triangulating relevant data and executing directives. When one enters a search query into Google, for example, algorithmic technologies filter and curate those results as per the stored lifetime history of use by that user. *See also* algorithmic authority; meaning-making machines.

algorithmic authority A novel type of authority, unique to the digital era, in which online leaders engender large followings and cultivate the power to sway decision-making on various sectors. This type of authority relies on a person's skill in navigating social media by manipulating algorithmic systems, soliciting audiences, and creating and promoting media content. A product of digital media, algorithmic authority is fragile and tenuous. *See also* algorithm; authority; influencers; religious digital creatives (RDCs). **Further Reading**: Heidi Campbell, *Digital Creatives and the Rethinking of Religious Authority* (2020a).

alterity Qualities of difference projected on people and social groups to which one does not belong. Alterity is a synonym for otherness and often comes to light within confrontations between powerful groups and more marginal ones, as groups historically tend to view others through lenses of suspicion, fear, control, and orientalism. Alterity has been a useful concept for anthropologists studying in colonial contexts, especially as modernizing Euro-American powers have categorized subjected peoples through strategies of alterity. *See also* boundary maintenance; cancel culture; digital orientalism; power. **Further Reading**: Michael Taussig, *Mimesis and Alterity* (1993).

apps Shorthand for "applications," referring to an entire range of digital programs downloadable to data phones, tablets, and personal computers to carry out tasks specific to the respective program. Apps can include word processors, money transfer programs, digital bibles, and games. **Further Reading**: 1. Rachel Wagner, "You Are What You Install: Religious Authenticity and Identity in Mobile Apps" (2013). 2. Jacqueline Fewkes, *Anthropological Perspectives on the Religious Uses of Mobile Apps* (2019).

authenticity and inauthenticity Authenticity at its simplest has to do with being real, true, and genuine. Criteria for attainment of authenticity as a state of being or identity are diverse and conflicting. Authenticity in the digital era is often a synonym for orthodoxy. Inauthenticity, alternatively, links to conceptions of heresy and the heterodox. Authenticity discourse is a primary form of boundary maintenance. To summarize, these are arbitrarily, culturally, and individually relative terms. *See also* boundary maintenance; heresy; heterodoxy; orthodoxy. **Further Reading**: 1. Kerstin Radde-Antweiler, "Authenticity" (2013). 2. Gunn Enli, *Mediated Authenticity: How the Media Constructs Reality* (2015). 3. David Chidester, *Authentic Fakes: Religion and American Popular Culture* (2005). 4. Russell Cobb, *The Paradox of Authenticity in a Globalized World* (2014).

authority In the classic Weberian conception, authority is the ability of a person to get other people to carry out their will despite resistance. Authority rests

on the legitimacy of the leader—his or her legitimate, authorized status—
and is closely linked to but not reducible in definition to power. In the digital
era, authority is under reconfiguration as the means to achieve it appears
to be undergoing horizontalization. New ways to generate and legitimate
authority seem to be increasing with the rise of social media. Authority is now
more fluidly networked than ever before and tends also to be fragile. *See also*
algorithmic authority; horizontalization; legitimacy; power. **Further Reading**:
1. Max Weber, *The Theory of Social and Economic Organization* (1964). 2. Stewart
Hoover, *The Media and Religious Authority* (2016). 3. Michel Foucault, *History of
Sexuality: An Introduction* (1978).

autodocumentation The reflexive practice of documenting one's own everyday life
through habitual use of social media apps. With Instagram, for example, some
users might upload pictures about their eating habits and fashion choices or
what they did throughout the day. To this effect, apps such as Instagram and
Facebook are the new more public-facing family photo albums. *See also* habitual
media; performative individualism.

binge religion As religious studies scholar Kathryn Lofton describes the term,
binge religion has to do both with the consumption of religious products and
the religious consumption of media during the late-capitalist era, wherein
instant gratification and speed are archvirtues. Binge religion may relate to
online and virtual church, for instance, but in Lofton's use it also has to do
with a religion of binge, as it were, or binge culture gone mainstream. **Further
Reading**: Kathryn Lofton, *Consuming Religion* (2017, 21–33).

blogs An abbreviated form of "weblog," a term coined in the late 1990s to
describe personal websites in the tradition of the personal journal or diary.
Contemporary blogs can be both personal and commercial but refer largely to
media-hosting websites that display their contents in chronological order with
the most recent post at the top. Blogs sometimes include comment sections
and have served as efficient and collaborative media for writers to cultivate
their voices and define a public brand. *See also* brand; collaborative media;
microblog; public. **Further Reading**: 1. Linda Kenix, "Blogs as Alternative"
(2009). 2. Jan Schmidt, "Blogging Practices" (2007). 3. Deborah Whitehead,
"The Evidence of Things Unseen: Authenticity and Fraud in the Christian
Mommy Blogosphere" (2015).

boundary maintenance A social process by which groups define their identities,
manage their bounds, and project alterity upon others. In subcultural identity
theory, boundary maintenance has as much to do with naming, labeling,
and categorizing otherness as it does clarifying internal definitions. Social
groupings can range from highly regulated institutions with legal bylaws that
define identity and participation to open-ended publics organized loosely and
informally around texts, discourse, and discussion. As groups define their
boundaries, they often do so through the use of hygienic metaphors. According

to anthropologist and social theorist Mary Douglas, groups identify "dirt" and "contagions" through applied standards of purity and danger. See also alterity; buffered self; cancel culture; digitally buffered self; dirt; heresy; orthodoxy. **Further Reading**: 1. Mary Douglas, *Purity and Danger* (1996). 2. Michael Schwalbe and Douglas Mason-Schrock, "Identity Work as Group Process" (1996).

brand In the neoliberal era, brands are marketed icons of selfhood and business. The self becomes business defined and understood as a brand. Conceptions of selfhood change as we view our identities and persons as projects to be invested in, developed skillfully, and made productive in a socioeconomic sense. *See also* blog; communicative capitalism; neoliberalism. **Further Reading**: Ilana Gershon, "Neoliberal Agency" (2011).

buffered self, the Charles Taylor coined this term to refer to modern subjectivities that contrast with medieval "porous selves." Whereas porous selves lived in enchanted worlds where the boundaries between the self and other entities— gods, spirits, and otherwise—were less than precise, the modern buffered self operates in a disenchanted, antimagic, rational realm. In the digital era, "buffering" takes on even more significance as selves are digitally constituted. *See also* boundary maintenance; digitally buffered self; secular; sensational forms. **Further Reading**: 1. Charles Taylor, *A Secular Age* (2007). 2. Taylor, "Buffered and Porous Selves" (2008).

cancel culture A recent tendency in contemporary society to use social media to publicly denounce and distance from people and things deemed morally, socially, or theologically suspect. Cancel culture is the new digital media empowered form of boundary maintenance. For religious users, cancel culture is akin to heresy and heterodoxy discourse. *See also* alterity; boundary maintenance; heresy; heterodoxy; media promiscuity. **Further Reading**: Jonah Bromwich, "Everyone Is Canceled" (2018).

cellphone Abbreviated from "cellular telephone," this type of personal technology served as the first major alternative to the landline in the late 1990s. The cellphone is a direct precursor to today's data phone, or smartphone, which connects to the internet and typically has a touch screen. Cellphones usually allowed for calling and texting as well as other more advanced features over time, such as photography. In popular parlance, cellphone is an umbrella category for mobile phone. By this logic, a data phone or smartphone is a cellphone, but a cellphone isn't necessarily a data phone or smartphone. *See also* data phone; habitual media; smartphone. **Further Reading**: 1. Anandam Kavoori and Noah Arceneaux, *The Cell Phone Reader: Essays in Social Transformation* (2006). 2. Paul Levinson, *Cellphone: The Story of the World's Most Mobile Medium and How It Has Transformed Everything!* (2004).

chaos rhetoric An applied form of boundary maintenance that occurs when a group attempts to persuade others that cherished social institutions, such as the family or the nation, are under attack by dangerous outsiders who hold different ideological views. Chaos rhetoric often works hand in hand with a declension narrative that retrospectively and nostalgically gestures back toward an ostensibly pure golden age. See also boundary maintenance; dirt. **Further Reading**: Leslie Smith, *Righteous Rhetoric: Sex, Speech, and the Politics of Concerned Women for America* (2014).

charisma A personality type, according to Max Weber, thought to be especially gregarious and likeable. If a person has charisma, he or she is likely to be able to generate followers and friends with relative ease. Charisma is often problematically conceived of as an innate, quasireligious quality bestowed at birth that makes someone a strong candidate for leadership and sets the person apart from others. See also authority; charismatic authority; power. **Further Reading**: Max Weber, *The Theory of Social and Economic Organization* (1964).

charismatic authority One of three ideal types of leadership outlined by Max Weber, the charismatic form is opposed to its bureaucratic and rational alternatives in its ability to break with the rules of history and tradition to blaze new territory. For Weber, charismatic authority has a sacredness to it as it deviates from the patterns of the profane and the everyday. Charismatic authority rests on the special abilities and endowments of the charismatic leader. This form of authority extends to the age of the social media influencers but mutates in strange and unpredictable ways, conflicting with Weber's understanding of the endowment as something natural that a person is born with. See also authority; charisma; power. **Further Reading**: Max Weber, *The Theory of Social and Economic Organization* (1964).

church plant The establishment of a new local church congregation. A church plant can result from a collaborative effort among existing churches, a denominational endeavor, or a pioneering independent exercise. See also mobile church.

circulation A biological metaphor that evokes the human circulatory system, circulation is the process by which textual artifacts and media generate shared reception within a reading public. To say that a text circulates is to say that it gets around, that it's repeatedly read and shared with others. The goal of promiscuous media, for instance, is to increase circulation and create and extend publics. Circulation in the era of new media is diverse and can include anything from sharing a book with a close friend to retweeting a controversial tweet online. See also counterpublics; promiscuous media; publics. **Further Reading**: David Beer, *Popular Culture and New Media: The Politics of Circulation* (2013).

collaborative media An umbrella concept that emphasizes social collaboration, cooperation, participation, and teamwork as its primary modus operandi, collaborative media in some uses can serve as a synonym for new social and digital media, with some important qualifications. Collaborative media is an expression of Web 2.0 and 3.0 technologies. *See also* digital media; new media; participatory media; social media; Web 3.0.

communicative capitalism Coined by theorist Jodi Dean, this concept describes the ways that capitalistic interests have commandeered online forms of communication, including individual blogging practices, in the neoliberal era. Communicative capitalism involves institutional practices of online surveillance. *See also* neoliberalism; panopticon. **Further Reading**: Jodi Dean, *Blog Theory: Feedback and Capture in the Circuits of Drive* (2010).

community cluster One of two models for explaining how group communication online takes place. For the community-cluster model, people share information in different, loosely defined conversations and may engage within multiple overlapping venues. The community cluster differs from the polarized crowd. *See also* polarized crowds. **Further Reading**: Marc Smith et al., "Mapping Twitter Topic Networks: From Polarized Crowds to Community Clusters" (2014).

continuity and complementarity, logic of One of two logics outlined by digital religion scholar Pauline Hope Cheong to describe scholars' stances on the influence of the internet and new media on religious groups. The logic of continuity and complementarity refers to that body of research whose findings situate the internet as something that extends and migrates the institution's previously existing endeavors. *See also* displacement and disjuncture, logic of. **Further Reading**: Pauline Cheong, "Authority" (2013).

counterpublic A form of embattled, initially marginal public that arises in opposition and resistance to a more widespread, dominant, and powerful one. This subgenre of public is cognizant of its status as subordinate to the more powerful public. *See also* public. **Further Reading**: Michael Warner, *Publics and Counterpublics* (2002).

corpus analysis A social scientific and textual research method that identifies and isolates a typically large body (corpus) of data to subject to close critical analysis. *See also* discourse analysis.

creative class, the A socioeconomic class unique to the contemporary era that is devoted to creating new forms and ideas across various occupational fields and subdisciplines. *See also* digital creatives; influencer; religious digital creatives (RDCs); tastemaker; taste regimes. **Further Reading**: Richard Florida, *The Rise of the Creative Class* (2002).

critical discourse analysis (CDA) The study of the explicit and implicit rules, ideologies, strategies, and agendas of how people communicate with each other in a society. CDA scholars study how discourse shapes society and culture. *See also* discourse. **Further Reading**: 1. Norman Fairclough, *Language and Power* (1989). 2. Lilie Chouliaraki and Norman Fairclough, *Discourse in Late Modernity: Rethinking Critical Discourse Analysis* (2005). 3. Noel Heather,

GLOSSARY 281

Religious Language and Critical Discourse Analysis (2000). 4. Michel Foucault, *The Archaeology of Knowledge: And the Discourse on Language* (2010). 5. Pierre Bourdieu, *Language and Symbolic Power* (1994).

cultural carrier When a symbol, object, group, or institution preserves and transports particular ideas and forms over time. As Dana Logan has argued, celebrity Gwyneth Paltrow's ascetic and elitist GOOP lifestyle brand is to some degree a cultural carrier of Reformed Calvinism. The internet is a cultural carrier of the Protestant critique of institutionalism and inheritor of the tension between media sincerity and promiscuity. Cultural carrier is in some cases used as a synonym to cultural logics. *See also* cultural logics; media promiscuity; media sincerity. **Further Reading**: 1. Dana Logan, "The Lean Closet: Asceticism in Postindustrial Consumer Culture" (2018). 2. Zachary Warren and Fathali Moghaddam, "Cultural Carriers" (2011).

cultural logics Embedded sociocultural values that directly or indirectly shape institutions. A cultural logic of the internet, for instance, is anti-institutionalism. *See also* affordances; cultural carrier; media ecology; media ideology. **Further Reading**: José van Dijck, *The Culture of Connectivity: A Critical History of Social Media* (2013).

data phone A form of mobile, cellular, smart technology that allows a cellular device to connect online. Although the data phone language was used by Bell Laboratories (e.g., the "Data-Phone 100") as early as the 1960s to refer to experimental new telephone technologies, the current use assumes that a device is internet enabled. *See also* mobile phone; smartphone.

democratization An antihierarchical, quasipopulist phenomenon that decentralizes power and in theory emphasizes voluntarism and self-organization. **Further Reading:** Nathan Hatch, *The Democratization of American Christianity* (1989).

determinism A strand of social and technological theory that emphasizes the rigidly structured aspects of social and technological systems and their decisive influence on humans. Technological determinism in its strongest pronouncements means that technology strictly influences how people act, interact, behave, and communicate. Although there are shades of applied determinism ranging from strong to weak, the media ecology school has often been labeled as deterministic, as has the concept of affordances. *See also* affordances; media ecology.

deterritorialized, viral ethnography Ethnographic research that is not tied to physical geographic locations but seeks to understand the social constructs of "place" and "space" as experienced by digital interlocuters in real life. Deterritorialized, viral ethnography is a messier, more ambiguous, network-focused practice of ethnography than anthropologists and sociologists have traditionally preferred. Ethnography in this sense includes so-called online worlds as well as those on ground and physical. *See also* ethnography; nonparticipative observation; participant observation. **Further Reading**: Victoria Bernal, *Nation as Network: Diaspora, Cyberspace & Citizenship* (2014).

digital abstinence A practice of strict "unplugging" or "fasting," which means disconnecting from the internet, logging off social media apps, and perhaps even powering down one's personal devices for a sustained, predetermined period. Digital abstinence is a form of media resistance. *See also* digital asceticism; digital minimalism; Luddite; media ambivalence. **Further Reading**: Trine Syvertsen, *Media Resistance: Protest, Dislike, Abstention* (2017).

digital age, the The most significant, latest development of the Industrial Age, the digital age (also called the Information Age and the new media age) began with the birth of personal computing and internet technologies in the second half of the twentieth century and continues to the present. **Further Reading**: 1. Johnny Ryan, *A History of the Internet and the Digital Future* (2010). 2. Stephen Segaller, *Nerds 2.0: A Brief History of the Internet* (1998).

digital asceticism In contrast to digital abstinence, digital asceticism is a more applied strategy that seeks to minimize and regulate rather than shut off digital media use altogether. Although not an exclusive list of practices, digital asceticism may include turning off one's data phone at a certain time in the evening, banning the use of technology at the dinner table, strictly policing children's screen time, among others. *See also* digital abstinence; digital minimalism; Luddite; media ambivalence. **Further Reading**: Trine Syvertsen, *Media Resistance: Protest, Dislike, Abstention* (2017).

digital creatives A global subclass of the creative class evolved for the digital era. Digital creatives focus primarily on producing digital content but in doing so have altered social and cultural configurations of power and authority. *See also* creative class; influencers; religious digital creatives (RDCs); tastemaking; taste regime. **Further Reading**: 1. Greg Hearn et al., *Creative Work beyond the Creative Industries: Innovation, Employment and Education* (2014). 2. Lev Manovich, "Notes on Instagrammism and Mechanisms of Contemporary Cultural Identity" (2016).

digital era *See* digital age.

digital fasts *See* digital abstinence.

digital immigrants People born and raised before mobile and digital technologies became an ingrained part of everyday life. *See also* digital natives. **Further Reading**: Marc Prensky, "Digital Natives, Digital Immigrants" (2001).

digital media Often called "new media," digital media are at base those forms of media composed of numeric digital code via computers and computer programming. *See also* new media. **Further Reading**: Lev Manovich, *The Language of New Media* (2001).

GLOSSARY 283

digital minimalism *See* digital asceticism.

digital natives People born and raised with mobile and digital technologies as part of everyday life. Digital natives, in public understanding, are often synonymous with millennials, or those born roughly between 1980 and 2000. *See also* digital immigrants. **Further Reading**: Marc Prensky, "Digital Natives, Digital Immigrants" (2001).

digital orientalism A form of cultural and often racial essentializing, stereotyping, and sometimes romanticizing of the other through a dominant Euro-American gaze via online discourse and interactions. *See also* alterity; boundary maintenance. **Further Reading**: 1. Trevor Jamerson, "Digital Orientalism: TripAdvisor and Online Travelers' Tales" (2017). 2. Edward Said, *Orientalism* (1979).

digital turn *See* digital age.

digitally buffered self Extrapolating from Charles Taylor's concept of the modern buffered self, the digitally buffered self refers to the intensifying of the boundaries of separation between social groups due to horizontalization and exposure in online interactions. People's understanding of others and of themselves changes as difference is encountered and classified via digital media. *See also* alterity; boundary maintenance; buffered self; horizontalization.

dirt According to social anthropologist Mary Douglas, dirt is disorder and contagion. Dirt is a hygienic metaphor for how social groups manage boundaries, cultivate identities, and identify and pronounce difference and otherness. *See also* alterity; boundary maintenance; digital orientalism. **Further Reading**: Mary Douglas, *Purity and Danger* (1966).

discourse Any form of social exchange and communicative back-and-forth, broadly conceived, be it face-to-face talk, letter writing, political speeches, sermons, or Facebook arguments. In academic parlance, discourse often implies interest in how communication and dialogue links to power and influences social structures, institutions, and practices. *See also* critical discourse analysis. **Further Reading**: 1. Greg Urban, *A Discourse-Centered Approach to Culture: Native South American Myths and Rituals* (1991). Pierre Bourdieu, *Language and Symbolic Power* (1994). 2. John Gumperz, *Discourse Strategies* (1982). 3. Michael Silverstein and Greg Urban, *Natural Histories of Discourse* (1996). 4. Lilie Chouliaraki and Norman Fairclough, *Discourse in Later Modernity: Rethinking Critical Discourse Analysis* (2005). 5. Crispin Thurlow and Kristine Mroczek, *Digital Discourse in the New Media* (2011).

discourse analysis *See* critical discourse analysis.

disembodied A charge levied by critics of new media against online communication forms. Because online worlds are different from physical, on-ground ones, they are thought to be lesser than. Virtual reality tech, however, is problematizing such an easy ableist distinction between live domains in the digital era, interfacing the digital onto the body in unique new ways. *See also* ableism; negative media ideologies; on ground vs. online.

displacement and disjuncture, logic of One of two logics outlined by digital religion scholar Pauline Hope Cheong to describe scholars' stances on the influence of the internet and new media on religious groups. The logic of displacement and disjuncture refers to that body of research whose findings conclude that the internet is something chaotic and dangerous regarding a religious organization's purposes and outlook. *See also* continuity and complementarity, logic of. **Further Reading**: Pauline Cheong, "Authority" (2013).

domestication A counter to strong forms of technological determinism, this theory suggests that people subtly shape and alter the technologies they use. In this view, technologies are subjected to and molded within powerful existing cultural contexts of uptake. If affordances exist, these affordances are interpreted and applied differently in different social and cultural contexts. *See also* affordances; determinism; social shaping of technology.

emerging church movement (ECM) An eclectic, boundary-defying, quasi-Protestant movement active in the late 1990s and early 2000s that might loosely be characterized by its preferences for theological and ecclesial inclusivity, ritual experimentalism and combination, postmodern and poststructural philosophy, and applied uses of new media for religious purposes. The ECM, in fact, is one of the first Protestant counterpublics that owes its very existence and organizational network to the internet. *See also* counterpublics; emerging evangelicals; exvangelicals; postevangelicals. **Further Reading**: 1. James Bielo, *Emerging Evangelicals: Faith, Modernity, and the Desire for Authenticity* (2011). 2. Gerardo Martí and Gladys Ganiel, *The Deconstructed Church: Understanding Emerging Christianity* (2014). 3. Travis Cooper, "Emerging, Emergent, Emergence: Boundary Maintenance, Definition Construction, and Legitimation Strategies in the Establishment of a Post-Evangelical Subculture" (2017).

emerging evangelicals There are two uses for this term, a broad one and a narrow one. First, the concept refers, in its widest possible definition, to contemporary evangelicals. Second, it refers to a narrow theologically and ideologically progressive subgroup of evangelicals with direct or indirect links to what had been called in the early 2000s the Emerging Church Movement (ECM). Emerging evangelicals in this second sense may actually reject the term "evangelical" to distance themselves from their conservative mainstream counterparts. Emerging evangelicals are active in post- or ex-evangelical publics initiated by writings from Rachel Held Evans and Rob Bell, among many others. *See also* counterpublics; emerging church movement (ECM); exvangelicals; postevangelicals.

entextualization When a stretch of discourse—e.g., a quoted speech, stretch of writing, or controversial tweet—is taken out of its context of origin and applied to a new discursive context. A retweet, for example, is akin to entextualization, as would be quoting something your mother told you to your best friend. *See also* discourse; reentextualization. **Further Reading**: Michael Silverstein and Greg Urban, "The Natural History of Discourse" (1996).

ethnography An immersive, long-term, firsthand, qualitative research method shared by social scientists and others that involves studying social actors in their native habitats. A key submethodology within the broader ethnographic method is participant observation, which typically involves living and participating with a designated sociocultural group for a designated period as observations are made and stored as fieldnotes and other scholarly data. Etymologically, *ethno-graphy* is literally people-writing or writing of people. The digital turn requires that anthropologists and others redefine ethnography to include studying nontraditional virtual domains enabled by the internet. *See also* deterritorialized ethnography; nonparticipant observation; participant observation.

exvangelical, ex-evangelical An emerging group of people who have rejected the conservative evangelical upbringing of their pasts and now posit their identities against evangelicalism proper. A clear example of a prominent ex-evangelical is the late Rachel Held Evans, who was raised in conservative Christianity but later attended an Episcopalian church. *See also* emerging evangelicals; emerging church movement; postevangelical. **Further Reading**: Dave Tomlinson, *The Post-Evangelical* (2003 [1995]).

face-to-face communication The gold standard of Western (and perhaps universal) interpersonal communication. Often assumed to be the purest, sincerest, and most sacred unmediated form of communication, conversing face-to-face is also inevitably mediated through the body and its postures, emotions, nonverbal cues, surrounding social and physical environments, among myriad other semiotic stimuli. Both Protestants and Western anthropologists alike are beholden to this media ideology of pureness and as such both are structured by the drive toward media sincerity. The preference for face-to-face communication is also part of a logocentric metaphysic and transport view of language, media, and communication. *See also* logocentrism; media ideology; media sincerity; transport view. **Further Reading**: John B. Thompson, *The Media and Modernity: A Social Theory of the Media* (1995, 82–87).

fear of missing out (FOMO) A folk expression for a tendency in the digital era for social media users to report feelings of anxiety, sadness, loneliness, and even despair when scrolling through feeds full of images of their friends and colleagues doing fun things in their own worlds (apart from them), such as going to parties, traveling, and other otherwise happy and exciting situations. *See also* digital media; social media.

flaming language An aggressive genre of combative, incendiary language online often found in public comment sections on news sites, blogs, and other new media where open dialogue is possible. Flaming language is often accredited to internet trolls and other types of online bullies because the language used is intentionally demeaning, offensive, and antagonistic toward a person or persons. Flaming language is related to what philosopher Byung-Chul Han describes as the rise of "the shitstorm" in online rhetoric. *See also* cancel culture; shitstorm; trolls. **Further Reading**: Peter Moor, "Conforming to the Flaming Norm in the Online Commenting Situation" (2007).

followers Quantified numerically, followers are "friends," loosely conceived, for the digital age. Followers may include close friends, family members, distant relatives, colleagues, associates, and complete strangers. Typically speaking, the higher the number of followers, the higher the cultural capital of the person with them. In some sense, a person's status as a public persona and even an authority can be gauged by the reach of their influence, that is, by the number of followers they have managed to cultivate. *See also* authority; friends; gatekeepers; influencers.

friends With the invention of the Facebook in the mid-2000s, a new form of extended sociality was born. The new genre of "friend" can include traditional friends under its purview but also complete strangers who one has never met or interacted with in everyday life outside of the internet. Facebook friends are like Instagram or Twitter followers, and the higher number of friends one has, the more influential and public facing a person is considered. *See also* authority; followers; gatekeepers; influencers.

gatekeepers Religious authorities who retain a significant degree of influence and power, enough to determine and enforce what is right and wrong and be taken seriously by followers. Gatekeepers are key nodes in the complex network of religious boundary maintenance that occurs online, although theological gatekeepers in the traditional, extradigital sense also exist. *See also* authority; influencers; power; religious digital creatives (RDCs).

green evangelicals A group of evangelical activists and theologians concerned with environmental issues and who seek alternative ways of living to help mitigate the energy crisis, global warming, and related issues. *See also* emerging church movement (ECM); emerging evangelicals; reflexive evangelicals; religious left. **Further Reading**: Harry Maier, "Green Millennialism: American Evangelicals, Environmentalism, and the Book of Revelation" (2010).

habitual media Various digital and social media of everyday life that are so ingrained into daily practices that they are no longer in any sense new. Habitual media practices range from smart watches that deliver text messages and Facebook notifications to the wearer's wrist, to data phones always at hand, to voice-activated Google Home devices, to smart washers and dryers that send

WiFi alerts to phones when clothes have finished their cycles. Habitual media are those technological practices that have become quotidian, commonplace, and embedded. *See also* Internet of Things (IOT); new media. **Further Reading**: Wendy Chun, *Updating to Remain the Same: Habitual New Media* (2016).

haptic devotionality Everyday rituals of viewing, scrolling, and seeing mediated through image-sharing platforms, such as Instagram, that beyond the consumption of aesthetically pleasing imagery appears to be shaping one's outlook in daily life. Socality, for instance, is a hybrid evangelical group that seeks to mediate the gap between the online and the offline worlds. Socality's primary media output consists of high-quality nature and outdoor photography meant to stir in viewers a sublime sense of communing with the divine.

hashtag A strategy of categorization online especially popular on Twitter and Instagram, a hashtag has the intent of increasing a post's views and expanding its potential publics. Hashtagging, in short, is digital-textual networking. Hashtags can be both formal and literal. For example, a person posting a picture of their pet via Instagram can hashtag the image with #cat or #catsofinstagram. Hashtags can also take on more creative and humorous iterations when users hashtag entire sentences all in lowercase to make an obnoxious point. Hashtags can also serve as points of stancetaking and critical microcommentaries on various subjects. *See also* publics; stancetaking. **Further Reading**: 1. Alice Daer, Rebecca Hoffman, and Seth Goodman, "Rhetorical Functions of Hashtag Forms across Social Media Applications" (2014). 2. Stamatios Giannoulakis and Nicolas Tsapatsoulis, "Evaluating the Descriptive Power of Instagram Hashtags" (2016).

hegemony A form of social and cultural power so ingrained and widespread that it becomes, in effect, invisible. As Antonio Gramsci theorized the concept, hegemony works behind-the-scenes, perhaps even at the level of the unconscious, to shape and direct people's actions. In the United States, Protestantism is a hegemonic force. Media ecologies are in some sense hegemonic as they operate in the background of human social lives. *See also* authority; media ecology; power. **Further Reading**: Jerome Karabel, "Revolutionary Contradictions: Antonio Gramsci and the Problem of Intellectuals" (2002), 30–36.

heresy An ancient form of social and religious labeling and boundary maintenance in which a belief, teaching, practice, or action is said to contradict an ecclesial structure's theological stance or official teaching on a doctrinal subject or subjects. In Christianity, where the term originated, heresy as an applied negative descriptor began to gain popularity after Irenaeus's *Contra Haereses*, a writing that circulated in the second century. For Irenaeus, heresy was that which was not Orthodox (from the Greek: *ortho*, "straight, conjoined" and *doxa*, "belief"). Whereas in premodern forms of Christianity official church trials could be held to determine an accused person's status as heretic, social media is changing how the term is conceived and applied. *See also* alterity; boundary maintenance; heterodoxy; horizontalization; orthodoxy. **Further Reading**: 1. Mark Edwards, *Catholicity and Heresy in the Early Church* (2009). 2. Jonathan Wright, *Heretics: The Creation of Christianity from the Gnostics to the Modern Church* (2011).

heterodoxy This concept means, literally, "different belief" (*hetero* + *doxa*). To be heterodox is to be heretical and profess deviant theology in either belief or practice or both. To be heterodox is to be pronounced as other. *See also* alterity; boundary maintenance; heresy; orthodoxy.

High Church vs. Low Church A distinction describing the differences in church service structure between formal liturgical styles and more informal evangelical Protestant styles. Such a distinction is oversimplistic and problematic, when applied during the contemporary era, for at least two reasons. First, evangelical revivalist forms standardize over time, becoming, in a sense, their own qualified form of Protestant liturgy. Second, contemporary churches, especially those who are part of experimental emerging evangelical circles, intentionally mix High Church liturgical aspects with Low Church informality.

horizontalization A key theory of the effects of the digital age on social and cultural configurations, horizontalization is the process by which religious groups are made to exist on a hypothetically level playing field online. Beyond this process of leveling are several subeffects. First, a horizontalized internet appears to be relativizing and exposing people to religious and nonreligious ideas different than their own. Second, horizontalization widens the parameters and expands the means for would-be authorities to seek power and influence. *See also* authority; power. **Further Reading**: Stewart Hoover, *The Media and Religious Authority* (2016).

hyperconnection An outcome of Facebook's aggressively social social networking platform, hyperconnection means simply to be overconnected and oversaturated in sociality. *See also* informational overload; informationism; media ambivalence; negative media ideologies. **Further Reading**: 1. Jesse Rice, *The Church of Facebook: How the Hyperconnected Are Redefining Community* (2009), 2. Niall Ferguson, "The False Prophecy of Hyperconnection: How to Survive the Networked Age" (2017b).

iconoclasm A religious tradition, broadly conceived, of denouncing and destroying imagery as heretical. For example, there has been a strong trend in the Protestant historical tradition to reject and demolish Catholic visual arts, such as stained glass, as ungodly (overly mediated). *See also* boundary maintenance; heresy; heterodoxy. **Further Reading**: Willem J. van Asselt et al., *Iconoclasm and Iconoclash: Struggle for Religious Identity* (2007).

imagined, the Building off of the work of Benedict Anderson on the place of mass print media's integral role in the modern invention of states as social nationalistic communities, the imaginary aspects of social groups refer to the ways identities and boundaries are not inherent, natural, or given but are inherently arbitrary, discursive, disputed, and subject to contestation and change over time. *See also* boundary maintenance; publics. **Further Reading**: 1. Benedict Anderson, *Imagined Communities: Reflections on the Origins and Spread of Nationalism* (1991). 2. Jean-François Bayart, *The Illusion of Cultural Identity* (2005).

incendiary posts *See* flaming language.

indexical bleaching When the link between an utterance and its repeating or reposting widens to the point that the connection to the original instance is broken or lost. *See also* entextualization; intertextual gap. **Further Reading**: Lauren Squires, "From TV Personality to Fans and Beyond: Indexical Bleaching and the Diffusion of a Media Innovation" (2014).

influencer A new genre of authority in the digital age, an influencer is a social media adept who cultivates a relatively large followership and thus exerts a tenuous sort of networked power. *See also* authority; charisma; gatekeeper; power.

Information Age *See* digital age.

informationalism Related to the Information Age, this malady involves consuming information for information's sake to the point of overload. *See also* information overload.

informational overload A type of semiotic malady and apparent product of the digital turn that occurs when social media users feel anxiety due to processing too many bits of information online coming from too many diverse sources. *See also* informationalism.

internet According to Tim Berners-Lee (2000, 18), the developer of foundational URL, HTTP, HTML, and the World Wide Web subprotocols, the internet is best thought of as a "network of networks." As defined by other influential internet engineers and historians, the internet "is at once a world-wide broadcasting capability, a mechanism for information dissemination, and a medium for collaboration and interaction between individuals and their computers without regard for geographic location." The earliest origins of the internet as a network linking computers date to memo discussions in 1962 where MIT's J. C. R. Licklider, the head of the Defense Advanced Research Projects Agency's (DARPA) computer research program, proposed a "Galactic Network" concept. **Further Reading**: 1. Barry Leiner et al., *The Internet Society* (1997). 2. Johnny Ryan, *A History of the Internet and the Digital Future* (2010). 3. Stephen Segaller, *Nerds 2.0: A Brief History of the Internet* (1998).

Internet of Things (IOT) A network of domestic or work-related physical technologies that all connect via the internet. An example of the IOT in a high-tech home might include smart appliances, such as WiFi-enabled washers, dryers, and dishwashers, televsions, lighting and heating services that are ran through data phone apps, not to mention the various PCs, tablets, printers, and mobile phones—all linked digitally together through WiFi. *See also* WiFi.

intertextual gap Linguistic anthropologist Richard Bauman defines the intertextual gap as a semiotic space generated when words and phrases are extracted from one context and exported to a new one of intertextual expression. New contexts inevitably change the original text. *See also* entextualization; indexical bleaching. **Further Reading**: 1. Richard Bauman, "Genre" (2000). 2. Ibid., *A World of Others' Worlds: Cross-Cultural Perspectives on Intertextuality* (2004). 3. Lauren Squires, "From TV Personality to Fans and Beyond: Indexical Bleaching and the Diffusion of a Media Innovation" (2014).

IRL (in real life) A folk expression and acronym for "in real life," that is, activities that are different than things that happen on social and digital media. IRL is used in expressions to accentuate the difference between types of communication, often implying that conversations and other interactions that occur outside of digital expression are more meaningful or valuable than those online. *See also* face-to-face; media ideology; transport view.

lifeworld According to existentialist anthropologist Michael Jackson (2013, 7), lifeworld is a more robust concept than "culture," "society," or "worldview" because it conveys how social fields exists "as a force field (*kraftfeld*), a constellation of both ideas and passions, moral norms and ethical dilemmas, the tried and true as well as the unprecedented, a field charged with vitality and animated by struggle." A lifeworld is an encompassing, intersubjective milieu of interactions, structures, identities, exchanges, traditions, values, and experiences. **Further Reading**: Michael Jackson, *Lifeworlds: Essays in Existential Anthropology* (2013).

local media The opposite of mass media or promiscuous media, local media intend for only a small immediate circulation, not the broadest possible one. Examples of local media include pamphlets, zines, billboards, flyers, and perhaps even letters to the editor of the local newspaper. *See also* mass media; promiscuous media; small media.

logocentrism Not unlike the tradition of media sincerity, logocentrism is the Western and Christian tendency to emphasize face-to-face talk as the gold standard of human communication According to Jacques Derrida, logocentrism downplays writing as secondary to what is thought to be more pure, authentic, and direct speech. The sincere-speaker model is a logocentric paradigm. *See also* face-to-face speech; media sincerity; transport view. **Further Reading**: 1. Jacques Derrida, *Of Grammatology* (1976). 2. Michael Harrison, "Logocentrism" (n.d.). 3. David Holmes, *Communication Theory: Media, Technology and Society* (2005, 123–124).

Luddite Commonly used as a synonym for a technophobe, this term has historical origins with a radical group of early-nineteenth-century English textile workers

GLOSSARY 291

who protested growing employment in the textile industry due to the rapid incorporation of industrial machines. Ned Ludd was a mythological character, akin to Robin Hood, who became the group's symbolic namesake. Today, the somewhat derisive Luddite (and occasionally self-applied) label means that a person distrusts and perhaps even rejects some forms of modern digital technology. *See also* digital asceticism; media abstinence; media ambivalence; technophobe. **Further Reading**: Trine Syvertsen, *Media Resistance: Protest, Dislike, Abstention* (2017).

mass media Multigenre media that reach or intend to reach a wide audience. The particular types of media that qualify as mass media include print publishing, television and radio broadcasting, the commercial film industry, and the internet, among other broadcast forms. Mass media are the opposite of small media and local media and trend toward media promiscuity. *See also* small media.

meaning-making machines According to media scholar Ganaele Langlois, this type of social machinery is at work behind-the-scenes of everyday internet operations filtering search results, classifying and presenting data, and tailoring online experiences and interactions—ultimately shaping conceptions of reality. *See also* algorithm; algorithmic authority. **Further Reading**: Ganaele Langlois, *Meaning in the Age of Social Media* (2014).

media Any and every vessel, widely construed, through which communication takes place. Media involve not just technological tools and material artifacts proper (e.g., televisions, computers, paper) but bodies, environments, facial expressions, infrastructures, environments, social media platforms, airwaves, internet networks, and the like. Mass media and digital media are subsets of the broader category. Whatever media are, they are inextricably human and inextricably social. "Media are so intrinsic to our nature," philosophers write, "that it seems legitimate to wonder if it really makes sense to speak of an immediate relation of human beings with the world" (Romele and Terrone 2018, 1–2). Beyond mere communication, media and technologies are also tools for social and religious order. Religions are intricately mediated and as such function as complex technologies and networks in and of themselves. In the other direction, some scholars claim, controversially, that media are inherently religious in that they contain built-in designs that may transcend or override the immediate aims of the user. **Further Reading**: 1. Roberto Romele and Enrico Terrone, eds. *Toward a Philosophy of Digital Media* (2018). 2. John Durham Peters, *The Marvelous Clouds: Toward a Philosophy of Elemental Media* (2015). 3. Jeremy Stolow, "Technology" (2008).

media ambivalence A restrained, suspicious, and uneasy approach to the use of technology that involves limiting certain platforms for varying periods of time. Occasionally, media ambivalence can border on media resistance. *See also* digital abstinence; digital asceticism; digital minimalism; Luddite. **Further**

Reading: 1. Rivka Ribak and Michele Rosenthal, "Smartphone Resistance as Media Ambivalence" (2015). 2. Trine Syvertsen, *Media Resistance Protest, Dislike, Abstention* (2017).

media ecology Both an influential and controversial school of media studies scholarship and a totalizing mediated environment consisting of people, tools, communication technologies, infrastructures, values, practices, and traditions. *See also* determinism; media ideology. **Further Reading**: 1. Lance Strate, "Understanding MEA" (1999) and "A Media Ecology Review" (2004). 2. Casey Lum, "Media Ecology: Concepts, Contexts, and Currents" (2014a).

media ideology Developed by anthropologist Ilana Gershon, this concept posits that there are culturally nuanced ideas about how media work and these shape how people actually put to use said media. For Gershon, media ideologies are normative ideas about appropriate (and inappropriate) use and often have to do with expressing what sorts of media are best (and least) suited for certain types of communication. Media ideologies, to summarize, strongly shape how technologies and communication media are employed. *See also* negative media ideologies. **Further Reading**: 1. Ilana Gershon, *The Breakup 2.0: Disconnecting over New Media* (2010a). 2. Gershon, "Media Ideologies: An Introduction" (2010b).

media promiscuity The second of two constitutive Protestant media ideologies, media promiscuity coincided with the rise of printing technologies during the Protestant Reformation's upheavals. Media promiscuity exploits mass media's capability to spread far and wide to the broadest publics possible. Promiscuous media clamor for the gaze of viewers; they are indiscriminate, evangelizing media. This genre is often controversial due to the wideness of its address and often has unanticipated consequences. Throughout the history of Protestantism and into the present, media promiscuity has conflicted and converged with media sincerity, creating unique new combinations and redefining time and time again what counts as authentic and orthodox. *See also* media sincerity.

media sincerity The first of two constitutive Protestant media ideologies, media sincerity is a deeply ingrained impulse born during the Protestant Reformation that emphasizes directness, immediacy, and authenticity and privileges face-to-face communication, advances the transport view, extends logocentrism, denigrates hierarchy, promotes the priesthood of all believers, and advocates for a particularly modern form of individual personhood. *See also* media promiscuity.

mediatization A reflexive process in which communicative technologies do not just present or depict information—nor behave neutrally—but actively and subtly shape society through the very process of adoption and use. *See also* affordance; media ecology. **Further Reading**: 1. Knut Lundby, *Mediatization: Concept, Changes, Consequences* (2009). 2. Ibid., *Mediatization of Communication* (2014). 3. André Jansson, *Mediatization and Mobile Lives: A Critical Approach* (2018).

GLOSSARY   293

megachurch A congregation whose members tally at least two thousand attendees per week. Congregations range from theologically conservative to progressive. **Further Reading**: 1. Scott Thumma and Dave Travis, *Beyond Megachurch Myths: What We Can Learn from America's Largest Churches* (2007). 2. Omri Elisha, *Moral Ambition: Mobilization and Social Outreach in Evangelical Megachurches* (2011). 3. Peter Schuurman, *The Subversive Evangelical: The Ironic Charisma of an Irreligious Megachurch* (2019).

meme A seemingly trivial yet culturally significant form of digital expression that juxtaposes various types of imagery with text to make points that range from humorous and lighthearted to heavily political and ideological. Memes often function as forms of boundary maintenance and involve shared insider knowledge, typically based on consumption of popular culture. If one doesn't understand the content of the image's origins, the textual commentaries make less sense. Memes exist because they are easily circulated online and have the propensity to go viral. *See also* stancetaking. **Further Reading**: Limor Shifman, *Memes in Digital Culture* (2014).

messiness A culture of church gathering preferred by some local emerging evangelical churches who reject megachurch professionalism and aspire for more authentic and true-to-life social and religious interactions. *See also* emerging church movement (ECM); emerging evangelicalism.

metaphor According to metaphor theorists George Lakoff and Mark Johnson (1980, 5), "The essence of metaphor is understanding and experiencing one kind of thing in terms of another." Metaphors are exceedingly important in that, as Lakoff and Johnson have argued, human thought, mental processing, and linguistic operations operate metaphorically. Metaphors are the very media by which people think, communicate, and argue. In the study of digital culture, for example, scholars, journalists, and engineers often employ aquatic metaphors to explain their vision of how the internet and new media operate. **Further Reading**: 1. George Lakoff and Mark Johnson, *Metaphors We Live By* (1980). 2. George Lakoff, "The Contemporary Theory of Metaphor" (1993). 3. John Durham Peters, *The Marvelous Clouds: Toward a Philosophy of Elemental Media* (2015).

microblogs Social media platforms such as personal Facebook pages or Twitter accounts. A Facebook comment, Instagram image, or tweet are smaller forms of blogging expressed via one of the previous digital platforms and not a blogging account proper (e.g., Blogger, Medium, or WordPress). *See also* blog; social media.

millennials A generational category that typically describes people born roughly between 1980 and 2000. Millennials are often depicted in popular commentary as being at odds with the postwar baby boomers born between the mid-1940s and the mid-1960s. *See also* digital immigrants; digital natives.

mobile church A congregation that does not have a permanent location or owns real estate but rents buildings or shares spaces with buildings designed for other uses. Examples of mobile churches might include a congregation that meets in a coffee shop, pub, theater, or elementary school gymnasium. *See also* church plant.

modified tweet (MT) A tweet shared from another Twitter account that has been slightly adjusted but still cites the source. An MT is typically followed up with the handle of the account of origin or reception and then the content itself. *See also* entextualization; reentextualization.

mommy blogs A niche genre of popular blogging involving writing about family, domestic affairs, and child-rearing, often mingled with reflections on faith and religion. *See also* blogs. **Further Reading**: Deborah Whitehead, "The Evidence of Things Unseen: Authenticity and Fraud in the Christian Mommy Blogosphere" (2015).

mutual submission A theology of gender that incorporates egalitarian impulses in terms of husband-and-wife domestic duties and that the hierarchy of power within marriage proposes that marriage is teamwork involving two coleaders who submit to each other's authority. **Further Reading**: R. Marie Griffith, *God's Daughters: Evangelical Women and the Power of Submission* (1997).

negative media ideologies Predisposed negative ideas, opinions, and discourses about media that tends to be critical—but usually insufficiently so. Although sometimes warranted, negative media ideologies pushed by scholars tend to function as a defense mechanism and ultimately help the commentator sidestep the more sustained difficult job of studying how technologies work and how they're adopted and repurposed within cultural systems. *See also* media ideologies.

neoliberalism A socioeconomic theory and applied system that advocates for freeing up individual entrepreneurial activities by creating a global-, institutional-, and state-level structure that sacralizes the free market and private property. Within the neoliberal purview, the market transcends to the level of self and identity, creating the neoliberal self. The person, in essence, becomes a business and brand as people cultivate themselves as bundles of entrepreneurial and marketable skills to compete in various markets. Neoliberalism is advanced capitalism for the digital era. *See also* brand; communicative capitalism. **Further Reading**: 1. David Harvey, *A Brief History of Neoliberalism* (2005). 2. Ilana Gershon, "Neoliberal Agency" (2011).

neoliberal self *See* neoliberalism.

netiquette Explicit and implicit rules for interacting online. These rules range from general expectations for manners in engagements to specific lists of approved and unapproved behaviors in blog comment sections, to formal user guides for Twitter and Facebook written in full legalese. Different social media platforms have different rules. These rules are often plastic and change over time. Manuals written about the internet and digital media also serve as more formal expressions of netiquette. Sometimes rules reflect one's broader moral codes, but other times they are adapted in the digital arena. *See also* idioms of practice; media ideologies.

network theory A social theory that sees power as flowing via decentralized, mostly horizontal nodes rather than top-down, vertical ones. Network theory emphasizes connection, social density, linkage, mapping, and collaboration among social actors. Networks are contagious and promiscuous. *See also* authority; power. **Further Reading**: 1. Niall Ferguson, *The Square and the Tower: Networks and Power, from the Freemasons to Facebook* (2017a). 2. Wendy Chun, *Updating to Remain the Same: Habitual New Media* (2016).

new media Broadly, new media is an arbitrary category for burgeoning media and technology systems. Narrowly, new media is a synonym for social, digital, and collaborative media. New media is a problematic designation in the manner of other temporal descriptors such as "modern" or "contemporary." These sorts of terminologies have very short shelf lives and quickly outdate themselves. *See also* collaborative media; social media. **Further Reading**: Lev Manovich, *The Language of New Media* (2001).

newness Like new media, newness as a qualifier is relatively short-lived and somewhat arbitrarily applied. Newness is also becoming problematic in that as a label it distracts from the fact social and digital media are becoming quite regular and habitual as an ingrained part of everyday life. *See also* new media. **Further Reading**: Ilana Gershon, *The Breakup 2.0: Disconnecting over New Media* (2010a, 78–83).

nonparticipative observation An ethnographic method of observation within a designated social space in which the researcher does not participate like an insider to that group (as one would attempt to do using traditional participant observation methods) but limits their activities mainly to observing and recording data. This method, for instance, has proven productive for digital anthropologists who want to observe social interactions online but not necessarily participate directly in them. *See also* deterritorialized ethnography; ethnography; participant observation.

on ground vs. online A helpful distinction proposed by anthropologists of digital media to move past the problematic and inaccurate binary of online vs. offline domains or virtual vs. real worlds. Due to advances in habitual wearable technologies in conjunction with the domestic Internet of Things, it becomes more and more difficult to distinguish between online and off. In some situations, and depending on one's technology choices, one many never be offline completely. In the same way, for some users, virtual worlds are just as real as physical, on-ground ones. On ground, in this direction, allows for difference between domains without proposing a normative critique against it. *See also* habitual media; Internet of Things (IOT). **Further Reading**: Jacqueline Fewkes, *Anthropological Perspectives on the Religious Uses of Mobile Apps* (2019).

opacity In reference to analyzing wide bodies of Twitter data, opacity refers to a tweet's potential for ambiguity regarding an author's stance. In other words, because of Twitter's affordance for concision, a person's stance on a subject they tweet or retweet is not always immediately clear given the tone and wording of the tweet alone. This unclearness is opacity.

open-source An expression that emphasizes the collaborative, participative, and decidedly social texture of some genres of online information. A good example of open-source media is Wikipedia, in which users following the guidelines can alter, edit, redact, and contribute to encyclopedia entries. Wikipedia is open-source because it is the product of millions of willing contributors. *See also* collaborative media.

oral media Utterances expressed vocally, audibly, live, and in person, such as a sermon or speech. Oral media are different in type, for example, from print media but could also be recorded and disseminated after the fact by digital media tools.

orthodoxy In theological parlance, to be orthodox is to be in right standing with church tradition and doctrine on a given matter. Etymologically, the word literally means "straight" (*ortho*) "belief" (*doxa*). Orthodoxy standards within Christianity reconfigure over time and differ according to the various subtraditions. Orthodoxy discourse and authenticity discourse often go hand in hand in religious contexts. *See also* authenticity; heresy; heterodoxy.

panopticon Emerging out of the writings of Michel Foucault, channeling Jeremy Bentham, the concept of the panopticon refers to an architectural feature in some prison designs in which inmates in cells below are observed from on high from a central tower. The key to the theory of the panopticon is architectural concealment and self-regulation. Prisoners could not be certain whether they were being surveilled from the tower, but the idea behind such an intentional unknown is that prisoners would govern themselves if they thought themselves being watched and their activities recorded. The concept of the panopticon has been applied to many parts of contemporary society, including to the internet itself. Facebook users will adjust their own behaviors and actions online keeping in mind that they are being monitored and recorded by some vague but powerful institutional other, whether that other be Big Brother, surveillance capitalism, the surveillance state, or at the very least one's social group. Social media is the new panopticon. *See also* communicative capitalism. **Further Reading**: 1. Michel Foucault, *Discipline & Punish: The Birth of the Prison* (1977, 201–202). 2. José Marichal, *Facebook Democracy: The Architecture of Disclosure and the Threat to Public Life* (2012, 75–76).

participant observation An ethnographic research method that involves firsthand observation, interaction, participation, and recording of fieldnotes within a designated social gathering or particular cultural setting or field. *See also* deterritorialized ethnography; ethnography; nonparticipant observation.

participatory media *See* collaborative media.

performative individualism Identity-oriented activities both online and offline, explicit and implicit, that range from everyday interpersonal interactions to posting articles from specific sources and linking to content, to dedicated self-curations of one's social media page aesthetics, to more mundane forms of autodocumentation regarding one's everyday habits and consumptive practices, to visual expressions of religiosity. One's activities online, rather than consisting of random, arbitrary acts, are ongoing projects of self-constitution. *See also* autodocumentation; digitally buffered self; habitual media. **Further Reading**: Erving Goffman, *The Presentation of Self in Everyday Life* (1990).

personal computer (PC) A form of computing made individual primarily by Silicon Valley entrepreneurs who sought to wrest the computer out of the hands of elite academics, technicians, and military personnel and turn it into an everyday household item. The traditional narrative is that these populist developments began in the 1970s but increased during the internet boom of the 1990s. More thorough recent histories of the computer, however, have complicated this story by looking to corresponding international developments outside of the United States and turning attention to time-sharing telephone- and-computer networks that predated the commercialization of the PC by at least ten years. **Further Reading**: Joy Rankin, *A People's History of Computing in the United States* (2018).

platform Most often used as to refer to social media programs and apps (e.g., Facebook, TikTok, etc.), in the neoliberal era, a platform is also a way of thinking about how one's online media serve to project one's voice and brand identity. One's platform includes those various media across which one's brand reaches.

polarized crowds One of two models for explaining how group communication online takes place. For the polarized-crowd model, people communicate within strictly defined bounds of like-mindedness and do not venture much beyond those boundaries. Communication is more insular. The polarized crowd differs from the community-cluster model. *See also* community cluster. **Further Reading**: Marc A. Smith et al., "Mapping Twitter Topic Networks: From Polarized Crowds to Community Clusters" (2014).

postevangelical A person who has a background in but has left, rejected, converted, or transitioned out of evangelicalism proper. Postevangelicals sometimes remain within the broad margins of what might count as evangelical but other times depart completely, rejecting the term as a meaningful category of identification. *See also* emerging church movement (ECM); emerging evangelicals; ex-evangelicals; progressive evangelicals. **Further Reading**: Dave Tomlinson, *The Post-Evangelical* (2003 [1995]).

power The likelihood, for Weber, that an authoritative figure can impose and then carry out his or her will even when subjects resist. Power has often been likened to force. Although authority shores up reservoirs of power, it can be seized and taken. In other words, due to how legitimacy works, one can be powerful without necessarily being an authorized legitimate leader. In the contemporary era, power appears to be even more fluid and network based. *See also* authority. **Further Reading**: 1. Max Weber, *The Theory of Social and Economic Organization* (1964). 2. Michel Foucault, *History of Sexuality: An Introduction* (1978).

priesthood of all believers A theological concept developed during the upheavals of the Protestant Reformation, this doctrine with a populist bent suggested that all baptized Christians were priests, of a sort, before God. The priesthood of all believers was a decidedly anti-Catholic concept that sought to strip the Catholic priestly hierarchy of authority and empower the individual Christian. **Further Reading**: Andrew Pettegree, *Brand Luther: How an Unheralded Monk Turned His Small Town into a Center of Publishing, Made Himself the Most Famous Man in Europe—and Started the Protestant Reformation* (2015).

progressive evangelicals Although terms like "progressive," "conservative," and "liberal" are arbitrary concepts, progressive here simply has to do with those evangelicals who operate on the margins of traditional evangelicalism by advancing progressive theologies and politics that may not align with the theologies and politics of the conservative mainstream. *See also* emerging church movement (ECM); emerging evangelicals.

public A social and textual community based on the consumption, circulation, and dialogue about shared texts. According to Michael Warner, publics are not institutional and depend entirely upon circulation, uptake, and discourse. Due to their open-ended constitution, publics can exist in varying degrees of size and influence. For example, counterpublics often form in opposition to what this marginal community would define as a powerful majority other. **Further Reading**: 1. Michael Warner, *Publics and Counterpublics* (2002). 2. Alex Fattal, "Hostile Remixes on YouTube: A New Constraint on Pro-FARC Counterpublics in Colombia" (2014). 3. Nancy Fraser, "Rethinking the Public Sphere: A Contribution to the Critique of Actually Existing Democracy" (1990).

public-use differentiation An activity that occurs in public places, such as church services, dinner at a restaurant, or even informal social gatherings, where cellphones are ironically considered antisocial distractions from the moment's in-person social exchanges, and therefore people tend to keep phones stowed away and out of sight. When this loose protocol is occasionally breached, such use is usually punctuated with apologies by the user and verbal explanations regarding the necessity of the phone's use at that time.

real world When employed by critics of technology, this term means the nondigital, offline, physical world. Such phrasing is problematic, however, in that it diminishes the value of digital social spaces and in some situations may even verge on being ableist. Qualifying something as real also misleadingly implies that digital interactions are less social and meaningful. One helpful alternative to bifurcating between the real and the digital would be to speak in terms of the online versus the on ground. *See also* on ground.

reentextualization If entextualization is the making of an utterance into a text to be shared, reentextualization is the moving of that text into a new context and introducing it there. *See also* entextualization; indexical bleaching; intertextual gap. **Further Reading**: Michael Silverstein and Greg Urban, "The Natural History of Discourse" (1996).

Reformed theology A modern Protestant tradition that links explicitly back to the Protestant Reformation and its rift with Roman Catholic ecclesiology, doctrine, and practice. Reformed theology professes *sola scriptura, sola gratia, sola fide,* and *sola Christus*—by scripture, grace, faith, and Christ alone. Reformed theology is considered in common parlance to be inseparable from Calvinist theology and its five points: total depravity, unconditional election, limited atonement, irresistible grace, and the perseverance and preservation of the saints. Many progressive evangelicals reject Reformed theology on multiple grounds. Depending on one's denominational upbringing, many influential evangelical groups also adhere to an Arminianism's doctrine of free will, which is the theological antithesis to major Calvinist tenets.

religious digital creatives (RDCs) As described by Heidi Campbell, RDCs include digital professionals who manage blogs, web pages, and social media platforms, create and edit online content, and otherwise mediate digitally between formal religious leaders and laypeople. RDCs are often in the employ of a church or ministry but also work as independent influencers. *See also* influencer. **Further Reading**: Heidi Campbell, *Digital Creatives and the Rethinking of Religious Authority* (2020a).

religious left An umbrella category that refers generally to religious progressives, whether Christian or not, who are opposed in various ways to the conservativism of the religious right. The emerging church movement (ECM) and progressive evangelicals, for instance, both qualify as part of this diffuse movement. *See also* emerging church movement; green evangelicals; progressive evangelicals (ECM). **Further Reading**: L. Benjamin Rolsky, *The Rise and Fall of the Religious Left: Politics, Television, and Popular Culture in the 1970s and Beyond* (2019).

retweet (RT) A discursive function on Twitter, to retweet is to repost a post submitted or forwarded by someone else. This retweeted post then shows up on the retweeter's own page with a double directional arrow icon. Users often (though not always) add the "RT" disclaimer to show that the information is not original to their handle.

Romanticism An eighteenth and nineteenth century cultural, artistic, musical, literary, and religious movement that emphasized nature, sublimity, feeling, and emotion over and against the cold and calculated rationality of the industrialized world. Key figures within the Romantic movement included writers Walt Whitman, Edgar Allan Poe, and Charlotte Brontë, musicians Franz Liszt and Ludwig von Beethoven, and painter Caspar David Friedrich. *See also* the sublime.

Second Reformation A religion- and media-oriented cultural shift brought about by the digital media turn and enabled by PC- and internet-mediated technologies. Some Protestant commentators writing in the late 1990s envisioned this shift as just as important and wide reaching in implication as the first Reformation.

secular Typically defined in sociology as differentiation from the religious sphere, secular entities are assumed to be free from the influence of religion. While recognizing that nonreligious people are indeed secular in this sense, recent historical studies have shown how the concept and milieu of the secular has been a product of Protestant contestations and may even represent an implicit hegemonic form of Christian power, especially in places such as the United States. *See also* hegemony. **Further Reading**: 1. Charles McCrary and Jeffrey Wheatley, "The Protestant Secular in the Study of American Religion" (2016). 2. Travis Cooper, "Objectivity Discourse, the Protestant Secular, and the Decolonization of Religious Studies" (2019b).

sensational forms As defined by Birgit Meyer (2011, 29), sensational forms are "relatively fixed modes for invoking and organising access to the transcendental, offering structures of repetition to create and sustain links between believers in the context of particular religious regimes." Sensational forms encompass habits, media, aesthetics, and modes of being, knowing, and communicating between religious people and those beings considered divine, sacred, or special. Sensational forms are a subclass of media ideologies. *See also* media ideologies. **Further Reading**: 1. Birgit Meyer, "Religious Sensations: Why Media, Aesthetics, and Power Matter in the Study of Contemporary Religion" (2007). 2. Ibid., "Mediation and Immediacy: Sensational Forms, Semiotic Ideologies and the Question of the Medium" (2011).

shitstorms Philosopher Byung-Chul Han's terminology for the rise of antagonistic exchanges, indecorum, and overall disrespect in online interactions. *See also* flaming language; negative media ideologies. **Further Reading**: Byung-Chul Han, *In the Swarm: Digital Prospects* (2017).

simulacra Jean Baudrillard's concept of how mediated signs, symbols, and signifiers construct reality as it is perceived. The media simulations and representations that surround us on all directions—the simulacra—do not serve as referents of some deeper, anchored meaning. The simulacra conceal the fact that in Baudrillard's view, there is no authentic truth being signified. In his estimation, the simulacra are the new, postmodern, postcapitalist hyperreality. *See also* communicative capitalism; informational overload. **Further Reading**: Jean Baudrillard, *Simulacra and Simulation* (1994).

simultaneity A unique affordance of the digital era, simultaneity is the ability to communicate instantaneously with one's online followership and friendship groups. Simultaneity has massive ramifications in terms of power and authority structures. **Further Reading**: Zynep Tufecki, *Twitter and Tear Gas: The Power and Fragility of Networked Protest* (2017).

sincere-speech paradigm *See* media sincerity.

sincerity/promiscuity paradigm Refers to the historic and ongoing tension in Protestantism between media sincerity and media promiscuity. The sincerity/promiscuity paradigm constitutes a robust and encompassing media ecology. *See also* media promiscuity; media sincerity.

slow church A religious philosophy and ecclesiology that applies Slow Movement principles to church culture and practices at the local congregational level. Slow church proponents advocate for rejecting all forms of capitalist advances made on religious life, including the rise of the megachurch, by treating mission as a business to be expanded and advanced. Slow church emphasizes simplicity and authenticity, embraces messiness and nonprofessionalism, and aspires toward a more robust form of religious life that is fulfilling and good. *See also* messiness. **Further Reading**: C. Christopher Smith and John Pattison, *Slow Church: Cultivating Community in the Patient Way of Jesus* (2014).

Slow Movement A minimalist social and cultural philosophy that rejects what it identifies as the cult of speed, which characterizes modern life and causes it to be hectic, chaotic, and otherwise unfulfilling. The Slow Food movement, one branch of the broader movement, applies the principles of slowness to the food industry, seeking to decommercialize foodways and relocalize them through farmer's markets, farm-to-table establishments, Slow Food fairs, protests against food industrialization, and other strategies. The Slow Movement, as a whole, reconsiders the role of technologies in everyday life, resists rapid industrialization and commercialization, and prioritizes rich local connections between people and their environments. *See also* slow church. **Further Reading**: Carl Honoré, *In Praise of Slowness: Challenging the Cult of Speed* (2004).

small media Media of various genres that emphasize activist participation and publicness but exist as alternatives to state-managed mass media or corporate-ran forms. Small media, then, are local media in that they serve local interests. Small media include newspapers, television, pamphlets, magazines, and so on. *See also* local media; mass media. **Further Reading**: Annabelle Sreberny-Mohammadi and Ali Mohammadi, *Small Media, Big Revolution: Communication, Culture, and the Iranian Revolution* (1994).

smartphone A form of mobile cellular telephone that connects to the internet and hosts internet-mediated apps as part of its affordances. Smartphone is often used as a synonym for data phone. *See also* cellular phone; data phone; mobile phone.

social media Technically all media are "social" in that they serve to communicate, but the more common use of this term refers to new digital, online media platforms that focus specifically on extending one's social connections. Social media, in other words, include microblog platforms, such as Facebook, Instagram, Twitter, TikTok, SnapChat, among many others. *See also* digital media; microblog; new media.

social shaping of technology A social constructionist and cultural approach to the study of technology, this school of thought stresses that social forces inevitably shape technologies, be it at the level of design or uptake and use. In short, people domesticate and culture their adopted technologies, sometimes expanding creatively beyond design intent. *See also* technological determinism. **Further Reading**: 1. Knut Lundby, "Theoretical Frameworks for Approaching Religion and New Media" (2013: 232–233). 2. Heidi Campbell, "Texting the Faith: Religious Users and Cell Phone Culture" (2006). 3. Ralph Schroeder, *Social Theory after the Internet: Media, Technology, and Globalization* (2018).

spreadable media This concept refers to the ability of media to be quickly and efficiently shared with others. A media's spreadability also links directly to its promiscuity. Spreadable media generate social publics and may sometimes engender unpredictable situations as a result of such effective sharing. *See also* media promiscuity. **Further Reading**: Henry Jenkins et al., *Spreadable Media: Creating Value and Meaning in a Networked Culture* (2013).

stance, stancetaking Sociolinguists define stancetaking as the "taking up a position with respect to the form or the content of one's utterance" (Jaffe 2009, 3). All expressions and utterances, in fact, are "stance-saturated" to varying degrees, as no entirely neutral relationship to one's expressions is possible. Applying these ideas, stance has to do with one's ideological position vis-à-vis some subject matter. **Further Reading**: Alexandra Jaffe, *Stance: Sociolinguistic Perspectives* (2009).

sublime, the Related to the Romantic movement and to broader aesthetic considerations, the sublime is a sense of emotive wonder experienced when one observes something other than or greater to oneself, such as nature. For example, in Caspar David Friedrich's famous 1817 oil painting, *Wanderer above the Sea of Fog*, the sublime is beheld as the natural expanse that spreads out like a vision beyond the explorer who contemplates it. *See also* Romanticism.

tastemaking *See* taste regime.

taste regime The ability of social media influencers to determine taste preferences in goods, decor, clothing, and food, effectively shaping the consumption practices of their followers. An example of a taste regime is when an institution, such as *Kinfolk*, establishes an entire aesthetic for millions of followers who then shape their tastes and adjust their preferences to align with it. *See also* communicative capitalism. **Further Reading**: 1. Zynep Arsel, "Down the #authenticity Hole with Socality Barbie" (2015). 2. Zynep Arsel and Jonathan Bean, "Taste Regimes and Market-Mediated Practice" (2012). 3. Pierre Bourdieu, *Distinction: A Social Critique of the Judgment of Taste* (1984).

technology Beyond a colloquial definition of technologies as practical tools and devices, such as cellphones, pencils, computers, and so on, defining the term is indeed "slippery," as Matthewman (2011, 9, 12–13) describes. In fact, one tradition of scholarship interprets technology as mediation between humans and the world. As I use the term in book, technology is closely analogous—and possibly identical to—media. *See also* media. **Further Reading**: Steve Matthewman, *Technology and Social Theory* (2011).

technology manual A guidebook in the self-help or how-to genre intended to assist readers in learning and applying new technologies. Technology manuals can also be categorized as theological writings on the appropriate place of technologies in Christian life.

technophobe A person who either fears technology to the point of not using it or rejects technological use for moral or religious reasons. Technophobia is a form of media resistance. *See also* digital asceticism; digital minimalism; Luddite; media ambivalence. **Further Reading**: Trine Syvertsen, *Media Resistance: Protest, Dislike, Abstention* (2017).

televangelism The accommodation of television broadcasting stations on the part of independent and networked evangelical revivalists who theologize the television as a divinely ordained medium for missionization and proselytization.

transport view A pervasive media ideology that conceives of communication as the transfer of information between two communicants and reifies the gold standard of face-to-face speech as the most direct and important form of authentic communication. This view takes a logocentric perspective that downplays anything beyond in-person speech—e.g., written text, published books, social media interactions, and the like—as lesser in quality. *See also* logocentrism. **Further Reading**: 1. David Holmes, *Communication Theory: Media, Technology and Society* (2005). 2. John Thompson, *The Media and Modernity: A Social Theory of the Media* (1995).

trolls Somewhat arbitrarily defined, these infamous digital creatures tend to police online comment sections and microblog discussion threads, frequently bullying and hounding users and dominating the interactions via flaming language. Some bloggers who encourage discussion among their readers post detailed rules for engagement that prohibit trolling activities and threaten to block trolls if the behavior is identified. Trolls infringe on the media ideology and general netiquette stipulation that conversation online should be civil and productive. *See also* flaming language; netiquette.

ubiquitous media *See* habitual media; spreadable media.

uptake The adoption or use of technologies, media, and apps.

vernacularization A populist activity of making media artifacts more accessible to a broader population. An example of this process is that following the upheavals of the Protestant Reformation, biblical texts were vernacularized as they were translated into less academic, everyday language to encourage reading by laypeople outside of monasteries and Catholic institutions.

vertical vs. lateral communication As described by anthropologist Debra Spitulnik, vertical communication is mass mediated in that it connects physically distant others across space. Lateral communication, on the other hand, has to do with person-to-person, face-to-face, local and immediate forms communication. *See also* horizontalization; mass media; transport view. **Further Reading**: Debra Spitulnik, "The Social Circulation of Media Discourse and the Mediation of Communities" (1996).

voice A communicative component linked to one's identity, voice is required for participation in discursive publics. In the neoliberal paradigm, voice is connected to platform and is used as a synonym for the brand/self and is measured by one's degree of influence, following, and reach. Voice, in a way, is the mediated digital self. *See also* communicative capitalism; neoliberalism; performative individualism. **Further Reading**: Laura Kunreuther, *Voicing Subjects: Public Intimacy and Mediation in Kathmandu* (2014).

wearable technology Communicative, habitual media devices that extend or layer upon the body. Examples include Google Glass, FitBits and smartwatches, earphones, and virtual reality headsets. Even the smartphone is to some degree "wearable" in that people tend to constantly carry it around with them on their person or stowed in a pocket, purse, or bag. *See also* habitual media. **Further Reading**: Adrianna de Souza e Silva, "Interfaces of Hybrid Spaces" (2006).

Web 3.0 Often used as a historical dating system for the development of the internet, Web 3.0 is the newest iteration of social, collaborative, internet-mediated communications occurring online. Web 3.0 encompasses cloud computing, the rise of mobile devices, the Internet of Things (IOT), habitual media, and other experimental augmented and virtual digital forms. Before Web 3.0, Web 2.0 began in the early 2000s and included the rise of public blogging and other personal uses of the internet. Web 1.0 included the very earliest days of the World Wide Web in the mid-1990s, before the internet became a popular everyday tool. **Further Reading**: Heidi Campbell and Stephen Garner, *Networked Theology: Negotiating Faith in Digital Culture* (2016, 44–48).

whiteness Often going unexamined in popular discourse and the public imagination, whiteness in the United States is a dominant sociological construct that functions invisibly and hegemonically as an unmarked register with applied religious, economic, social, and political ramifications. An example of whiteness's power, for instance, are the myriad forms of implicit, explicit, and institutionalized racism to which marginalized Americans categorized as existing outside of bounds of whiteness are subjected. *See also* hegemony; power. **Further Reading**: 1. John Hartigan Jr., *Race in the 21st Century: Ethnographic Approaches* (2015). 2. Khyati Joshi, *White Christian Privilege: The Illusion of Religious Equality in America* (2020). 3. Anthea Butler, *White Evangelical Racism: The Politics of Morality in America* (2021).

WiFi Often misunderstood to be an abbreviation for "wireless fidelity" (similar to hi-fi, or high fidelity), WiFi is a gibberish term that originated in 1999 as the name for a network service that met IEEE 802.11 technical specifications. Today, WiFi is synonymous with wireless internet and is the crucial mediated backdrop for the development of the Internet of Things (IOT) and habitual media. *See also* habitual media; Internet of Things (IOT). **Further Reading**: David Pogue, "What Wi-Fi Stands For—And Other Wireless Questions Answered" (2012).

wikimodel A genre of social, collaborative, and informational media ran by a contributor base or fan group. The most important online encyclopedia, Wikipedia, is perhaps the clearest example of a wikimodel. Etymologically, "wiki" comes from Ward Cunningham's *WikiWikiWeb*, the first media of this type created in 1994. Cunningham named the project "Wiki" after a "wiki wiki" airport bus system in Hawaii, a synonym for "quick." **Further Reading**: Ward Cunningham, "Correspondence on the Etymology of Wiki" (2003).

BIBLIOGRAPHY

Abdel-Fadil, Mona. 2016. "Conflict and Affect among Conservative Christians on Facebook." Online: *Heidelberg Journal of Religions on the Internet* 11: 1–27.
Albanese, Catherine L. 1990. *Nature Religion in America from the Algonkian Indians to the New Age*. Chicago: University of Chicago Press.
Albert, Brian. 2011. "Farewell Rob Bell Part One." *Confessions of a Doxaholic* (blog), March 29, 2011. http://confessionsofadoxaholic.blogspot.com/2011/03/farewell-rob-bell-part-one.html.
Alper, Meryl. 2017. *Giving Voice: Mobile Communication, Disability, and Inequality*. Cambridge, MA: MIT Press.
Altman, Michael. 2019. "'Religion, Religions, Religious' in America: Toward a Smithian Account of 'Evangelicalism.'" *Method and Theory in the Study of Religion* 31: 71–82.
Anderson, Benedict. 1991. *Imagined Communities: Reflections on the Origins and Spread of Nationalism*. London: Verso.
Anderson, Dianna E. 2015. *Damaged Goods: New Perspectives on Christian Purity*. New York: Jericho.
———. 2016a. "Unsettled." *Dianna E. Anderson* (blog), November 18, 2016. http://diannaeanderson.net/blog/2016/11/unsettled.
———. 2016b. "On Being Better, On Doing Better." *Dianna E. Anderson* (blog), March 27, 2016. http://diannaeanderson.net/blog/2016/3/on-being-better-on-doing-better.
———. 2016c. "Whiteness as the Background Radiation of Gender." *Dianna E. Anderson* (blog), May 14, 2016. http://diannaeanderson.net/blog/2016/5/whiteness-as-the-background-radiation-of-gender.
———. 2016d. "Some Honest Questions for the People Who Keep Asking Me Questions About." *Dianna E. Anderson* (blog), May 20, 2016. http://diannaeanderson.net

/blog/2016/5/some-honest-questions-for-the-people-who-keeping-asking-me-questions-about-panic-issue-here.

———. 2016e. "You Aren't a Different Person When You Drink." *Dianna E. Anderson* (blog), June 10, 2016. http://diannaeanderson.net/blog/2016/6/you-arent-a-different-person-when-you-drink.

———. 2016f. "On Pride in the Wake of Pain." *Dianna E. Anderson* (blog), June 12, 2016. http://diannaeanderson.net/blog/2016/6/on-pride-in-the-wake-of-pain.

———. 2016g. "Brexit and the Humiliation of the Exit." *Dianna E. Anderson* (blog), July 1, 2016. http://diannaeanderson.net/blog/2016/7/brexit-and-the-humiliation-of-the-expert.

———. 2017a. "Home." *Dianna E. Anderson* (blog). http://diannaeanderson.net/.

———. 2017b. "None of This Is Normal." *Dianna E. Anderson* (blog), January 22, 2017. http://diannaeanderson.net/blog/2017/1/none-of-this-is-normal.

———. 2018. *Problematic: How Toxic Call-Out Culture Is Destroying Feminism.* Lincoln, NE: Potomac.

Apkon, Stephen. 2013. *The Age of the Image: Redefining Literacy in a World of Screens.* New York: Farrar, Straus and Giroux.

Apostolidis, Paul. 2000. *Stations of the Cross: Adorno and Christian Right Radio.* Durham, NC: Duke University Press.

Appadurai, Arjun. 1991. "Global Ethnoscapes: Notes and Queries for a Transnational Anthropology." In *Interventions: Anthropologies of the Present*, edited by R. G. Fox, 191–210. Santa Fe, NM: School of American Research.

Arsel, Zeynep. 2015. "Down the #authenticity Hole with Socality Barbie." *University of Concordia News*, September 18, 2015. http://www.concordia.ca/cunews/main/stories/2015/09/18/socality-barbie-instragram-social-media-zeynep-arsel.html.

Arsel, Zeynep, and Jonathan Bean. 2013. "Taste Regimes and Market-Mediated Practice." *Journal of Consumer Research* 39: 899–917.

Arterburn, Stephen, and Fred Stoker. 2002. *Every Young Man's Bible: Strategies for Victory in the Real World of Sexual Temptation.* Colorado Springs, CO: WaterBrook.

Asad, Talal. 1993. *Genealogies of Religion: Discipline and Reasons of Power in Christianity and Islam.* Baltimore, MD: Johns Hopkins University Press.

Aslam, Salman. 2018. "Twitter by the Numbers: Stats, Demographics & Fun Facts." *Omnicore*, January 1, 2018. https://www.omnicoreagency.com/twitter-statistics/.

Attanasi, Katherine, and Amos Young. 2012. *Pentecostalism and Prosperity: The Socio-Economics of the Global Charismatic Movement.* New York: Palgrave Macmillan.

Au, Wagner James. 2019. "If an Actual Pastor Simulates a Baptism in VR, Is It Spiritually Real? Here Comes the Theology." *New World Notes*, May 22, 2019. https://nwn.blogs.com/nwn/2019/05/vrchat-baptism-theology.html.

Baab, Lynne M. 2012. "Toward a Theology of the Internet: Place, Relationship, and Sin." In *Digital Religion, Social Media and Culture: Perspectives, Practices and Futures*, edited by Pauline Hope Cheong, Peter Fischer-Nielsen, Stefan Gelfgren, and Charles Ess, 277–291. New York: Peter Lang.

Bacovcin, Helen. 2003. *The Way of a Pilgrim and a Pilgrim Continues His Way.* New York: Doubleday.
Bailey, Sarah Pulliam. 2011. "Rob Bell's Upcoming Book on Heaven & Hell Stirs Blog, Twitter Backlash on Universalism." *Christianity Today,* February 26, 2011. http://www.christianitytoday.com/gleanings/2011/february/rob-bells-upcoming-book-on-heaven-hell-stirs-blog-twitter.html?paging=off.
Bakewell, Sarah. 2016. *At the Existentialist Café: Freedom, Being, and Apricot Cocktails—with Jean-Paul Sartre, Simone De Beauvoir, Albert Camus, Martin Heidegger, Karl Jaspers, Edmund Husserl, Maurice Merleau-Ponty, and Others.* New York: Other.
Bakhtin, M. M. 1981 [1934–1935]. *The Dialogic Imagination: Four Essays.* Edited by Michael Holquist and Caryl Emerson. Translated by Michael Holquist. Austin: University of Texas Press.
Bakken, Scott. 2015. "Socality Response Regarding Account: @socalitybarbie." *Socality,* September 7, 2015. http://www.socality.org/journal/2015/9/7/socality-response-socalitybarbie.
———. 2017. "The Socality Story." *Socality.* http://www.socality.org/socality-story.
Balbier, Uta Andrea. 2009. "Billy Graham's Crusades in the 1950s: Neo-evangelicalism between Civil Religion, Media, and Consumerism." *Bulletin of the GHI* 44: 71–80.
Barlow, John Perry. 1996. "A Declaration of the Independence of Cyberspace." *Electronic Frontier Foundation.* February 8, 1996. https://www.eff.org/cyberspace-independence.
Bartkowski, John P. 2001. *Remaking the Godly Marriage: Gender Negotiation in Evangelical Families.* New Brunswick, NJ: Rutgers University Press.
Barthes, Roland. 1981. *Camera Lucida: Reflections on Photography.* Translated by Richard Howard. New York: Hill and Wang.
Barton, Bernadette. 2012. *Pray the Gay Away: The Extraordinary Lives of Bible Belt Gays.* New York: New York University Press.
Baudrillard, Jean. 1994. *Simulacra and Simulation.* Translated by Sheila Faria Glaser. Ann Arbor: University of Michigan Press.
Bauman, Richard. 2000. "Genre." *Journal of Linguistic Anthropology* 9 (1–2): 84–87.
———. 2004. *A World of Others' Words: Cross-Cultural Perspectives on Intertextuality.* Malden, MA: Blackwell.
Bayart, Jean-François. 2005. *The Illusion of Cultural Identity.* Translated by Steven Rendall, Janet Roitman, and Jonathan Derrick. London: Hurst & Company.
Beaujon, Andrew. 2006. *Body Piercing Saved My Life: Inside the Phenomenon of Christian Rock.* Cambridge, MA: Da Capo.
Bebbington, David W. 1990. "Evangelical Christianity and Romanticism." *Crux* 26 (1): 9–15.
———. 1994. "Evangelicalism in Its Settings: The British and American Movements since 1940." In *Evangelicalism: Comparative Studies of Popular Protestantism in North America, the British Isles, and Beyond, 1700–1990,* edited by Mark A Noll,

David W. Bebbington, and George A. Rawlyk, 365–388. New York: Oxford University Press.
———. 2005. *The Dominance of Evangelicalism: The Age of Spurgeon and Moody.* Downers Grove, MI: InterVarsity.
Beer, David. 2013. *Popular Culture and New Media: The Politics of Circulation.* New York: Palgrave Macmillan.
Bell, Catherine. 2009. *Ritual Theory, Ritual Practice.* New York: Oxford University Press.
Bell, Rob. 2005. *Velvet Elvis: Repainting the Christian Faith.* Grand Rapids, MI: Zondervan.
———. 2007. *Sex God: Exploring the Endless Connections between Sexuality and Spirituality.* New York: HarperCollins.
———. 2008. *Jesus Wants to Save Christians: A Manifesto for the Church in Exile.* Grand Rapids, MI: Zondervan.
———. 2011a. "Love Wins." *Vimeo*, February 22, 2011. https://vimeo.com/20272585.
———. 2011b. *Love Wins: A Book about Heaven, Hell, and the Fate of Every Person Who Ever Lived.* New York: HarperCollins.
———. 2017a. *How to Be Here: A Guide to Creating a Life Worth Living.* New York: HarperOne.
———. 2017b. *What Is the Bible? How an Ancient Library of Poems, Letters, and Stories Can Transform the Way You Think and Feel about Everything.* New York: HarperOne.
Benjamin, Walter. 1969. "The Work of Art in an Age of Mechanical Reproduction." In *Illuminations*, edited by Walter Benjamin, 217–252. New York: Schocken.
Bennett, Gena R. 2014. *Using Corpora in the Language Learning Classroom Corpus Linguistics for Teachers.* Ann Arbor: University of Michigan Press.
Bernal, Victoria. 2014. *Nation as Network: Diaspora, Cyberspace & Citizenship.* Chicago: University of Chicago Press.
Bernard, H. Russell. 2011. *Research Methods in Anthropology: Qualitative and Quantitative Approaches.* 5th ed. Lanham, MD: AltaMira.
Berners-Lee, Tim. 2000. *Weaving the Web: The Original Design and Ultimate Destiny of the World Wide Web by Its Inventor.* New York: HarperCollins.
Bessey, Sarah. 2008. "In Which Black and White Collide." *Sarah Bessey* (blog), January 4, 2000. http://sarahbessey.com/in-which-black-and-white-collide/.
———. 2009. "In Which I Am Still Emerging." *Sarah Bessey* (blog), July 1, 2009. http://sarahbessey.com/in-which-i-am-still-emerging/.
———. 2013a. *Jesus Feminist: An Invitation to Revisit the Bible's View of Women.* New York: Howard.
———. 2013b. "I Am Damaged Goods." *A Deeper Story* (blog), January 29, 2013. http://deeperstory.com/i-am-damaged-goods/.
———. 2013c. "In Which I Am Damaged Goods." *Sarah Bessey*, January 29, 2013. http://sarahbessey.com/in-which-i-am-damaged-goods/.

———. 2014. "In Which I Am Retiring 'In Which' and a Few Other Decisions about Blogging." *Sarah Bessey* (blog), August 19, 2014. http://sarahbessey.com/decisions-about-blogging/.
———. 2015. *Out of Sorts: Making Peace with an Evolving Faith*. New York: Howard.
Bialecki, Jon. 2017. *A Diagram for Fire: Miracles and Variation in an American Charismatic Movement*. Oakland: University of California Press.
Bielo, James. 2009. *Words upon the Word: An Ethnography of Evangelical Group Bible Study*. New York: New York University Press.
———. 2011. *Emerging Evangelicals: Faith, Modernity, and the Desire for Authenticity*. New York: New York University Press.
———. 2015. *Anthropology of Religion: The Basics*. London: Routledge.
Bossy, John. 1985. *Christianity in the West: 1400–1700*. New York: Oxford University Press.
Bourdieu, Pierre. 1994. *Language and Symbolic Power*. Edited by John B. Thompson. Translated by Gino Raymond and Matthew Adamson. Cambridge, MA: Harvard University Press.
———. 1984. *Distinction: A Social Critique of the Judgment of Taste*. Cambridge, MA: Harvard University Press.
———. 1977. *Outline of a Theory of Practice*. Translated by Richard Nice. Cambridge, MA: Cambridge University Press.
Bourgeois, David T. 2013. *Ministry in the Digital Age: Strategies and Best Practices for a Post-Website World*. Downers Grove, IL: IVP.
Bowler, Kate. 2020. *The Preacher's Wife: The Precarious Power of Evangelical Women Celebrities*. Princeton, NJ: Princeton University Press.
Boy, John D., and Justus Uitermark. 2016. "How to Study the City on Instagram." *PLoS ONE* 11 (6): 1–16.
Brasher, Brenda E. 2001. *Give Me That Online Religion*. New Brunswick, NJ: Rutgers University Press.
Brehm, Stephanie N. 2019. *America's Most Famous Catholic (according to Himself): Stephen Colbert and American Religion in the 21st Century*. New York: Fordham University Press.
Brekus, Catherine A., and W. Clark Gilpin, eds. 2011. *American Christianities: A History of Dominance and Diversity*. Chapel Hill: University of North Carolina Press.
Bridle, James. 2018. *New Dark Age: Technology and the End of the Future*. London: Verso.
Briggs, Kate. 2017. *This Little Art*. London: Fitzcarraldo Editions.
Bromwich, Jonah Engel. 2018. "Everyone Is Canceled." *New York Times*, June 28, 2018. https://www.nytimes.com/2018/06/28/style/is-it-canceled.html.
Brown, Candy Gunther. 2004. *The Word in the World: Evangelical Writing, Publishing, and Reading in America, 1789–1880*. Chapel Hill: University of North Carolina Press.

Brobst, Scout. 2021. "'Exvangelicals' Are Living a Uniquely American Crisis." *Vice*, March 16, 2021. https://www.vice.com/en/article/akdbee /what-its-like-to-leave-the-evangelical-community-exvangelicals.

Bruner, Edward M. 2005. *Culture on Tour: Ethnographies of Travel*. Chicago: University of Chicago Press.

Bryant, Don. 2014. "My Response to John Pavlovitz's Article, 'The Continued Crucifying of Rob Bell, and What It Says about the State of Modern Christianity.'" *Don Bryant* (blog), December 12, 2014. https://donbryant.wordpress. com/2014/12/12/my-response-to-john-pavlovitzs-article-the-continued -crucifying-of-rob-bell-and-what-it-says-about-the-state-of-modern-christianity/.

Bucar, Elizabeth M. 2011. *Creative Conformity: The Feminist Politics of US Catholic and Iranian Shi'i Women*. Washington, DC: Georgetown University Press.

———. 2017. *Pious Fashion: How Muslim Women Dress*. Cambridge, MA: Harvard University Press.

Buettel, Cameron. 2011. "Rob Bell Takes Off His Sheep Suit—And John Piper Bids Him 'Farewell.'" *Once upon a Cross* (blog), March 9, 2011. http://onceuponacross .blogspot.com/2011/03/rob-bell-takes-off-his-sheep-suit.html.

Bunt, Gary R. 2018. *Hashtag Islam: How Cyber-Islamic Environments Are Transforming Religious Authority*. Chapel Hill: University of North Carolina Press.

Buonanno, Milly. 2008. *The Age of Television: Experiences and Theories*. Translated by Jennifer Radice. Chicago: University of Chicago Press.

Burningham, G. 2016. "Father of the Internet Worries Our Digital History Is Disappearing." *Newsweek*, June 9, 2016. http://www.newsweek.com/father -internet-worries-our-digital-history-disappearing-468642.

Butler, Anthea. 2007. *Women in the Church of God in Christ: Making a Sanctified World*. Chapel Hill: University of North Carolina Press.

———. 2021. *White Evangelical Racism: The Politics of Morality in America*. Chapel Hill: University of North Carolina Press.

Calhoun, Adele Ahlberg. 2005. *Spiritual Disciplines Handbook: Practices That Transform Us*. Downers Grove, IL: InterVarsity.

Campbell, Heidi A. 2005. *Exploring Religious Community Online: We Are One in the Network*. New York: Peter Lang.

———. 2006. "Texting the Faith: Religious Users and Cell Phone Culture." In *The Cell Phone Reader: Essays in Social Transformation*, edited by Anandam Kavoori and Noah Arceneaux, 139–154. New York: Peter Lang.

———. 2010a. *When Religion Meets New Media*. New York: Routledge.

———. 2010b. "Religious Authority and the Blogosphere." *Journal of Computer-Mediated Communication* 15: 251–276.

———, ed. 2013a. *Digital Religion: Understanding Religious Practice in New Media Worlds*. New York: Routledge.

———. 2013b. "Community." In *Digital Religion: Understanding Religious Practice in New Media Worlds*, edited by Heidi A. Campbell, 57–71. New York: Routledge.

———. 2013c. "Evangelicals and the Internet." In *Evangelical Christians and Popular Culture: Pop Goes the Gospel, Volume 1*, edited by Robert H. Woods Jr., 277–291. Santa Barbara, CA: Praeger.

———. 2020a. *Digital Creatives and the Rethinking of Religious Authority*. New York: Taylor & Francis Group.

———, ed. 2020b. *Religion in Quarantine: The Future of Religion in a Post-Pandemic World*. Digital Religion Publications: An Imprint of the Network for New Media, Religion & Digital Culture Studies. Ebook.

Campbell, Heidi A., and Stephen Garner. 2016. *Networked Theology: Negotiating Faith in Digital Culture*. Grand Rapids, MI: BakerAcademic.

Cantwell, Christopher D. 2018. "@Preacher_Bot: An Experiment in Evangelical Speech Making." *Religion* 48 (2): 276–290.

Carey, Jesse. 2014. "The Rob Bell Show Premier Was about the Cross." *Relevant*, December 22, 2014. https://relevantmagazine.com/culture/-rob-bell-show-premiere-was-about-cross.

———. 2018. "How to Know Your Facebook Post Is about to Go Very, Very Wrong." *Relevant* 91: 83.

Carlton, Bobby. 2018. "Tech-Savvy Pastor Uses VR to Deliver Virtual Baptisms." *VR Scout*, May 27, 2018. https://vrscout.com/news/pastor-delivers-vr-baptisms/#.

Carpenter, Joel A. 1997. *Revive Us Again: The Reawakening of American Fundamentalism*. New York: Oxford University Press.

Cavanagh, Sarah Rose. 2017. "No, Smartphones Are Not Destroying a Generation." *Psychology Today*, August 6, 2017. https://www.psychologytoday.com/blog/once-more-feeling/201708/no-smartphones-are-not-destroying-generation.

Cerf, Vinton. 2002. "The Internet Is for Everyone." *Internet Engineering Task Force*, April. Accessed January 2, 2022. http://www.ietf.org/rfc/rfc3271.txt.

———. 2012. "Freshwater Will Be the New Oil." *European*. September 27, 2012. http://www.theeuropean-magazine.com/vint-cerf/6083-the-future-of-the-internet.

Challies, Tim. 2011. "Bell, Hell and What We Did Well." *Challies* (blog), June 30, 2011. http://www.challies.com/articles/bell-hell-and-what-we-did-well.

———. 2015 [2011]. *The Next Story: Faith, Friends, Family, and the Digital World*. Grand Rapids, MI: Zondervan.

Chancey, Jennie, and Stacy McDonald. 2007. *Passionate Housewives Desperate for God*. San Antonio, TX: Vision Forum.

Chaves, Mark. 2011. *American Religion: Contemporary Trends*. Princeton, NJ: Princeton University Press.

Chayka, Kyle. 2016. "The Last Lifestyle Magazine: How *Kinfolk* Created the Dominant Aesthetic of the Decade with Perfect Lattes and Avocado Toast." *Racked*, March 14, 2016. http://www.racked.com/2016/3/14/11173148/kinfolk-lifestyle-magazines.

Cheong, Pauline Hope. 2012. "Twitter of Faith: Understanding Social Media Networking and Microblogging Rituals as Religious Practices." In *Digital Religion*,

Social Media and Culture: Perspectives, Practices and Futures, edited by Pauline Hope Cheong, Peter Fischer-Nielsen, Stefan Gelfgren, and Charles Ess, 191–206. New York: Peter Lang.

———. 2013. "Authority." In *Digital Religion: Understanding Religious Practice in New Media Worlds*, edited by Heidi A. Campbell, 72–87. New York: Routledge.

———. 2014. "Tweet the Message? Religious Authority and Social Media Innovation," *Journal of Religion, Media, and Digital Culture* 3 (3): 1–19.

———. 2016. "Religious Authority and Social Media Branding in a Culture of Religious Celebrification." In *The Media and Religious Authority*, edited Stewart M. Hoover, 81–102. University Park: Pennsylvania State University Press.

Cheong, Pauline Hope, and Charles Ess. 2012. "Introduction: Religion 2.0? Relational and Hybridizing Pathways in Religion, Social Media, and Culture." In *Digital Religion, Social Media and Culture: Perspectives, Practices and Futures*, edited by Pauline Hope Cheong, Peter Fischer-Nielsen, Stefan Gelfgren, and Charles Ess, 1–21. New York: Peter Lang.

Cherney, James L. 2019. *Ableist Rhetoric: How We Know, Value, and See Disability*. University Park: Pennsylvania State University Press.

Chidester, David. 2005. *Authentic Fakes: Religion and American Popular Culture*. Berkeley: University of California Press.

Chin, Mallory. 2016. "Artist Paweł Kuczyński Shows Us His Satirical Take on 'Pokémon GO.'" *Hypebeast*, July 29, 2016. https://hypebeast.com/2016/7/pawel-kuczynski-pokemon-go.

Chomsky, Noam. 2017. *Global Discontents: Conversations on the Rising Threats to Democracy—Interviews with David Barsamian*. New York: Metropolitan.

Chouliaraki, Lilie, and Norman Fairclough. 2005. *Discourse in Late Modernity: Rethinking Critical Discourse Analysis*. Edinburgh, Scotland: Edinburgh University Press.

Chumley, Norris J. 2011. *Mysteries of the Jesus Prayer: Experiencing the Presence of God and a Pilgrimage to the Heart of an Ancient Spirituality*. New York: HarperOne.

Chun, Wendy Hui Kyong. 2016. *Updating to Remain the Same: Habitual New Media*. Cambridge, MA: MIT Press.

Claridge, Claudia and Wilson, Andrew. 2002. "The Stylistic Evolution of the English Sermon, ca. 1640–2000." In *Sounds, Words, Texts, Change*, edited by Teresa Fanego, Belén Méndez-Naya, and Elena Seoane, 25–44. Selected papers from the 11th International Conference on English Historical Linguistics (11 ICEHL): Current Issues in Linguistic Theory. Amsterdam, The Netherlands: John Benjamins.

Clark, Lynn Schofield. 2013. *The Parent App: Understanding Families in the Digital Age*. New York: Oxford University Press.

Cmiel, Kenneth, and John Durham Peters. 2020. *Promiscuous Knowledge: Information, Image, and Other Truth Games in History*. Chicago: University of Chicago Press.

Cobb, Russell. 2014. *The Paradox of Authenticity in a Globalized World*. New York: Palgrave Macmillan.

Cochran, Pamela. 2005. *Evangelical Feminism: A History*. New York: New York University Press.
Coffman, Elesha. 2017. "'You Cannot Fool the Electronic Eye:' Billy Graham and Media." In *Billy Graham: American Pilgrim*, edited by Andrew Finstuen, Grant Wacker, and Anne Blue Wills, 197–215. New York: Oxford University Press.
Coleman, Simon. 2006. "When Silence Isn't Golden: Charismatic Speech and the Limits of Literalism." In *The Limits of Meaning: Case Studies in the Anthropology of Christianity*, edited by Matthew Engelke and Matt Tomlinson, 39–61. New York: Berghahn.
Coleman, Simon, and Rosalind I. J. Hackett, eds. 2015. *The Anthropology of Global Pentecostalism and Evangelicalism*. New York: New York University Press.
Connable, Sean. 2016. "The 'Christian Nation' Thesis and the Evangelical Echo Chamber." In *The Electronic Church in the Digital Age: Cultural Impacts of Evangelical Mass Media*, edited by Mark Ward, Sr., 183–203. Santa Barbara, CA: Praeger.
Cooper, Travis Warren. 2010. "A Tale of Two Churches: Walmartization, Cultural Accommodation, and Modernization in Two Ozarks Area Megachurches." Unpublished paper, presented at Missouri State University's Graduate Interdisciplinary Forum, Springfield, MO.
———. 2011. "Ecstasy and the Kinesthetic Body: An Ethnographic Study of Contemporary Pentecostal Worship." MA thesis, Missouri State University.
———. 2013. "'Cooking with Gordon:' Food, Health, and the Elasticity of Gender Roles (and Belt Sizes) on the 700 Club." *Religion & Gender* 3 (1): 108–124.
———. 2014. "Benny Hinn's Media Empire: Image and Presence in Global Televangelism." *Symposia* 6: 1–14.
———. 2016. "Media Ideologies, Contested Authenticities, and Socality Barbie." *Bulletin for the Study of Religion*, January 8, 2016. http://bulletin.equinoxpub.com/2016/01/media-ideologies-contested-authenticities-and-socality-barbie/.
———. 2017a. "Taxonomy Construction and the Normative Turn in Religious Studies." *Religions* 8: 1–15.
———. 2017b. "Worship Rituals, Discipline, and Pentecostal-Charismatic 'Techniques du Corps' in the American Midwest." In *Annual Review of the Sociology of Religion: Volume 8: Pentecostals and the Body*, edited by Michael Wilkinson and Peter Althouse, 77–101. Boston: Brill.
———. 2017c. "Emerging, Emergent, Emergence: Boundary Maintenance, Definition Construction, and Legitimation Strategies in the Establishment of a Post-Evangelical Subculture." *Journal for the Scientific Study of Religion* 56 (2): 398–417.
———. 2017d. "New Media (and) Ritual." *Studying Religion in Culture: Ongoing Discussions at the University of Alabama* (blog), January 26, 2017. https://religion.ua.edu/blog/2017/01/26/new-media-and-ritual/.
———. 2018. "Boutique Industrial Capitalism from *Goop* to *Kinfolk* Magazine: A Reply to Dana Logan." *Bulletin for the Study of Religion* 47 (3–4): 7–13.

———. 2019a. Theses on New Media. *anthro{dendum}* (blog), March 28, 2019. https://anthrodendum.org/2019/03/28/theses-on-method-new-media-social-technologies-and-the-anthropology-of-digital-worlds/.

———. 2019b. "Objectivity Discourse, the Protestant Secular, and the Decolonization of Religious Studies." *Method and Theory in the Study of Religion.* Advanced Articles, March 20, 2019. https://doi.org/10.1163/15700682-12341463.

Cottle, Simon. 2006. *Mediatized Conflict: Developments in Media and Conflict Studies.* New York: Open University Press.

Couldry, Nick, and Andreas Hepp. 2017. *The Mediated Construction of Reality.* Malden, MA: Polity.

Craig. 2015. "Interview // Scott Bakken." *Lens Distortions,* July 27, 2015 https://lensdistortions.com/interview-scott-bakken/.

Crawford, Terrace. 2012. *#GoingSocial: A Practical Guide on Social Media for Church Leaders.* Kansas City, MO: Beacon Hill.

Crouch, Ian. 2014. "The Great American Twitter Novel." *New Yorker,* July 23, 2014. https://www.newyorker.com/books/page-turner/great-american-twitter-novel.

Crystal, David. 2008. *Txtng: The Gr8 Db8.* New York: Oxford University Press.

Cunningham, Ward. 2003. "Correspondence on the Etymology of Wiki." *C2.* Accessed January 2, 2022. http://c2.com/doc/etymology.html.

Curtis, Finbarr. 2012. "The Study of American Religions: Critical Reflections on a Specialization." *Religion* 42 (3): 355–372.

Cyzewski, Ed. 2018. *Why Evangelicals Need the Wilderness.* Amazon Digital Services. Ebook.

Daer, Alice R., Rebecca Hoffman, and Seth Goodman. 2014. "Rhetorical Functions of Hashtag Forms across Social Media Applications." *Proceedings of the 32nd ACM International Conference on the Design of Communication* 16: 1–3.

Davidson, Bruce W. 2017. "The Perils of Religious Romanticism." *American Thinker.* February 12, 2017. https://www.americanthinker.com/articles/2017/02/the_perils_of_religious_romanticism.html.

Dawson, Lorne L., and Douglas E. Cowan, eds. 2004. *Religion Online: Finding Faith on the Internet.* New York: Routledge.

De Seta, Gabriele. 2018. "Three Lies of Digital Ethnography." *anthro{dendum}* (blog), February 7, 2018. https://anthrodendum.org/2018/02/07/three-lies-of-digital-ethnography/.

De Souza e Silva, Adriana. 2006. "Interfaces of Hybrid Spaces." In *The Cell Phone Reader: Essays in Social Transformation,* edited by Anandam Kavoori and Noah Arceneaux, 19–43. New York: Peter Lang.

Deal, William E., and Timothy K. Beal. 2004. *Theory for Religious Studies.* New York: Routledge.

Dean, Jodi. 2010. *Blog Theory: Feedback and Capture in the Circuits of Drive.* Malden, MA: Polity.

DelBene, Ron, Mary Montgomery, and Herb Montgomery. 1992. *The Breath of Life: A Simple Way to Pray.* Eugene, OR: Wipf and Stock.

Delight in Truth. 2013. "Farewell, Rob Bell." *Delight in Truth* (blog), March 23, 2013. http://delightintruth.com/2013/03/23/farewell-rob-bell/.
Deloitte. 2017. "2017 Global Mobile Consumer Survey: US Edition." *Deloitte Development LLC* 1–15.
Derrida, Jacques. 1976. *Of Grammatology*. Translated by Gayatri Chakravorty Spivak. Baltimore, MD: Johns Hopkins University Press.
DeRogatis, Amy. 2014. *Saving Sex: Sexuality and Salvation in American Evangelicalism*. New York: Oxford University Press.
Design You Trust. 2015. "Kamil Kotarba Explores the Lack of Human Interaction in the Digital Age." *Design You Trust*, September. Accessed January 2, 2022. https://designyoutrust.com/2015/09/kamil-kotarba-explores-the-lack-of-human-interaction-in-the-digital-age/.
Detweiler, Craig. 2013. *iGods: How Technology Shapes Our Spiritual and Social Lives*. Grand Rapids, MI: Brazos.
———. 2018. *Selfies: Searching for the Image of God in a Digital Age*. Grand Rapids, MI: Brazos.
Dick, Michael. 2011. "Twenty Years of Unnecessary Forward Slashes: Critiquing Narratives of the Development of the Web." In *The Long History of New Media: Technology, Historiography, and Contextualizing Newness*, edited by David W. Park, Nicholas W. Jankowski, and Steve Jones, 145–159. New York: Peter Lang.
Diehl, Kristin and Gal Zauberman. 2016. "How Taking Photos Increases Enjoyment of Experiences." *Journal of Personality and Social Psychology* 111 (2): 119–140.
Dillenberger, John, ed. 1962. *Martin Luther: Selections from His Writings*. New York: Anchor.
Douglas, Mary. 1966. *Purity and Danger: An Analysis of the Concepts of Pollution and Taboo*. New York: Routledge.
Drescher, Elizabeth. 2011. *Tweet If You* ♥ *Jesus: Practicing Church in the Digital Reformation*. New York: Morehouse.
Duerringer, Christopher M. 2016. "The 'War on Christianity' and the Construction of Identity in Evangelical Media." In *The Electronic Church in the Digital Age: Cultural Impacts of Evangelical Mass Media*, edited by Mark Ward Sr., 205–225. Santa Barbara, CA: Praeger.
Du Mez, Kristin Kobes. 2020. *Jesus and John Wayne: How White Evangelicals Corrupted a Faith and Fractured a Nation*. New York: Liveright.
Dyer, John. 2011. *From the Garden to the City: The Redeeming and Corrupting Power of Technology*. Grand Rapids, MI: Kregel.
Ebersole, Samuel E. 2013. "Evangelicals and Social Media." In *Evangelical Christians and Popular Culture: Pop Goes the Gospel, Volume 1*, edited by Robert H. Woods Jr., 307–322. Santa Barbara, CA: Praeger.
Eck, Diana L. 2001. *A New Religious America: How a "Christian Country" Has Now Become the World's Most Religiously Diverse Nation*. San Francisco, CA: HarperSanFrancisco.

Edwards, Mark. 2009. *Catholicity and Heresy in the Early Church*. Burlington, VT: Ashgate.

Einstein, Mara. 2013. "GodTube." In *Evangelical Christians and Popular Culture: Pop Goes the Gospel, Volume 1*, edited by Robert H. Woods Jr., 292–306. Santa Barbara, CA: Praeger.

Elisha, Omri. 2011. *Moral Ambition: Mobilization and Social Outreach in Evangelical Megachurches*. Berkeley: University of California Press.

Emerson, Michael O., and Christian Smith. 2001. *Divided by Faith: Evangelical Religion and the Problem of Race in America*. New York: Oxford University Press.

Enli, Gunn. 2015. *Mediated Authenticity: How the Media Constructs Reality*. New York: Peter Lang.

Entwistle, Joanne. 2000. *The Fashioned Body: Fashion, Dress and Modern Social Theory*. Malden, MA: Blackwell.

Espinosa, Gastón. 2014. *Latino Pentecostals in America: Faith and Politics in Action*. Cambridge, MA: Harvard University Press.

Estes, Douglas. 2009. *SimChurch: Being the Church in the Virtual World*. Grand Rapids, MI: Zondervan.

Evans, Leighton. 2015. *Locative Social Media: Place in the Digital Age*. New York: Palgrave Macmillan.

Evans, Rachel Held. 2009. "The Book, the Blog, the Elusiveness of Joy." *Rachel Held Evans* (blog), April 6, 2009. http://rachelheldevans.com/blog/the-book-the-blog-the-elusiveness-of-joy?rq=writing.

———. 2010a. *Evolving in Monkey Town: How a Girl Who Knew All the Answers Learned to Ask Questions*. Grand Rapids, MI: Zondervan.

———. 2010b. "Ask Your Writing/Publishing Questions." *Rachel Held Evans* (blog), April 7, 2010. http://rachelheldevans.com/blog/publishing-questions?rq=ask%20your%20writing%2Fpublishing%20questions.

———. 2011a. "Guest Post Guidelines." *Rachel Held Evans* (blog), February 1, 2011. http://rachelheldevans.com/blog/guest-post-guidelines?rq=writing.

———. 2011b. "How to Write a Controversial Blog Post with No Regrets." *Rachel Held Evans* (blog), March 2, 2011. http://rachelheldevans.com/blog/controversial-blog-post-tips?rq=How%20to%20write%20a%20controversial%20blog%20post%20with%20no%20regrets.

———. 2011c. "How to Build a Better Writing Platform by Being Yourself." *Rachel Held Evans* (blog), June 1, 2011. http://rachelheldevans.com/blog/writing-platform-be-yourself?rq=writing.

———. 2011d. "On Getting Published." *Rachel Held Evans* (blog), June 4, 2011. http://rachelheldevans.com/blog/on-getting-published?rq=on%20getting%20published.

———. 2011e. "Theresa of Avila on Blogging." *Rachel Held Evans* (blog), October 10, 2011. http://rachelheldevans.com/blog/teresa-of-avila-on-blogging?rq=on%20blogging.

―――. 2011f. "What They Didn't Tell Me at the Young Author's Conference." *Rachel Held Evans* (blog), November 4, 2011. http://rachelheldevans.com/blog/young-authors-conference.

―――. 2012a. *A Year of Biblical Womanhood: How a Liberated Woman Found Herself Sitting on Her Roof, Covering Her Head, and Calling Her Husband "Master."* Nashville, TN: Thomas Nelson.

―――. 2012b. "10 Tips for Dealing with Online Criticism." *Rachel Held Evans* (blog), April 25, 2012. http://rachelheldevans.com/blog/10-tips-online-criticism?rq=negative.

―――. 2012c. "10 Cool Things We've Done in 1,000 Posts." *Rachel Held Evans* (blog), September 24, 2012. http://rachelheldevans.com/blog/1000-post?rq=on%20blogging.

―――. 2012d. "Why 'A Year of Biblical Womanhood' Is a NYT Bestseller." *Rachel Held Evans* (blog), November 16, 2012. http://rachelheldevans.com/blog/why-a-year-of-biblical-womanhood-is-a-nyt-bestseller.

―――. 2013. "Why Millennials Are Leaving the Church." *CNN Belief Blog*, July 27, 2013. http://religion.blogs.cnn.com/2013/07/27/why-millennials-are-leaving-the-church/?iref=allsearch.

―――. 2014. *Faith Unraveled: How a Girl Who Knew All the Answers Learned to Ask Questions*. Grand Rapids, MI: Zondervan.

―――. 2015. *Searching for Sunday: Loving, Leaving, and Finding the Church*. Nashville, TN: Thomas Nelson.

―――. 2018. *Inspired: Slaying Giants, Walking on Water, and Loving the Bible Again*. Nashville, TN: Thomas Nelson.

―――. n.d. "Modesty: I Don't Think It Means What You Think It Means." *Q Ideas* (blog). Accessed January 2, 2022. http://208.106.253.109/blog/modesty-i-dont-think-it-means-what-you-think-it-means.aspx.

Fairclough, Norman. 1989. *Language and Power*. New York: Longman.

Fattal, Alex. 2014. "Hostile Remixes on YouTube: A New Constraint on Pro-FARC Counterpublics in Colombia." *American Ethnologist* 41 (2): 320–335.

Fea, John. 2020. *Believe Me: The Evangelical Road to Donald Trump*. Grand Rapids, MI: William B. Eerdmans.

Ferguson, Niall. 2017a. *The Square and the Tower: Networks and Power, from the Freemasons to Facebook*. New York: Penguin.

―――. 2017b. "The False Prophecy of Hyperconnection: How to Survive the Networked Age." *Foreign Affairs*, August 15, 2017. https://www.foreignaffairs.com/articles/2017-08-15/false-prophecy-hyperconnection.

Fessenden, Tracy. 2007. *Culture and Redemption: Religion, the Secular, and American Literature*. Princeton, NJ: Princeton University Press.

Fewkes, Jacqueline H. 2019. "Piety in the Pocket: An Introduction." In *Anthropological Perspectives on the Religious Uses of Mobile Apps*, edited by Jaqueline H. Fewkes, 1–16. New York: Palgrave Macmillan.

Fischer-Nielsen, Peter. 2012. "Pastors on the Internet: Online Responses to Secularization." In *Digital Religion, Social Media and Culture: Perspectives, Practices and Futures*, edited by Pauline Hope Cheong, Peter Fischer-Nielsen, Stefan Gelfgren, and Charles Ess, 115–130. New York: Peter Lang.

Fischer-Nielsen, Peter, and Stefan Gelfgren. 2012. "Conclusion: Religion in a Digital Age: Future Developments and Research Directions." In *Digital Religion, Social Media and Culture: Perspectives, Practices and Futures*, edited by Pauline Hope Cheong, Peter Fischer-Nielsen, Stefan Gelfgren, and Charles Ess, 293–305. New York: Peter Lang.

Fisher, Jennifer. 2016. "Curators and Instagram: Affect, Relationality and Keeping in Touch." *Journal of Curatorial Studies* 5 (1): 100–123.

Fisher, Linford D. 2016. "Evangelicals and Unevangelicals: The Contested History of a Word, 1500–1950." *Religion and American Culture: A Journal of Interpretation* 26 (2): 184–226.

Florida, Richard. 2002. *The Rise of the Creative Class: And How It's Transforming Work, Leisure, Community and Everyday Life*. New York: Basic.

Fore, William F. 1987. *Television and Religion: The Shaping of Faith, Values, and Culture*. Minneapolis, MN: Augsburg.

Foucault, Michel. 1977. *Discipline & Punish: The Birth of The Prison*. New York: Pantheon.

———. 1978. *History of Sexuality: An Introduction (Volume I)*. Translated by Robert Hurley. New York: Vintage.

———. 1997. *Ethics: Subjectivity and Truth*. Translated by Robert Hurley et al. Harmondsworth, UK: Penguin.

———. 2010. *The Archaeology of Knowledge: And the Discourse on Language*. Translated by A. M. Sheridan Smith. New York: Vintage.

Frankl, Razelle. 1998. "Televangelism." In the *Encyclopedia of Religion and Society*. Edited by William H. Swatos Jr. Walnut Creek, CA: AltaMira. http://hirr.hartsem.edu/ency/Televangelism.htm.

Fraser, Nancy. 1990. "Rethinking the Public Sphere: A Contribution to the Critique of Actually Existing Democracy." *Social Text* 25/26: 56–80.

French, Kristen. 2018. "This Pastor Is Putting His Faith in a Virtual Reality Church." *Wired*, February 2, 2018. https://www.wired.com/story/virtual-reality-church/.

Fuchs, Christian. 2014. *Social Media: A Critical Introduction*. Thousand Oaks, CA: Sage.

Gardner, Christine J. 2011. *Making Chastity Sexy: The Rhetoric of Evangelical Abstinence Campaigns*. Berkeley: University of California Press.

Gasaway, Brantley W. 2014. *Progressive Evangelicals and the Pursuit of Social Justice*. Chapel Hill: University of North Carolina Press.

Geertz, Clifford. 1973. *The Interpretation of Cultures: Selected Essays*. New York: Basic.

Geiger, Antoine. 2015. "'SUR-FAKE' (Paris, 2015)." Accessed January 2, 2022. https://antoinegeiger.com/SUR-FAKE.

Gelfgren, Stefan. 2012. "'Let There Be Digital Networks and God Will Provide Growth?' Comparing Aims and Hopes of 19th-Century and Post-Millennial Christianity." In *Digital Religion, Social Media and Culture: Perspectives, Practices and Futures*, edited by Pauline Hope Cheong, Peter Fischer-Nielsen, Stefan Gelfgren, and Charles Ess, 227–242. New York: Peter Lang.

Gershon, Ilana. 2010a. *The Breakup 2.0: Disconnecting over New Media*. Ithaca, NY: Cornell University Press.

———. 2010b. "Media Ideologies: An Introduction." *Journal of Linguistic Anthropology* 20 (2): 283–293.

———. 2011. "Neoliberal Agency." *Current Anthropology* 52 (4): 537–555.

Gershon, Ilana, and Paul Manning. 2006. "Converting Meanings and the Meanings of Conversion in Samoan Moral Economies." In *The Limits of Meaning: Case Studies in the Anthropology of Christianity*, edited by Matthew Engelke and Matt Tomlinson, 147–163. New York: Berghahn.

Giannoulakis, Stamatios, and Nicolas Tsapatsoulis. 2016. "Evaluating the Descriptive Power of Instagram Hashtags." *Journal of Innovation in Digital Ecosystems* 3: 114–129.

Gillespie, Kelli. 2015. "Intentionally Inclusive: Meet Socality Founder Scott Bakken." *Risen Magazine*. Accessed January 2, 2022. http://www.risenmagazine.com/scott-bakken/.

Gin Lum, Kathryn, and Paul Harvey. 2018. *The Oxford Handbook of Religion and Race in American History*. London: Oxford University Press.

Glascock, Taylor. 2015. "Hipster Barbie Is So Much Better at Instagram Than You." *Wired*, September 3, 2015. https://www.wired.com/2015/09/hipster-barbie-much-better-instagram/.

Gloege, Timothy E. W. 2015. *Guaranteed Pure: The Moody Bible Institute, Business, and the Making of Modern Evangelicalism*. Chapel Hill: University of North Carolina Press.

Goetz, Rebecca Anne. 2012. *The Baptism of Early Virginia: How Christianity Created Race*. Baltimore, MD: Johns Hopkins University Press.

Goffman, Erving. 1981. *Forms of Talk*. Philadelphia: University of Pennsylvania Press.

———. 1990. *The Presentation of Self in Everyday Life*. New York: Anchor.

Goldsmith, Kenneth. 2016. *Wasting Time on the Internet*. New York: Harper Perennial.

Google. 2018 "Vincent G. Cerf." https://research.google.com/pubs/author32412.html.

Gould, Meredith. 2011. "Christ Has No Online Presence but Yours." *Ignatian Spirituality*. Accessed January 2, 2022. http://www.ignatianspirituality.com/8704/christ-has-no-online-presence-but-yours.

Gravity. 2018. "Breath Prayer." *Gravity: A Center for Contemplative Activism*. Accessed January 2, 2022. https://gravitycenter.com/practice/breath-prayer/.

Greenfield, Adam. 2017. *Radical Technologies: The Design of Everyday Life*. London: Verso.

Gregory, Brad S. 2012. *The Unintended Reformation: How a Religious Revolution Secularized Society.* Cambridge, MA: Belknap of Harvard University Press.
Greif, Mark. 2016. *Against Everything: Essays.* New York: Pantheon.
Grieve, Gregory Price, and Daniel Veidlinger, eds. 2015. *Buddhism, the Internet, and Digital Media: The Pixel in the Lotus.* New York: Routledge.
Griffith, R. Marie. 1997. *God's Daughters: Evangelical Women and the Power of Submission.* Berkeley: University of California Press.
———. 2004. *Born Again Bodies: Flesh and Spirit in American Christianity.* Berkeley: University of California Press.
———. 2017. *Moral Combat: How Sex Divided American Christians and Fractured American Politics.* New York: Basic.
Gumperz, John J. 1982. *Discourse Strategies.* New York: Cambridge University Press.
Gupta, Akhil, and James Ferguson. 1997. "Discipline and Practice: 'The Field' as Site, Method, and Location in Anthropology." In *Anthropological Locations: Boundaries and Grounds of a Field Science*, edited by Akhil Gupta and James Ferguson, 1–46. Berkeley: University of California Press.
Hall, David D., ed. 1997. *Lived Religion: Toward a History of Practice.* Princeton, NJ: Princeton University Press.
Haller, Beth A. 2010. *Representing Disability in an Ableist World: Essays on Mass Media.* Louisville, KY: Advocado.
Han, Byung-Chul. 2017. *In the Swarm: Digital Prospects.* Cambridge, MA: MIT Press.
Handman, Courtney. 2015. *Critical Christianity: Translation and Denominational Conflict in Papua New Guinea.* Berkeley: University of California Press.
Hanks, William F. 1996. "Exorcism and the Description of Participant Roles." In *Natural Histories of Discourse*, edited by Michael Silverstein and Greg Urban, 160–200. Chicago: University of Chicago Press.
Harari, Yuval Noah. 2017. *Homo Deus: A Brief History of Tomorrow.* New York: Harper.
Harding, Susan. 2000. *The Book of Jerry Falwell: Fundamentalist Language and Politics.* Princeton, NJ: Princeton University Press.
Harfoush, Rahaf. 2009. *Yes We Did! An Inside Look at How Social Media Built the Obama Brand.* Berkeley, CA: New Riders.
Harris, Joshua. 1997. *I Kissed Dating Goodbye.* New York: Multnomah.
Harrison, Michael. n.d. "Logocentrism." *Chicago School of Media Theory.* Accessed January 12, 2018. https://lucian.uchicago.edu/blogs/mediatheory/keywords/logocentrism/.
Hart, D. G. 2004. *Deconstructing Evangelicalism: Conservative Protestantism in the Age of Billy Graham.* Grand Rapids, MI: Baker Academic.
———. 2011. "Hello, Rob Bell." *Old Life* (blog), March 24, 2011. http://oldlife.org/2011/03/hello-rob-bell/.
Hartigan, John, Jr. 2015. *Race in the 21st Century: Ethnographic Approaches.* New York: Oxford University Press.

Harvey, David. 2005. *A Brief History of Neoliberalism*. New York: Oxford University Press.
Harvey, Paul. 2016. *Christianity and Race in the American South: A History*. Chicago: University of Chicago Press.
Hatch, Nathan O. 1989. *The Democratization of American Christianity*. New Haven, CT: Yale University Press.
Haveman, Heather A. 2015. *Magazines and the Making of America: Modernization, Community, and Print Culture, 1741–1860*. Princeton, NJ: Princeton University Press.
Hawkins, J. Russell, and Phillip Luke Sinitiere. 2013. *Christians and the Color Line: Race and Religion after Divided by Faith*. New York: Oxford University Press.
Haywood, Jacob. 2020. "3 Ways Cancel Culture Can Strengthen the Church." *LifeWay—Facts & Trends*, October 7, 2020. https://factsandtrends.net/2020/10/07/3-ways-cancel-culture-can-strengthen-the-church/.
Hearn, Greg, Ruth Bridgstock, Ben Goldsmith, and Jess Rodgers. 2014. *Creative Work beyond the Creative Industries: Innovation, Employment and Education*. Cheltenham, UK: Edward Elgar.
Heather, Noel. 2000. *Religious Language and Critical Discourse Analysis*. New York: Peter Lang.
Hedstrom, Matthew S. 2013. *The Rise of Liberal Religion: Book Culture and American Spirituality in the Twentieth Century*. New York: Oxford University Press.
Heidegger, Martin. 1977. *The Question Concerning Technology and Other Questions*. Translated by William Lovitt. New York: Garland.
Helland, Christopher. 2000. "Religion Online/Online Religion and Virtual Communitas." In *Religion on the Internet: Research Prospects and Promises (Religion and Social Order 8)*, edited by Jeffery K. Hadden and Douglas E. Cowan, 205–224. London: JAI.
———. 2005. "Online Religion as Lived Religion: Methodological Issues in the Study of Religious Participation on the Internet." *Online—Heidelberg Journal of Religions on the Internet 1.1*. Accessed January 2, 2022. https://core.ac.uk/download/pdf/32579519.pdf.
———. 2015. "Virtual Religion: A Case Study of Virtual Tibet." *Oxford Handbooks Online*. Accessed January 2, 2022. https://www.oxfordhandbooks.com/view/10.1093/oxfordhb/9780199935420.001.0001/oxfordhb-9780199935420-e-43.
Hendershot, Heather. 2004. *Shaking the World for Jesus: Media and Conservative Evangelical Culture*. Chicago: University of Chicago Press.
Henderson, Harry. 2002. *Pioneers of the Internet*. Detroit, MI: Lucent.
Henry, Andre. 2018. "Audrey Assad Opens Up about Her Lost-And-Found Faith on Her New Album." *Relevant*, January 11, 2018. https://relevantmagazine.com/culture/music/audrey-assad-opens-lost-found-faith-new-album/.
Hewitt, Rachel. 2019. "A Way Out of Cancel Culture in the Church." *Relevant*, July 15, 2019. https://www.relevantmagazine.com/culture/a-way-out-of-cancel-culture-in-the-church/.

Hillerbrand, Hans Joachim. 1968. *The Protestant Reformation*. New York: Macmillan.
Hindmarsh, D. Bruce. 2018. *The Spirit of Early Evangelicalism: True Religion in a Modern World*. New York: Oxford University Press.
Hinn, Benny. 1999. *He Touched Me: An Autobiography*. Nashville, TN: Thomas Nelson.
———. 2012. "Spiritual Warfare, Part 1." *bennyhinn*, July 3, 2012. http://www.bennyhinn.org/media/2012-7-3.asx.
Hinojosa, Felipe. 2014. *Latino Mennonites: Civil Rights, Faith, and Evangelical Culture*. Baltimore, MD: Johns Hopkins University Press.
Hipps, Shane. 2005. *The Hidden Power of Electronic Culture: How Media Shapes Faith, the Gospel, and Church*. Grand Rapids, MI: Zondervan.
———. 2009. *Flickering Pixels: How Technology Shapes Your Faith*. Grand Rapids, MI: Zondervan.
Hochman, Nadav, and Raz Schwartz. 2012. "Visualizing Instagram: Tracing Cultural Visual Rhythms." *AAAI Technical Report* 12 (3): 6–9.
Hogan, Bernie, and Barry Wellman. 2012. "The Immanent Internet Redux." In *Digital Religion, Social Media and Culture: Perspectives, Practices and Futures*, edited by Pauline Hope Cheong, Peter Fischer-Nielsen, Stefan Gelfgren, and Charles Ess, 43–62. New York: Peter Lang.
Højsgaard, Morten, and Margit Warburg, eds. 2005. *Religion and Cyberspace*. London: Routledge.
Holmes, David. 2005. *Communication Theory: Media, Technology and Society*. London, New Delhi, and Thousand Oaks, CA: Sage.
Honoré, Carl. 2004. *In Praise of Slowness: Challenging the Cult of Speed*. New York: HarperCollins.
Hooton, Christopher. 2014. "New Banksy Art Sees Love and Smartphones at Odds, but Where in the UK Is It?" *Independent*, April 14, 2014. https://www.independent.co.uk/arts-entertainment/art/news/new-banksy-art-sees-love-and-smartphones-at-odds-but-where-in-the-uk-is-it-9259358.html.
Hoover, Stewart. 2012. "Foreword: Practice, Autonomy, and Authority in the Digitally Religious and Digitally Spiritual." In *Digital Religion, Social Media and Culture: Perspectives, Practices and Futures*, edited by Pauline Hope Cheong, Peter Fischer-Nielsen, Stefan Gelfgren, and Charles Ess, vii–xii. New York: Peter Lang.
———, ed. 2016. *The Media and Religious Authority*. University Park: Pennsylvania University Press.
Horsfield, Peter. 2015. *From Jesus to the Internet: A History of Christianity and Media*. New York: Wiley-Blackwell.
Horst, Heather A., and Daniel Miller. 2006. *The Cell Phone: An Anthropology of Communication*. Oxford and New York: Berg.
———, eds. 2013. *Digital Anthropology*. New York: Bloomsbury Academic.
Howard, Robert Glenn. 2011. *Digital Jesus: The Making of a New Christian Fundamentalist Community on the Internet*. New York: New York University Press.

Hu, Yuheng, Lydia Manikonda, and Subbarao Kambhampati. 2014. "What We Instagram: A First Analysis of Instagram Photo Content and User Types." *Proceedings of the 8th International Conference on Weblogs and Social Media, ICWSM*: 595–598.

Huang, Y-H., and Y-F. Lot. 2012. "What Makes Blogging Attractive to Bloggers: A Case of College-Level Constituency Users." *Journal of Computer Assisted Learning* 28: 208–221.

Hunt, Zach (@ZaackHunt). 2017. "Lord, for the gift of @youtube car repair tutorials, we give thanks." Twitter, January 13, 2017. https://twitter.com/ZaackHunt /status/819965104800354305.

Hunter, James Davidson. 1987. *Evangelicalism: The Coming Generation*. Chicago: University of Chicago Press.

Hurd, Seth Tower. 2017. "The Theology Debate That's Dividing Christian Hip-Hop." *Relevant*, August 4, 2017. https://relevantmagazine.com/article /the-theology-debate-thats-dividing-christian-hip-hop/.

Hutchby, Ian. 2001. "Technologies, Texts, and Affordances." *Sociology* 35 (2): 441–456.

Hutcheon, S. J. 2007. "Q&A with Google's Chief Internet Evangelist." *Sydney Morning Herald*, March 8, 2007. http://blogs.smh.com.au/mashup /archives/010255.html.

Hutchings, Tim. 2013. "Considering Religious Community through Online Churches." In *Digital Religion: Understanding Religious Practice in New Media Worlds*, edited by Heidi A. Campbell, 164–172. New York: Routledge.

———. 2015. "Now the Bible Is an App: Digital Media and Changing Patterns of Religious Authority." In *Religion, Media, and Social Change*, edited by Kenneth Granholm, Marcus Moberg, and Sofia Sjö, 143–161. New York: Routledge.

———. 2017. *Creating Church Online: Ritual, Community and New Media*. New York: Routledge.

Ingersoll, Julie. 2003. *Evangelical Christian Women: War Stories in the Gender Battles*. New York: New York University Press.

Internet World Stats. 2010. "United States." Usage and Population Statistics. Accessed July 4, 2021. https://www.internetworldstats.com/ unitedstates.htm.

Isaacson, Walter. 2011. *Steve Jobs*. New York: Simon and Schuster.

Jackson, Michael. 2013. *Lifeworlds: Essays in Existential Anthropology*. Chicago: University of Chicago Press.

Jaffe, Alexandra, ed. 2009. *Stance: Sociolinguistic Perspectives*. New York: Oxford University Press.

Jamerson, Trevor. 2017. "Digital Orientalism: TripAdvisor and Online Travelers' Tales." In *Digital Sociologies*, edited by Jessie Daniels, Karen Gregory, and Tressie McMillan Cottom, 119–135. Bristol, UK: Polity.

Jansson, André. 2018. *Mediatization and Mobile Lives: A Critical Approach*. New York: Routledge.

Jenkins, Henry, Sam Ford, and Joshua Green, eds. 2013. *Spreadable Media: Creating Value and Meaning in a Networked Culture*. New York: New York University Press.
Jobson, Christopher. 2010. "Ghost Life." *Colossal*, December 20, 2010. http://www.thisiscolossal.com/2010/12/ghost-life/.
Johns, Mark D. 2013. "Ethical Issues in the Study of Religion and New Media." In *Digital Religion: Understanding Religious Practice in New Media Worlds*, edited by Heidi A. Campbell, 238–250. New York: Routledge.
Johnson, Emily Suzanne. 2019. *This Is Our Message: Women's Leadership in the New Christian Right*. New York: Oxford University Press.
Johnson, Sylvester A. 2015. *African American Religions, 1500–2000: Colonialism, Democracy, and Freedom*. Cambridge, UK: Cambridge University Press.
Jones, Robert P. 2016. *The End of White Christian America*. New York: Simon and Schuster.
Joshi, Khyati J. 2020. *White Christian Privilege: The Illusion of Religious Equality in America*. New York: New York University Press.
The Junia Project. 2014. "About the Junia Project." http://juniaproject.com/about-2/.
Kahn, Jonathon S., and Vincent W. Lloyd, eds. 2016. *Race and Secularism in America*. New York: Columbia University Press.
Karabel, Jerome. 2002. "Revolutionary Contradictions: Antonio Gramsci and the Problem
of Intellectuals." In *Antonio Gramsci: Critical Assessments of Leading Political Philosophers, Volume II: Intellectuals, Culture and the Party*, edited by James Martin, 7–52. London: Routledge.
Kavoori, Anandam, and Noah Arceneaux, eds. 2006. *The Cell Phone Reader: Essays in Social Transformation*. New York: Peter Lang.
Keane, Webb. 2002. "Sincerity, 'Modernity,' and the Protestants." *Cultural Anthropology* 17 (1): 65–92.
———. 2006a. "Epilogue: Anxious Transcendence." In *The Anthropology of Christianity*, edited by Fenella Cannell, 308–324. Durham, NC: Duke University Press.
———. 2007. *Christian Moderns: Freedom and Fetish in the Mission Encounter*. Oakland: University of California Press.
Kenix, Linda Jean. 2009. "Blogs as Alternative." *Journal of Computer-Mediated Communication* 14: 790–822.
Kennedy, Matt. 2011. "The McLaren Moment: What John Piper Meant by 'Farewell Rob Bell.'" *Stand Firm in Faith* (blog). http://standfirminfaith.com/?/sf/page/27308.
Kidd, Thomas. 2020. *Who Is an Evangelical?: The History of a Movement in Crisis*. New Haven, CT: Yale University Press.
Kim-Kort, Mihee. 2012. *Making Paper Cranes: Toward an Asian American Feminist Theology*. St Louis, MO: Chalice.
———. 2014a. *Yoked: Stories of a Clergy Couple in Marriage, Ministry, and Family (with Andy Kort)*. Lanham, MD: Rowman & Littlefield.

———, ed. 2014b. *Streams Run Uphill: Conversations with Clergywomen of Color.* Valley Forge, PA: Judson.

———. 2014c. "#FaithFeminisms: Flash Mob." *Mihee Kim-Kort* (blog), July 21, 2014. http://miheekimkort.com/2014/07/21/faithfeminisms-flash-mob/.

———. 2014d. "#BlackLivesMatter and Standing in Solidarity." *Mihee Kim-Kort* (blog), December 15, 2014. http://miheekimkort.com/2014/12/15/blacklivesmatter-and-standing-in-solidarity/.

———. 2015a. "Deeper Story: Girls, Modesty-Shaming, and Jesus Feminism." *Mihee Kim-Kort* (blog), February 17, 2015. http://miheekimkort.com/2015/02/17/deeper-story-girls-modesty-shaming-and-jesus-feminism/.

———. 2015b. "Not an Ally: Getting to Work." *Mihee Kim-Kort* (blog), June 19, 2015. http://miheekimkort.com/2015/06/19/dont-call-me-an-ally-getting-to-work/.

———. 2015c. "When Spiking Your Best Friend's Drink Is Okay." *Mihee Kim-Kort* (blog), November 11, 2015. http://miheekimkort.com/2015/11/11/when-spiking-your-best-friends-drink-is-okay/.

———. 2018. *Outside the Lines: How Embracing Queerness Will Transform Your Faith.* Minneapolis, MN: Fortress.

Kim-Kort, Mihee, Emily Rice, and Suey Park. 2014. "Killjoy Prophets, Asian America, Evangelicalism (Part 2)." *Mihee Kim-Kort* (blog), October 28, 2014. http://miheekimkort.com/2014/10/28/killjoy-prophets-asian-america-evangelicalism-part-2/.

Konnikova, Maria. 2013. "How Facebook Makes Us Unhappy." *New Yorker*, September 10, 2013. https://www.newyorker.com/tech/elements/how-facebook-makes-us-unhappy.

Krishna, Golden. 2015. *The Best Interface Is No Interface: The Simple Path to Brilliant Technology.* San Francisco, CA: New Riders.

Kuczyński, Paweł. 2016. "Dinner." Facebook, June 2, 2016. https://www.facebook.com/pawelkuczynskiart/photos/pb.228849284410325.-2207520000.1471125268./1291599707535272/?type=3&theater.

Kunreuther, Laura. 2014. *Voicing Subjects: Public Intimacy and Mediation in Kathmandu.* Berkeley: University of California Press.

Kuster, Thomas. 2018. "VR6: A Virtual Baptism?" *Christ in Media Institute*, June 3, 2018. http://christinmedia.org/vr6-a-virtual-baptism/.

Lakoff, George. 1993. "The Contemporary Theory of Metaphor." In *Metaphor and Thought*, edited by Andrew Ortony, 202–251. Cambridge, UK: Cambridge University Press.

Lakoff, George, and Mark Johnson. 1980. *Metaphors We Live By.* Chicago: University of Chicago Press.

———. 2016. "Understanding Trump's Use of Language." *georgelakoff* (blog), August 19, 2016. https://georgelakoff.com/2016/08/19/understanding-trumps-use-of-language/.

Langlois, Ganaele. 2014. *Meaning the Age of Social Media.* New York: Palgrave Macmillan.

Latour, Bruno. 1993. *We Have Never Been Modern.* Translated by Catherine Porter. Cambridge, MA: Harvard University Press.
Laver, James. 1969. *Modesty in Dress: An Inquiry into the Fundamentals of Fashion.* London: William Heinemann.
Leaver, Tama, Tim Highfield, and Crystal Abidin. 2020. *Instagram: Visual Social Media Cultures.* Medford, MA: Polity.
Leiner, Barry M., Vinton G. Cerf, David D. Clark, Robert E. Kahn, Leonard Kleinrock, Daniel C. Lynch, Jon Postel, Larry G. Roberts, and Stephen Wolff. 1997. "Brief History of the Internet." *Internet Society.* Accessed January 2, 2022. https://www.internetsociety.org/internet/history-internet/brief-history-internet/.
Lenhart, Amanda, and Susannah Fox. 2006. "Bloggers: A Portrait of the Internet's New Storytellers." *Pew Internet and American Life Project,* July 19, 2006. http://www.pewinternet.org/files/old-media/Files/Reports/2006/PIP%20Bloggers%20Report%20July%2019%202006.pdf.pdf.
Leonardi, Paul, Marianne E. Leonardi, and Elizabeth Hudson. 2006. "Culture, Organization, and Contradiction in the Social Construction of Technology: Adoption and Use of the Cell Phone across Three Cultures." In *The Cell Phone Reader: Essays in Social Transformation,* edited by Anandam Kavoori and Noah Arceneaux, 205–225. New York: Peter Lang.
Levin, Sam. 2017. "Mark Zuckerberg: I Regret Ridiculing Fears over Facebook's Effect on Election." *Guardian,* September 27, 2017. https://www.theguardian.com/technology/2017/sep/27/mark-zuckerberg-facebook-2016-election-fake-news.
Levinson, Paul. 2004. *Cellphone: The Story of the World's Most Mobile Medium and How It Has Transformed Everything!* New York: Macmillan.
Leys, Ruth. 2011. "The Turn to Affect: A Critique." *Critical Inquiry* 37 (3): 434–472.
Lindsey, Andrew. 2011. "'Farewell Rob Bell:' A 'Dastardly' or Apostle-like Response? *Call to Die* (blog), March 28, 2011. http://alindsey4.blogspot.com/2011/03/farewell-rob-bell-dastardly-or-apostle.html.
Lindsey, Rachel McBride. 2017. *A Communion of Shadows: Religion and Photography in Nineteenth-Century America.* Chapel Hill: University of North Carolina Press.
Lloyd, Vincent W. 2016. "Introduction: Managing Race, Managing Religion." In *Race and Secularism in America,* edited by Jonathon S. Kahn and Vincent W. Lloyd, 1–19. New York: Columbia University Press.
Loechner, Erin. 2016. *Chasing Slow: Courage to Journey Off the Beaten Path.* Grand Rapids, MI: Zondervan.
Lofton, Kathryn. 2011. *Oprah: The Gospel of an Icon.* Berkeley: University of California Press.
———. 2017. *Consuming Religion.* Chicago: University of Chicago Press.
Logan, Dana. 2017. "The Lean Closet: Asceticism in Postindustrial Consumer Culture." *Journal of the American Academy of Religion* 85 (3): 600–628.
Logan, Robert K. 2010. *Understanding New Media: Extending Marshall McLuhan.* New York: Peter Lang.

Longinow, Michael A. 2008. "Publishing Books for the Tribe and Beyond." In *Understanding Evangelical Media: The Changing Face of Christian Communication*, edited by Quentin J. Schulze and Robert H. Woods Jr., 85–97. Downers Grove, IL: IVP.
Lövheim, Mia. 2013. "Identity." In *Digital Religion: Understanding Religious Practice in New Media Worlds*, edited by Heidi A. Campbell, 41–56. New York: Routledge.
Luhrmann, T. M. 2012. *When God Talks Back: Understanding the American Evangelical Relationship with God*. New York: Vintage.
Lum, Casey Man Kong. 2014a. "Media Ecology: Concepts, Contexts, and Currents." In *The Handbook of Media and Mass Communication Theory*, edited by Robert S. Fortner, P. Mark Fackler, 137–153. Hoboken, NJ: Wiley-Blackwell.
———. 2014b. "Media Ecology." *Key Concepts in Intercultural Dialogue* 35. https://centerforinterculturaldialogue.files.wordpress.com/2014/10/key-concept-media-ecology.pdf.
Lundby, Knut, ed. 2009. *Mediatization: Concept, Changes, Consequences*. New York: Peter Lang.
———. 2013. "Theoretical Frameworks for Approaching Religion and New Media." In *Digital Religion: Understanding Religious Practice in New Media Worlds*, edited by Heidi A. Campbell, 225–237. New York: Routledge.
———, ed. 2014. *Mediatization of Communication*. Berlin: De Gruyter Mouton.
Lynerd, Benjamin T. 2014. *Republican Theology: The Civil Religion of American Evangelicals*. New York: Oxford University Press.
Mahmood, Saba. 2005. *The Politics of Piety: The Islamic Revival and the Feminist Subject*. Princeton, NJ: Princeton University Press.
Maier, Harry. 2010. "Green Millennialism: American Evangelicals, Environmentalism, and the Book of Revelation." In *Ecological Hermeneutics: Biblical, Historical, and Theological Perspectives*, edited by David G. Horrell, Cherryl Hunt, Christopher Southgate, and Francesca Stavrakopoulou, 246–265. New York: T&T Clark International.
Manovich, Lev. 2001. *The Language of New Media*. Cambridge, MA: MIT Press.
———. 2016. "Notes on Instagrammism and Mechanisms of Contemporary Cultural Identity." In *Instagram and Contemporary Image*, 1–25. Self-published ebook.
Marichal, José. 2012. *Facebook Democracy: The Architecture of Disclosure and the Threat to Public Life*. New York: Routledge.
Martí, Gerardo, and Gladys Ganiel. 2014. *The Deconstructed Church: Understanding Emerging Christianity*. New York: Oxford University Press.
Martin, Craig. 2012. *A Critical Introduction to the Study of Religion*. Bristol, CT: Equinox.
Martin, James (@JamesMartinSJ). 2020. "Dear friends: Here is the Benediction I prayed last night at the @DemConvention: a prayer for a nation where every life is sacred, all people are loved and all are welcome." Twitter, August 21, 2020. https://twitter.com/JamesMartinSJ/status/1296798445328576513.

Marty, Martin E. 1973. "The Protestant Press: Limitations and Possibilities." In *The Religious Press in America*, 5–63. New York: Holt, Rinehart and Winston.
Mathewes-Green, Frederica. 2009. *The Jesus Prayer: The Ancient Desert Prayer That Tunes the Heart to God*. Brewster, MA: Paraclete.
Mathews, Mary Beth Swetnam. 2017. *Doctrine and Race: African American Evangelicals and Fundamentalism between the Wars*. Tuscaloosa: University of Alabama Press.
Matlock, Mark (@MarkMatlock). 2018. "Out of the overflow of the heart the thumbs tweet." Twitter, August 16, 2018. https://twitter.com/markmatlock/status/1030130944685092864.
Matthewman, Steve. 2011. *Technology and Social Theory*. New York: Palgrave Macmillan.
Matthews, Bob, and Liz Ross. 2010. *Research Methods: A Practical Guide for the Social Sciences*. London: Pearson.
Mayer, Robert. 2017. *Walter Scott and Fame: Authors and Readers in the Romantic Age*. New York: Oxford University Press.
Maynard, Emily. 2012. "I'm-terview." *Emily Is Speaking Up* (blog), October 4, 2012. http://www.emilyisspeakingup.com/?page=9#sthash.2RqoTp8R.dpuf.
———. 2013a. "Girl Power." *Emily Is Speaking Up* (blog), February 4, 2013. http://www.emilyisspeakingup.com/blog/2013/2/8/girl-power.
———. 2013b. "Thoughts on Christianity and the Gender Wars." *Emily Is Speaking Up* (blog), February 8, 2013. http://www.emilyisspeakingup.com?page=8#sthash.UZdNVJFd.dpuf.
———. 2013c. "Stepping Down, Speaking Up." *Emily Is Speaking Up* (blog), February 12, 2013. http://www.emilyisspeakingup.com/blog/2013/2/12/stepping-down-speaking-up.
———. 2013d. "Things I Actually Like, 2–22." *Emily Is Speaking Up* (blog), February 22, 2013. http://www.emilyisspeakingup.com/blog/2013/2/22/things-i-actually-like-2-22.
———. 2013e. "The Fires of Feminism." *Emily Is Speaking Up* (blog), February 27, 2013. http://www.emilyisspeakingup.com/blog/2013/2/27/the-fires-of-feminisms.
———. 2013f. "Things I Actually Like, 3–8." *Emily Is Speaking Up* (blog), March 8, 2013. http://www.emilyisspeakingup.com/blog/2013/3/8/things-i-actually-like-3-8.
———. 2013g. "Grief and Resolutions." *Emily Is Speaking Up* (blog), April 8, 2013. http://www.emilyisspeakingup.com/blog/2013/4/8/grief-and-resolutions.
———. 2013h. "Sunshine and Modesty: Brief Thoughts." *Emily Is Speaking Up* (blog), May 17, 2013. http://www.emilyisspeakingup.com/blog/2013/5/17/sunshine-modesty-brief-thoughts.
———. 2013h. "The One Where I Get in Grad School, Part II." *Emily Is Speaking Up* (blog), June 5, 2013. http://www.emilyisspeakingup.com/blog/2013/6/4/the-one-where-i-get-in-grad-school-part-ii.

———. 2014. "God Has a Body." *Emily Is Speaking Up* (blog), April 21, 2014. http://www.emilyisspeakingup.com/blog/2014/4/20/god-has-a-body.

———. 2015a. "It Can Be Different." *Emily Is Speaking Up* (blog), July 21, 2015. http://www.emilyisspeakingup.com/blog/2015/2/21/it-can-be-different.

McAuley, Louis Kirk. 2013. *Print Technology in Scotland and America, 1740–1800.* Lewisburg, PA: Bucknell University Press.

McCrary, Charles, and Jeffrey Wheatley. 2016. "The Protestant Secular in the Study of American Religion: Reappraisal and Suggestions." *Religion* 47 (2): 1–21.

McCutcheon, Russell T. 2002. "The Study of Religion as an Anthropology of Credibility." In *Religious Studies, Theology, and the University: Conflicting Maps, Changing Terrain*, edited by Linell E. Cady and Delwin Brown, 13–30. Albany: State University of New York Press.

———. 2014. *Entanglements: Marking Place in the Field of Religion.* Bristol, UK: Equinox.

McDannell, Colleen. 1995. *Material Religion: Religion and Popular Culture in America.* New Haven, CT: Yale University Press.

McDanell, Kyle. 2015. "Can We Now Say, 'Farewell, Rob Bell?'" *Kylemcdanell* (blog), December 2015. http://www.kylemcdanell.com/2015/01/can-we-now-say-farewell-rob-bell.html.

McGuire, Meredith. 2008. *Lived Religion: Faith and Practice in Everyday Life.* New York: Oxford University Press.

McHargue, Mike. 2016. *Finding God in the Waves: How I Lost My Faith and Found It Again through Science.* New York: Convergent.

McKnight, Scot. 2007. "Five Streams of the Emerging Church: Key Elements of the Most Controversial and Misunderstood Movement in the Church Today." *Christianity Today*, January 19, 2007. http://www.christianitytoday.com/ct/2007/February/11.35.html.

McLuhan, Marshall. 1969. *Counterblast.* New York: Harcourt, Brace & World.

———. 2001. *Understanding Media: The Extensions of Man.* Cambridge, MA: MIT Press.

Menzies, Heather. 2005. *No Time: Stress and the Crisis of Modern Life.* Vancouver, Canada: Douglas & McIntyre.

Merelli, Analisa. 2015. "Socality Barbie Hits Uncomfortably Close to Home: A Tongue-in-Cheek Instagram Account Underscores the Paradox of Social-Media Authenticity." *Atlantic*, September 9, 2015. https://www.theatlantic.com/entertainment/archive/2015/09/hipster-socality-barbie-shows-the-cliche-of-instagram-authenticity/404431/.

Merritt, Carol Howard. 2011. "Rob Bell and Tall Steeples." *Faith & Leadership*, March 7, 2011. https://www.faithandleadership.com/carol-howard-merritt-rob-bell-and-tall-steeples.

Messina-Dysert, Gina, Jennifer Dobair, and Amy Levin. 2015. *Faithfully Feminist: Jewish, Christian, and Muslim Feminists on Why We Stay.* Ashland, OR: White Cloud.

Meyer, Birgit. 2007. "Religious Sensations: Why Media, Aesthetics, and Power Matter in the Study of Contemporary Religion." In *Religion: Beyond a Concept*, edited by Hent De Vries, 704–723. New York: Fordham University Press, 2007.

———. 2011. "Mediation and Immediacy: Sensational Forms, Semiotic Ideologies and the Question of the Medium." *Social Anthropology/Anthropologie Sociale* 19 (1): 23–39.

———. 2015. "Picturing the Invisible: Visual Culture and the Study of Religion." *Method and Theory in the Study of Religion* 27: 333–360.

Micah, Jory. 2016. "The Rise of Evangelical Feminism: A Conversation for Gender Equality Month." *Relevant Magazine*, March 29, 2016. http://www.relevantmagazine.com/god/god-our-generation/rise-evangelical-feminism.

Miles, Margaret R. 1998. "Image." In *Critical Terms for Religious Studies*, edited by Mark C. Taylor, 160–172. Chicago: University of Chicago Press, 1998.

Miller, Daniel. 2018. "The Anthropology of Social Media." *Scientific American*, February 15, 2018. https://blogs.scientificamerican.com/observations/the-anthropology-of-social-media/.

———. 2014. "Facebook and the Origins of Religion." In *Framing Cosmologies: The Anthropology of Worlds*, edited by Allen Abramson and Martin Holbraad, 244–260. Manchester, UK: Manchester University Press.

———. 2011. *Tales from Facebook*. Malden, MA: Polity.

Miller, Daniel, Elisabetta Costa, Nell Haynes, Tom McDonald, Razvan Nicolescu, Jolynna Sinanan, Juliano Spyer, Shriram Venkatraman, and Xinyuan Wang. 2016. *How the World Changed Social Media*. London: University College of London Press.

Miller, Donald. 2003. *Blue Like Jazz: Nonreligious Thoughts on Christian Spirituality*. Nashville, TN: Thomas Nelson.

Modern, John Lardas. 2011. *Secularism in Antebellum America*. Chicago: University of Chicago Press.

Mohler, Albert. 2011. "'A Massive Shift Coming in What it Means to Be a Christian?'—TIME Magazine Considers Rob Bell." *Albert Mohler*, April 15, 2011. http://www.albertmohler.com/2011/04/15/a-massive-shift-coming-in-what-it-means-to-be-a-christian-time-magazine-considers-rob-bell/.

Moor, Peter. 2007. "Conforming to the Flaming Norm in the Online Commenting Situation." Unpublished Bachelor's Thesis, University of Twente, 1–7. http://essay.utwente.nl/58838/1/scriptie_P_Moor.pdf.

Morgan, David. 2007. *The Lure of Images: A History of Religion and Visual Media in America*. London: Routledge.

———. 2013. "Religion and Media: A Critical Review of Recent Developments." *Critical Research on Religion* 1 (3): 347–356.

Mortensen, Mette, Christina Neumayer, and Thomas Poell, eds. 2019. *Social Media Materialities and Protest: Critical Reflections*. New York: Routledge. VitalSource ebook.

Moss, Candida. 2014. *The Myth of Persecution: How Early Christians Invented a Story of Martyrdom*. New York: HarperOne.
Mullen, Lincoln A. 2017. *The Chance of Salvation: A History of Conversion in America*. Cambridge, MA: Harvard University Press.
Murray, Joddy. 2009. *Non-Discursive Rhetoric: Image and Affect in Multimodal Composition*. Albany: State University of New York.
Musa, Bala A. 2015. "Mediating Faith through Popular Culture: The Voice of Aimee Semple McPherson in the New Media Marketplace." In *From Twitter to Tahrir Square: Ethics in Social and New Media Communication*, edited by Bala A. Musa and Jim Wallis, 87–101. Santa Barbara, CA: Praeger.
Myers, Greg. 2009. *Discourse of Blogs and Wikis*. New York: Continuum.
Natale, Simone, and Diana Pasulka, eds. 2020. *Believing in Bits: Digital Media and the Supernatural*. New York: Oxford University Press.
Nathan, Richard, and Linda Nathan. 2006. "'Christian' Romanticism, the INKLINGS, and the Elevation of Mythology." *Kjos Ministries*, August 7, 2006. http://www.crossroad.to/articles2/006/nathan/romanticism.htm.
Nelson, Ted. 1974. *Computer Lib: You Can and Must Understand Computers Now*. Stroud, UK: Tempus. Self-Published.
Neo, Perpetua. 2015. "Does Facebook Make You Depressed?" *HuffPost*, November 5, 2015. https://www.huffingtonpost.com/dr-perpetua-neo/does-facebook-make-you-de_b_8474654.html.
Newport, Cal. 2019. *Digital Minimalism: Choosing a Focused Life in a Noisy World*. New York: Portfolio/Penguin.
Niequist, Shauna. 2016. *Present over Perfect: Leaving behind Frantic for a Simpler, More Soulful Way of Living*. New York: HarperCollins.
Noble, Alan. 2018. *Disruptive Witness: Speaking Truth in a Distracted Age*. Downers Grove, IL: InterVarsity.
Noble, David F. 1997. *The Religion of Technology: The Divinity of Man and the Spirit of Invention*. New York: Alfred A. Knopf.
Noll, Mark. 2001. *American Evangelical Christianity*. Malden, MA: Blackwell.
———. 2007. "Protestant Evangelicals and Recent American Politics." *Journal of American and Canadian Studies* 25: 3–18.
Nord, David Paul. 2004. *Faith in Reading: Religious Publishing and the Birth of Mass Media in America*. New York: Oxford University Press.
Northcutt, Peter. 2017. "4 Bad Reasons Christians Call Each Other 'Heretics.'" *Relevant*, March 2, 2017. https://relevantmagazine.com/article/4-bad-reasons-christians-call-each-other-heretics/.
Ockenga, Harold J. 1942. "The Unvoiced Multitudes." In *Evangelical Action! A Report of the Organization of the National Association for Evangelicals for United Action*, 26–27. Boston: United Action.
Olson, Roger E. 2016. "The Emerging Divide in Evangelical Theology." In *The Future of Evangelicalism in America*, edited by Candy Gunther Brown and Mark Silk, 92–123. New York: Columbia University Press.

Orsi, Robert A. 2005. *Between Heaven and Earth: The Religious Worlds People Make and the Scholars Who Study Them*. Princeton, NJ: Princeton University Press.

Osmann, Murad, and Nataly Zakharova. 2016. *Follow Me To: A Journey around the World through the Eyes of Two Ordinary Travelers*. New York: Skyhorse.

Pettegree, Andrew. 2015. *Brand Luther: How an Unheralded Monk Turned His Small Town into a Center of Publishing, Made Himself the Most Famous Man in Europe—and Started the Protestant Reformation*. New York: Penguin.

Peters, John Durham. 2015. *The Marvelous Clouds: Toward a Philosophy of Elemental Media*. Chicago: University of Chicago Press.

Pew Research Center. 2015a. "Americans' Internet Access: 2000–2015." *Religion & Public Life*, June 26, 2015. http://www.pewinternet.org/2015/06/26/americans-internet-access-2000-2015/#main-findings.

———. 2018. "Social Media Use in 2018." *Religion & Public Life*, March 1, 2018. http://www.pewinternet.org/2018/03/01/social-media-use-in-2018/.

Pickersgill, Eric. 2016. "Removed." *Ericpickersgill*, October 12, 2016. http://www.removed.social/2015/10/12/cameron.

Pink, Sarah, Heather Horst, John Postill, Larissa Hjorth, Tania Lewis, and Jo Tacchi. 2015. *Digital Ethnography: Principles and Practices*. Thousand Oaks, CA: Sage.

Platypus: The CASTAC Blog. 2019. "About." Accessed January 2, 2022. http://blog.castac.org/about/.

Pogue, David. 2012. "What Wi-Fi Stands For—And Other Wireless Questions Answered." *Scientific American*, May 1, 2012. https://www.scientificamerican.com/article/pogue-what-wifi-stands-for-other-wireless-questions-answered/.

Porterfield, Amanda. 2012. *Conceived in Doubt: Religion and Politics in the New American Nation*. Chicago: University of Chicago Press.

Prensky, Marc. 2001. "Digital Natives, Digital Immigrants." *On the Horizon* 9 (5): 1–6.

Priestly, Theo. 2015. "Is Social Media Just Another Bad Habit to Break?" *Forbes*, August 30, 2015. https://www.forbes.com/forbes/welcome/?toURL=https://www.forbes.com/sites/theopriestley/2015/08/13/is-social-media-just-another-bad-habit-to-break/&refURL=&referrer=#179dfd546f99.

Rabinow, Paul. 2007. *Reflections on Fieldwork in Morocco*. Berkeley: University of California Press.

Radde-Antweiler, Kerstin. 2013. "Authenticity." In *Digital Religion: Understanding Religious Practice in New Media Worlds*, edited by Heidi A. Campbell, 83–103. New York: Routledge.

Rankin, Joy Lisi. 2018. *A People's History of Computing in the United States*. Cambridge, MA: Harvard University Press.

Rasche, Tuhina Verma. 2016. "Day One/Fuck/Matthew 24:44." *Medium*, November 26, 2016. https://medium.com/fuckthisshit/fuckthisshit-an-advent-devotional-b33fd0a79831.

Raser, Timothy. 2015. *Baudelaire and Photography: Finding the Painter of Modern Life*. New York: Modern Humanities Research Association and Routledge.

Relevant Magazine. 2015. "Why the Girl Behind @Socalitybarbie Called It Quits." *Relevant* 79 (January–February): 20.
———. 2018a. "'Heresy' Is Having Its Hollywood Moment." *Relevant* 92 (March–April): 20.
———. 2018b. "10 People Who Changed the Faith Conversation." *Relevant* 92 (March–April): 46–47.
RelevantMagazine.com. 2014. "The Return of Rob Bell." June 24, 2014. https://relevantmagazine.com/culture/tv/return-rob-bell.
Rey, Jessica. 2013. "The Evolution of the Swimsuit." YouTube video, June 17, 2013. http://www.youtube.com/watch?v=WJVHRJbgLz8.
Reynolds, Frank, and David Tracy, eds. 1992. *Discourse and Practice*. Albany: State University of New York Press.
Ribak, Rivka, and Michele Rosenthal. 2015. "Smartphone Resistance as Media Ambivalence." *First Monday: Peer-Reviewed Journal on the Internet* 11 (2). Accessed January 2, 2022. https://firstmonday.org/ojs/index.php/fm/article/view/6307/5136.
Rice, Jesse. 2009. *The Church of Facebook: How the Hyperconnected Are Redefining Community*. Colorado Springs, CO: David C. Cook.
Robbins, Joel. 2012. "Some Things You Say, Some Things You Dissimulate, Some Things You Keep to Yourself: Linguistic, Material, and Marital Exchange in the Construction of Melanesian Societies." In *The Scope of Anthropology: Maurice Godelier's Work in Context*, edited by Laurent Dousset, Serge Tcherkézoff, 25–45. New York: Berghahn.
Robinson, Brett T. 2013. *Appletopia: Media Technology and the Religious Imagination of Steve Jobs*. Waco, TX: Baylor University Press.
Rolsky, L. Benjamin. 2019. *The Rise and Fall of the Religious Left: Politics, Television, and Popular Culture in the 1970s and Beyond*. New York: Columbia University Press.
Romele, Roberto, and Enrico Terrone, eds. 2018. *Towards a Philosophy of Digital Media*. New York: Palgrave Macmillan.
Roose, Kevin. 2017. "Facebook's Frankenstein Moment." *New York Times*, September 11, 2017. https://www.nytimes.com/2017/09/21/technology/facebook-frankenstein-sandberg-ads.html.
Rosenthal, Michele. 2007. *American Protestants and TV in the 1950s: Responses to a New Medium*. New York: Palgrave Macmillan.
———. 2012. "Commercial Television News, Crisis, and Collective Memory." In *The Oxford Handbook of Religion and the American News Media*, edited by Diane Winston, 141–156. New York: Oxford University Press.
Rouse, Richard W. 1999. "Technology and a New Reformation." *Evangelical Lutheran Church in America*. Accessed January 2, 2022. http://download.elca.org/ELCA%20Resource%20Repository/LP_Technology_New_Reformation.pdf.
Royce, Anya Peterson. 2002. "Learning to See, Learning to Listen: Thirty Years of Fieldwork with the Isthmus Zapotec." In *Chronicling Cultures: Long-Term Field*

Research in Anthropology, edited by Robert V. Kemper and Anya Peterson Royce, 8–33. Lanham, MD: AltaMira.

Russmann, Uta, and Jakob Svensson. 2016. "Studying Organizations on Instagram." *Information* 7 (58): 1–12.

Ryan, Johnny. 2010. *A History of the Internet and the Digital Future.* London: Reaktion.

Sack, Daniel. 2000. *Whitebread Protestants: Food and Religion in American Culture.* New York: Palgrave.

Said, Edward W. 1979. *Orientalism.* New York: Vintage.

Saint Hoax. 2015. "Contemporary Fairy Tale." *Instagram*, September 7, 2015. https://www.instagram.com/p/7VZn_IQYdS/.

Sánchez Walsh, Arlene M. 2003. *Latino Pentecostal Identity: Evangelical Faith, Self, and Society.* New York: Columbia University Press.

Sanjek, Roger, and Susan W. Tratner. 2016. *eFieldnotes: The Makings of Anthropology in the Digital World.* Philadelphia: University of Pennsylvania Press.

Sawers, Paul. 2013. "Internet Pioneer Vint Cerf Talks Online Privacy, Google Glass and the Future of Libraries." *Next Web*, July 12, 2013. https://thenextweb.com/insider/2013/07/12/vint-cerf/.

Schaefer, Donovan O. 2015. *Religious Affects: Animality, Evolution, and Power.* Durham, NC: Duke University Press.

———. 2019. *The Evolution of Affect Theory: The Humanities, the Sciences, and the Study of Power.* Cambridge, UK: Cambridge University Press.

Schlafly, Phyllis. 2003. *Feminist Fantasies.* Dallas, TX: Spence.

Schmelzer, Dave. 2017. *Blue Ocean Faith: The Vibrant Connection to Jesus That Opens Up Insanely Great Possibilities in a Secularizing World—and Might Kick Off a New Jesus Movement.* Ann Arbor, MI: Front Edge.

Schmidt, Jan. 2007. "Blogging Practices: An Analytical Framework." *Journal of Computer-Mediated Communication* 12: 1409–1427.

Schmucker, Nathaniel. 2012. "Why We Long for the Ideal: Caspar David Friedrich and General Revelation." *Dartmouth Apologia: A Journal of Christian Thought.* http://www.dartmouthapologia.org/apologia/why-we-long-for-the-ideal-caspar-david-friedrich-and-general-revelation-2/.

Schroeder, Ralph. 2018. *Social Theory after the Internet: Media, Technology, and Globalization.* London: UCL.

Schultze, Quentin J. 1990. "The Invisible Medium: Evangelical Radio." In *American Evangelicals and the Mass Media: Perspectives on the Relationship between American Evangelicals and the Mass Media*, edited by Quentin J. Schultze, 171–195. Grand Rapids, MI: Zondervan.

———. 2002. *Habits of the High-Tech Heart: Living Virtuously in the Information Age.* Grand Rapids, MI: Baker Academic.

Schultze, Quentin J., and Robert H. Woods Jr., eds. 2008. *Understanding Evangelical Media: The Changing Face of Christian Communication.* Downers Grove, IL: InterVarsity.

Schuurman, Peter J. 2019. *The Subversive Evangelical: The Ironic Charisma of an Irreligious Megachurch*. Montreal: McGill-Queen's University Press.
Schwalbe, Michael L., and Douglas Mason-Schrock. 1996. "Identity Work as Group Process." *Advances in Group Processes* 13 (113): 115–49.
Schwartz, David R. 2012. *Moral Minority: The Evangelical Left in an Age of Conservatism*. Philadelphia: University of Pennsylvania Press.
Scolari, Carlos A. 2015. "From (New) Media to (Hyper)mediations: Recovering Jesús Martín-Barbero's Mediation Theory in the Age of Digital Communication and Cultural Convergence." *Information, Communication & Society* 18:9: 1092–1107.
Sebek, Petra P. 2019. *Spirituality in the Selfie Culture of Instagram*. Eugene, OR: Wipf & Stock.
Segaller, Stephen. 1998. *Nerds 2.0.: A Brief History of the Internet*. New York: TV Books.
Seigworth, Gregory J., and Melissa Gregg. 2009. "An Inventory of Shimmers." In *The Affect Theory Reader*, edited by Melissa Gregg and Gregory J. Seigworth, 1–25. Durham, NC: Duke University Press.
Selka, Stephen. "Morality in the Religious Marketplace: Evangelical Christianity, Candomblé, and the Struggle for Moral Distinction in Brazil. *American Ethnologist* 37 (2): 291–307.
Shepard, Ben. 2004. "Affect." *University of Chicago Theories of Media Glossary*. http://csmt.uchicago.edu/glossary2004/affect.htm.
Shifman, Limor. 2014. *Memes in Digital Culture*. Cambridge, MA: MIT Press.
Silva, Ken. 2011a. "Farewell, Rob Bell." *Apprising Ministries*, June 20, 2011. http://apprising.org/2011/06/20/farewell-rob-bell/.
———. 2011b. "Rob Bell, Farewell." *Apprising Ministries*, June 27, 2011. http://apprising.org/2011/06/27/rob-bell-farewell/.
Silverstein, Michael, and Greg Urban. 1996. "The Natural History of Discourse." In *Natural Histories of Discourse*, edited by Michael Silverstein and Greg Urban, 1–17. Chicago: University of Chicago Press.
Simpson, James. 2019. *Permanent Revolution: The Reformation and the Illiberal Roots of Liberalism*. Cambridge, MA: Belknap of Harvard University Press.
Sircar, Atish, and Jennifer Rowley. 2016. "Social Media and Megachurches." *International Federation for Information Processing* I3E: 695–700.
Smith, Andrea. 2008. *Native Americans and the Christian Right: The Gendered Politics of Unlikely Alliances*. Durham, NC: Duke University Press.
Smith, C. Christopher, and John Pattison. 2014. *Slow Church: Cultivating Community in the Patient Way of Jesus*. Downers Grove, IL: IVP.
Smith, Christian. 1998. *American Evangelicalism: Embattled and Thriving*. Chicago: University of Chicago Press.
Smith, Christian, and Melinda Lundquist Denton. 2005. *Soul Searching: The Religious and Spiritual Lives of American Teenagers*. New York: Oxford University Press.
Smith, Jonathan Z. 1982. "In Comparison a Magic Dwells." In *Imagining Religion: From Babylon to Jonestown*. Chicago: University of Chicago Press.

———. 1990. "On Comparison." In *Drudgery Divine: On the Comparison of Early Christianity and the Religions of Late Antiquity*. Chicago: University of Chicago Press.

Smith, Leslie Dorrough. 2014. *Righteous Rhetoric: Sex, Speech, and the Politic of Concerned Women for America*. New York: Oxford University Press.

———. 2020a. *Compromising Positions: Sex Scandals, Politics, and American Christianity*. New York: Oxford University Press.

———. 2020b. "What the Falwell Saga Tells Us about Evangelicals and Gender Roles." *Conversation*, August 26, 2020. https://theconversation.com/what-the-falwell-saga-tells-us-about-evangelicals-and-gender-roles-145018.

Smith, Marc A., Lee Rainie, Ben Schneiderman, and Itai Himelboim. 2014. "Mapping Twitter Topic Networks: From Polarized Crowds to Community Clusters." *Pew Research Center*, February 20. 2014. http://www.pewinternet.org/2014/02/20/mapping-twitter-topic-networks-from-polarized-crowds-to-community-clusters/.

Smith, Nils. 2013. *Social Media Guide for Ministry*. Springfield, MO: Group.

Smith, Wilbur M. 2014. *A Voice for God: The Life of Charles E. Fuller*. Eugene, OR: Wipf & Stock.

Smolan, Sandy, dir. 2016. *The Human Face of Big Data*. Against All Odds Productions & Luminous Content, 2014. PBS Distribution, 2016. 60 minutes. DVD.

Socality. 2017. http://www.socality.org/.

Spitulnik (Vidali), Debra. 1996. "The Social Circulation of Media Discourse and the Mediation of Communities." *Journal of Linguistic Anthropology* 6 (2): 161–187.

Squires, Lauren. 2014. "From TV Personality to Fans and Beyond: Indexical Bleaching and the Diffusion of a Media Innovation." *Journal of Linguistic Anthropology* 24 (1): 42–62.

Sreberny-Mohammadi, Annabelle, and Ali Mohammadi. 1994. *Small Media, Big Revolution: Communication, Culture, and the Iranian Revolution*. Minneapolis: University of Minnesota Press.

Stacey, Judith, and Susan Elizabeth Gerard. 1990. "'We Are Not Doormats: The Influence of Feminism on Contemporary Evangelicals in the United States." In *Uncertain Terms: Negotiating Gender in American Culture*, edited by Faye Ginsburg and Anna Lowenhaupt Tsing, 98–117. Boston: Beacon.

Stavrositu, Carmen, and S. Shyam Sundar. 2010. "Does Blogging Empower Women? Exploring the Role of Agency and Community." *Journal of Computer-Mediated Communication* 17: 369–386.

Sterling, Christopher H. 2005. "Radio: AM, FM, Analog, Digital." In *Encyclopedia of 20th-Century Technology*, edited by Colin A. Hempstead and William E. Worthington, 633–635. New York: Routledge.

Stolow, Jeremy. 2008. "Technology." In *Keywords in Religion, Media and Culture*, edited by David Morgan, 187–197. New York: Routledge.

Stout, Harry. 1991. *The Divine Dramatist: George Whitefield and the Rise of Modern Evangelicalism*. Grand Rapids, MI: Wm. B. Eerdmans.

Strang, Cameron. 2017. "Welcome to the New Era." *Relevant* 86 (March–April): 10–11.
Strate, Lance. 1999. "Understanding MEA." *In Medias Res* 1:1 (October).
———. 2004. "A Media Ecology Review." *Communication Research Trends* 23 (2): 3–48.
Streensland, Brian, and Philip Goff, eds. 2014. *The New Evangelical Social Engagement*. New York: Oxford University Press.
Stutz, Chad P. 2009. "Christians, Critics, and Romantics: Aesthetic Discourse among Anglo-American Evangelicals, 1830–1900." PhD diss., Boston College.
Sullivan, Winnifred Fallers. 2005. *The Impossibility of Religious Freedom*. Princeton, NJ: Princeton University Press.
Supp-Montgomerie, Jenna. 2021. *When the Medium Was the Mission: The Atlantic Telegraph and the Religious Origins of Network Culture*. New York: New York University Press.
Suslak, Daniel F. 2009. "The Sociolinguistic Problem of Generations." *Language & Communication* 29: 199–209.
Sweet, Leonard. 2012. *Viral: How Social Networking Is Poised to Ignite Revival*. Colorado Springs, CO: WaterBrook.
Syrmor. 2020. "Real Pastor in Virtual Reality Baptizes an Anime Girl." YouTube video, May 19, 2020. https://www.youtube.com/watch?v=N_88DBmdnNA&vl=en.
Syvertsen, Trine. 2017. *Media Resistance: Protest, Dislike, Abstention*. Cham, Switzerland: Palgrave Macmillan.
Tarango, Angela. 2014. *Choosing the Jesus Way: American Indian Pentecostals and the Fight for the Indigenous Principle*. Chapel Hill: University of North Carolina Press.
Taussig, Michael. 1993. *Mimesis and Alterity: A Particular History of the Senses*. New York: Routledge.
Taylor, Charles. 2007. *A Secular Age*. Cambridge, MA: Belknap of Harvard University Press.
———. 2008. "Buffered and Porous Selves." *Immanent Frame*, September 2, 2008. https://tif.ssrc.org/2008/09/02/buffered-and-porous-selves/.
Taylor, Justin. 2011. "Rob Bell: Universalist?" *Gospel Coalition*, February 26, 2011. http://www.thegospelcoalition.org/blogs/justintaylor/2011/02/26/rob-bell-universalist/.
Teusner, Paul Emerson. 2013. "Formation of a Religious Technorati: Negotiations of Authority among Australian Emerging Church Blogs. In *Digital Religion: Understanding Religious Practice in New Media Worlds*, edited by Heidi A. Campbell, 182–189. New York: Routledge.
Thomas, Todne. 2021. *Kincraft: The Making of Black Evangelical Sociality*. Durham, NC: Duke University Press.
Thompson, John B. 1995. *The Media and Modernity: A Social Theory of the Media*. Stanford, CA: Stanford University Press.
Thumma, Scott, and Dave Travis. 2007. *Beyond Megachurch Myths: What We Can Learn from America's Largest Churches*. New York: John Wiley & Sons.

Thumma, Scott, and Warren Bird. 2015. "Recent Shifts in America's Largest Protestant Churches: Megachurches 2015 Report." *Leadership Network & Hartford Institute*. Accessed January 2, 2022. http://hirr.hartsem.edu/megachurch/2015 _Megachurches_Report.pdf.

Thurlow, Crispin, and Kristine Mroczek, eds. 2011. *Digital Discourse: Language in the New Media*. New York: Oxford University Press.

Tomlinson, Dave. 2003 [1995]. *The Post-Evangelical*. El Cajon, CA: emergentYS.

Tomlinson, Matt. 2006. "The Limits of Meaning in Fijian Methodist Sermons." In *The Limits of Meaning: Case Studies in the Anthropology of Christianity*, edited by Matthew Engelke and Matt Tomlinson, 129–146. New York: Berghahn.

Tomlinson, Matt, and Matthew Engelke. 2006. "Meaning, Anthropology, Christianity." In *The Limits of Meaning: Case Studies in the Anthropology of Christianity*, edited by Matthew Engelke and Matt Tomlinson, 1–37. New York: Berghahn.

Trammell, Jim Y. 2016. "Jesus? There's an App for That! Tablet Media in the 'New' Electronic Church." In *The Electronic Church in the Digital Age: Cultural Impacts of Evangelical Mass Media*, edited by Mark Ward, Sr., 219–237. Santa Barbara, CA: Praeger.

Tranby, Eric, and Douglas Hartmann. 2008. "Critical Whiteness Theories and the Evangelical 'Race Problem:' Extending Emerson and Smith's 'Divided by Faith.'" *Journal for the Scientific Study of Religion* 47 (3): 341–359.

Tufecki, Zynep. 2017. *Twitter and Tear Gas: The Power and Fragility of Networked Protest*. New Haven, CT: Yale University Press.

Turkle, Sherry. 1997. *Life on the Screen: Identity in the Age of the Internet*. New York: Touchstone.

———. 2011. *Alone Together: Why We Expect More from Technology and Less from Each Other*. New York: Basic.

Turner, Fred. 2006. *From Counterculture to Cyberculture: Stewart Brand, the Whole Earth Network, and the Rise of Digital Utopianism*. Chicago: University of Chicago Press.

Tweed, Thomas A. 2006. *Crossing and Dwelling*. Cambridge, MA: Harvard University Press.

Twenge, Jean M. 2017. "Are Smartphones Destroying a Generation?" *Atlantic*, September 2017. https://www.the atlantic.com/magazine/archive/2017/09 /has-the-smartphone-destroyed-a-generation/534198/.

Twitter. 2018. "About verified accounts." https://help.twitter.com/en/managing -your-account/about-twitter-verified-accounts.

Untold. 2018. "'The Heretic'—Official Trailer—Rob Bell Documentary." YouTube video, December 31, 2018. https://www.youtube.com/watch?time_continue =55&v=fQ3HYWFhoKg.

Urban, Greg. 1991. *A Discourse-Centered Approach to Culture: Native South American Myths and Rituals*. Austin, TX: University of Texas Press.

Vaca, Daniel. 2012. "Book People: Evangelical Books and the Making of Contemporary Evangelicalism." PhD diss., Columbia University.
———. 2019. *Evangelicals Incorporated: Books and the Business of Religion in America.* Cambridge, MA: Harvard University Press.
van Asselt, Willem J., Paul Van Geest, Daniela Muller, and Theo Salemink, eds. 2007. *Iconoclasm and Iconoclash: Struggle for Religious Identity.* Leiden, The Netherlands: Brill.
van Dijck, José. 2013. *The Culture of Connectivity: A Critical History of Social Media.* New York: Oxford University Press.
van Prooyen, Kristina. 2004. "The Realm of the Spirit: Caspar David Friedrich's Artwork in the Context of Romantic Theology, with Special Reference to Friedrich Schleiermacher." *Journal of the Oxford University History Society* 1: 1–16.
Vance, Deborah Clark. 2016. "The Flesh and the Spirit: Communicating Evangelical Identity via 'Christian Radio.'" In *The Electronic Church in the Digital Age: Cultural Impacts of Evangelical Mass Media,* edited by Mark Ward, Sr., 27–51. Santa Barbara, CA: Praeger.
Vander Hart, Shane. 2013. "Bye, Bye Rob Bell." *Caffeinated Thoughts,* March 19, 2013. https://caffeinatedthoughts.com/2013/03/bye-bye-rob-bell/.
Vermeer, Danielle. 2011. "The Christian Way of Relating." *From Two to One: Reflections on Marriage, Faith, and Feminism,* January 29, 2011. http://www.fromtwotoone.com/2011_01_01_archive.html.
———. 2012. "The Modesty Myth." *From Two to One: Reflections on Marriage, Faith, and Feminism,* May 14, 2012. http://www.fromtwotoone.com/2012/03/modesty-myth.html.
———. 2013a. "Why I Think Secular Feminists Need Feminists of Faith." *Role Reboot: Life off Script,* March 27, 2013. http://www.rolereboot.org/culture-and-politics/details/2013-03-why-i-think-secular-feminists-need-feminists-of-faith.
———. 2013b. "Moving On from Blogging as I've Known It." *From Two to One: Reflections on Marriage, Faith, and Feminism,* September 30, 2013. http://www.fromtwotoone.com/?zx=51607fe904824018.
Vial, Stéphane. 2019. *Being and the Screen: How the Digital Changes Perception.* Cambridge, MA: MIT Press.
Virtual Church. 2020a. "Leadership." Accessed January 2, 2022. https://www.vrchurch.org/board.
———. 2020b. "Beliefs." Accessed January 2, 2022. https://www.vrchurch.org/beliefs.
Voskuil, Dennis N. 1990. "The Power of the Air: Evangelicals and the Rise of Religious Broadcasting." In *American Evangelicals and the Mass Media: Perspectives on the Relationship between American Evangelicals and the Mass Media,* edited by Quentin J. Schultze, 69–95. Grand Rapids, MI: Zondervan.
Wacker, Grant. 2014. *America's Pastor: Billy Graham and the Shaping of a Nation.* Cambridge, MA: Harvard University Press.

———, ed., with Andrew Finstuen and Anne Blue Wills. 2017. *Billy Graham: American Pilgrim*. New York: Oxford University Press.
Wagner, Phillip E. 2016. "And on the Eighth Day, God Created TBN: Evangelical Television in the Digital Age." In *The Electronic Church in the Digital Age: Cultural Impacts of Evangelical Mass Media*, edited by Mark Ward, Sr., 53–76. Santa Barbara, CA: Praeger.
Wagner, Rachel. 2012. *Godwired: Religion, Ritual and Virtual Reality*. London: Routledge.
———. 2013. "You Are What You Install: Religious Authenticity and Identity in Mobile Apps." In *Digital Religion: Understanding Religious Practice in New Media Worlds*, edited by Heidi A. Campbell, 199–206. New York: Routledge.
Wang, Amy B. 2017. "Former Facebook VP Says Social Media Is Destroying Society with 'Dopamine-Driven Feedback Loops.'" *Washington Post*, December 12, 2017. https://www.washingtonpost.com/news/the-switch/wp/2017/12/12/former-facebook-vp-says-social-media-is-destroying-society-with-dopamine-driven-feedback-loops/?utm_term=.ea171dfee23e.
Ward, Mark Sr. 2014. "Give the Winds a Mighty Voice: Evangelical Culture as Radio Ecology." *Journal of Radio & Audio Media* 21 (1): 115–133.
———. 2017. *The Lord's Radio: Gospel Music Broadcasting and the Making of Evangelical Culture, 1920–1960*. Jefferson, NC: McFarland & Company.
Warner, Michael. 2002. *Publics and Counterpublics*. New York: Zone.
Warren, Zachary, and Fathali M. Moghaddam. 2011. "Cultural Carriers." *The Encyclopedia of Peace Psychology*. https://doi.org/10.1002/9780470672532.wbepp073.
Waters, Kenneth E. 2008. "Pursuing New Periodicals in Print and Online." In *Understanding Evangelical Media: The Changing Face of Christian Communication*, edited by Quentin J. Schulze and Robert H. Woods Jr., 71–84. Downers Grove, IL: IVP.
Watts, Joel L. 2015. "Farewell, Rob Bell." *Unsettled Christianity*, February 19, 2015. http://unsettledchristianity.com/farewell-rob-bell/.
Weber, Max. 1964. *The Theory of Social and Economic Organization*. Edited by Talcott Parsons. New York: The Free Press.
Weiner, Isaac. 2014. *Religion Out Loud: Religious Sound, Public Space, and American Pluralism*. New York: New York University Press.
Weisenfeld, Judith. 2017. *New World A-Coming: Black Religion and Racial Identity during the Great Migration*. New York: New York University Press.
Wellman, James K. 2012. *Rob Bell and a New American Christianity*. Nashville, TN: Abingdon. Ebook.
Wells, Kathleen. 2011. *Narrative Inquiry*. New York: Oxford University Press.
Wenger, Tisa. 2009. *We Have a Religion: The 1920s Pueblo Indian Dance Controversy and American Religious Freedom*. Chapel Hill: University of North Carolina Press.

Whitehead, Deborah. 2015. "The Evidence of Things Unseen: Authenticity and Fraud in the Christian Mommy Blogosphere." *Journal of the American Academy of Religion* 83 (1): 120–150.

———. 2018. *Christian Evangelicals and Digital Media: Mediating the Gospel in Contemporary America*. New York: Routledge.

Wilcox, W. B. 2004. *Soft Patriarchs, New Men: How Christianity Shapes Fathers and Husbands*. Chicago: University of Chicago Press.

Williams, Mariam. 2010a. "The Sacred Vow." *Redbone Afropuff and Black GRITS* (blog), June 9, 2010. http://www.redboneafropuff.com/2010/06/09/the-sacred-vow/.

———. 2010b. "Thrivalerious Outsider, but Not Alone." *Redbone Afropuff and Black GRITS* (blog), October 23, 2010. http://www.redboneafropuff.com/2010/10/13/thrivalerious-outsider-but-not-alone/.

———. 2011. "Rape Is Never Funny." *Redbone Afropuff and Black GRITS* (blog), October 9, 2011. http://www.redboneafropuff.com/2011/10/09/rape-is-never-funny/.

———. 2012a. "Another 'F' Voice Emerges in 2012." *Redbone Afropuff and Black GRITS* (blog), January 1, 2012. http://www.redboneafropuff.com/2012/01/01/another-f-voice-emerges-in-2012/.

———. 2012b. "When Man-Made Laws Protect Us from Bad Faith." *Redbone Afropuff and Black GRITS* (blog), February 20, 2012. http://www.redboneafropuff.com/2012/02/20/when-man-made-laws-protect-us-from-bad-faith/.

———. 2012c. "Virginity as a Social Construct." *Redbone Afropuff and Black GRITS* (blog), June 2, 2012. http://www.redboneafropuff.com/2012/06/02/virginity-as-a-social-construct/.

———. 2012d. "Bringing Feminism into Sexual Morality." *Redbone Afropuff and Black GRITS* (blog), July 3, 2012. http://www.redboneafropuff.com/2012/07/03/bringing-feminism-into-sexual-morality/.

———. 2012e. "When Christianity and Feminism Don't Get Along." *Redbone Afropuff and Black GRITS* (blog), August 31, 2012. http://www.redboneafropuff.com/2012/08/31/when-christianity-and-feminism-dont-get-along/.

———. 2012f. "Called to Love in Election 2012." *Redbone Afropuff and Black GRITS* (blog), November 2, 2012. http://www.redboneafropuff.com/2012/11/02/called-to-love-in-election-2012/.

———. 2013a. "Looking for Love the Christian Way Doesn't Always Lead to Happiness." *National Catholic Reporter*, January 13, 2013. https://www.ncronline.org/blogs/intersection/finding-love-christian-way-doesnt-always-lead-happiness.

———. 2013b. "Feminism and the Future of Whiteness." *Redbone Afropuff and Black GRITS* (blog), February 23, 2013. http://www.redboneafropuff.com/2013/02/23/feminism-and-the-future-of-whiteness/.

———. 2013c. "How to Be a Black Feminist." *Redbone Afropuff and Black GRITS* (blog), September 19, 2013. http://www.redboneafropuff.com/2013/09/19/how-to-be-a-black-feminist/.

———. 2013d. "Why I'm Blogging Like Crazy." *Redbone Afropuff and Black GRITS* (blog), November 1, 2013. http://www.redboneafropuff.com/2013/11/01/why-im-blogging-like-crazy/.

———. 2013e. "Pure Black Power." *Redbone Afropuff and Black GRITS* (blog), November 8, 2013. http://www.redboneafropuff.com/2013/11/08/pure-black-power/.

———. 2013f. "First Lady Love (the Other First Lady)." *Redbone Afropuff and Black GRITS* (blog), November 15, 2013. http://www.redboneafropuff.com/2013/11/15/first-lady-love-the-other-first-lady/.

———. 2013g. "What Makes Me a Feminist." *Redbone Afropuff and Black GRITS* (blog), November 26, 2013. http://www.redboneafropuff.com/2013/11/26/what-makes-me-a-feminist/.

———. 2013h. "The Jesus in Grandmama's House." *Redbone Afropuff and Black GRITS* (blog), December 22, 2013. http://www.redboneafropuff.com/2013/12/22/the-jesus-in-grandmamas-house/.

———. 2013i. "Why Mrs. Carter Will Not Set You Free." *Redbone Afropuff and Black GRITS* (blog), December 27, 2013. http://www.redboneafropuff.com/2013/12/27/why-mrs-carter-will-not-set-you-free/.

———. 2014a. "At the Intersection: Christianity and Feminism Need Not Be Mutually Exclusive." *Redbone Afropuff and Black GRITS* (blog), June 20, 2014. http://www.redboneafropuff.com/2014/06/20/at-the-intersection-christianity-and-feminism-need-not-be-mutually-exclusive/.

———. 2014b. "I Know I've Been Changed." *Redbone Afropuff and Black GRITS* (blog), December 22, 2014. http://www.redboneafropuff.com/2014/12/22/i-know-ive-been-changed/.

———. 2015a. "Feminist Masquerade." *Redbone Afropuff and Black GRITS* (blog), February 17, 2015. http://www.redboneafropuff.com/2015/02/17/feminist-masquerade/.

———. 2015b. "For Mother Emanuel." *Redbone Afropuff and Black GRITS* (blog), June 19, 2015. http://www.redboneafropuff.com/2015/06/19/for-mother-emanuel/.

———. 2016. "About." *Redbone Afropuff and Black GRITS* (blog). Accessed August 20, 2016. http://www.redboneafropuff.com/about-2/.

Wilson, Andrew. 2015. "Twenty Twitter Tips." *Think Theology* (blog), February 4, 2015. https://thinktheology.co.uk/blog/article/twenty_twitter_tips.

Wilson-Hartgrove, Jonathan. 2010. *The Wisdom of Stability: Rooting Faith in a Mobile Culture*. Brewster, MA: Paraclete.

Wise, Justin. 2014. *The Social Church: A Theology of Digital Communication*. Chicago: Moody.

Wong, Janelle S. 2018. *Immigrants, Evangelicals, and Politics in an Era of Demographic Change*. New York: Russell Sage Foundation.

Wood, Connor. 2016. "Social Media Is Toxic. Religious Studies Tells Us Why." *Science on Religion (Patheos)*, December 21, 2016. https://www.patheos.com/blogs/scienceonreligion/2016/12/social-media-toxic-religious-studies-tells-us/.

Woods, Robert H., Jr., ed. 2013. *Evangelical Christians and Popular Culture: Pop Goes the Gospel, Volume 1*. Santa Barbara, CA: Praeger.

Workman, Jane E., and Beth W. Freeburg. 2009. *Dress and Society*. New York: Fairchild.

Worthen, Molly. 2014. *The Crisis of Authority in American Evangelicalism*. New York: Oxford University Press.

Wrench, Jason S. 2016. "Setting the Evangelical Agenda: The Role of 'Christian Radio.'" In *The Electronic Church in the Digital Age: Cultural Impacts of Evangelical Mass Media*, edited by Mark Ward, Sr., 173–192. Santa Barbara, CA: Praeger.

Wright, Jamie. 2018a. "Divorce, Death, and Resurrection." *The Very Worst Missionary*, July 31, 2018. https://theveryworstmissionary.com/2018/07/divorce-death-and-resurrection/.

———. 2018b. *The Very Worst Missionary: A Memoir or Whatever*. New York: Convergent.

Wright, Jonathan. 2011. *Heretics: The Creation of Christianity from the Gnostics to the Modern Church*. Boston: Houghton Mifflin Harcourt.

Wuthnow, Robert. 1988. *The Restructuring of American Religion: Society and Faith since World War II*. Rutgers, NJ: Princeton University Press.

———. 2015. *Inventing American Religion: Polls, Surveys, and the Tenuous Quest for a Nation's Faith*. New York: Oxford University Press.

Yagoda, Maria. 2015. "5 Lessons We Can All Learn about Insta from Socality Barbie." *People*, September 7, 2015. http://people.com/celebrity/hipster-barbie-parody-account-takes-on-millenials/.

Yawn, Byron. 2013. "The Curious Case of Rob Bell." *Trajectory*. http://thetrajectory.org/the-curious-case-of-rob-bell.

Young, Philip and Maria Åkerström. 2016. "Meet the Digital Naturals." In *Strategic Communication, Social Media and Democracy: The Challenge of the Digital Naturals*, edited by W. Timothy Coombs, Jesper Falkheimer, Mats Heide and Philip Young, 1–10. New York: Routledge.

Yukich, Grace, and Penny Edgell. 2020. *Religion Is Raced: Understanding American Religion in the Twenty-First Century*. New York: New York University Press.

Žižek, Slavoj. 1999. *The Plague of Fantasies*. London: Verso.

@ajfernando. 2015. "Who's in Indiana? @thepastorstephen is hosting a dinner in collaboration with Socality x HungerFree in NW Indiana on the 17th. Head to his page to find more details." *Socality*. Instagram photo, November 8, 2015. https://www.instagram.com/p/92c3w_Oesd/.

@andrewwilson. 2015. *Socality*. Instagram photo, January 6, 2015. https://www.instagram.com/p/xgCai3Oeor/.

@anthaang. 2015. "Love what you do." *Socality*. Instagram photo, April 12, 2015. https://www.instagram.com/p/1Yt14vOetS/.

@amandaseeyoudarrr. 2015. "I loved you at your darkest." *Socality*. Instagram photo, May 4, 2015. https://www.instagram.com/p/2RyoX1Oei_/.

@bertymandagie. 2014. "We are so proud of our friend @bobxdalton who founded @sackclothxashes as his story was featured on @instagram today. Bob has created the Socality collection and when you buy a blanket, a twin fleece is donated to your local homeless shelter." *Socality*. Instagram photo, November 26, 2014. https://www.instagram.com/p/v4ADAIuelP/.

@bethelredding. 2016. "The ministry of the gospel is not merely speaking with words, but emitting (His) presence wherever you are - @bethelredding - Bill Johnson. #ThisIsMyCommunity." *Socality*. Instagram photo, February 27, 2016. https://www.instagram.com/p/BCTPuNEOes7/.

@bluegerri. 2015. "We only have this moment. Photo by @lennartpagel #socality #thisismycommunity." *Socality*. Instagram, December 7, 2015. https://www.instagram.com/p/BNvjbMIBbMi/.

@bradleymountain. 2015. "Socality x @bradleymountain. This Socality Scout bag is limited edition and will be available only until the end of August. Visit our store on our site to find it. We love working with local artists and sharing their story. @bradleymountain is committed to making high quality leather goods, crafted and made in the USA." *Socality*. Instagram, August 7, 2015. https://www.instagram.com/p/6FpWv8uerd/.

@brandoneckroth. 2015. "It's not always easy standing up for what you believe in or standing out in a way that is not most popular. A moment shared by @iamshpak and captured by @brandoneckroth." *Socality*. Instagram photo, June 19, 2015. https://www.instagram.com/p/4IdwZ9ueqr/.

@brenton_clarke. 2015. "'We all desire a people, a place and a purpose.' - @samindecapolis 'The Table' a new 3 part series on the journal. Link in bio. Photo by @brenton_clarke #socality #socalitywashington #thisismycommunity." *Socality*. Instagram photo, December 9, 2015. https://www.instagram.com/p/_FDmufuetz/.

@brightong. 2016. "I lift my eyes up. Photo by @brightong #socality #thisismycommunity." *Socality*. Instagram photo, October 2, 2016. https://www.instagram.com/p/BLEPt_XhWX-/?utm_source=ig_share_sheet&igshid=5bioyy5k5ai3.

@dansmoe. 2015. "all things new. Photo by @dansmoe #socality #easter #risen." *Socality*. Instagram photo, April 5, 2015. https://www.instagram.com/p/1HfURtuep9/.

———. 2017. *Socality*. Instagram photo, May 25, 2017. https://www.instagram.com/p/BUhkl1DD39d/.

@davey_gravey. 2015. "make every moment count. Photo by @davey_gravy #socality." *Socality*. Instagram photo, May 13, 2015. https://www.instagram.com/p/2oBGP9uere/.

@dinelianoel. 2015. "Shout out to the amazing @dinelianoel and the entire crew in Sacramento who put together a #socalityhungerfree event tonight. You guys are

killing it!" *Socality*. Instagram photo, October 25, 2015. https://www.instagram.com/p/9SKFGfOev9/.
@dirka. 2016a. "Two years ago today was #socalitypdx in Portland! This gets us excited to soon announce events for 2017! Where do you think it should be?!" *Socality*. Instagram photo, October 26, 2016. https://www.instagram.com/p/BMDQSxKhsUQ/.
———. 2016b. "What are the things that drive us away from community and into isolation? #ThisIsMyCommunity." *Socality*. Instagram photo, April 11, 2016. https://www.instagram.com/p/BEDEwHHOeh6/.
———. 2016c. "Exploring the beautiful streets of the Holy Land. Photo by @dirka #socality #israelcollective." *Socality*. Instagram photo, June 28, 2016. https://www.instagram.com/p/BHNROmcB2J1/.
@dyerandjenkins. 2015. "California!! You have been good to us. We want to thank @dyerandjenkins for supporting the #forgeyourownpathtour. We will be sharing photos and stories over the next week from all the incredible people we encountered the last 10 days." *Socality*. Instagram photo, March 10, 2015. https://www.instagram.com/p/0DUcpLuen1/.
@erwnchow. 2015. *Socality*. Instagram photo, May 18, 2015. https://www.instagram.com/p/214b8HOety/.
@estherlecler. 2016. "Happy Memorial Day. Grateful for those who gave up their lives for our freedom today. US #ThisIsMyCommunity." *Socality*. Instagram photo, May 31, 2016. https://www.instagram.com/p/BGDtRI8uenc/.
@evan.boutte. 2015. "Express Yourself.. Photo by @evan.boutte #socality." *Socality*. Instagram photo, July 21, 2015. https://www.instagram.com/p/5azNgquejV/.
@fabiooliveira. 2017. *Socality*. Instagram photo, April 2, 2017. https://www.instagram.com/p/BSZEt2mDoTX/?taken-by=socality.
@filmography. 2015a. *Socality*. Instagram photo, July 10, 2015. https://www.instagram.com/p/4lssquemM/.
———. 2015b. "OKLAHOMA!! You've got a #socalityhungerfree event happening in your state! Get in touch with the awesome @filmography for more details or head over to Socality.org/hungerfree to see the current list of gatherings." *Socality*. Instagram photo, November 12, 2015. https://www.instagram.com/p/-AWHM_OeqJ/.
@giffinlamb. 2015. *Socality*. Instagram photo, April 27, 2015. https://www.instagram.com/p/2AFdpMOen8/.
@haleyswinth. 2015. "where is your favourite adventure spot you have ever been? Photo by @haleyswinth #socality." *Socality*. Instagram photo, March 28, 2015. https://www.instagram.com/p/0ypaKJOert/.
@hankhazen. 2016. "If we are to live our lives fully and well, we must learn to embrace the opposites, to live in a creative tension between our limits and our potentials. We must honor our limitations in ways that do you not distort our nature, and we must trust and use our gifts in ways that fulfill the potential's God gave us. - Parker Palmer. #ThisIsMyCommunity. Photo by @hankhazen

#Socality." *Socality*. Instagram photo, March 31, 2016. https://www.instagram.com/p/BDmtHm8ueul/?taken-by=socality.

@hipturelife. 2016. "Frame your world. So pumped to have @hipturelife at Socality. For those at the event, grab a frame from @monikergroup warehouse and get your frame for free. Take creative pics throughout the event and tag @hipturelife and they have some incredible prizes for you! Photo by @robstrok #socality #socalitylivesd." *Socality*. Instagram photo, July 30, 2016. https://www.instagram.com/p/5xKbnKueki?/.

@ianandrewnelson. 2015. "We are honoured to welcome @instagram Community Manager of North America @jeffreydgerson with us for Socality San Diego. In addition to hosting a workshop, Jeffrey will be hanging and getting to know all of those at the event. Jeffrey is passionate about #communityfirst and is an incredible story teller and communicator. His insight on social media and building authentic community is inspiring!! Socality San Diego starts in 2 days! Find details on our site for full itinerary and to register! Photo by @ianandrewnelson #socality #socalitylivesd." *Socality*. Instagram photo, July 27, 2015. https://www.instagram.com/p/5qJ2kyuerg/.

@ianandrewnelson. 2016. *Socality*. Instagram photo, June 9, 2016. https://www.instagram.com/p/BGa66H6ueon/.

@ineverstoppedlooking. 2015. *Socality*. Instagram photo, May 31, 2015. https://www.instagram.com/p/3WZQ8bOeuw/.

@jamieout. 2016. "We can be the change. Photo by @jamieout #socality #thisismycommunity #restartfreedom." *Socality*. Instagram photo, November 27, 2016. https://www.instagram.com/p/BNVxxKYhcQI/.

@jeremyklefeker. 2015. Cafe captures. A moment shared by @jeremyklefeker. Congratulations on being a finalist in the Socality X @moment_lens. The photo with the most likes will win a set of Moment lenses.Voting closes Tomorrow night at 11:59 pm. #sharemymoment #socality." *Socality*. Instagram photo, July 17, 2015. https://www.instagram.com/p/5Q1Mxquesg/.

@jguzmannn. 2017. *Socality*. Instagram photo, July 10, 2017. https://www.instagram.com/p/BWZEg6g1sP/.

@jkwinders. 2017. "If you can imagine it, you can achieve it. If you can dream it, you can become it. - William Arthur Ward. Photo by @jkwinders #socality #thisismycommunity." *Socality*. Instagram photo, February 17, 2017. https://www.instagram.com/p/BQmbGPljRn4/?taken-by=socality.

@jollejolle. 2015. "You know what a community values by what it celebrates. Photo by @jollejolle #socality #socalitynorway." *Socality*. Instagram photo, July 3, 2015. https://www.instagram.com/p/4rozYluen7/.

@jonathanzoeteman. 2015. "Update: Part of our team is in Peru this week with the @krochetkids team working on a special project. Here's a capture and story from @jonathanzoeteman. '14,000+ feet, hundreds of Alpacas, Peruvian Andes, and a couple days I won't soon forget. It's been a great start here in Peru with @

tannerwendell, @philipleclerc, @estherleclerc, and some amazing guys from @krochetkids. Huge thanks to @robdonegan and @blakegoodfellow for leading this trip and representing such a great organization so well. Pretty stoked for everyone to see what we've been working on in the coming weeks!' #kkintl #kkperu #socality #socalityperu." *Socality*. Instagram photo, September 24, 2015. https://www.instagram.com/p/8CEwNXuenC/.

———. 2016. *Socality*. Instagram photo, June 27, 2016. https://www.instagram.com/p/BHK4hFLh7fM/.

@jontaylorsweet. 2014. *Socality*. Instagram photo, November 29, 2014. https://www.instagram.com/p/v_c_k9ueko/.

@justin_02. 2015. "get out of the ordinary. Photo by @justin_02 #socality." *Socality*. Instagram photo, June 6, 2015. https://www.instagram.com/p/3l8-oouehX/.

@lance_asper. 2015. "Socality San Diego starts tomorrow!!! Photo by @lance_asper #socality #socalitylivesd." *Socality*. Instagram photo, July 19, 2015. https://www.instagram.com/p/5tbfXquekd/.

@lebackpacker. 2016. "Happy Thanksgiving! This is where family and friends gather and reflect on what they are thankful for. It's also a season where we prepare for generosity! This week we are supporting an incredible cause and encouraging people to GIVE this #givingtuesday. @ijm is launching a campaign next week to stop cybersex trafficking. We have always been about using social media collectively for good and we would love if you would join your voice with us this Monday as we SHARE and Tuesday as we GIVE! Monday we share a powerful video telling the stories of those who are in need of rescue and we hope that you can help us in the mission! If you are on our email list we will be sharing more on how you can support and #restartfreedom! You can also click link in bio to learn more. You guys are the best! #socality #thisismycommunity #givingtuesday Photo by @lebackpacker." *Socality*. Instagram photo, November 25, 2016. https://www.instagram.com/p/BNOJ4-qBHLU/.

@lennart. 2017. "A light to guide you home. Photo by @lennart #socality #thisismycommunity." *Socality*. Instagram photo, February 3, 2017. https://www.instagram.com/p/BQCfLkDhZt1/.

@lennartpagel. 2016. "We only have this moment. Photo by @lennartpagel #socality #thisismycommunity." *Socality*. Instagram photo, December 7, 2016. https://www.instagram.com/p/BNvjbMIBbMi/.

@lidiagulyas. 2014. "where is on your list to travel in 2015? Photo by @lidiagulyas #socality." *Socality*. Instagram photo, December 11, 2014. https://www.instagram.com/p/wfMbv9OemY/.

@littlecoal. 2017. "What does it take to bring cultural impact and inspire a generation? We recently sat down with @russell.evans and @saymevans of @planetshakers to discuss! Link in bio. Photo by @littlecoal #socality #thisismycommunity #planetshakers." *Socality*. Instagram photo, March 17, 2017. https://www.instagram.com/p/BRv7EgnjpqH/?taken-by=socality.

@loveinjustin. 2016. "Where stories are shared, bread is broken, and family is formed. #ThisIsMyCommunity. Photo by @loveinjustin #socality." *Socality*. Instagram photo, June 10, 2016. https://www.instagram.com/p/BGdeh_MOem_/.

@mark_whail. 2014. "what are you fighting for? New video up on site featuring our Instameet in Seattle and blog about fighting for community. You can watch and read by clicking link in bio. Photo by @mark_whail #socality #socalityrattlesnake." *Socality*. Instagram photo, January 29, 2014. https://www.instagram.com/p/ycYm2fueiO/.

@matteoewing. 2015. "Hey Dallas! Tonight we are excited to be at The Venue and to have @scottcbakken sharing about Socality and its story. See you @ venuecolleyville at 7pm. Register for free online at www.socality.org.#socality #socalitydallas Photo by @matteoewing." *Socality*. Instagram photo, May 28, 2015. https://www.instagram.com/p/3Omx9suegN/.

@mattzoeteman. 2015. "find your inspiration. Photo by @mattzoeteman #socality." *Socality*. Instagram photo, April 26, 2015. https://www.instagram.com/p/18XoBnuekt/.

@matt_kuma. 2015. "take it to the top. Photo by @matt_kuma #socality." *Socality*. Instagram photo, February 16, 2015. https://www.instagram.com/p/zLtS7GOenE/.

@mrvalography. 2015. *Socality*. Instagram photo, May 21, 2015. https://www.instagram.com/p/29zdpEOev6/.

@muradosmann. 2015. *Instagram*. https://www.instagram.com/muradosmann/?hl=en.

@naomi4nn. 2016. "Words from the team: @jonathanzoeteman 'I don't think we realize just how much our fear controls us. How much we worry about the future, about all the things that could go wrong. Crafting back-up plans and safety nets. Making contingency plans and insurance policies. We like the idea of being fearless, but we like the safety that living in our fear provides. Living in fear is often comfortable. Safe. It's very difficult to feel truly alive from a place of comfort and safety. So instead of spending so much time and energy on all the areas in our lives where we could fail, where something could go wrong, where we could build another buffer or safety net, let's ask ourselves what life looks like on the other side of our fear. What would you do, create, be? Where would you go, what would you say to those who matter most from a position of fearlessness? Maybe it's time to set plan b aside. We weren't made to live comfortably on the crash mat, we were made to take great leaps, to fall, to get back up, to do it all over again. We were made to live, and living truly begins at the point where our fear ends.' @jonathanzoeteman #ThisIsMyCommunity. Photo by @naomi4nn #socality." *Socality*. Instagram photo, April 14, 2016. https://www.instagram.com/p/BEKxKXhOeu3/.

@ownthelight. 2015. *Socality*. Instagram photo, July 1, 2015. https://www.instagram.com/p/4lIwePuehP/.

@patrickjjohnson. 2017. *Socality*. Instagram photo, March 24, 2017. https://www.instagram.com/p/BDUoSSauevF/.

@philipleclerc. 2015a. "We are a community committed to sharing God's love and truth in every space of life. The Gospel is about being accepted as you are and being transformed into who God says you are. See our interview today with Christian Post and how we are committed to seeing the love of Christ go beyond walls and into the hearts of humanity. Click link in bio to read. Photo by @philipleclerc #socality #thisismycommunity." *Socality*. Instagram photo, September 3, 2015. https://www.instagram.com/p/7LbHxuOesz/.

———. 2015b. "400 people will now have clean water because of you. We are blown away by this community. Together there were 20 Instameets, 24 individual campaigns, over 500 unique donations and over 1000 people in attendance for World Wide Instameet and together we raised $12,000.00. 400 lives are changed because you gave. Never under estimate the power of one. One person, one gift, one life, joined together as one. You can read more on our site by clicking link in bio. You guys are truly incredible. All for eternity #socality. Photo by @philipleclerc." *Socality*. Instagram photo, March 31, 2015. https://www.instagram.com/p/o4OYYeOegy/.

———. 2016a. "Words are a powerful tool. With them we can literally speak life or death. Read 'Lost in Translation' Journal by musical artist @sebell at SOCALITY.org. Photo by @philipleclerc in Old Jerusalem. #socality #thisismycommunity #israelcollective." *Socality*. Instagram photo, July 27, 2016. https://www.instagram.com/p/BIXq65khpGP/.

———. 2016b. "We're so pumped! Today our team is flying from Canada and Texas to meet up for an amazing week of vision and planning down in San Diego. Couldn't be more excited to share with you all for what's ahead in 2016! #ThisIsMyCommunity Photo by @philipleclerc #socality." *Socality*. Instagram photo, February 7, 2016. https://www.instagram.com/p/BBfpYoEOetB/.

@philipplitvin. 2015. *Socality*. Instagram photo, August 5, 2015. https://www.instagram.com/p/5_ZRyFues6/.

@reachalana. 2015. *Socality*. Instagram photo, December 25, 2015. https://www.instagram.com/p/_vecXjuess/.

@ryan_field_. 2016. "This looks like the perfect afternoon to us! Photo by @ryan_field_ #socality #thisismycommunity." *Socality*. Instagram photo, November 17, 2016. https://www.instagram.com/p/BM8EzKuBoVu/.

@sawyerkey. 2015. "it's 2015. Where we going? Photo by @sawyerkey #socality." *Socality*. Instagram photo, January 1, 2015. https://www.instagram.com/p/xUrCl2Oeud/.

@scottcbakken. 2016. *Socality*. Instagram, June 30, 2016. https://www.instagram.com/p/BHRFZOBD2h/.

———. 2017. "We had an awesome day filming our first educational series coming in March. The sunrise wasn't bad either! Photo by @scottcbakken #socality #thisismycommunity." *Socality*. Instagram photo, January 29, 2016. https://www.instagram.com/p/BP23wFIBSe2/.

@shopboutonne. 2015. "GIVEAWAY: today we are excited to announce @ shopboutonne as a sponsor of Socality San Diego. This amazing San Diego shop makes fine leather goods and will give away this fold top messenger bag (leather and raw denim). To enter, follow us both and tag a friend below. Winner announced Thursday. #socality #shopboutonne." *Socality*. Instagram photo, May 26, 2015. https://www.instagram.com/p/3KoonIOegT/.
@silassao. 2015. "let's get into the weekend. Photo by @silassao edit by @romanspataro #socality." *Socality*. Instagram photo, June 5, 2015. https://www.instagram.com/p/3kPNGtOei1/.
@sindreglaso. 2015. "into the fog. Photo by @sindreglaso #socality." *Socality*. Instagram photo, May 22, 2015. https://www.instagram.com/p/3AN_LYueky/.
@skylerwagoner. 2017. "Hey Monday! We got this. Photo by @skylerwagoner #socality #thisismycommunity #motivationmonday" *Socality*. Instagram photo, May 7, 2017. https://www.instagram.com/p/BP5pOzuBjqn/.
@socality. 2015a. "We are excited to announce Socality Live San Diego. An all-new live experience. July 29 - August 1. Our first line of guests announced with much more to come! Register for early bird rates. Link in bio. #socality #socalitylive." *Socality*. May 7, 2015. https://www.instagram.com/p/2ZAwViuemw/.
———. 2015b. "For the month of February we've chosen Health as our theme of focus. As humans we're made up of body, mind, and soul, and each of these areas are critically important as we seek to create lives that influence and impact the world around us. This month we'll be sharing thoughts, stories, and ideas around health in a relational, physical, mental, financial, and spiritual context. We're challenging our community to come together around the issues and ideas that matter to you. To take some tangible steps in your own life and as a community to see positive change in one of these areas. Link in bio for more info and some ideas. #socalityhealthproject #socality." *Socality*. Instagram photo, February 1, 2015. https://www.instagram.com/p/yladVouetj/.
———. 2016. "Socality Live SD: As we celebrate our 2nd birthday this week, we're looking back at our favorite moments of this past year: Today we look back to some of the greatest several days of 2015 that took place in sunny San Diego, California #SocalityliveSD - we truly believe something incredible took place along these beaches and throughout this city as we gathered from all over the world in this place! Something we'll never forget. #ThisIsMyCommunity #socality #sandiego." *Socality*. Instagram photo, January 25, 2016. https://www.instagram.com/p/BA8zGXjuerd/.
@socalitybarbie. 2015. *Socalitybarbie*. Instagram photo. https://www.instagram.com/p/9rFl36HjIc/.
———. 2017. *Socalitybarbie*. Instagram photo. https://www.instagram.com/socalitybarbie/.
@tannerwendell. 2017. "Seattle showed up even despite the rain for one amazing day. The fog made for a great background on top of Rattlesnake Ledge. We couldn't get

everyone in this shot and all in all about 150 came out to hang and create together! After the hike, everyone enjoyed pizza thanks to our friends @moment! Thanks to all our hosts and co-hosts @tannerwendell @mariawendellstewart @kylekotajarvi @charlottelittlewolf @zach_reed @joellefriend @hannah.aspen @zmelhus @jermzlee. Check out our IG story for more. Photo by @tannerwendell #socality #socalityseattle #thisismycommunity." *Socality.* Instagram photo, April 2, 2017. https://www.instagram.com/p/BSXtb35DOGE/.
@tarynstine. 2016. "Happy Good Friday! #ThisisMyCommunity @tarynstine #socality." *Socality.* Instagram photo, March 25, 2016. https://www.instagram.com/p/BDZqMzvuejb/.
@technopaul. 2015a. "ONE HOUR LEFT to help fix 6 wells in Uganda with @TheAdventureProject for Earth Day and #SocalityRestoreProject. We are asking you to donate $10 and then tag 5 friends to do the same. Together #LetsFixSix!" *Socality.* Instagram photo, April 22, 2015. https://www.instagram.com/p/1zWWsGueqo/.
———. 2015b. *Socality.* Instagram photo, February 3, 2015. https://www.instagram.com/p/yqLIN9Oehk/.
———. 2016. "California Classics by @technopaul #ThisIsMyCommunity #socality." *Socality.* Instagram photo, April 6, 2016. https://www.instagram.com/p/BD4fH-yOegk/.
@temi.coker. 2015. "love like no other. Photo by @ryan_eger #socality." *Socality.* Instagram photo, April 11, 2015. https://www.instagram.com/p/1WTcyqOeiS/.
@tri_art. 2015. "California!! You have been good to us. We want to thank @dyerandjenkins for supporting the #forgeyourownpathtour. We will be sharing photos and stories over the next week from all the incredible people we encountered the last 10 days. Thanks to every single person who showed up and made all the community events and gatherings. The last few days were unreal and we are all full of excitement and vision for the future ahead. Stay tuned for more. Photo by tri_art_ #socality #socalityelmatador." *Socality.* Instagram photo, March 10, 2015. https://www.instagram.com/p/oDUcpLuen1/.
@wildrecollection. 2015. *Socality.* Instagram photo, April 27, 2015. https://www.instagram.com/p/2AFdpMOen8/.
@winniestranero. 2015. "Maps. A moment shared by @winniestranero. Congratulations on being a finalist in the Socality X @moment_lens. The photo with the most likes will win a set of Moment lenses.Voting closes Tomorrow night at 11:59 pm. #sharemymoment #socality." *Socality.* Instagram photo, July 3, 2015. https://www.instagram.com/p/4smBgtueh3/.
@winnterfresh. 2015. "3 days left to raise $3628 to build one well and give clean water to a community in need. Click the link in bio and donate $1 to help. The craziest thing we can do is nothing. Photo by @winnterfresh #socality #idonatedadollar. (shirt available at @perspectivesca)." *Socality.* Instagram photo, March 29, 2015. https://www.instagram.com/p/ooRRufOev5/.

@zmelhus. 2016. *Socality*. Instagram photo, December 22, 2016. https://www
.instagram.com/p/BOWMXF3BoB/.
@8thgod. 2015. "the way to paradise. Photo by @8thgod #socality." *Socality*.
Instagram photo, June 7, 2015. https://www.instagram.com/p/3pgDkPOeky/.
@_joshes. 2015. *Socality*. Instagram photo, December 20, 2015. https://www
.instagram.com/p/_hQ-K.

INDEX

ableist discourse, 243–244, 275, 283–284, 298–299
Adam, Ansel, 157–158, 161
affect, 116, 147–169, 183, 235n12, 276; affect theory, 161–164
affordance, 6–7, 37, 42–44, 57, 67, 77, 79, 81, 85, 94, 96, 102, 103, 105, 116, 119, 121n10, 123, 127, 128, 137, 139, 151, 153, 161, 163, 189, 195, 219, 224, 226, 231, 242, 243, 247, 249, 254, 255, 257, 259, 274n26, 275, 276, 281, 284, 296, 301
algorithm, the, 6–8, 84, 195, 199, 227, 262, 263, 275
alterity, 11, 103, 275–276, 277, 283
Amazon, 82, 197, 262; Amazon Echo, 17, 181
ancient-future, 201n7, 204, 232
Anderson, Dianna, xii, 124, 130–131, 133, 134, 135, 136, 137, 138, 140, 146n10
Android, 181
anthropology, 3, 4, 9, 11, 19–22, 28n6, 29n21, 42–44, 130, 177–179, 196, 201n5, 201n9, 205, 235n3, 235n11, 261–262, 265, 275–276, 277–278, 281–282, 283, 285, 290, 295
apps, 26, 42, 43, 67, 84, 203, 213–216, 230, 234, 245, 255, 256, 276, 277, 301–302
aquatic metaphors, 81–84, 147, 293
authentic, authenticity, definitions of, 7–10, 28n9, 29n16, 84–87, 88–89, 97, 149, 152, 177, 276, 296
authority, definitions of, 5–10, 276–277, 279
autodocumentation, 147, 153, 167, 277, 297

Babylon Bee, the, 251
Bakken, Scott, 25, 148–169, 169n1, 241, 252, 265–266, 273nn18, 24
baptism, 10, 13, 27, 238–244
Baptists, 10, 13, 14, 115, 178, 185, 186
Barlow, John Perry, 62, 64–65
Barthes, Roland, 155, 156, 162, 169n4
Baudrillard, Jean, 165, 300–301
Bazan, David, 102, 120n1
Bell, Rob, 24, 96, 101–121, 148–149, 224–226, 284; *Love Wins*, 24, 101–106
Bergson, Henri, 162
Berners-Lee, Tim, 181, 255, 259n5, 289
Berry, Wendell, 92–93
Bessey, Sarah, xii, 9, 124, 126, 129, 131, 133, 136, 137, 138, 139, 145
Bialecki, Jon, 38, 178, 180, 190, 201n8, 222, 235n8, 236n20
Bible reading, 26, 34, 40, 50, 52, 67, 72, 182–183, 198, 203, 204, 207; *digital Bible apps*, 213–216
big data, 20
binge religion, 94, 277
bivocational pastors, 191, 201n8
Black Lives Matter, 12, 208
blogs, 9, 17, 67, 112–115, 122–146, 264–265, 277
Blogger, 9, 25, 293
Bloomington, Indiana, xii, 26, 173–237
books, 9, 16, 22, 45n3, 50, 71–98, 262–264
book burning, 36, 45n3

355

Bourdieu, Pierre, 167, 179, 201n9, 235n7, 281, 283, 303
Bourgeois, David T., 73, 74, 80, 94–95, 263, 264
boundary maintenance, 10–16, 22, 24, 25, 41, 49, 50, 57, 58, 69n4, 76–81, 96, 102–103, 110, 116, 168, 198, 220, 222, 223, 234, 240, 241, 250, 254, 276, 277–278, 279, 286, 288, 293
Boyd, Greg, 224, 225
bra burning, 122–124
brand, 11, 33, 37, 124, 129, 139–140, 144–145, 153, 169, 190–191, 249, 269, 273n22, 277, 278, 294, 297, 304. *See also* platform, voice.
Brand, Russell, 62
Breathe Prayer Exercise, 209–210
Bridle, James, 256, 258
Buddhism, 17, 255–256
buffered self, the, 11, 278; *the digitally buffered self*, 6, 11–13, 82, 103, 105, 112, 115, 198, 199, 250, 254, 283

Campbell, Heidi, 6, 7, 8, 17, 43, 67, 68, 84, 102, 113, 127, 128, 151, 225, 244–245, 299
cancel culture, 240, 248–252, 278
Catholicism, 12, 14, 17, 18, 27, 28n13, 33–41, 44, 45n3, 49, 119, 125, 131, 205, 232, 235n8, 304; anti-Catholic rhetoric, 63, 66, 79, 242, 288, 298, 299
cellphone, 3, 92, 278, 298
Cerf, Vincent, 62, 65–66
Challies, Tim, 73–121, 262–264
chaos rhetoric, 126–127, 258, 278–279
charisma, 5, 13, 55, 105, 232, 235n6, 279
charismatic authority, 5, 279
children's technology use, 75, 228–231
Christian Left, the, 16
Christians for Biblical Equality, 125
Christianity Today, 51, 105
Chun, Wendy, 3, 19, 28n7, 29n22, 35, 62, 84, 199, 287, 295
Church on the Margins, xi, 26, 101, 173–202, 203–237, 244–248
church plant, 176, 224, 279
circulation, 15, 23, 33–36, 40, 41, 49, 50, 78, 103, 104, 116, 117, 123, 137, 141, 144, 151, 166, 168, 279, 290, 298
Cisneros, Darby, 150, 164, 169. *See also* Socality Barbie

clothing, 110, 124, 132, 134, 143, 176, 264, 270, 303–304
Cole, Thomas, 159
Colorado Springs, Colorado, 10
collaborative media, 245, 277, 279, 295, 296
comments sections, 141–142
Committee on the Anthropology of Science, Technology, and Computing (CASTAC), 261
Communication Decency Act, 64
communicative capitalism, 139, 278, 280, 295, 296. *See also neoliberal self, the*
community cluster, 108, 236n15, 280, 297. *See also polarized crowd*
Council on Biblical Manhood and Womanhood, 125
Covid-19 pandemic, x, 9–10, 27, 239, 244, 252
creative class, the, 225, 280, 282. *See also digital creatives*
cultural logic, 62, 253, 259n3, 281. *See also cultural carrier*

data phone, 17, 21, 22, 25, 42, 67, 76, 92, 93, 116, 176, 181–185, 200–201, 206, 213, 215, 228, 230, 234, 235n2, 245, 251, 254, 276, 281, 282, 286. *See also cellphone*
democratization, 79, 281
Detweiler, Craig, 74, 75, 77, 78, 82, 89, 93, 94, 262, 263, 264, 273n5
digital abstinence, 92, 230–231, 282
digital asceticism, 204, 233, 234,
digital age, 1, 6, 81, 152, 226, 249, 282
digital evangelicals, the, definition of, 16
digital fasting, 230–231
digital minimalism, 91. *See also digital asceticism*
digital orientalism, 6, 112, 283
digital natives vs. digital immigrants, xi, 75–76, 282, 283
digitally buffered self, the, 6, 11–13, 82, 103, 105, 112, 164, 198, 199, 209, 250, 253, 254, 283. *See also boundary maintenance, buffered self, the*
dirt, 10–12, 112, 277–278, 283. *See also heresy, heterodoxy*
disembodied, disembodiment, 3, 64, 89, 241, 273n18, 275, 283–284
distraction, 3, 83, 91, 92, 159, 182, 215, 230, 251, 298
Dobson, James, 10, 127

INDEX

Drumsy, 238–244
communion, digital, 10, 27, 76, 238–248
corpus analysis, 22, 24, 25, 29n23, 97, 106–115, 262, 264, 268–272, 280
critical discourse analysis, 29n23, 280–281. See also discourse
Crawford, Terrace, 73, 74, 76, 83, 88, 89, 94, 263, 264
cultural carrier, 61–62, 70n14, 255, 281
depression, 18–19, 168, 229
determinism, biological-sexual, 135–136, 143; technological, 34, 41–44, 82, 186, 281, 284
Drescher, Elizabeth, 73, 74, 77, 80, 95, 97, 262–264
Dyer, John, 74, 75, 77, 81, 88, 91, 92, 263

email, 8, 17, 66, 187, 191, 230, 349
embodiment, 124, 131, 132, 136, 162
emerging church movement (ECM), ix, 97, 191, 223, 236n19, 284. See also exvangelical, postevangelical
Emerson, Ralph Waldo, 272n1
entextualization, 109, 112, 285, 299. See also indexical bleaching, reentextualization
ephemerality vs. disability in blogging, 142–143, 150, 213
Estes, Douglas, 74, 76, 180
ethnography, xi, xii, 3, 7, 12, 19–27, 28n10, 29n21, 67, 173–202, 203–237, 239, 245–248, 251–252, 259, 285; deterritorialized, viral ethnography, 20, 281; digital ethnography, 29n21; multisite ethnography, 20, 27
Evangelical Women's Caucus, 125
evangelicalism, definitions of x, 10–16, 252–253
Evans, Rachel Held (RHE), xii, 9, 119, 124, 126, 129–130, 134–135, 137, 139, 141–142, 143, 145, 146n9, 284, 285
exvangelical, 16, 284, 285. See also postevangelical, reflexive evangelical, progressive evangelical

face-to-face communication, 4, 9, 19, 29n16, 45n1, 50, 54, 87, 89, 90, 119, 144, 153, 166, 169, 189, 216, 217, 227, 228, 230, 232, 283, 285. See also IRL, logocentrism, media sincerity, transport view
Falwell, Jerry, 10, 56, 127; Falwell, Jerry Jr., 248, 249, 259n1

farewell, Rob Bell, 24, 101-120. See also hashtag
fear of missing out (FOMO), 87, 168, 285
Federal Council of Churches, 59
feminism, xi, 24, 120, 122–146, 149, 150, 202n11, 212, 251, 264–265, 273n22
flaming language, 212, 286. See also incendiary posts, shitstorms, trolls
followers, 88, 104, 107, 200, 216, 286; cultivation of, 6, 8, 148, 153, 154, 161, 279, 286. See also friends, influencer
food, 185, 204–205, 220, 223, 225, 268–272, 302; foodies, 165, 175; Slow Food movement, 92–93, 301
friendship, 26, 89, 97, 119, 195, 196, 203, 216; Friends[1] vs. Friends[2], 216–219, 233–234, 265
Foucault, Michel, 5–6, 199, 277, 281, 296, 298
Friedrich, Caspar David, 159, 160, 161, 268, 300, 302. See also Romanticism, the sublime
Fuck This Shit: An Advent Devotional, 200, 202n11
Fuller, Charles, 23, 52–54, 95

gatekeepers, 8, 9, 29n16, 77, 79, 80, 106, 127, 135, 138, 144, 149, 152, 251, 252, 253, 267, 286
Geertz, Clifford, 178
gender, 51, 73, 75, 123–145, 146n8, 146n10, 178, 210, 259n1, 294
Gershon, Ilana, x, 19, 36, 43, 72, 84, 94, 103, 127, 139, 175, 195, 278, 292, 294, 295. See also media ideologies, the neoliberal self, newness
glitches, 9, 26, 188, 190
GodTube, 67
Google, 65, 75, 77, 79, 82, 89, 184, 189, 190–191, 245, 262, 275; Google Glass, 304; Google Home, 17, 181, 286; Google Nest 17
Gospel Coalition, the, 96, 104, 134, 251
Graham, Billy, 14, 23, 51, 54–57, 70n5, 95, 118
Great Commission, the, 95, 256
green evangelicals, 169n6, 286. See also religious left, progressive evangelicals
Greenfield, Adam, 257–258
Gutenberg, Johannes, 34,
Gutenbergers vs. the Googlers, 75, 89

habitual media, xi, 17, 68, 72, 147, 150, 153, 185, 201, 231, 258, 286–287, 304, 305
Han, Byung-Chul, 28n4, 29n19, 257–259, 286, 300. See also shitstorms

haptic devotionality, 25, 150, 163, 164, 167, 169, 287
HarperCollins, 104
hashtags, 24, 103, 107, 109, 117, 148, 154, 166, 169, 265, 266, 287
hegemony, 59, 70n6, 70n7, 287
heterodoxy, 10, 19, 39, 85, 102, 103, 106, 107, 144, 222, 226, 252, 258, 267, 276, 288. *See also alterity, authenticity, boundary maintenance, heresy, orthodoxy*
heresy, 9, 12, 80, 101–121, 134, 249, 251, 252, 277, 278, 287–288
High Church vs. Low Church, 173, 205, 232, 241, 288
Hillsong Church, 149, 179, 248–249
Hinn, Benny, 23, 56, 57, 95
Hipps, Shane, 73, 74, 75, 81, 83, 88, 89, 91, 263, 264
hipsters, 120n1, 165, 175, 177, 180, 222
horizontalization, 6, 10, 102–103, 117, 251, 253, 256, 277, 283, 288
Howard, Robert Glenn, 17–18, 67, 259n2
Humbard, Rex, 54, 56
hyperconnection, 72, 82, 87, 288. *See information overload*
hypertext, 62–63, 77, 128

iconoclasm, 288
iGods, 74, 77, 81–85
image, the, 147–148, 169
imagined, the, 11, 15, 64, 72, 116, 254, 289
in real life (IRL), 146n15, 217, 219, 243, 281, 290
incendiary posts, 212, 286. *See also flaming language*
indexical bleaching, 120n6, 289. *See also reentextualization*
individualism, performative, 199, 297
influencers, 5, 8, 37, 62, 154, 249, 279, 299, 302–303
information overload, 72, 81–83, 182. *See also hyperconnection, informationalism*
Information Age, 76, 83, 208, 282. *See also digital age*
informationalism, 289
Instagram, xi, xii, 8, 9, 10, 16, 21, 22, 24, 25, 37, 43, 93, 147–169, 179, 191–198, 200, 207, 210, 216, 241, 248, 251, 252, 261, 265–266, 267–272, 272n4, 273nn6-26

internet, the origins of, 61–66, 289
internet of things, the, 17, 189–290, 295, 304, 305
intertextual gap, 120n6, 290. *See also indexical bleaching, reentextualization*
iPhone, 165, 181, 183, 185, 189; apps, 148; origins, 17; as religious object, 201n7
Islam, 146n7, 256; islamophobia, 236n19

Jameson, Fredric, 162
Jobs, Steve, 255
Jones, Andrew "Tall Skinny Kiwi," 97

Keane, Webb, 37–38, 178
Kimball, Dan, 97
Kim-Kort, Mihee, xii, 124, 130, 131, 136, 137, 139, 145, 146n10
Kinfolk magazine, 92–93, 165, 268, 273n18, 302–303
Kinkade, Thomas, 159, 161
kinship, 21, 26, 125, 176, 190, 195, 196–197
Kuczyński, Paweł, 1–3; *Dinner*, 1–3, 238

Lakoff, George, 120n7, 293
lateral communication, 45n1, 304. *See also vertical communication*
Lear, Norman, 56
lectio divina, 232
Lewis, C. S., 267
LGBT[QIA+], 12
lifeworld, 38, 166, 290
Liberty University, 10, 248
LISTSERV, the, 8, 17, 191
Liturgists, the, 225, 251
liturgy, 39, 227, 232, 288
local media, 19, 26, 35, 290, 301. *See also small media*
Lofton, Kathryn, xi, 70n14, 94, 124, 191, 277
logic of continuity and complementarity, 219–220, 223, 280
logic of displacement and disjuncture, 219–220, 224, 284
logocentrism, 236n17, 285, 290, 292, 303
Luddite, 90–93, 290–291
lust, sexual, 124, 132, 135
Luther, Martin 33–41, 44, 45nn1, 3, 47, 48, 55, 64, 72, 80, 248; Ninety-Five Theses, the, 33–35, 40

INDEX   359

magazines, 16, 49–51
markets, 11, 34, 41, 48, 50, 51, 52, 59, 60, 67, 71,
    139, 148, 197, 214, 244, 256, 294
materiality, 65, 143; of Catholic ritual, 37–39,
    232; non-materiality, 64; of print, 69n2,
    213-216, 234, 236n17; of technology, 169n7,
    255, 273n18
Maynard, Emily, xii, 122–123, 124, 126, 135, 137,
    138, 139, 141, 142, 145
McKnight, Scot, 87, 97, 236n19
McLuhan, Marshall, 41–43, 75, 77, 84, 162,
    180, 196
McPherson, Aimee Semple, 52
mediatization, 19, 43, 60, 68, 292
MeToo, 249
millennials, 51, 69n2, 151–152, 190, 283, 293
Miller, Daniel, 19, 29n21, 70n11, 180, 195, 196,
    199, 233, 235n11; *Why We Post* project, 43
meaning-making machines, 7, 84, 291. *See also*
    algorithm
media ambivalence, 73, 203–237, 245,
    291–292. *See also technological abstinence,*
    technological asceticism
media ecology, 15, 23, 34, 46–70, 78, 123, 180,
    248, 250–251, 255, 259n3, 292; definition of,
    41–44
media ideologies, definition of, 19, 43, 292
mass media, 16, 35, 45n1, 54, 59, 66, 176, 290,
    291, 292, 301. *See also media promiscuity*
oral media, 48, 226, 296
negative media ideologies, 27, 257–259,
    262, 294
media sincerity and promiscuity, definitions
    of, 4, 34–39, 292
mediatization, 19, 43, 60, 68, 276, 292
megachurch, the, 26, 101, 126, 176, 179, 180, 189,
    190, 191, 228, 241, 193, 301
meme, 13, 116, 248, 268, 269, 270, 271, 293
messiness, 9, 26, 184, 204, 219, 221–224, 231,
    232–234, 245, 246, 293, 301
microblogs, 24, 96, 103, 113, 115, 116, 127, 128,
    145, 149, 264, 293, 302, 303
Midwest, the, xii, 3, 9, 20, 22, 25, 26, 91, 93, 101,
    116, 122, 132, 136, 173–237, 244–248, 252
miscommunication, 189
misinformation, 82
missional, 191. *See emerging church movement*
mobile church, 185, 279, 293–294

modesty culture, 24, 122–146
Modesty Police, the, 135, 136
modified tweet (MT), 120n4, 294
Moody, Dwight L., 262, 267
mutual submission, 126, 127, 129, 294
Muir, John, 157

National Association of Evangelicals, the,
    14, 28n14
negative media ideologies, 27, 257–259,
    262, 294
Nelson, Ted, 62–64, 65, 70n15
neoevangelicalism, 14, 125, 130
neoliberal, neoliberalism, 123, 139–140, 144,
    145, 146n11, 153, 179, 206, 227, 254, 258, 278,
    280, 294, 297, 304; neoliberal self, the,
    139, 294. *See also brand, communicative*
    capitalism, platform, voice
netiquette, 88, 91, 119, 294, 303;
network theory, 6, 295
newness, 94, 103, 137, 239, 254, 295
nonparticipative observation, 19, 295
nonreligiosity, 27, 59, 60, 62, 69n4, 70n9, 255,
    288, 300. *See also secular, the protestant*
    secular

Oculus, 241
on ground vs. online, 28n6, 157, 241, 282,
    283–284, 295, 299
opacity, 106–108, 296
open-source, 79, 296. *See also Wiki model*
Orsi, Robert, 178, 201n5
orthodoxy, 8, 9, 24, 41, 72, 77, 79, 85, 88, 95,
    96, 97, 101–121, 149, 152, 165, 167, 168, 177,
    205, 242, 255, 257, 258, 276, 296. *See also*
    authenticity, heterodoxy

panopticon, postpanopticon, 199,
    258, 296
Parler Free Speech Network, 249
pentecostalism, x, 13, 56, 57, 115, 205, 211,
    222, 239
persecution rhetoric, 60–61
personal computer (PC), 18, 23, 61–70, 255,
    276, 297
Piper, John, 101–121, 134
plasticity, 19, 133, 142, 144, 149, 195, 201, 210,
    216, 220, 274n26, 294

podcasts, 9, 26, 67, 101, 138, 180, 182, 191, 198, 199, 203, 204, 224–228, 233, 234, 237nn21–22, 251

polarized crowds, 108, 236n15, 280, 297. *See also community cluster*

postevangelical, 16, 102, 191, 202n11, 236n19, 285, 297,

power, definition of, 5, 297–298

Power Point, 184, 186, 187, 190, 222

prayer, 1, 12, 28n12, 38, 54, 56, 186, 191, 195, 196, 198, 199, 204, 205, 208, 236n13; proximal intercessory prayer, 57, 92, 174; via Skype, 177, 187–188, 190; via iPhones, 183; via Zoom, 246

priesthood of all believers, the, 40, 79–80, 258, 292, 298

print culture, 25, 48–54, 59, 69n2, 71–98

printing press, the, 33, 34, 35, 44, 46, 48, 59, 60, 66, 70n13

progressive evangelicals, 24–25, 67, 102, 120n1, 182, 219, 247, 252, 298, 299

pub theology, 204–205, 234n1

public, the, 15–16, 21, 22, 24, 34, 36, 37, 41, 50, 57, 58, 61, 67, 103, 106, 117, 130, 136, 137, 138, 139, 141, 142, 144, 145, 147–150, 161, 164, 199, 252, 253, 254, 259n3, 262, 279, 280, 287, 298; counterpublic, 44, 117, 123, 124, 136, 143, 144, 145, 250, 251, 259, 259n3, 265, 280, 298

public-use differentiation, 229, 234, 298

purity culture. *See modesty culture*

race, racism, 28n15, 64, 70n6, 130, 131, 136, 175, 209; whiteness, 304–305

radio broadcasting, 11, 16, 23, 29n17, 44, 47, 51–54, 55, 57, 58, 59, 67, 69, 69nn3–4, 71, 94, 151, 225, 291

reentextualization, 285, 294, 299. *See also entextualization*

Reformation, the, 9, 14, 25, 28n8, 33–41, 44, 46, 49, 50, 59, 60, 62, 66, 68, 78, 79, 80, 213, 292, 298, 299, 300, 304

Reformed theology, 96, 299

Relevant Magazine, 51, 118–119, 145, 165–166, 237n21, 250,

religious left, the, 56, 299

resistance, 5, 8, 38, 48, 73, 79, 92, 96, 109, 120, 123, 131, 143, 166, 169, 203, 205, 234, 255, 276–277, 280, 282

retweet (RT), 107, 285, 296, 299

revivalism, revivalists, 18, 46–70, 71, 87, 158, 253, 267, 273n22, 288

Rice, Jesse, 73, 74, 82, 86, 87, 92, 97, 262, 263, 288

religious digital creatives (RDCs), 8, 179, 249, 275, 299

Roberts, Oral, 51, 54, 56, 57

Robertson, Pat, 56, 57

Romanticism, 150, 156–161, 266–267

Sankey, Ira D., 267

Schlafly, Phyllis, 125

Schultze, Quentin J., 16, 52, 73, 74, 77, 81, 82, 85, 86, 87, 88, 90, 93, 96, 262–263

Science Mike, 225

Scopes Trial, the, 59

screen, 83, 84, 196, 200, 215, 228, 254, 255, 273n18, 278; children's screen time, 228–230, 282; television screen, 57; materiality of screen, 169n7; mobile phone, 180–185; projector screen, 173–174, 185–187, 189–190, Zoom screen sharing, 246–247

Second Reformation, the, 61, 300

secular, secularity, 11, 18, 23, 27, 29n18, 58, 60, 61, 68–69, 70n6, 70n8, 70n14, 73, 86, 92, 129, 251, 255, 300; the Protestant Secular, 300

selfies, 164, 268, 269, 273n5

sensational forms, 57, 300

sensory overload, 204, 204–209

sermon discourse, 26, 121n11, 206, 211, 221, 225, 228

Sesame Street, 13

shitstorm, 28n4, 258, 286

simulacra, 165, 300–301

Six Streams of Historic Christianity, 235

simultaneity, 6–7, 249, 301

sincere-speech paradigm, 4, 301,

Skype, 9, 25, 26, 176–177, 187–190, 200, 203, 233

slow church, 93, 228–231, 236n19, 301

Slow Movement, the, 92–94, 228–231, 301

small media, 34–35, 291, 301. *See also local media*

smartphone, 147, 156, 157, 181–184, 214, 220, 228, 230, 273n18, 278, 281, 301, 304. *See also data phone, cellphone*

Smith, Nils, 73, 74, 76, 89, 94, 95

Socality, 25, 147–169, 198, 241, 265–274, 287
Socality Barbie, ix, 164–169
social shaping of technology, 43, 302. *See also* domestication
soft patriarchy, 146n3
Soto, D. J., 238–244
speed, 36, 45n2; culture or cult of, 92–93
spiritual disciplines, 9, 207, 235n8
spreadable media, 191, 302. *See also media promiscuity*
Springfield, Missouri, x, 10, 104
stancetaking, 72, 105, 106–113, 166, 287, 302
Star Wars, 13
Strang, Cameron, 69n2
sublime, the, 155, 156–161, 167, 168, 287, 302
surveillance, 131, 146n7, 199, 214, 257, 280, 296. *See also panopticon*
Sweet, Leonard, 74, 75, 79, 83, 89, 97, 263, 264

Taylor, Justin, 96, 104–105, 107, 114
taste, tastemaking, taste regimes, 163, 167, 302–303. *See also creative class*
Teams, Microsoft, 9, 10, 27, 188, 199, 245, 247
Thoreau, Henry David, 159, 272n1
technological asceticism, 90–93
technological optimism, 90, 94–95
technological redemption, 90, 93–94
technophobe, 90, 290–291, 303. *See also Luddite*
television, 11, 16, 23, 44, 47, 51, 54–61, 63, 67, 69, 71, 83, 91, 94, 151, 181, 186, 206, 225, 263, 291, 301, 303. *See also televangelism*
televangelism, x, 16, 56, 57, 303
theoblogians, 8, 37, 149
therapeutic spirituality, 61, 158, 272n1
transport view, the, 19, 236n18, 285, 292, 303
Tolkien, J. R. R., 267
trolls, 25, 141–142, 286, 303. *See also flaming language*
Trump, Donald, 118, 120, 138, 209, 221, 230, 236n14, 249
Turkle, Sherry, 29n16, 29n19, 180, 258
Twitter, x, xi, 6, 8, 9, 21, 22, 24, 25, 37, 42, 43, 67, 73, 79, 83, 96, 98, 101–121, 127, 134, 138, 142, 146n7, 147, 148, 149, 152, 179, 191, 192, 195, 196, 197, 198, 207, 209, 211, 216, 251, 264, 265, 274n26, 286, 287, 293, 294, 296, 299, 302
Twitter pastors, 8, 37, 224–228

ubiquitous media, 68, 84, 147, 150, 181, 187, 204, 303
uptake, 15, 19, 34, 35, 36, 42, 43, 56, 68, 123, 127, 128, 141, 225, 256, 284, 298, 302, 304

Vermeer, Danielle, xii, 124, 128, 129, 132, 133, 137, 138, 145
vernacularization, 40, 304
vertical communication, 45n1, 304
Vineyard Movement, the, 180, 205, 222–223, 234n1, 235n8
viral, virality, 20, 27, 36, 74, 77, 79, 89, 97, 134, 238, 268, 281, 293,
Virtual Church, 76–77, 88, 90, 95, 238–248, 252, 277
virtual reality (VR), 240-241, 283, 304
visio divina, 232
voice, 24, 46–47, 51, 54, 66, 69n3, 77, 96, 106, 108, 120, 123, 127, 128, 137, 138–139, 141, 144, 145, 153, 211, 212, 233, 277, 297, 304

Wanderer Above the Sea of Fog. See Friedrich, David Caspar
wearable technology, 82, 240, 245, 295, 304
Web 2.0, 67, 128, 179, 280, 304
Web 3.0, 225, 304
Weber, Max, 5–6, 7, 276–277, 279, 297–298
Wesley, John, 39, 46–47
White Horse Inn, the, 251
Whitefield, George, 23, 46–48, 59
whiteness, 58–59, 70n6, 130, 136, 304–305
Whole Earth Catalog, the, 62
Wifi, 1, 93, 187, 189, 251, 287, 289–290, 305
wikimodel, 305. *See also open-source*
Wikipedia, 71, 76–81, 138, 296, 305
wilderness, the, 93, 155, 158–159
Williams, Marian, xii, 124, 130–131, 132, 136, 137, 138, 139, 140, 142, 146n6, 146n10
Wimber, John, 205, 222
Wise, Justin, 73, 74, 75, 77, 80, 81, 82, 88, 92, 118, 138, 263, 264
WordPress, 25, 191, 192, 293

YouTube, 42, 67, 83, 116, 120, 200, 224, 225, 238, 265

Zahnd, Brian, 224, 225
Zoom, x, 9, 10, 27, 188, 238, 244–248, 252

TRAVIS WARREN COOPER is Research Associate in the Department of Anthropology at Indiana University Bloomington.

www.ingramcontent.com/pod-product-compliance
Lightning Source LLC
Chambersburg PA
CBHW020308240426

43673CB00039B/738